THE SELECTED WORKS OF GORDON TULLOCK

VOLUME 5

The Rent-Seeking Society

THE SELECTED WORKS OF GORDON TULLOCK

VOLUME 1 *Virginia Political Economy*

VOLUME 2 *The Calculus of Consent: Logical Foundations of Constitutional Democracy* (with James M. Buchanan)

VOLUME 3 *The Organization of Inquiry*

VOLUME 4 *The Economics of Politics*

VOLUME 5 *The Rent-Seeking Society*

VOLUME 6 *Bureaucracy*

VOLUME 7 *The Economics and Politics of Wealth Redistribution*

VOLUME 8 *The Social Dilemma: Of Autocracy, Revolution, Coup d'Etat, and War*

VOLUME 9 *Law and Economics*

VOLUME 10 *Economics without Frontiers* (includes a cumulative index for the series)

Gordon Tullock

THE SELECTED WORKS OF GORDON TULLOCK

VOLUME 5

The Rent-Seeking Society

GORDON TULLOCK

Edited and with an Introduction by

CHARLES K. ROWLEY

Liberty Fund

This book is published by Liberty Fund, Inc., a foundation established to encourage study of the ideal of a society of free and responsible individuals.

The cuneiform inscription that serves as our logo and as the design motif for our endpapers is the earliest-known written appearance of the word "freedom" (*amagi*), or "liberty." It is taken from a clay document written about 2300 B.C. in the Sumerian city-state of Lagash.

Printed in the United States of America

Paperback cover photo courtesy of the *American Economic Review*
Frontispiece courtesy of Center for Study of Public Choice, George Mason University, Fairfax, Virginia

15 18 19 20 21 C 6 5 4 3 2
19 20 21 22 23 P 7 6 5 4 3

Library of Congress Cataloging-in-Publication Data
Tullock, Gordon.
The rent-seeking society / Gordon Tullock ; edited and with an introduction by Charles K. Rowley.
p. cm.—(The selected works of Gordon Tullock ; v. 5)
Includes bibliographical references and index.
ISBN 978-0-86597-524-8 (alk. paper)—
ISBN 978-0-86597-535-4 (pbk. : alk. paper)
1. Rent (Economic theory). 2. Social choice. I. Rowley, Charles Kershaw. II. Title. III. Series: Tullock, Gordon, Selections, 2005 ; v. 5.
HB401.T7926 2004
330.01′2—dc22 2004040868

LIBERTY FUND, INC.
11301 North Meridian Street
Carmel, Indiana 46032

CONTENTS

Introduction, *by Charles K. Rowley* ix

1. RENT SEEKING: AN OVERVIEW

Rent Seeking: The Problem of Definition 3

Rent Seeking 11

2. MORE ON EFFICIENT RENT SEEKING

Efficient Rent-Seeking Revisited 85

Back to the Bog 88

Another Part of the Swamp 93

Still Somewhat Muddy: A Comment 95

3. THE ENVIRONMENTS OF RENT SEEKING

Rent Seeking as a Negative-Sum Game 103

Industrial Organization and Rent Seeking in Dictatorships 122

Transitional Gains and Transfers 136

Rents and Rent-Seeking 148

Why Did the Industrial Revolution Occur in England? 160

Rent Seeking and Tax Reform 171

Rent-Seeking and the Law 184

Excise Taxation in the Rent-Seeking Society 196

4. THE COST OF RENT SEEKING

The Costs of Rent Seeking: A Metaphysical Problem 203

Rents, Ignorance, and Ideology 214

Efficient Rent Seeking, Diseconomies of Scale, Public Goods, and Morality 231

Are Rents Fully Dissipated? 236

Where Is the Rectangle? 241

Which Rectangle? 253

5. EXCHANGES AND CONTRACTS 261

6. FUTURE DIRECTIONS FOR RENT-SEEKING RESEARCH 295

INDEX 313

INTRODUCTION

The Rent-Seeking Society brings together the main body of Gordon Tullock's contributions to a field that he pioneered during the late 1960s and early 1970s. Although Anne Krueger coined the name "rent seeking" in 1974, Tullock provided the initial insight in 1967.[1]

An important characteristic of competitive market equilibrium is the equality that exists between marginal consumption benefits and marginal production costs. Such an equality implies that competitive markets maximize consumers' surplus over cost. Harberger triangles occur whenever market prices are distorted by taxes, tariffs, or monopolistic practices that drive wedges between marginal benefits and marginal costs, thus cutting off mutually beneficial transactions.

Economists had long thought that welfare losses could be approximated by the magnitude of such triangles. Jules Dupuit is generally credited with the initial insight concerning the notion that welfare effects of price changes could be estimated from demand and supply conditions. Indeed, the welfare loss triangles were known as Marshallian triangles, in honor of the famous Cambridge economist Alfred Marshall, as early as the late nineteenth century.[2]

Yet before 1954, no one had ever calculated the magnitude of welfare losses from actual distortions within an economy. In 1954 Arnold Harberger proceeded to do so, using a general equilibrium framework in which demand curves were more nearly Hicksian (based on compensating variations) than Marshallian (ignoring the income effects of price changes). In consequence, the welfare loss triangles are now referred to as Harberger triangles.[3]

Tullock's rent-seeking insight came as a negative reaction to Harberger's 1954 paper in which he measured the welfare loss from monopoly in the United States at a mere 0.1 percent of gross national product. Instinctively

1. Anne O. Krueger, "The Political Economy of the Rent-Seeking Society," *American Economic Review* 64 (1974): 291–303; Gordon Tullock, "The Welfare Costs of Tariffs, Monopolies, and Theft," *Western Economic Journal* 5 (1967): 224–32.

2. A. Jules Dupuit, "De la Mesure de l'utilité des travaux publics," *Annales des Ponts et Chaussées*, 2d ser., 8 (1844); Alfred Marshall, *Principles of Economics* (London: Macmillan, 1890).

3. Arnold C. Harberger, "Monopoly and Resource Allocation," *American Economic Review* 44 (May 1954): 77–87.

Tullock recoiled from the notion that the measured welfare loss from monopoly could be so low. Creatively he set about determining why he felt his instinct was correct.

To this end, Tullock shifted attention away from the welfare triangle to the rectangle depicting the supernormal profits available as the monopolist reduces output below and elevates price above the competitive market equilibrium. If supernormal profits are available from a monopoly position, Tullock argues, surely potential monopolists will expend resources through the political process in a competitive race to secure that monopoly.

If such rent seeking is efficient, in the sense that resources expended equal the present value of monopoly profits, then, Tullock argues, the profit rectangle must be added to the Harberger triangle to identify the full trapezoid of the welfare cost to monopoly. For this insight, economists now identify the profit rectangle as the "Tullock rectangle" in the literature on rent seeking.

The Rent-Seeking Society consists of six parts, each depicting a separate component of the field.

Part 1, "Rent Seeking: An Overview," brings together two papers that focus on problems of defining rent-seeking behavior and outline the nature of the ongoing research program in a suitable historical perspective.

"Rent Seeking: The Problem of Definition" represents Tullock's proposed restraining order on those economists who view all forms of competitive behavior as rent seeking. As Tullock notes, most forms of competitive behavior are wealth enhancing, even when they result in the elimination of less-efficient firms from the marketplace. Let us restrict the rent-seeking concept, he argues, to only those cases in which individuals and organizations expend resources on lobbying government for special privileges that reduce the wealth of society. In such instances, both the resources expended on lobbying and the special privileges obtained are wasteful of scarce resources, and, further, we know for certain we are dealing with behavior that is harmful to society as a whole.

Rent Seeking is Tullock's widely acclaimed monograph depicting the intellectual history of the rent-seeking research program and describing the hazards confronted by any scholar who challenges conventional wisdom in public policy, most especially when that challenge threatens strongly entrenched ideological positions. Tullock explains in some detail the nature of Harberger's 1954 contribution and Harvey Leibenstein's 1966 modification of that paper in the form of the concept of x-inefficiency (the notion that monopolies may fail to function on their outer-bound production frontiers because of the absence of strong competitive pressure).[4] He outlines the nature of his own alternative approach from the perspective of rent seeking and carefully summarizes the sequence of steps that he took during the early 1970s to flesh out the implications of the basic model before Anne Krueger labeled rent seeking, the behavior identified by Tullock's program of research.

Tullock devotes the middle part of the monograph to integrating rent-seeking behavior into a more general public choice model of democratic political markets. The model that he uses will be familiar to those who have read *The Economics of Politics*, volume 4 of this series. For those who have not, suffice it to say that the public choice model is one that implies political market failure when more-powerful interest groups and self-seeking senior bureaucrats rent seek to shift legislative outcomes away from the median preferences of relatively ill-informed voters. By so doing, scarce resources are wasted in the implementation of wealth-reducing policies in clear and costly violations of the Pareto principle.

In the final section of the monograph, Tullock explores an interesting menu of potential constitutional and institutional reforms designed to mitigate the significant welfare costs of the rent-seeking society.

Part 2, "More on Efficient Rent Seeking," contains four contributions in which Tullock elaborates on his famous 1980 article on efficient rent seeking (published in volume 1 of the series).[5]

"Efficient Rent-Seeking Revisited" formalizes and classifies an efficient rent-seeking problem using the example of a true lottery. Tullock assumes that potential rent seekers are permitted to purchase as many tickets as they wish in a rent-seeking lottery. The tickets are placed in a hat. The winning ticket is randomly selected and provides a rent seeker with a predetermined prize. The paper demonstrates that, except for an infinite number of players and constant marginal costs, the market does not clear. The rent seekers in aggregate will lay out sums either in excess of or less than the available prize. In this sense, rent seeking is not efficient.

In "Back to the Bog," "Another Part of the Swamp," and "Still Somewhat

4. Harvey Leibenstein, "Allocative versus X-Efficiency," *American Economic Review* 56 (1966): 392–415.

5. Gordon Tullock, "Efficient Rent Seeking," in *Toward a Theory of the Rent-Seeking Society*, ed. James M. Buchanan, Robert D. Tollison, and Gordon Tullock (College Station: Texas A&M University Press, 1980), 97–112.

Muddy: A Comment," Tullock plays out his self-appointed role of confounding anyone who claims to have resolved his efficient rent-seeking paradox. These short papers demonstrate the robustness of his original efficient rent-seeking insight.

Part 3, "The Environments of Rent Seeking," consists of eight papers that together display the wide reach of the rent-seeking concept.

In "Rent Seeking as a Negative-Sum Game," Tullock explains that when an individual invests in something that will not actually improve, but indeed will more likely lower, productivity, he engages in rent seeking. The "rent" is the income that the individual seeks to secure as a consequence of the special privilege or monopoly power that his investments target. Typically government and its bureaucracy are the focus of such rent-seeking activity. Tullock explains why this type of rent seeking wastes resources overall, even though the successful rent seeker increases his own net wealth. He continues with an explanation of how the existence of privilege and monopoly purchased through government generates attempts by others to avoid the payment of the rents they now confront. Such rent avoidance itself diverts resources from productive to nonproductive activities. Tullock points out the harmful economic consequences that may occur when corporations hire political manipulators, rather than entrepreneurs, as their chief executives, and when they locate high-level executives in Washington specifically to mitigate the harmful consequences of unproductive laws and regulations.

In "Industrial Organization and Rent Seeking in Dictatorships," Tullock shifts his attention from democracies to evaluate the relevance of rent seeking in dictatorships (in 1986 still the most dominant form of government worldwide). He observes that the dictator typically extracts significant rents from his subjects. The existence of such high rents attracts rent seekers among the high officials, guards, policemen, and military, who endlessly plot for the dictator's overthrow through coup d'état. The dictator rationally responds by dispensing rents and privileges (as well as killings) in order to disperse coalitions before they are in a position to oust him. The social cost of rent seeking, therefore, is at least as high under dictatorship as under conditions of democracy.

"Transitional Gains and Transfers" attempts to explain why governments rarely transfer the benefits from an exhaustible resource (for example the discovery of oil reserves) efficiently across the citizenry. Instead of providing citizens with a property right in the oil revenues, or making direct cash transfers to existing citizens, governments typically resort to public expenditure programs that carry high excess burdens, even when they are at all productive. Tullock's explanation rests on an unfortunate combination of ignorance at the highest level of government and of self-seeking by bureaucrats and corporations who stand to gain from such public expenditure programs. In consequence, the transfers of windfall benefits usually are so inefficient that only the initial transitional gain is real.

In "Rents and Rent-Seeking," Tullock sets out to distinguish clearly between what he calls "good rents" and what he calls "bad rent-seeking." Innovations typically attract quasi rents in a competitive private market system. These rents are good rents, even though successful innovations drive the owners of preexisting capital out of business. A situation in which the government seeks to restrict innovations because they damage existing producers is highly undesirable. On the other hand, the seeking of rents through the lobbying of government for special privileges of any sort is also undesirable. Such rent seeking reduces the overall wealth of society.

In "Why Did the Industrial Revolution Occur in England?" Tullock notes that the industrial revolution was well under way, if not completed, before Adam Smith's *Wealth of Nations* had significant influence on government policy. Tullock argues that the conditions for the industrial revolution in England were established as a consequence of the civil war and its aftermath, culminating in the Glorious Revolution of 1688, which made it more difficult for individuals to seek special privileges from crown and church alike.

In "Rent Seeking and Tax Reform," Tullock explores the possibility of reducing through tax reform rent seeking and other kinds of government waste. He argues that efficient tax reform, designed to reduce excess burdens and to close special-interest tax loopholes, is best pursued as a general bargain in which everyone loses some special privilege than by piecemeal methods that will meet fierce, highly specific rent-protection lobbying.

In "Rent-Seeking and the Law," Tullock outlines, for example, the opportunities provided by the American adversary legal system for wasteful rent seeking by attorneys using expert witnesses. He suggests that such a costly system can be justified, by comparison with a civil code system, only if it is substantially more accurate in its outcomes. Tullock notes that American courts are in error in at least one case in eight.

In "Excise Taxation in the Rent-Seeking Society," Tullock notes that taxes imposed on such supposed luxury goods as cigarettes and alcohol do not significantly reduce consumption of either product. They are both products for which demand is price inelastic. Such taxes are imposed, he argues, because they raise significant tax revenues while avoiding counterlobbying by groups that have been vilified. Considerations of public choice, rather than of sound social policy, dominate excise tax impositions in the rent-seeking society.

Part 4, "The Cost of Rent Seeking," comprises six papers that address a number of important issues about the cost of rent seeking to society as a whole.

In "The Costs of Rent Seeking: A Metaphysical Problem," Tullock challenges head-on the implications of rent seeking, one of his most important scholarly contributions. The general normative thrust of the rent-seeking literature before this paper had been that rent-seeking behavior distorted political outcomes from those preferred by the median voter in favor of outcomes favored by concentrated interests and that such distortions were welfare reducing. Tullock further questions this judgment in "The Costs of Rent Seeking." Given that we accept that the majority of the electorate is rationally ignorant, Tullock asks why should we prefer political outcomes that curry favor to ignorant voters over those that favor the votes of members of a highly informed special-interest group?

In "Rents, Ignorance, and Ideology" and "Efficient Rent Seeking, Diseconomies of Scale, Public Goods, and Morality," Tullock attempts to explain the small size of the rent-seeking industry. His explanations are the following: that to fool voters, rent seeking typically assumes very inefficient forms, thus providing but small rents to successful lobbyists; that there are diseconomies of scale in lobbying; and that some individuals are endowed with an ethical dislike of rent seeking. For the most part, the small scale of the rent-seeking industry does not imply that the social cost of rent seeking is low. Inefficient rent-seeking mechanisms—for example, quotas rather than tariffs in trade protection or in-kind rather than cash transfers—are extremely costly in terms of resource misallocation.

Finally, in three short papers, "Are Rents Fully Dissipated?" "Where Is the Rectangle?" and "Which Rectangle?" Tullock fine-tunes his thinking on the high cost of rent seeking. He notes that rent-seeking waste is exacerbated by instability in rent-seeking coalitions and results in rotating majorities among groups that seek special privileges. He suggests that the voters themselves are badly—or asymmetrically—informed rent seekers, logrolling among themselves, each in pursuit of an intensely desired special privilege. He further suggests that government subsidies—for example, to farmers—lower the cost of production and thus increase the size of the available Tullock rectangle by comparison with the usual constant-cost welfare loss diagram.

Part 5 is Tullock's short monograph *Exchanges and Contracts*, in which he develops a systematic theory of exchange in political markets, identifying with such exchange serious weaknesses in the form of externalities, rational ignorance, rent seeking, and other transaction costs. Since these political market failures correspond to, in form, and are more insidious, in nature, than the transaction costs typically ascribed to ordinary markets, this monograph succeeds in reestablishing the strong presumption against resorting to politics originally argued by Adam Smith in his masterpiece, *The Wealth of Nations.*[6] The monograph offers a refreshing free-market perspective to counterbalance the interventionist predilections of most modern neoclassical economists.

In part 6, "Future Directions for Rent-Seeking Research," Tullock focuses on the importance of information in the political marketplace. He notes that in 1600 rent seeking was overwhelmingly the most common way of becoming wealthy. The mercantilist society was a society organized on the basis of rent seeking. The free market ideas advanced by Adam Smith and David Ricardo led to the dismantling in England of the mercantilist system and brought about the industrial revolution. Unfortunately this good information was suppressed from the late nineteenth century, allowing political markets to revert to mercantilism. The future direction of rent-seeking research, Tullock argues, should target modern mercantilism with the objective of returning advanced economies to free markets.

Tullock's original rent-seeking insight and his subsequent extensive follow-up research in this field have opened a major research program in economics and public choice.

CHARLES K. ROWLEY

Duncan Black Professor of Economics, George Mason University

Senior Fellow, James M. Buchanan Center for Political Economy, George Mason University

General Director, The Locke Institute

6. Adam Smith, *The Wealth of Nations* (1776; London: Methuen, 1904).

PART I

RENT SEEKING: AN OVERVIEW

RENT SEEKING

THE PROBLEM OF DEFINITION

Some time ago, I received a paper for comment arguing that the current patent process generated rent seeking. The author's point was that because a patent would be a monopoly, and, in many cases a valuable one, a considerable number of people would engage in attempting to get the patent, and this would be a wasteful duplication of research. In essence, as result of this waste, scientific progress was "too fast."

Most people think it is not possible for scientific progress to be too fast, but most economists would disagree. The realization that too many resources may be invested in something that is in itself desirable is one of the insights provided by economics. In this case, however, oddly enough there may be underinvestment because of competitive research. Thus, the waste might go either way.

In order to see how the research might be undesirably slow, assume that we have a number of people who have decided that some particular patent would be desirable and have undertaken research to achieve it. Each of them, however, realizes that he is not alone; hence, there is only some probability of getting the patent, instead of certainty. Suppose each of them feels that even if he works as fast as possible, he has only a one-in-three chance of being the first person to achieve the goal.

Under these circumstances, he would plan on investing resources of one-third or less of the patent's true value. However, all three of these people will keep their research secret. Under the circumstances, it is certain that there will be duplication, i.e., literally that the different people who are engaging in it will perform the same experiments, undertake the same tests, and so on, and this, if one looks at it from the eye of God, would be wasteful.

Although the various people engaging in this research will invest resources up to, roughly speaking, the value of the patent, much of this resource investment will be duplicative; therefore, the total amount learned might be considerably less than we would achieve if somehow the whole thing had been allocated to one researcher who had then invested the full

Reprinted, with kind permission of Kluwer Academic Publishers, from *The Economics of Special Privilege and Rent Seeking* (Boston/Dordrecht/London: Kluwer Academic Publishers, 1989), 49–57.

value of the patent. Scientific research can progress too slowly as well as too rapidly. In this case, it might end up costing as much as the efficient pattern while producing a great deal less.

What does this have to do with rent seeking? The answer is that my colleague who sent me the paper thought it was an example of rent seeking, and, indeed, it does look somewhat like it.[1] The paper actually took the view that probably something should be done about the matter in the case of patents, but it did not have any positive recommendations. I personally am a proponent of patents,[2] but I must admit that there is a resemblance between the two situations.

A resemblance is not confined to patents. Consider the efforts undertaken by producers to sell their products, whether in the form of advertising or simply providing a pleasant environment in which to buy.[3] These things tend to be, to some extent, self-cancelling in the same way that one person's secret research tends to duplicate another's.

An example of what can be done in this area is the recent change in the billboards along the interstates. They used to be large and conspicuous. As a result of legislation, they are now rather small plaques attached to an information board put up by the highway department. I do not argue that this is an ideal system, but I have no doubt that it is an improvement. Information of the same sort that the billboards produced is now available at a much lower cost, both to the advertiser and to the driver, who has an unimpeded view of the scenery.

It is not obvious that there is true waste in the sales effort or the invention cases, because it may be that nothing better can be done. In the case of sales effort, I believe something better could be done. I think a heavy tax on advertising would mean that the government could obtain funds, and there would be substantially no cost to the advertisers themselves because everyone's advertising would be cut back by about the same amount. The experience with the restrictions on TV advertising of alcoholic beverages and then

1. Note that in this entire chapter I am ignoring the mathematical difficulties raised by the series of articles beginning with my "Efficient Rent Seeking."

2. See my "Intellectual Property," in *Direct Protection of Innovation*, ed. William Kingston (Dordrecht: Kluwer Academic Publishers, 1987), pp. 171–200; and *The Organization of Inquiry* (Durham: Duke University Press, 1966; and New York: University Press of America, 1987).

3. Expensive restaurants do indeed provide superior food, but they spend much more money on "ambiance."

on cigarettes seems to indicate that the producers of these goods were themselves delighted at what amounted to a cartelization that reduced the total investment in advertising. As far as I know, the people who formerly put up billboards along the highways are satisfied with the present arrangement under which they simply put placards on a large board arranged by the highway department.

It is unlikely that any such tax would go through, because the media themselves are immensely influential in our society and would object to this cut in a large part of their income. We do not know whether society as a whole would gain or lose from this partial conversion of the support of the media from the advertisers to the people who are actually consuming. Surely the readers would have to pay somewhat higher prices, but, on the other hand, the government would have a significant source of revenue.

The problem here is one of definition. Should we regard the competitive research, competitive sales effort, and so on, as equivalent to rent seeking?

Assume here that we have obtained divine guidance: we know everything about some particular set of transactions and can make calculations on the basis of this perfect knowledge. Suppose we examine a simple sales case, not an invention, but a sales case, in which a number of people are trying to sell substantially identical brands of soap. Note, I have said substantially identical. Certainly technological progress has been made in the manufacture of soap, which the advertising and sales process no doubt accelerates. One of the benefits from advertising, I would imagine a quite small one, is the acceleration of technical developments in the product.[4]

We can now, with our divine knowledge, make calculations as to the cost: first, the cost of producing the soap; second, the cost of distribution at minimum cost levels; and third, the cost of informing the purchasers of the soap and its possible superiority over other brands. The sale of the soap in "nice" boxes and the provision of the supermarkets where it is purchased should also here be counted as genuine cost.

I think our divine knowledge would indicate that the customers would be just as well off, and technological progress would go on just as fast. The total cost would be lower if the various parties producing soap were somehow forced to follow an optimal policy of coordination in their advertise-

4. There are a lot of cases in which the soap is simply changed without any improvement, and then the advertisers claim improvement. But, nevertheless, over time there is no doubt that these changes do effect an improvement, even if the improvement is not great.

ments, and so on. The policy coordination, however, would also require divine knowledge because no one now has any idea what an optimal policy would be.

What we can do is work out a humanly possible plan of coordination and inquire whether it would be cheaper than the present system. Undoubtedly it would be, although such a plan might suffer from the fact that there would be substantially no motive for any human being to actually carry it out. Furthermore, there would be many motives for human beings to use the plan as a subtle, or possibly, not-so-subtle, method of cartelizing the industry.

In a way, then, the people who are advertising, and so on, in the soap industry are trying to create monopolistic competitive gains which do, indeed, resemble in a small way the gains obtained by setting up a formal cartel or getting government regulation. Should we call this rent seeking?

As the reader has probably already deduced, my answer is "no." What I would like, however, is some kind of continuous function in which the costs of competition, and there are costs, were set off against the gains of competition, as opposed to monopolistic activity. For this purpose our divine knowledge, i.e., knowing what would happen if, instead of competition, we had an ideally designed program in which the desires of the consumers were not only known but anticipated by some gigantic super computer, is possibly a useful intellectual construct even though there is no prospect of its being more.

To give an idea of the difficulty, I am dictating this chapter in a room at the Charlottesville Holiday Inn. The bathroom has a note from the management that says: "If you have forgotten or are in the need of essential toiletries (shaving cream, razor, comb, toothbrush, and toothpaste), call our front desk and we will get you a complimentary replacement right away."

The reason that the management does this is not necessarily that they think their guests are nice people who should be helped. Basically, they are attempting to engage in a little monopolistic competition with the idea that in the future I am more likely to stop at a Holiday Inn than at another hotel. In this case they have chosen, as hotels tend to choose, a very minor advantage because such minor advantages are hard to advertise nationally. Almost the only way people could find out if Quality Courts also do this is through personal experience or word-of-mouth advertising.

This convenience for their customers is also a competitive technique. Is it true that as a result of having this service (which, of course, the customers pay for), the toughness of the competition between them and other hotels is somewhat eased? Will customers pay more for their hotel accommodations than they would prefer to? I do not know, nor can I think of any way of calculating it. Nevertheless, if we are attempting to determine the costs of competition, this would be part of the problem. I do not even see any way of determining whether the customers would prefer to have this service provided, or have a trifling reduction in their bill.

In competition, it is likely that other hotels will choose to do the same thing. Thus, we might expect sometime in the future that this kind of service is universal for all except the cheapest hotels. Would this be a good or bad thing? I cannot say, but I also do not think that the hotel management themselves have either the appropriate motives or the ability to calculate it. This makes it impossible for them to answer that question any better than I can.

Let us think of the patent case. Suppose, for example, there is some potential new invention that will be worth $1 million if it is made and if a monopoly is granted to its designer. At the moment, the discovery of this invention would require the solution of 12 problems, and we shall assume that an advance cost estimate for solving each of these problems is $100,000. Under the circumstances, it clearly is not desirable for people to engage in research for this particular invention. It might be true that, socially, the invention is desirable because the monopolized invention would be worth less to society than a competitive use of the same product, but we will put that aside temporarily.

With time, however, science progresses, and let us assume that after a while, two of the 12 problems have been solved. At this point, one can imagine someone undertaking research to make the invention. One can imagine, that several different companies would undertake that research and that one of them would achieve the patent. Let us assume that if all the estimates of $100,000 turn out to be true, it is just a question of speed, and Company A spending $1 million achieves the patent which is worth $1 million, while Companies B and C each spend $800,000 and solve eight of the problems but do not achieve the patent. The social loss here seems to be quite severe.

But assume that Companies A, B, and C, instead of taking that particular action, say to themselves: "It is likely that if we start working on that, at least two other people will also start. Their scientists are as good as ours. It is likely that we will not win the race except maybe one time in three, so our laboratories should not begin work on this particular project until there has been further scientific progress." Under these circumstances, all three of them would wait until another set of problems had been solved by someone else. At that point, all three of the laboratories would start working. One of them would beat the other two out and receive something worth $1 million for an investment of $300,000. The other two would make investments of, say, $300,000 again, but would get to the patent office a little late. Under these circumstances, we have a socially desirable invention, but note that we have it considerably later than we could have had it with perfect planning. Further, the discovery depends on the sort of accidental production elsewhere of knowledge that turns out to be useful.

It certainly looks as though starting off the research as soon as the two outside experiments have been done, having only one company do it, and having that company achieve the invention much earlier would be a desirable thing from the standpoint of society. Thus, we have here a case in which it appears superficially that competition has led to a bad outcome. Further, we might say that, in this case, rent seeking is the cause of the bad outcome, because, after all, the return on the patent is a rent.

Try to imagine what kind of institutional structure would lead to bettering this outcome. It is true that if we assume that there is some government bureau, perfectly informed and motivated to work hard, that with consistent correctness makes up its mind as to when an invention has become feasible and then assigns it to the appropriate company, we could do better than the market assuming that the government bureau had a zero or very little cost. Immediately after World War II, the British aircraft industry attempted to overcome the advantage of the competing American aircraft manufacturers by this exact pattern. One of their products, the Concord, is still flying. In general, the experience was a disaster.

It turned out that government officials were not good at making this kind of guess. There is no reason they should be. They were not subject to the kind of discipline that the private market forces on research organizations. In any event, it is not a good idea to have the initiation of new discoveries monopolized by anyone. Science works best if a number of people, all of whom are independently pushing for things that they think are desirable, are using methods that they choose. Again, the Russian and, to a lesser extent, the French scientific communities stand as examples. The Russians actually spend more than the Americans do on science, but they make very little progress, because of the central planning mechanism. In their case, this means that all the brightest people in their laboratories are attempting to manipulate the central planning system, and only the second level people are actually doing the research.

Nothing I have said is intended to imply that the competitive market, whether it is the market for selling hotel rooms or for making inventions, is waste free. I have even recommended a reform: a tax on advertising. But it is difficult to think of an institution that would work better. We motivate people to seek out entrepreneurial opportunities, invest in them, work hard, and abandon them when the cost-benefit projections seem to go negative. Even granted that competition does have the defects we see, it still seems better than its alternatives.

This is also true in the case of competition for the favor of a government. A government does not, in general, just go about the world doing good. It has to be pushed into it. Consider, for example, the gigantic to-do that accompanied the construction of almost every single interstate route. The problem was where the highway would go and where its entries would be. Big private investments were made in attempting to influence those decisions. I presume that the investments were not actually larger than the value of the service. But this was basically a way of seeing to it that the government did a somewhat better job than it would do if it were simply planning in advance. Indeed, the decision by the government to do just about anything is the result of various people engaging in influential efforts.

A government planning bureau, the purpose of which is to plan the government, is difficult to set up. We must try to organize the matter in such a way that the optimal set of incentives, which is not likely to be perfect, are given to optimal people.

This brings me to my definition of *rent seeking.* Instead of attempting to take, say, the total cost of a project, including all of the sales and maneuvering costs, and set that off against the total benefit, I have a more modest proposal. Clearly, that total cost is what we would like to do but cannot. My suggestion is that we use the term "rent seeking" (and I always have) solely for cases in which whatever is proposed has a negative social impact.

Consider a clear-cut case. Suppose that a steel manufacturing company in difficulty (as steel manufacturing companies tend to be at the moment) has a choice between two different operations, both of which will cost the same and, according to experts, have equal prospects of success and have equal effects on its profits. The first proposal is to invest a large amount of money in getting the government to ban the import of Korean steel on the purported grounds that it is environmentally dangerous. The result of this would be the rise in the price of steel, and most people in the United States will be at least slightly worse off than they were before. (I assume that the environmental charge is false.)

The alternative proposal is to introduce some new machinery in its plant which will increase its efficiency enough so that it will make the same amount of additional profits. Indeed, in this case, it may acquire a little bit of semimonopoly power, because its costs would be lower than that of its competitors. Clearly, the net effect on society is that the cost of steel is somewhat lower, and most people are somewhat better off. Needless to say, the steel company's competitors are not. I use "rent seeking" for the first and not for the second. This is not, however, to repeat a denial that competition may have costs and that individuals investing in it may be consciously aware of the fact that they are damaging their competitors.

I offer this definition because I can do no better. In general, economists can recognize institutions and institutional changes that are harmful in themselves. We cannot recognize institutions that are beneficial in themselves but which, through the competitive process, cost too much. Again, we frequently recognize wasteful expenditures. The expenditures of the people who are attempting to make the invention and who fail because someone else beats them to it are wasted in the sense that they have no positive output.

Socially, giving people an incentive to compete in a race may be a good thing even though we know that many will lose. *Subspecies eternitas*, if we somehow could pick out the winner in advance and get him to work just as hard (and, in the case of the invention, start him earlier), no doubt the world would be better off. It is one of the many cases where, if we had knowledge and institutions that we do not have, we would be better off. It would also be convenient if we could fly. We cannot detect that kind of a situation nor can we measure the resources "wasted." Let us, then, confine ourselves to what we can do and engage in rent-seeking research only in cases where the institution to be created is, in and of itself, undesirable.

In that case, it is very clear. The resources are wasted in producing it, and the institution itself imposes cost. If we confine ourselves to that issue, we will be dealing with a problem that we can handle, not engaging in Utopian dreams.

RENT SEEKING

Early Beginnings

One of the first lessons that I learned when I began to study price theory was that the main effects of monopoly were to misallocate resources, to reduce aggregate welfare, and to redistribute income away from consumers in favour of the monopolist. I observed that a significant number of academic economists, both in the United States and elsewhere, devoted much of their time to such issues, analysing a formidable list of monopolistic practices and estimating the degree to which production and distribution were concentrated in the hands of a small number of firms. I further noted that students of monopoly power focused their attention almost exclusively on unregulated private markets. The presumption appeared to be that once government invaded monopolistic markets, whether through regulation or through public ownership, market failures would be rectified.

Such a preoccupation with monopoly in the burgeoning literature of industrial organization during the late 1950s and early 1960s, for me, presented something of a paradox. Perhaps instinctively, or perhaps because of my early price theory training, I shared the prevailing view that monopoly was a significant evil, worthy of the attention that it produced. Yet, I was aware of two widely cited papers that had determined that the loss of economic welfare caused by monopoly in the United States was very small, perhaps of the order of one-tenth of one per cent of gross national product. Since this conflict between my instinct and my observation eventually triggered my 1967 paper on rent seeking, let me begin this book by revisiting Harberger's contribution.[1]

Harberger defined the loss of economic welfare associated with monopoly as the excess of the loss of consumers' surplus over the gain to the monopolist. The gain to the monopolist was his net profit, which, in the constant

Reprinted, by permission, from *The Shaftesbury Papers*, vol. 2 (Aldershot, U.K., and Brookfield, Vt.: Edward Elgar, 1993), 1–98.

1. A. C. Harberger, "Monopoly and Resource Allocation," *American Economic Review* 44 (1954): 77–87; A. C. Harberger, "Using the Resources at Hand More Effectively," *American Economic Review* 49 (1959): 134–46; G. Tullock, "The Welfare Costs of Tariffs, Monopolies, and Theft," *Western Economic Journal* 5 (1967): 224–32.

cost model, is the difference between his price and the competitive price multiplied by the quantity sold at the monopoly price. For purposes of illustration, Harberger assumed that the point elasticity of demand for the industry's product was unity throughout the output range. Figure 1 defines the welfare loss from monopoly under these conditions in terms of the shaded triangle (now known as the "Harberger triangle").

Harberger proceeded to estimate the magnitude of such welfare losses for the U.S. economy utilizing statistics on the rate of return of capital for 73 manufacturing industries for the years 1924 to 1928 compiled by Ralph Epstein. Epstein's study was based on a sample of 2046 corporations accounting for 45 per cent of the sales and capital in manufacturing industry.[2] Harberger calculated that in order to equalize the profit rate in all the industries covered, it would be necessary to transfer $550 million in resources from low-profit to high-profit industries. To take account of total manufacturing, this figure must be augmented to $1.2 billion. On this basis, the resource misallocation in U.S. manufacturing could have been eliminated by a net transfer of 4 per cent of the resources in the manufacturing industry, or 1.5 per cent of the total resources of the economy.

If such a transfer of resources had been effected, by how much would people have been better off? Using Epstein's data, but this time estimating the counterpart of the shaded triangle in Figure 1 for each industry, Harberger determined that the total improvement in consumer welfare to be derived with reference to Epstein's sample of firms amounted to $26.5 million. This figure must be augmented for the whole economy to $59 million—less than one-tenth of one per cent of the national income. For a variety of reasons, Harberger concluded that this figure was something of an underestimate and that the correct gain might be slightly in excess of one-tenth of one per cent. Harberger confessed that he was amazed at this result and that he himself had laboured under the delusion that monopoly distortions to the resource structure were much higher than they really were.

Of course, statistics for the 1920s are very sketchy by modern standards, and Harberger's assumptions of constant costs and unit demand elasticity are not immune to criticism. Yet, a variety of studies, calculating the welfare loss to monopoly and tariffs in a range of countries, came up with equally minute

2. R. C. Epstein, *Industrial Profits in the United States* (New York: National Bureau of Economic Research, 1934).

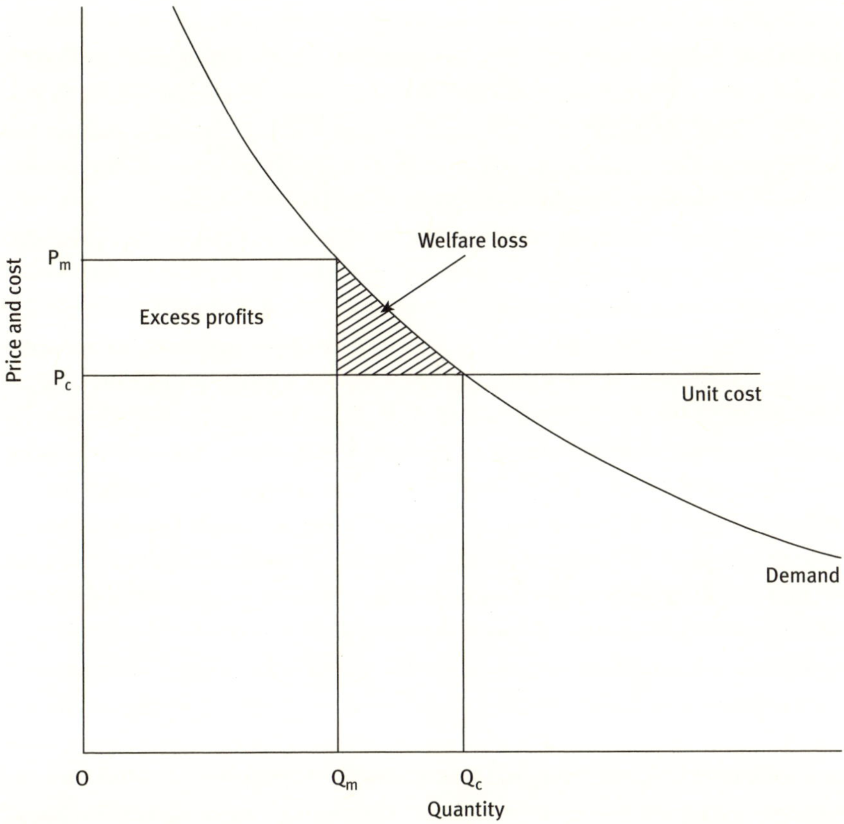

FIGURE 1
Harberger's measure of the welfare loss from monopoly

magnitudes.[3] Let us play around with some numbers to see why this is not really surprising. Suppose that half of the national output is produced in monopolized industries, that the price differential is 20 per cent, and that the average elasticity of demand is 1.5 per cent.[4] Now the welfare loss to monop-

3. H. G. Johnson, "The Gains from Freer Trade with Europe: An Estimate," *Manchester School of Economic and Social Studies* 26 (1958): 247–55; J. Wemelsfelder, "The Short-Term Effect of Lowering Import Duties in Germany," *Economic Journal* 60 (1960): 94–104; D. Schwartzman, "The Burden of Monopoly," *Journal of Political Economy* 68 (1960): 727–29.

4. H. Leibenstein, "Allocative Efficiency vs. X-Efficiency," *American Economic Review* 56 (1966): 392–415.

oly turns out to be 1.5 per cent. But we used enormous figures to generate this result. Given that private monopoly accounts for a much smaller percentage of national output and that monopoly prices, according to most estimates, appear to be no more than 8 per cent, on the average, above competitive prices, Harberger's results do not seem to be much of an underestimate.

The notion that the social cost of monopoly is approximately captured by the sum of the Harberger triangles remained the conventional wisdom of mainstream neoclassical economics until the mid 1970s, despite well-based challenges by Leibenstein and by myself.[5] I even taught such orthodoxy myself, though not often, since the particular courses for which I was responsible had little need for it. Prior to 1967, I would have taught it without concern had my courses required it. In this respect, I was little different from my fellow economists. In retrospect, it is interesting to note that economics students in general disliked Harberger's result, probably because of their instinctive distrust of monopoly power and of what they perceived to be its adverse implications for income distribution. It turns out that they were right, though for incorrect reasons, and that most professional economists (including myself before 1967), in some cases well into the 1970s, were simply wrong.

Leibenstein's Challenge to the Harberger Presumption

The first major challenge to the notion that welfare loss to monopoly is confined to the allocative inefficiencies characterized by Harberger triangles came in 1966 with Harvey Leibenstein's concept of "X-inefficiency." Leibenstein had a great deal of difficulty persuading the editors of the *American Economic Review* to publish this paper, and even now it remains a controversial issue among welfare economists. As I shall suggest later, editorial resistance to radically new ideas is a predictable consequence of the organization of economic inquiry. Normal science jealousy guards its carefully cultivated terrain.[6]

Leibenstein acknowledged that the welfare effects of reallocation typically must be relatively small, since allocative inefficiency involves only the net

5. Leibenstein, "Allocative Efficiency"; G. Tullock, *Toward a Mathematics of Politics* (Ann Arbor: University of Michigan Press, 1967), and Tullock, "Welfare Costs of Tariffs."

6. Leibenstein, "Allocative Efficiency"; G. Tullock, *The Organization of Inquiry* (Durham: Duke University Press, 1966).

marginal effects. The basic assumption of the conventional approach is that every firm purchases and utilizes all its inputs efficiently. What is left is simply the consequences of price and quantity distortions. While some specific price and quantity distortions may be large, it seems unlikely that all relative price distortions would be exceptionally large. However, if firms in fact do not purchase and utilize their inputs efficiently, as a consequence of managerial difficulties, the potential loss of welfare may be many magnitudes greater.

Leibenstein identified three causes of X-inefficiency in firms that are not subjected to high competitive pressures, namely:

1. contracts for labour that are incomplete;
2. production functions that are not completely specified or known; and
3. inputs that are not marketed or, if marketed, are not available on equal terms to all buyers.[7]

In such circumstances, the assumption of cost minimization by all firms is simply incorrect. In consequence, firms and economies will not operate on outer-bound production possibility surfaces consistent with their resources. Rather, they actually work on production surfaces that are well within that outer bound:

> This means that for a variety of reasons people and organizations normally work neither as hard nor as effectively as they could. In situations where competitive pressure is light, many people will trade the disutility of greater effort, of search, and the control of other people's activities for the utility of feeling less pressure and of better interpersonal relations. But in situations where competitive pressures are high, and hence the costs of such trades are also high, they will exchange less of the disutility of effort for the utility of freedom from pressure, etc. . . . The data suggest that in a great many instances the amount to be gained by increasing allocative efficiency is trivial while the amount to be gained by increasing X-efficiency is frequently significant.[8]

It is now possible to show the additional welfare losses imposed by monopoly when a shift from competition to monopoly increases production costs by increasing X-inefficiency. Figure 2 illustrates two alternative out-

7. For an explicit model, see M. A. Crew, M. Jones-Lee, and C. K. Rowley, "X-Theory versus Management Discretion Theory," *Southern Economic Journal* 37 (1971): 173–84.

8. Leibenstein, "Allocative Efficiency," 413.

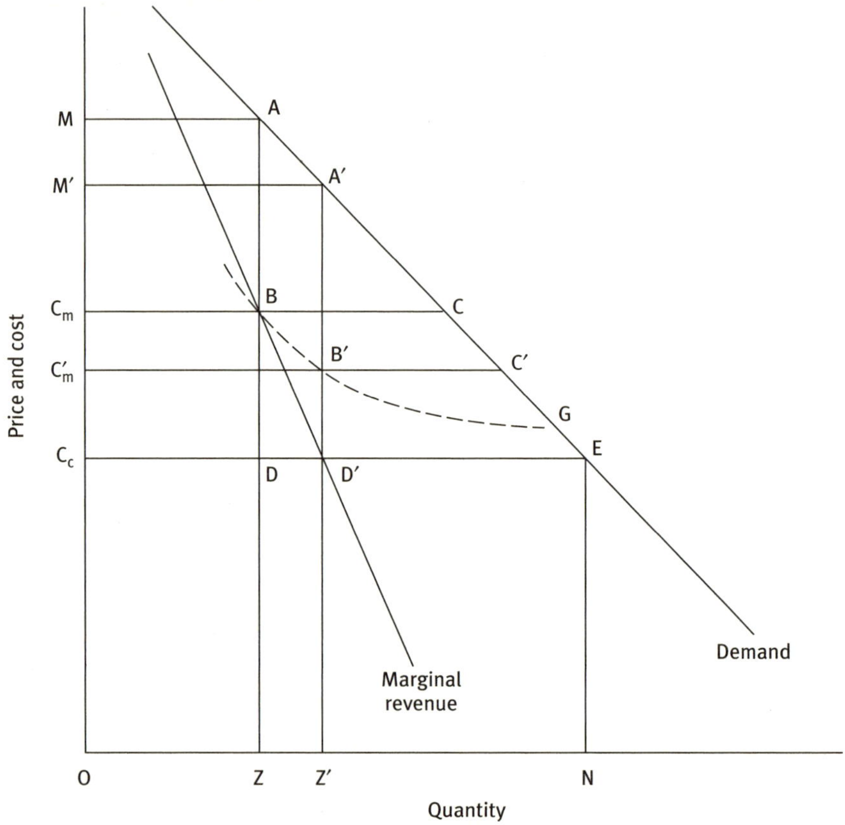

FIGURE 2
The Crew-Rowley model of X-inefficiency welfare losses

comes and is based upon a diagram initially presented by Crew and Rowley.[9] In one interpretation of this diagram, a shift from competition to monopoly increases average (and marginal) cost from C_c to C_m and raises price from C_c to M. Output falls from ON to OZ units. The welfare loss due to allocative inefficiency is depicted by the triangle ADE, which is considerably larger than the triangle that Harberger attempted to measure, ABC. To this welfare loss must be added the loss due to X-inefficiency depicted by the rectangle C_mC_cDB which itself typically will be much larger than the loss due to resource misallocation.

9. M. A. Crew and C. K. Rowley, "On Allocative Efficiency, X-Efficiency and the Measurement of Welfare Loss," *Economica* 38 (1971): 199–203.

In a second interpretation, X-inefficiency manifests itself as an overhead effect and does not strike at marginal cost. In such circumstances, the monopoly output rate is OZ′ > OZ, and the monopoly price is OM′ < OM. Average cost inclusive of overhead X-inefficieney is derived from the rectangular hyperbola constructed through B, which cuts demand at G. In this case, the average cost of producing the monopoly output OZ′ is OC'_m. In such circumstances, the welfare loss from X-inefficiency is depicted by the rectangle $C'_mC_cD'B'$, which is identical to C_mC_cDB in the first case. The welfare loss due to allocative inefficiency is depicted by the triangle A′D′E, which is clearly less than that defined in the first case.[10]

On the basis of this kind of analysis, Leibenstein concluded that "(m)icroeconomic theory focusses on allocative efficiency to the exclusion of other types of efficiencies that, in fact, are much more significant in many instances." Having read Leibenstein's paper, my attention was alerted to the welfare loss issue. I was not convinced by the X-inefficiency argument. Yet, I was equally not prepared to accept Mundell's pessimistic comment that "someone will inevitably draw the conclusion that economics has ceased to be important."[11]

Instead, I determined to explore the other route explored by Mundell, namely, "a thorough theoretical re-examination of the validity of the tools upon which these (welfare loss) studies are founded." I was absolutely certain that the classical economists were not concerning themselves with trifles when they argued against tariffs, and that the U.S. Department of Justice was not dealing with a minuscule problem in its attacks on monopoly. This time, it turned out that my intuition was not misdirected.

The Welfare Costs of Tariffs, Monopolies, and Theft

As in the case of Leibenstein, the point of departure for my paper "The Welfare Costs of Tariffs, Monopolies, and Theft" was the conventional welfare loss to monopoly associated with Harberger's famous triangle. Although my article dealt with tariffs and theft as well as with the monopoly problem, I shall draw here entirely on the monopoly example to outline the nature of

10. C. K. Rowley, *Antitrust and Economic Efficiency* (London: Macmillan, 1973).

11. Leibenstein, "Allocative Efficiency," 392; see also G. J. Stigler, "Xistence of X-efficiency," *American Economic Review* 66 (1976): 213–16; R. A. Mundell, "A Review of L. H. Janssen: Free Trade, Protection, and Customs Unions," *American Economic Review* 52 (1962): 622.

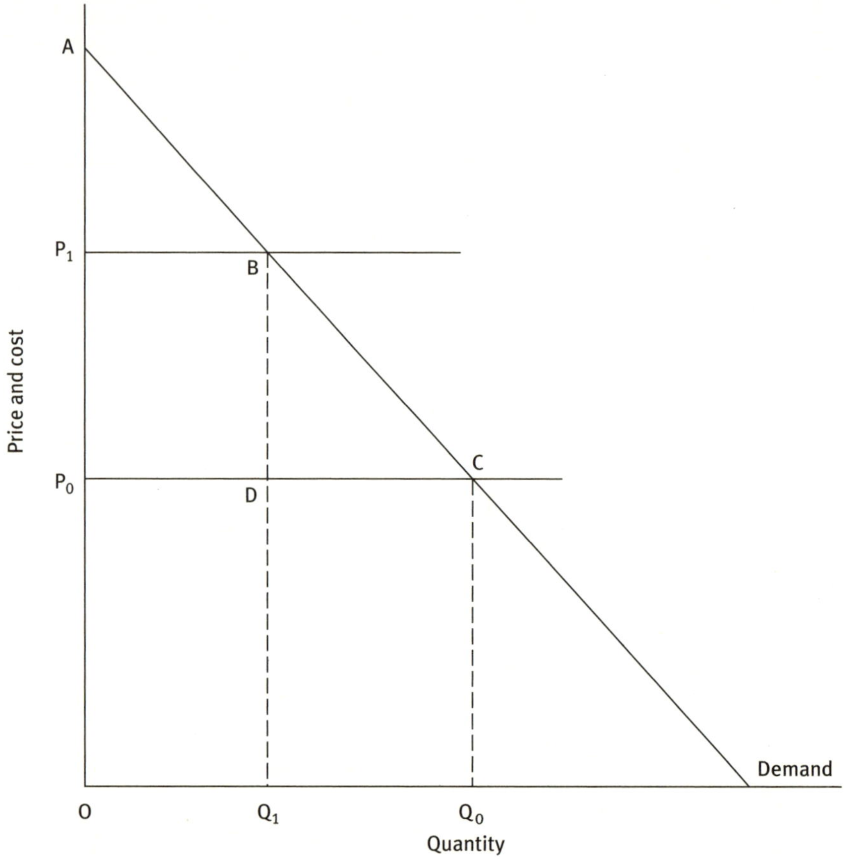

FIGURE 3
Tullock's model of the welfare loss from monopoly

my contribution, and I shall refer to my original diagram, reproduced here as Figure 3.

In Figure 3, a competitive industry is assumed to produce output OQ_0 at price OP_0, which is equal to marginal cost, thus generating a total (consumers') surplus depicted by the triangle AP_0C. The monopolist reduces output to OQ_1 and raises price to OP_1, reducing consumers' surplus to AP_1B. According to Harberger, the rectangle P_1BDP_0 depicts a simple transfer of surplus from consumers to monopolist, leaving a net loss of welfare depicted by the triangle BDC.

If the rectangle P_1BDP_0 in Figure 3 is the income transfer that a successful monopolist can extort from his customers, surely we would expect potential monopolists, with so large a prize dangling before them, to invest large resources in the activity of monopolizing. Indeed, the capital value, properly discounted for risk, of the monopoly transfer is much greater than the rectangle suggests, since the latter represents only a single period transfer. Entrepreneurs should be willing to invest resources in attempts to form a monopoly until the marginal cost equals the properly discounted marginal return. Potential customers should be interested in preventing the transfer and should be willing to make large investments to that end.

Even when a monopoly is established, continual efforts to break it up or to muscle into it would be predictable, once again involving a considerable investment of scarce resources. Such attacks predictably would induce the monopolist to invest resources in defence of its monopoly powers. The welfare triangle method of measurement ignores these important costs and hence greatly understates the welfare loss of monopoly. Evidently, the "Tullock rectangle" must be added, in whole or in part, to the "Harberger triangle" when calculating the potential loss of welfare associated with monopoly.

Although the point that I made in "Welfare Costs of Tariffs, Monopolies, and Theft," in retrospect was very simple, no one had recognized it before, and it was extremely important from the perspective both of formulating policy and of understanding the behaviour of government. The paper eventually made quite an impact on the economics profession. By April 1990, it had been cited 241 times, according to the Institute for Scientific Information.[12] Yet, I experienced considerable difficulty in getting it published.[13] First, I submitted it to the *American Economic Review*, where it was rejected by John Gurley, the editor, with the following remarks:

> You will no doubt note that the referee neglects your point regarding the amount of real resources devoted to establishing, promoting, destroying etc., monopolies. However, I have noted it and while I think it is certainly valid, it does not appear significant enough (as a theoretical contribution) to overthrow the referee's recommendation.[14]

12. G. C. Durden, L. V. Ellis, and S. W. Millsaps, "Gordon Tullock: His Journal and His Scholarship," *Public Choice* 71 (1991): 171–96.

13. G. Brady and R. D. Tollison, "Gordon Tullock: Creative Maverick of Public Choice," *Public Choice* 71 (1991): 141–48.

14. John Gurley, letter to author, 16 August 1966.

The paper was also rejected by the *Southern Economic Journal.* Robert E. Gallman, the managing editor, stated that "Tullock's main point that the 'small' triangle does not adequately measure welfare loss in the absence of perfect competition is well understood." He also argued that I had inadvertently misinterpreted the spirit of Harberger's paper, and erroneously concluded that "[w]hile Harberger called the small triangle the welfare loss, he also took account of the rectangle but called it, I think, misallocated resources."[15]

If somewhat chastened, I remained unshaken in my insight and submitted the paper yet again, this time to a relatively obscure journal, the *Western Economic Journal*, where it was finally recognized and published in June 1967. Probably because the journal did not circulate widely, my simple idea only slowly penetrated the economics profession, despite my presenting the paper at a number of professional meetings. Interestingly, following my presentation of the paper at George Washington University, I was approached by a member of the audience, Donald S. Watson, the editor of a widely circulated book of student readings, who asked my permission to reprint it in a revised edition. In view of the relative obscurity of the *Western Economic Journal* and the large circulation of Watson's *Book of Readings*, it seems likely that there was a considerable period of time during which my idea was known and understood by first-year economics students, but not known at all by the average professor of economics.[16]

It is interesting to speculate upon why my 1967 paper encountered such inflexible resistance from the leading journals of economics which yet published large numbers of essentially ephemeral and insignificant contributions. I believe that a number of factors played a role, many of which I had anticipated in my 1966 book, *The Organization of Inquiry*, and others that I learned after I embarked on my own editorial career, also in 1966, with the first publication of *Papers on Non-Market Decision Making.*[17]

To understand the behaviour of journal editors, it is necessary to take account of the non-market environment which is central to their operations.

15. Harberger, "Monopoly and Resource Allocation"; Robert E. Gallman, letter to author, 6 February 1967.

16. D. S. Watson, *Price Theory in Action: A Book of Readings* (1965; Boston: Houghton Mifflin, 1969).

17. G. Tullock, *Papers on Non-Market Decision Making* (Charlottesville: Thomas Jefferson Center for Political Economy, University of Virginia, 1966); see C. K. Rowley, "Gordon Tullock: Entrepreneur of Public Choice," *Public Choice* 71 (1991): 149–70.

The large majority of academic journals are non-profit organizations brokering a "market" in published scholarship which is made up of individual scholars who themselves are either public employees or employees of non-profit organizations. This is not an environment in which entrepreneurship predictably can thrive. The often unpaid editors of journals no doubt are motivated to do their best to select the most promising articles from among the contributions they receive; but their best may not be all that good. For, as I observed in 1966, "the job of journal editor, although respectable, is not one of sufficient attraction to get the very best personnel."[18]

Where editors are respected, but ordinary contributors to the literature in which their journals trade, and where they are unpaid or lowly paid servants of non-profit journals, they may lack both the skills and incentives to identify the unusual, original articles that cross the editorial desk. They may be attracted more by high technology than by creative scholarship.[19] Such a bias will not be countered by reliance upon unpaid anonymous referees who, under the shield of anonymity, are not under any great pressure to reach the correct decision. Both editor and referee have incentives to play safe, to accept high-technology articles that make a marginal contribution to a well-established field, but to deny publication to papers that threaten to pull down the pack of cards of normal science. As I noted in 1966, "[t]he prestige of a journal is affected by the articles it prints; it is not affected by those it turns down. This probably leads the editors to some degree, at any rate, to play safe."[20]

In any event, my 1967 article was simple, low tech, and brief, factors that evidently did not enamour it to the editors of two leading economics journals. Random factors in the choice of referees may have played a role. However, I suspect that my experience was not unusual, as Leibenstein's difficulties with the *American Economic Review* tend to confirm. Such inefficiencies may not matter much as long as the journal market remains reasonably competitive. In my case, I suspect that editorial inefficiencies retarded the dissemination of the rent-seeking insight by no more than seven years. Leibenstein, perhaps as a result of greater stubbornness, was able to wear down the editor into revising his initial rejection decision.

18. Tullock, *Organization of Inquiry.*

19. Rowley, "Gordon Tullock."

20. Tullock, *Organization of Inquiry*, 147.

The Cost of Transfers and Competing for Aid

In 1971, I returned to the theme of my 1967 paper, which as yet had made little headway in mainstream economics. Drawing on my discussion of theft, rather than of tariffs and monopoly, I directed attention to the cost of transfers. The welfare economics literature at that time was awash with notions of interdependent utility functions and of utility-enhancing income redistributions. Governments were accredited with a major role in such transfer processes, allegedly because of the public good characteristics of the charitable motive.[21]

The strong implicit assumption in such analysis was that transfers were effected costlessly from rich to poor individuals by impartial and well-advised governments that determined the size and composition of their transfer programmes by reference to the charitable preferences of the rich. Such arguments seemed to me to bear little relationship to the realities of the political process. My paper set out to bring a dash of reality to the redistribution literature.[22]

The problem is that, although the actual operation of charitable giving is profitable to all parties, its mere possibility sets off behaviour on the part of all parties, aimed at improving their respective utilities, but wasteful of scarce resources. Suppose that individual T perceives that individual K may make a charitable gift. Under these circumstances, he would be well advised to invest in becoming a more suitable object of K's charity. In cases with which I am familiar—Chinese beggars—such behaviour may lower the utility of all concerned. When I was in China, occasionally I would see beggars who had deliberately and usually horribly mutilated themselves in order to increase their charitable take. Even though I might be disposed to supply the charity that they sought, I always found that their mutilations inflicted a considerable negative utility on me.

In the Western world, such drastic measures are less frequent. However, many would-be recipients of charity do engage in a certain amount of resource expenditure to improve their receipts. Granted that the potential ob-

21. G. Tullock, "The Cost of Transfers," *Kyklos* 24 (1971): 629–43; Tullock, "Welfare Costs of Tariffs"; H. M. Hochman and J. R. Rogers, "Pareto Optimal Redistribution," *American Economic Review* 59 (1969): 542–57.

22. Tullock, "The Cost of Transfers."

jects of charity may behave in such a manner, the political donors feel obliged to invest resources in attempting to control such subterfuges. Such interactions are not simply a modern phenomenon. The hiring of almsmongers by medieval princes was an early effort to reduce the wastage of resources in attempts to attract charity by potential beneficiaries of the royal largesse.

The problem worsens sharply when private charity gives way to government redistribution of income. Of course, such government transfers are only in part involuntary. Presumably, taxpayer-citizens are interested in making charitable gifts to other persons and may choose to use the state as a cooperative instrument for that end. It seems likely, however, that government income redistribution is carried well beyond the point where those who are paying for the redistribution benefit. In my view, perhaps 90 per cent of all income transfers through the state are of this involuntary nature. They are the result of lobbying activities on the part of recipients, combined with ignorance and/or political weakness on the part of those individuals who supply the transfers. Transfers in the form of farm subsidies and of import protection for domestic steel producers and motor car manufacturers clearly fall into this category.

Much more clearly than in 1967, my 1971 paper focused on the resource cost of competitive lobbying of politicians and bureaucrats, both by those who sought to extract government transfers and those who sought to prevent them. One side or the other will win each such battle; but, from the social standpoint, the resources invested in the conflict between the two interest groups are entirely wasted. The fact that the transfer game itself is clearly a negative sum does not imply that those who engage in such political battles are behaving irrationally. It is just one example of a prisoners' dilemma in the oft-times inconvenient world in which we find ourselves.

In 1974, I was prompted by some probing criticisms from Edgar Browning to sharpen my 1971 insight and to further segment the government transfer process. Browning's commentary focused attention on examples of broad-based tax reform that transferred income from one group of millions of people to another group of similarly large size. With some justice, he claimed that voluntary contributions to lobbying often were not evident as the motive force for such redistributions. This led me to reflect upon the publicness characteristics of certain kinds of income redistribution and the free-riding that such characteristics implied. This phenomenon offered an explanation for the fact that, in democracies, there occurs a very large amount of self-cancelling transfers of income back and forth within the middle-income groups.[23]

One kind of transfer process—the kind that I had earlier outlined—clearly was subject to what I now call Wagner-type lobbying, in which politicians respond to well-defined interest groups within their districts and show more interest in brokering benefits to those groups than almost anything else, at immense cost in terms of legislative commitments.[24] The actual effect of this kind of lobbying is far greater than the direct resource costs involved, because a great many people who are not involved in lobbying find themselves affected by the outcome. My 1971 article talked mainly about transfers of this sort: decisions on appropriations or programmes that had a fairly concrete and narrow direct effect for some limited groups of people.

Another kind of transfer, however, involves large numbers of individuals, most of whom do not view the effect to be sufficiently large as to justify the investment in lobbying resources. In such circumstances, the outcome is apt to be random. For some such changes they benefit, for some they lose. We might anticipate that, over the population as a whole, individuals who are not involved in active lobbying would tend to gain about as much as they lose. I should add that transfers from the wealthy to the poor do not feature much in this kind of random redistribution.

My 1974 reflections led me to conclude that the population either invests in lobbying or participates in a lottery. For the first group, which is probably small, my original description is more or less correct. For the second, and much larger group, there is an excess burden but, on the average, no net transfer of income or wealth. It is interesting to note that the cost of transfers debate was conducted in *Kyklos* and not in the *American Economic Review*, since George H. Borts, the managing editor of the latter journal, had rejected my 1971 paper citing the following referee's remarks:

> This paper does not have anything useful to offer. Its principal point is that the possibility of income or wealth transfers has the unfortunate consequence that people invest resources either to abstain or to prevent them.[25]

23. E. K. Browning, "On the Welfare Costs of Transfers," *Kyklos* 27 (1974): 374–77; G. Tullock, "More on the Welfare Cost of Transfers," *Kyklos* 27 (1974): 378–81.

24. R. E. Wagner, "Price Groups and Political Entrepreneurs: A Review Article," *Papers on Non-Market Decision Making* (Charlottesville: Thomas Jefferson Center for Political Economy, University of Virginia, 1966): 161–70.

25. George H. Borts, letter to author, 18 February 1971.

In 1975, I extended my analysis of transfers to demonstrate that wasteful competition over transfers was not restricted to individuals but also occurred among the various levels of government within a multi-layer system. In "Competing for Aid," I illustrated my thesis by reference to public road rebuilding programmes. I discussed a situation, common in the United States, in which a higher level of government programme provided assistance to lower-level government organizations in accordance with their "need." I showed how lower-level organizations would respond to such a set of incentives by deliberately neglecting road repairs in order to qualify for higher-level subsidies. My arguments were not hypothetical. I showed how the city of Blacksburg had deliberately skewed road repair contracts away from its most damaged roads in order to be targeted for repair by the Commonwealth of Virginia. I showed how the development of divided centre, limited access toll highways during the early 1950s was almost completely self-aborted once President Eisenhower introduced the federally subsidized interstate system.[26]

The local community that allows its road system to deteriorate in order to qualify for state subsidies or that runs down its hospital system in the expectation that the federal government will replace it is in exactly the same situation as the Chinese beggar who mutilates himself to obtain charity from passers-by. In both cases, the action is rational. In both cases, the effect is to lower the welfare of those involved.

The Concept of Rent Seeking

The reader will be aware that the term "rent seeking" was not applied in any of my early contributions to the welfare cost literature. The term was invented in 1974 by Anne Krueger in a paper published in the *American Economic Review.* The author was unaware of my contributions to the subject, no doubt because they had been published in relatively obscure journals, and therefore did not cite them in her paper. The fact that her article was published in a major economics journal, together with the catchy nature of her term, "rent seeking," undoubtedly speeded up the dissemination of the basic idea within the economics profession.[27]

26. G. Tullock, "Competing for Aid," *Public Choice* 21 (1975): 41–52.

27. A. O. Krueger, "The Political Economy of the Rent-Seeking Society," *American Economic Review* 64 (1974): 291–303.

Krueger's article focused attention upon market-oriented economies in which government restrictions upon economic activity are pervasive facts of life. Such restrictions give rise to rents in a variety of forms; and people often compete for rents. Sometimes such competition is perfectly legal. In other instances, rent seeking takes illegal routes, such as bribery, corruption, smuggling, and black markets. Krueger developed a model of competitive rent seeking for the important case when rents originate from quantitative restrictions upon international trade. In this case, she inferred that:

1. competitive rent seeking leads to the operation of the economy inside its transformation curve;
2. the welfare loss associated with quantitative restrictions is unequivocally greater than the loss from the tariff equivalent of those restrictions; and
3. competitive rent seeking results in a divergence between the private and social costs of certain activities.

She provided estimates of the value of rents from import licences from India and Turkey, finding them to be large relative to the gross national products of those countries.

It is interesting to speculate as to why Krueger's paper was accepted by the *American Economic Review* following the journal's rejection of my two earlier articles on an almost identical theme. It does not seem to me that the intrinsic randomness of the refereeing process was entirely responsible. I believe that three factors contributed to the editorial decision. First, Krueger's paper was somewhat more lengthy and a little more technical than either of my two papers. Second, the paper contained some statistical measures, albeit very crude, of the magnitude of rents involved. Third, and most significant in my judgement, was the fact that her analysis focused on rent seeking in India and Turkey, whereas my articles utilized examples clearly relevant to the United States. Referees tend to be less troubled in recognizing insights that challenge the status quo if such insights appear to be directed at far distant lands. They become much less comfortable when acknowledging that they have been teaching their students falsehoods that impact directly on an understanding of their own domestic economies. In any event, Anne Krueger's forceful and well-written article served an invaluable purpose in publicizing the basic idea of rent seeking widely across the English-speaking economics profession.

It is perhaps noteworthy that three early contributors to the rent-seeking literature—myself, Anne Krueger, and Jagdish Bhagwati—have all spent a good deal of time in the Far East, where there coexists a number of immensely successful cultures capable of generating high-quality art, literature, etc. Yet, many of these civilizations, despite their cultural successes, are economically backward, even though they evidence no shortage of highly intelligent, well-educated, and highly motivated individuals.[28]

The *émigré* Chinese of southeast Asia and the United States perform extremely well, as do the *émigré* Indians of Africa. Only in their own homelands do they fail to perform well. The phenomenon is not peculiar to Chinese, Indian, or Islamic cultures, but rather is located in the traditional governmental institutions of these various backward societies. Rent seeking offers a powerful general explanation of this apparent paradox. It is not surprising that our common exposure to economic failure in culturally advanced societies led Krueger, Bhagwati, and myself to the rent-seeking explanation.

It used to be customary in the lumbering industry to cut down the trees, roll them into a stream, and float them down to the mill. There was a tendency for some of the tree trunks to get caught in gigantic jams that actually dammed up the waters of the stream. The breaking of these dams, a highly dangerous activity, involved, at least in myth, the locating of the key log. When the key log was removed, the logjam was broken and the downstream movements of the logs recommenced.

It would appear that the rent-seeking concept was a key log in certain areas of economic research. In these areas, progress was retarded by the existence of such a jam. Once rent seeking was discovered, there followed an immense florescence of research, taking the form of an exponential curve, as relevant ideas began to disseminate throughout economics. Of course, the rent-seeking concept has now found its way well beyond economics into the litany of political science and sociology. It has found its way onto the pages of the *Wall Street Journal* and even into the speeches of better-educated members of Congress. Interestingly enough, such congressmen do not appear to be unduly perturbed when they confront the real implications of their professional life.

This rapid intellectual advance has been well chronicled in two volumes of

28. J. N. Bhagwati, "Lobbying and Welfare," *Journal of Public Economics* 14 (1980): 355–63; J. N. Bhagwati, R. A. Brecher, and T. N. Srinivasan, "DUP Activities and Economic Theory," in *Neoclassical Political Economy*, ed. D. C. Colander (Cambridge: Ballinger, 1984), 17–32.

readings. The first volume—*Toward a Theory of the Rent-Seeking Society*—was edited in 1980 by Buchanan, Tollison, and Tullock and contained a large majority of the articles on rent seeking that had been published up to that time. The second volume—*The Political Economy of Rent-Seeking*—edited in 1988 by Rowley, Tollison, and Tullock could afford to be a good deal more selective and encompassed a much smaller percentage of the incremental output of papers. The major introduction to the second volume, by Charles Rowley and myself, could and did present a much more comprehensive picture, and a better-balanced assessment of the research that had been completed up to that point.[29]

On the whole, what has been done since that time has been an extension of the same basic concepts into other areas. The use of resources to obtain through the political process special privileges in which the injury to other people arguably is greater than the gain to the people who obtain rents is now a major subject in economics. It has spread well beyond economics, into political science, orientalism, and sociology.

This raises certain problems which require clarification. The first of these is that investing resources in order to obtain a rent is not necessarily rent seeking. For example, if I were to invest resources in research and invent a cure for cancer, which I then were to patent, I should certainly become wealthy on the rents that would be generated. This, however, is not really what we mean by rent seeking. The result of my resource investment not only is that I am better off, but so is almost everyone else.

When I was editor of *Public Choice* I used to receive, on average, twice a year an article by a young assistant professor or sometimes a graduate student who would excitedly point out that research and patents were examples of rent seeking. It is true that resources are invested and that rents are derived, but some activities bear little resemblance to the overall welfare losses that are imposed by the artificial creation of tariff barriers. If, on the other hand, I were to invest resources in obtaining a law prohibiting the import of a newly devised cure for cancer, because I am myself a manufacturer of an older and

29. J. M. Buchanan, R. D. Tollison, and G. Tullock, eds., *Toward a Theory of the Rent-Seeking Society* (College Station: Texas A&M University Press, 1980); C. K. Rowley, R. D. Tollison, and G. Tullock, *The Political Economy of Rent-Seeking* (Boston: Kluwer Academic Publishers, 1988); C. K. Rowley and G. Tullock, introduction to Rowley, Tollison, and Tullock, *Political Economy of Rent-Seeking*, 3–14.

less effective one, then I might gain, but almost everyone else would lose. This is the kind of thing that we mean by rent seeking.

The second limitation of most of the rent-seeking literature is that it deals with the manipulation of democratic governments in order to obtain rents through injuring other people. The U.S. farm programme is an example. Speaking as the only person in public choice who has actually written a book on dictatorships, I can assure readers that these impositions are not restricted to democracies. Indeed, what is called socialism in much of the backward world is simply an elaborate mechanism for transferring rents to friends and close supporters of the dictator.[30]

It is an unfortunate fact that recent events which signal the death throes of socialism and the rebirth of what is designated as capitalism have not brought about very great improvements from the rent-seeking perspective. In what is called "crony capitalism," the man who in the past would have been a rather inept manager of a government-owned sugar central is now the owner. He is still inept and still requires special government protection to support his activities. In both cases, typically, he does very well for himself.

Attempts to measure the scope of rent seeking, which will be discussed later, have not led to any definite conclusions. Superficial examination would seem to indicate that rent seeking is much more important in dictatorships than it is in democracies.[31] This book will primarily concern itself with rent seeking where it involves manipulating democratic governments. This is not because democratic governments are particularly prone to rent seeking. It is because most of the research has been done in this area; and, in fact, it is much easier to do research in the relatively open situation of democracies than it is in the murky environment of most dictatorships.

Another restriction is that I shall not write much about rent seeking in the form of private seeking of private monopolies. This is essentially because I do not consider such activities to be economically significant at the present time, though they have been important in the past.[32] Today it is very difficult indeed for a private group, without government aid, to obtain a monopoly by any method except by providing commodities at low prices and with good-quality service.

30. G. Tullock, *Autocracy* (Boston: Kluwer Academic Publishers, 1987).

31. Ibid.

32. Rowley and Tullock, introduction.

This is partly because there are antitrust laws (which in fact sometimes inconveniences companies that are sole producers because they are simply cheaper and better). But more important is the fact that the economy is large, transportation and communication are easy, and almost any monopoly obtaining excess profits is likely to attract competitors. For the most part, private markets are highly contestable. In small corners of society we may still find companies producing some commodity for which the total demand is low enough so that it is unlikely to attract a competitor even though it is selling at wide price-cost margins. But this is the exception and not the general rule.

For the most part, companies do not make the kind of excess profits that they would make if they had a private monopoly. Nor is there much evidence that X-inefficiency raises private costs in allegedly protected markets.[33] As we shall see, publicly sponsored monopolies also frequently do not make very large profits, although the fact that the businessmen, labour unions, and academics seek them out indicates they are certainly better from the owner's standpoint than a purely competitive situation.

For the rest of this book, we shall primarily concern ourselves with the manipulation of democratic governments to obtain special privileges under circumstances where the people injured by these privileges are hurt more than the beneficiary gains. We shall also evaluate the behaviour of individuals who attempt to defend themselves against such monopolies and of people who engage in lobbying activity for the purpose of dismantling them. The latter activity I would not call rent seeking; but there are some people who would.

The Political Market in Rent Seeking

As it happens, the rent-seeking research programme, for the most part, has followed the public choice tradition of which my own work is a part. Anne Krueger's paper has stimulated a separate research programme labelled by Jagdish Bhagwati as "directly unproductive profit-seeking."[34] Both pro-

33. But see R. Franz, "X-Efficiency and Allocative Efficiency: What Have We Learned?" *American Economic Review* 82 (1992): 434–38.

34. Krueger, "Rent-Seeking Society"; Bhagwati et al., "DUP Activities and Economic Theory"; Bhagwati, "Lobbying and Welfare."

grammes focus attention upon individual or group economic behaviour of a rational, self-seeking nature which nevertheless destroys rather than enhances the resources available to society. Both programmes have radically changed our understanding of the behaviour of political and bureaucratic markets and may have shifted the views of many individuals on the value of constitutional constraints. Yet the two approaches differ significantly, most particularly with respect to the role of political markets in the rent-seeking society.[35]

My initial 1967 paper directed the attention of welfare loss scholars away from private and towards publicly created monopolies and away from Harberger triangles towards Tullock rectangles. But only in one sentence did I hint at the public choice implications of these insights, noting that governments usually do not introduce tariffs in the absence of interest group lobbying in favour of this instrument of trade protection. In retrospect, somewhat surprisingly, I failed to develop this implication as a central feature of my paper, thus delaying the public choice linkage for some four years.

The public choice linkage came in 1971 with my paper on the cost of transfers. I emphasized in that paper that the opportunity to effect wealth transfers through the machinery of government, on at least a partially coercive basis, encourages lobbying and counter-lobbying in a negative sum game as individuals and groups invest resources in attempts to obtain transfers or to resist transfers away from themselves.

The crucial public choice aspect of this insight is the notion that the mere possibility of transfers attracts rent-seeking and rent-protection outlays that will condition the nature of the transfer outcome. More generally, the particular rents made available by government fiat ***are determined by and do not determine*** the level and composition of rent-seeking outlays. The political process is itself endogenous to the rent-seeking process. In contrast, DUP analyzes rent seeking in terms of exogenously determined rents, paying little or no attention to the public choice characteristics of that market. In this book, I emphasize the public choice approach to rent seeking and ignore the DUP approach (though I do rather like the term DUP). In this section, I shall briefly review the principal actors in the political market for rents, the voters, the media, the interest groups, and the bureaucrats. First, I must review the role of those who broker that market in exchange for votes, cam-

35. C. K. Rowley, "Rent-Seeking versus Directly Unproductive Profit-Seeking Activities," in Rowley, Tollison, and Tullock, *Political Economy of Rent-Seeking*.

paign contributions, and other perquisites of office, namely the politicians at all levels of the federal system.

THE LEGISLATORS

In the public choice research programme, politicians are modelled as providing a brokering function in the political market for wealth transfers. Special-interest groups capable of effective organization "demand" such transfers. Other more general groups, including many individual voters, incapable of such effective economic organization, "supply" such transfers, albeit sometimes after an ineffective struggle. Politicians affect political market equilibrium, balancing their own benefits against their costs at the margin, maximizing their individual utilities, variously weighted in terms of expected wealth and expected votes.[36] It is within the framework of this basic model that I shall review the behaviour of U.S. legislators. With minor adjustments, the approach applies to democratic legislators worldwide.

Let me start with a quotation from Republican Congressman Armey, who recently proposed an amendment to the Agricultural Act providing that farmers with more than $125,000 a year of non-farm income would not receive any government subsidies. His amendment was defeated 2–1 on the floor of the House of Representatives by a recorded vote. The immediate reaction of someone not schooled in public choice is that two-thirds of the U.S. congressmen had lost their minds. Imagine voting in favour of giving government subsidies to farmers who are so wealthy that their non-farm income exceeds $125,000 a year. Armey, however, explained the matter:

> There are no weak sisters on the agricultural committee. They do what the committees do very well. They spend five years filling their silos with chits and then they call them in.

Anyone paying attention to Congress can think of very many other similar cases. Senator John Warner, a rather conservative legislator from Virginia, for example, for many years succeeded in preventing the army from closing down a fort which was so antique that it actually had a moat. I am happy to say that it was finally closed down; but only by being converted into a national monument and museum with almost as many employees as the fort had supported.

36. C. K. Rowley, W. F. Shughart, and R. D. Tollison, "Interest Groups and Deficits," in *Deficits*, ed. J. M. Buchanan, C. K. Rowley, and R. D. Tollison (Oxford: Basil Blackwell, 1987), 263–80.

As one of the co-authors of *The Calculus of Consent*, I am not arguing that "log-rolling" trades of this sort are always rent seeking. Indeed, in many circumstances they actually lead to a better result than would be obtained if no such trade existed. It can however be used, as in the two cases cited above, to generate rents.[37]

Indeed, in some cases, bills without any log-rolling potential at all, but which are clearly of a rent-seeking nature, pass through the legislature. The various legislative expansions of Medicare in the United States are examples. Here, of course, there is a powerful special interest group in the form of doctors and other medical service providers; however, it seems fairly certain that congressmen are more interested in the very large number of voters who benefit from these services, and who do not realize that they are paying taxes to finance them.

The United States is a particularly convenient place for empirical research in this area because it can be subdivided into the 50 states, 48 of which are contiguous to each other. Although the legislative institutions bear considerable resemblance, they are not identical. The situation is ideal for cross-sectional research, and the very detailed statistical data available make quite elaborate research of this sort possible. McCormick, Tollison, and Crain have been especially prolific in researching these issues.[38]

Legislative trades even occur in local government. Recently, a bond issue was defeated in an election vote in Pima County, Arizona (which includes Tucson). The apparent reason was that the various road-repair projects did not include anything for the southwest district. The city council and the county board of supervisors redrafted it so that there was something for everybody. In this case it is likely to be one of the cases where log-rolling leads to a superior outcome. Each of the individual road repairs would certainly be defeated if voted on all by itself; but the package which will contain mainly road repair and improvements which are indeed socially desirable or at least very close to socially desirable got through.

Thus, this example may not constitute rent seeking, in our definition of that concept, even though there are trades. Legislative trades are not in and of themselves rent seeking or undesirable. It is only when the trades are used

37. J. M. Buchanan and G. Tullock, *The Calculus of Consent: Logical Foundations of Constitutional Democracy* (Ann Arbor: University of Michigan Press, 1962).

38. R. E. McCormick and R. D. Tollison, *Politicians, Legislation, and the Economy: An Inquiry into the Interest Group Theory of Government* (Boston: Martinus Nijhoff, 1981); W. M. Crain and R. D. Tollison, *Predicting Politics* (Ann Arbor: University of Michigan Press, 1990).

to produce wealth-reducing commodities like the farm programme or to maintain useless army posts which are surrounded by moats that the issue comes up.

A particularly striking example of this kind of thing is the decision by the Democratic Party in the U.S. Congress not to push for significant reductions in American defence after the collapse of the Soviet empire. The explanation given by congressmen in public speeches, and mentioned in all the newspapers, is that the congressmen are worried about losing military bases or contracts to defence industries in their districts. Thus, the real purpose of maintaining the military will not be buying insurance in the event that the Soviets should revert to Cold War strategies, but buying votes in a large number of different congressional districts.

In addition to the more-or-less straightforward cross-section regression studies carried out by Tollison in association with numerous research associates, a number of other scholars have done excellent work. Peltzman and Stigler are names that immediately come to mind. Stigler is primarily famous for having been the first person to point out that government regulatory agencies are normally not "captured" by the people they regulate. Normally what happens is they are set up by the people they regulate. As he once put it, complaining about a regulatory commission protecting the people regulated from falling prices is very much like complaining about dentists because they work on teeth. In both cases they are doing their job. Such regulatory agencies are usually driven by specialized interest groups and are by no means as profitable to the companies that they regulate as some of the literature suggests. One problem, first discussed by Posner, is that these agencies are primarily employed to transfer money back and forth among politically powerful groups.[39]

There is a particularly clear-cut example of this. The regulation of telephones by the Federal Communications Commission was largely the result of lobbying by AT&T, which was beginning to find competition cutting into its profits. Nevertheless, AT&T was only one, comparatively minor, beneficiary. During the period when the telephones were regulated by the Federal Communications Commission in a centralized way, the price of long-distance calls was kept artificially high in order to subsidize local callers. It

39. S. Peltzman, "Toward a More General Theory of Regulation," *Journal of Law and Economics* 19 (1976): 211–40; Stigler, "Xistence of X-efficiency"; R. A. Posner, "The Social Costs of Monopoly and Regulation," *Journal of Political Economy* 83 (1975): 807–27.

was, in essence, a tax on part of the economy in order to subsidize a large number of voters. It is particularly interesting because it is not obvious that the voters who were subsidized actually gained.

The long-distance calls which were held at an artificially high price were partly ordinary citizens' calls, and only partly business calls. Although the poorly informed voter thought he was getting a subsidy from the business calls, in a competitive economy, even those would eventually be reflected in higher prices of consumer goods. Thus the individual who found a dollar taken off his local phone bill by this subsidy, paid for by high prices on long-distance calls, in all probability would pay a dollar or more per month extra in higher prices on various consumer goods. The regulation generated an invisible tax funding a rather visible subsidy, to the benefit of vote-seeking politicians.

Even this, however, is a little too superficial. It is not at all obvious that most people receiving this subsidy knew that they were receiving it, let alone that they were paying a tax. It was only when rival interests began talking about eliminating it that the real situation became clear to the average voter. Nevertheless, the average voter did want low prices on his local telephone bill, and brought political pressure to bear both on his congressman and on the Commission. He probably failed to realize that there was an offsetting cost.

Peltzman's work has been directly connected with income transfers, and he has argued more or less that politically powerful people, essentially in the middle class, have used the government structure to transfer funds from the wealthy to the poor. Actually, to say that they transfer resources to the poor is not literally true. What happens is that the poor do not get very much of the largesse of the welfare state, indeed, probably less than their votes would normally entitle them to.[40] It is unfortunately true that both Stigler and Peltzman, prominent economists to say the least, made a fundamental mistake. They talked about the whole process in terms of its welfare transfer outcomes and did not discuss at all the rent-seeking cost of the process.

This is a particularly impressive lacuna in the case of Stigler, who talked about regulatory bodies as being set up for the specific purpose of benefiting the interests that had arranged them, but never discussed the cost of this process. Recognition that such costs exist is of course the heart of rent seeking.

40. G. Tullock, *The Economics of Special Privilege and Rent Seeking* (Boston: Kluwer Academic Publishers, 1989).

Becker, who wrote a very good article on interest group competition in which he pointed out that the result of certain groups pushing for special privileges and other groups counter-pressuring to avoid being victimized should lead to a balance which is at least arguably some kind of political optimum, failed to emphasize the rent-seeking cost of this exercise.[41]

What do congressmen get out of all of this? Since they are engaging in rent seeking they must get something, but I suspect usually not very much. There is talk about campaign contributions, and it is true that congressmen can privatize some of the contributions. No doubt this has an important influence on their behaviour; but it is very small compared with the value of the privileges they hand out. It is not the major rent-seeking cost.

More important is the careful courting of the congressmen by lobbyists. The many expense-account restaurants and night clubs found not only in Washington, D.C., but in the state capitals are evidence of that. Once again, however, such outlays are relatively low compared with the value of the gifts that congressmen hand out. The major cost of rent seeking must be found elsewhere. It seems likely from the standpoint of the congressmen that the principal reward they seek is simply being re-elected. Each pressure group argues strongly that it can sway at least some votes, and provide some campaign monies, and that the congressman had better therefore pay careful attention to its requests.

The congressmen, or for that matter the state representative or even the city council member, is normally convinced that he is vulnerable at the next election and that he must pay careful attention to various small groups of voters. This being so, his staffers spend a great deal of time on such matters. This work is particularly impressive because frequently the congressman represents a number of different groups, each of which wants something and each of which to some extent objects to the requests of other groups. He must forge some cautious compromise in which everybody gets a little something. The net effect of this may be that, for each of these groups, the gain that they receive, minus the cost of all the gifts to the others, is actually modest or even negative, once rent-seeking costs are accounted for.

Thus the bulk of the cost of a specific policy output is not the rent seeking that triggered it but the unsuccessful outlays by other groups that the congressman trades off in order to implement it. Unfortunately, this has so far es-

41. G. S. Becker, "A Theory of Competition among Pressure Groups for Political Influence," *Quarterly Journal of Economics* 47 (1983): 371–400.

caped measurement; and I have no suggestion as to how to make such measurements. The fact that it is difficult to measure does not imply that it is qualitatively insignificant.

The complexity of the various pieces of legislation that now wind their way through the legislature, each of which is normally an immense pastiche of specific provisions dealing with specific problems in accord with the wishes of some small group, is a major cost for the country as a whole. Most of the gigantic volume of laws, and for that matter the even more gigantic volume of regulations, are never read by the nominal decision-makers, or indeed by any single individual inside or outside the legislature. They are closely scrutinized by attorneys seeking to use them for private advantage. The congressman or the secretary simply does not have the time to read all of this detail, and, in addition, he would probably not fully understand it should he do so. The Internal Revenue Act is an informative example. There used to be, before the Reagan reforms, 17 pages in the Internal Revenue Act dealing with the raising of racehorses. This provision had been introduced successfully by lobbyists for the racehorse "industry" and carefully surveyed by officials from the Internal Revenue Service who wanted to see to it that political revenues were not damaged excessively. It is doubtful whether more than four or five people actually fully understood those pages.

In this case we know that the clauses must have been very favourable for the horse-racing industry, because when the Reagan reforms abolished those sections, the racehorse industry immediately experienced a severe economic depression. The price of prime stallions, for example, fell catastrophically. Thus, this was a case in which, quite inconspicuously, a group of very wealthy men, most of whom in fact were pursuing the raising of racehorses as a hobby, obtained very great tax reductions from special-interest legislation. The cost of such secretive lobbying, however, is extremely difficult to measure.

It is not at all obvious that the congressman regards the fact that he does not read most of the bills he passes as immoral, or the fact that he would not understand them if he did as pitiful. After all, all his colleagues legislate in a similar fashion, and his own lack of attention to detail is protected by the rational ignorance of the electorate.

The cost to society as a whole, however, from this professional ineptitude must be very great indeed. One of the functions of government is to provide a national co-ordinated policy programme. If policy, in fact, is a very large collection of special provisions which are never co-ordinated, or for that matter not even all read by any one person, then this function fails.

One of the duties of the courts is to deal with acts of Congress that are inconsistent, either internally or with each other. Fortunately for the courts, but unfortunately for each of the rest of us, most of these provisions are simply gifts to individual interest groups, and hence they are not strictly speaking inconsistent. They cause difficulty only by raising the federal deficit and increasing regulatory intervention; and the courts are not responsible directly for these outcomes.

One of the characteristics shown by American public opinion polls is that most Americans distrust and dislike Congress but trust and like their own Congress person. This is a fairly clear example of the role of the Congress person in a rent-seeking society. The average American realizes that the whole bundle of bills that I have been describing serves to his disadvantage. He also realizes that his representative is seeing to it that among the large collection of wealth-reducing bills there are a good many which he himself benefits from.

Assume, just for sake of argument, that each congressman in the House of Representatives can influence 1/435 of the total legislation. The individual voter feels that 1/435 is influenced in his favour by the congressman. The other 434/435, on the other hand, most likely are to his net disadvantage. Since he cannot influence Congress as a whole, he tends to dislike Congress and yet to like his own congressman. This dichotomy is entirely rational.

THE VOTERS

The first thing to be said about voters is that typically they are very badly informed. Any specialist who discusses policy issues even with well-educated citizens quickly realizes that this is true. One illustration of this is that public opinion pollsters usually encounter quite appalling ignorance if they choose to question people in detail on almost any issue. For example, should they ask questions like: "Which is the fissionable kind of uranium?" they may find something of the order of one-tenth of one per cent of the population is correctly informed. If they change to another form of questioning such as: "Do you feel informed about atomic energy?" they find that large majorities of those polled are informed. In political polls they always find that a significant minority do not know the name of their President.

The majority of voters do not even know the name of their congressional representative. Louis Harris & Associates have responded to this ignorance by asking not for the name, but for the voter's opinion on whether he knows it. Even here they get only 65 per cent who say they know.[42] This lack of information tends to irritate political scientists. Statements like "You have a duty to cast an informed vote" are frequently included in American government classes. Perhaps the average voter does have such a duty; but it is clear that he pays little practical attention to it.

One of the first contributions of public choice to this field was the demonstration, first by Anthony Downs and then elaborated on to some extent by myself, that the average voter may recognize his civic duty, and may in fact feel guilty if he does not become well informed.[43] However, in strict cost-benefit terms he is rational to be ignorant. The reason for this is simply that the influence his individual vote has on almost any election is so small that even very modest information costs swamp expected net benefits from informed voting. Thus, the average voter makes a correct calculation to remain potentially unaware, even if his professor of American government does not approve of his rational calculus. He may even make the correct calculation to avoid the polling booths come election day.

There are, of course, a number of people who are well informed, and I presume the bulk of the readers of this book will be among them. They are to a large extent people who are pursuing a hobby of politics or, in my case, of international affairs.

With these hobbyists, however, it is notable that political information does not seem to have very much effect on their vote behaviour. Polling information indicates that the more information a person has, the less likely he is to switch from one political party to another. Thus, it would appear that he acquires the information for the purpose of carrying on conversations with other people, feeling superior, and, more important than either of these, cheering on his team. Baseball used to be more important as a national sport than it is now. Fans then memorized immense volumes of statistics about various baseball teams. They never let that affect the question of which team they supported.

This lack of political information is of very great importance when we speak of rent seeking. Unfortunately, it is not simple straightforward random ignorance. It is biased ignorance. An individual is likely to have a good deal of information about a few narrow subjects which concern him deeply.

42. *American Enterprise*, May–June, 1992, 102.

43. A. Downs, *An Economic Theory of Democracy* (New York: Harper and Row, 1957); Tullock, *Toward a Mathematics of Politics*.

A farmer probably knows a good deal about his particular crops and, in general, has been informed by the various agricultural journals he reads about the political programme for those crops and what his congressman has done about it. This is the ideal arrangement for a pressure group since the farmer almost never has much information about other aspects of the overall political programme. For example, a proposal to cut back the acreage of U.S. farmland ultimately may cause starvation in parts of Africa. The agricultural journals will never note the relationship between cause and effect, not least because such a linkage would make their readers feel guilty and they might switch to another publication.

Such biased ignorance is not restricted to farmers. I myself am an academic and have listened to a good many speeches by political candidates of one sort or another directed at academic audiences. Such speeches normally include at least something about the public good aspects of education, with the general drift of argument somewhat to the left of centre because that is judged to be what an academic audience wants. Always they include comments about the importance of education, the need to have good teachers, and the need to pay them well.

Name recognition is of great importance in elections. Both professional politicians and political scientists agree that one of the problems of a candidate who is not a current incumbent is simply to get his name recognized. The incumbent usually already has such recognition. The elaborate mailing out of campaign literature, officially listed as information, in the period between elections is to a large extent an effort simply to get voters to recognize the name of their congressman.

To repeat, this information is distributed asymmetrically and is not just the property of the well-established interest groups. Congressmen are fairly continuously approached by people who want a specific favour or some project in their particular area carried out. An important example of this is the complaint by senior citizens that their social security check has not arrived or that the Social Security Administration has made some kind of error.

In general, in this area it seems likely that congressional intervention makes the citizen service of the Social Security Administration better than it would otherwise be. Whether this improvement in service is worth the cost is something on which, as far as I know, there are no studies; but I would guess that it is cost effective. A large part of any congressman's staff is engaged in tasks rather similar to this and for that matter in simply responding to letters from constituents.

In general, the fact that a congressman says he is on a particular elector's side is pleasurable; but if he does not actually bring home the pork, get whatever favour is requested, he is likely to be remembered for that rather than for his politeness. Most congressmen have a large staff which, in addition to dealing with what we might call the wholesale market, the major pressure groups, also attempts to accumulate votes on a one-for-one basis by taking care of various minor problems.

The question of whether dealing with these minor problems benefits the country as a whole is open; and whether the benefit is worth the cost is an even more difficult question. It should be pointed out that the cost is not just the salaries and other perquisites of office of the congressional staff. As a general rule, most government bureaucracies give any inquiries from a congressional office top priority; and hence, one of the costs of congressional intervention is that many other things, some of which may be more important, are put aside until the office has responded to the congressional inquiry.

The result of all this is that voters are, to a considerable extent, a major source of rent seeking. It should be pointed out, however, that for some types of policy determination a system of direct popular votes or referenda is superior to log-rolling within the legislature. Well-organized pressure groups can frequently manoeuvre the legislature into enacting legislation that would never get through a popular vote.

The countervailing problem is that a direct popular vote puts the issue before a large number of voters, most of whom do not know anything much about the issue, who have at least some tendency to vote either for or against the issue entirely in terms of their confidence in the governmental process. But it is very hard to look at the results of referenda in areas where pressure groups operate without feeling that the referenda do reduce the frequency with which severe costs are imposed.

Yet voters who, let us say, vote against a quota on eggs are often the very same voters who are apt to push the congressman into providing them with special privileges. Only when the subject is so transparent that even the badly informed voter notices what is going on will referenda tend to drive out special privileges for small minorities.

There is a good deal of talk in the popular press, as well as in public choice literature, about campaign contributions both by individuals and by political action committees (PAC). There is no doubt that these outlays influence congressmen. There is also no doubt that such outlays are very small compared with the value of gifts that congressmen distribute.[44] Therefore, it seems fairly certain that the effective pressure exerted on congressmen is not by way of campaign contributions. Indeed, it may well be that the principal reason congressmen are interested in campaign contributions is that the latter are viewed as a good measure of the political influence of the pressure group and hence of the number of vote gains or losses that they can provide.

Thus, the voter is a rather shaky reed upon which to depend if the object is to achieve good government and a government which in particular only spends money on things that are generally worth purchasing. The average voter benefits from the activities of those pressure groups of which he is a member, although the benefit may be much smaller than he thinks it is. On the other hand he is injured by all the other pressure groups, and the net effect is that he is actually worse off than without any of them. The limits of his information, however, mean that he is actually only able to function effectively by promoting pressure groups. In consequence, the outcome is that there is a good deal more wasteful rent seeking than there would be if somehow or other people were able to vote in terms of their long-term interest.

Let me conclude this discussion of the relative weakness of voters in the rent-seeking market-place on a more formal note by setting out the model of rational voter abstention and rational voter ignorance on which this judgement rests. I am aware that certain Chicago economists, notably Peltzman, do not accept these models and argue that all voters are fully and rationally informed on political matters. I am aware of no theoretical contribution that they can rely on to overcome the problem defined by the model that I now outline, and which originated with Downs as finessed by Tullock.[45]

Suppose that an individual is possessed of some political information that leads him to favour the Democratic Party candidate in a particular election (whether for the presidency, for the Senate, or for the House of Representatives). The pay-off to the individual from voting in that election is given by the expression

$$BDA - C = P \tag{1}$$

where B = benefit expected to be derived from the success of the individual's favoured candidate, D = probability that the individual's vote will be decisive

44. Tullock, *Economics of Special Privilege.*

45. S. Peltzman, "How Efficient Is the Voting Market?" *Journal of Law and Economics* 33 (1990): 27–64; Downs, *An Economic Theory of Democracy*; Tullock, *Toward a Mathematics of Politics.*

in the election, A = probability that the individual's political information is accurate, C = cost of voting for the individual, and P = pay-off. Certain aspects of this expression merit further discussion. B refers, of course, not to the absolute advantage of having one party or candidate in office, but to the difference between the candidate and his opponent. The factor A is often omitted from models of this kind. It is included here because I wish to consider variations in the amount of information acquired by an individual; and the principal effect of being better informed is that an individual's judgement is more likely to be correct. In essence, A is a subjective variable, which ranges from minus to plus one in value.

The factor D reflects the probability that an individual's vote will make a difference in the election. For a U.S. presidential election, this probability typically is less than one in ten million. The factor for C is the cost in money, time, and inconvenience of registering and voting in an election. For some individuals, this may be negative, since they obtain pleasure (perhaps in the sense of relief from the social pressure to vote). If voting is perceived to be an instrumental act, however, then the decision to vote or to abstain will depend on the weighing of costs and benefits as above outlined.

For most individuals, the cost of registration and voting is probably in excess of \$10, and for some, it will exceed \$100. For most individuals, the value of the factor ABD, in almost any election, will be less than one cent, and for very few will it be more than \$1. It follows from this that only those individuals who experience pleasure from voting (i.e., whose valuation of C is zero or negative) should rationally choose to vote. No doubt this explains why fewer than 50 per cent of voters turn out to the polls in U.S. elections, although it does not really explain the sizeable turnouts that do occur, since D remains very high even at the reduced voting levels that are observed. Evidence certainly supports the view that individuals are more likely to vote in close elections.[46] Probably those who enjoy politics, and for whom C is negative, are well represented in the set of active voters.

Even for those who decide to vote, however, it is by no means evident that they will decide to become well informed. The factor A presumably increases as the quantity and/or the quality of an individual's political information increases; but so does the magnitude of C as the relevant costs of information are added to the cost of voting. Whatever happens to A, its impact is always cushioned by the low value of D, which is an inescapable consequence of the

46. Y. Barzel and E. Silberberg, "Is the Act of Voting Rational?" *Public Choice* 16 (1973): 51–58.

indivisibility of political markets. Herein is to be found the crucial weakness of democracy, the principal determinant of the evident bias of the political process in favour of voters who are concentrated and well informed on issues that are significantly relevant to them and against voters who are dispersed and ill informed on issues that are less directly relevant. Herein, also, is to be found the reason for the political vacuum into which the special interests penetrate in order to rent seek, to the general detriment of society as a whole.

THE MEDIA

In terms of the model outlined in equation 1, let us assume, for each political issue, that the voter is either ignorant, casually informed, or well informed, thus simplifying the reality of a continuous variation across this spectrum. In order to distinguish between these three states of knowledge, it is necessary to analyze the behaviour of the mass media, through which most voters obtain what information they have on political issues. This analysis focuses attention on *the politics of persuasion* and on *the economics of lying*.[47]

Most of the mass media, when they carry any political information at all, combine it with a great deal of other information carefully balanced to reflect the tastes of their respective customers. The typical reader, listener, or viewer does not pay equal attention to all items that the media supply, but rather focuses upon those of particular interest, largely tuning out the rest. Moreover, he does not necessarily remember over any significant period of time the information that initially attracts his attention. Even that which is retained may not be given much, if any, serious thought when the voter commits his vote.

At the time of voting, therefore, the individual may be in a state of complete ignorance on many, indeed on most, issues, either because he has not been exposed effectively to the relevant information or because he has not been sufficiently impressed as to retain and/or to make use of such information. Alternatively, he may be aware of the issue and have some amount of factual information about it as the result of essentially casual receipt of information together with an evaluation of that information that led him to remember it. I shall refer to this state as *casually informed*, and this state will be the principal concern of this section on the media. Thirdly, the individual may be extremely knowledgeable about the issue because its outcome is expected to impact significantly on his utility. In such circumstances, the voter predictably will be impervious to media persuasion or to the lies of

47. Tullock, *Toward a Mathematics of Politics.*

politicians, even if he will not always prove capable of forming accurate judgements on the issues concerning which he is well informed. The well-informed voter is the pressure group voter *par excellence*, a rare yet highly predictable phenomenon, casting his vote very largely in terms of the particular issues of great interest to him.

The pattern of behaviour which this picture of the information held by voters dictates for the politician essentially is that described by log-rolling. Politicians will follow widely and strongly held opinions, and will promise to confer simple, easily perceived benefits on small groups. They will attempt to disburse the costs of such policies lightly across the rationally ignorant and rationally casually informed electorate. They will attempt to access the mass media in order to influence casually informed voters to vote for their policy platforms. Let me now return to the model defined by equation 1 to outline the role played by persuasion in political markets characterized by casually informed voters. Equation 2 reflects the new situation:

$$BD_pA - C - C_p = P \tag{2}$$

where C_p is the cost of effort invested in persuasion, and D_p is the likely effect of such persuasion on the probability that a voter's vote will be decisive. Even if voting itself has a negative pay-off, efforts to persuade may not, since advocacy is more likely to affect the outcome of an election than is a single vote. Of course, there will be great variation in the magnitude of D_p from person to person. It is important to note that C_p is very small for certain categories of voter. In particular, individuals engaged professionally in providing material for the mass media may be able to insert considerable persuasive effort at almost zero cost.

The stockholders of the mass media will place limits on this process where it threatens to lower the net worth of their stock. If there exists any principal-agent problem, however, management characterized by specific political agendas may invade the mass media specifically to engage in political persuasion, and then will actively encourage propaganda favourable to their causes. This phenomenon is even more characteristic of the class media, which not infrequently exist primarily for the purpose of political advocacy. Teachers, especially those in higher education, are also well placed to push political agendas at little or no cost to themselves, especially where such views are left-leaning and conform to the politically correct dogmas of the large majority of college administrators.

In communicating in order to persuade, inaccuracy in information is important only if it is likely to be exposed to the targeted recipients. In this respect, media competition plays an important constraining role. In dictatorships, or in environments characterized by media monopoly, false information may exert a powerful influence. Fortunately, the information revolution has significantly weakened the prospects for such manipulation, quite contrary to the expectations of George Orwell and Aldous Huxley.

For the political propagandist of any persuasion it is rational to lie if the anticipated benefits exceed the anticipated costs. From this perspective, important deductions follow. The more expert the recipient, the less beneficial is the lie. The more important the political issue to the recipient, the more likely it is that the lie will be detected. The more frequent the transactions with the recipient, the more costly long-term is the ultimately to be detected lie. All this renders the casually informed voter extremely vulnerable to lies, especially since there are no stringent laws protecting voters from false advertising by politicians or by the media. In particular, the ability of major newspapers to protect the anonymity of information sources and the increasing difficulty for "public" personalities to sue newspapers successfully even for gross libel, enable propagandists to manipulate the media as a source of politically productive lies at a relatively low cost.

THE INTEREST GROUPS

The rationally casually ignorant voter is a very slender reed on which to build the foundations of democratic politics. He is much more likely to be the recipient of the dispersed costs than of the concentrated benefits of the legislative process. He is much more likely to suffer the net costs of random prisoners' dilemmas than to enjoy the systematic gains-from-trade outlined in *The Calculus of Consent.*[48] Is it legitimate, in such circumstances, to infer that the forces of supply and demand in political markets are driven not by individual voters but by interest groups; that collective action replaces individual action in the battle over the spoils of politics that is the *raison d'être* of democratic politics? If so, what predictions can be made about the rent-seeking consequences of competition among pressure groups for political influence?

The relatively optimistic, rose-tinted-spectacles scenario of interest group competition is that advanced by Gary Becker in two elegant and highly influential articles. In this model, Becker presents a theory of the political redis-

48. Buchanan and Tullock, *Calculus of Consent.*

tribution of income and of other public policies that builds on competition among pressure groups for political favours. Active groups produce pressure to raise their political influence, where all influences are jointly determined by the pressures produced by all groups. The political budget equation between the total amount raised in taxes and the total amount available for subsidies implies that the sum of all influences is zero. This itself is seen to have a significant effect on the competition among pressure groups.[49]

Each group is assumed to maximize the income of its members under the Cournot-Nash assumption that additional pressure does not affect political expenditures of other groups. Political equilibrium depends on the efficiency of each group in producing pressure, the effect of additional pressure on their influence, the number of persons in different groups, and the deadweight costs of taxes and subsidies.

Efficiency in producing pressure is determined in part by the cost (recognized though not emphasized by Becker) of controlling free-riding among members. Greater control over free-riding raises the optimal pressure by a group and thus increases its subsidy or reduces its taxes. Efficiency is also determined by the size of a group, not only because its size affects free-riding, but also because small groups may not be able to take advantage of scale economies in the production of pressure.

Becker places considerable emphasis on the deadweight costs of taxes and subsidies and the fact that such costs generally rise at an increasing rate as taxes and subsidies increase. He suggests that an increase in the deadweight cost of a subsidy discourages pressure by the subsidized group, while an increase in the deadweight cost of a tax encourages pressure by taxpayers. Consequently, deadweight costs give taxpayers an intrinsic advantage in the competition for influence. Groups that receive large subsidies presumably manage to offset their intrinsic disadvantage by efficiency, optimal size, or easy access to political influence.

In Becker's analysis, all groups favour and lobby for efficient taxes, whereas efficient methods of subsidization raise subsidies and benefit recipients, but harm taxpayers unless recipients are induced to produce less pressure by a sufficiently rapid increase in their deadweight costs as their subsidy increases. He claims relevance for his theory not only to taxes and subsidies that redistribute income, but also to regulations and quotas, as well as to poli-

49. Becker, "Theory of Competition"; G. S. Becker, "Public Policies, Pressure Groups, and Dead Weight Costs," *Journal of Public Economics* 28 (1985): 329–47.

cies that raise efficiency by the production of public goods and the curtailment of other market failures. In his view, policies that raise efficiency are likely to win out in the competition for influence because they produce gains rather than deadweight costs, so that groups benefited have an intrinsic advantage compared with groups harmed. In Becker's world, where there is open competition between interest groups, together with free entry and exit, inefficient transfer mechanisms will not be widespread in political market equilibrium.

For a number of reasons, I do not share Becker's optimism regarding the impact of interest groups in democratic politics, at least in the absence of important constitutional constraints. Let me start with the free-rider problem emphasized by Mancur Olson in his seminal discussion of the logic of collective action.[50] The free-rider proposition asserts that in a wide range of situations, individuals will fail to participate in collectively profitable activities in the absence of coercion or of individually appropriable inducements.[51] This proposition is easily illustrated.

Let the gain to an individual be equal to G if a collective activity is undertaken. For instance, G may be the individual's gain from a tariff which might be obtained by an effective interest group lobby. The cost of the collective action is C, and there are n identical self-seeking individuals. By hypothesis, the joint action is collectively profitable, so $nG > C$. However, the individual will refrain from joining the collective action if n is of some appreciable size, given his judgement that the viability of the action does not depend on his participation. If enough individuals free ride in this manner, the collective action will not be taken. Even though rides, like lunches, are never completely free, if n is large the free-rider problem is widely believed to be endemic.

Mancur Olson set out to prove logically that free-riding was not a universal problem for collective action but rather that it struck differentially at particular types of interest groups, thereby providing unequal or asymmetric access to the political process. The paradox that he presented is that (in the absence of special arrangements or circumstances) large groups, at least if they are composed of rational individuals, will *not* act in their group interest.[52] The reason for this is to be found in the publicness characteristics of the benefits that flow from successful collective action. In such circumstances, in-

50. M. Olson, *The Logic of Collective Action* (Cambridge: Harvard University Press, 1965).

51. G. J. Stigler, "Free Riders and Collective Action: An Appendix to Theories of Economic Regulation," *Bell Journal of Economics and Management Science* 5 (1974): 359–65.

52. Olson, *Logic of Collective Action*.

terest groups will not exist unless individuals support them for some reason *other* than for the collective goods that they may provide.[53]

In the case of government, of certain professional associations, and of labour unions that have secured the political privilege of the closed shop, free-riding is overcome by the coercive powers that can be deployed against recalcitrant individuals. These coercive powers are usefully subsumed under the more general concept of *selective incentive* which explains almost all successful collective action in the case of large groups of individuals. A selective incentive is one that applies selectively to individuals, depending on whether or not they contribute to the provision of the collective good.

A selective incentive may be positive or negative. Tax payments, for example, are obtained with the help of negative selective incentives, since those who are found not to have paid their taxes must suffer taxes, accumulated interest, and additional penalties. Most of the dues extracted by strong trade unions are obtained through union shop, closed shop, or agency shop arrangements which make dues-paying more or less compulsory. Positive selective incentives are also commonplace. For example, many of the members of American farm lobbies have their dues deducted automatically from the "patronage dividends" of farm co-operatives or included in the insurance premia paid to mutual insurance companies associated with the farm lobbies.[54] Any number of organizations with urban clients provide selective incentives in the form of insurance policies, publications, group air fares, and other private goods made available at special discounts only to members.

Stigler has questioned Olson's by-product theory of selective incentives by challenging the assertion that an interest group would be able to charge more than the cost of the services supplied in the case of services that are appropriable as private goods.[55] Surely, if an interest group seeks to add a charge for the provision of collective action, a rival supplier of those services, that undertakes no collective action, can undersell it. Even if those services, such as the collection of information, possess great economies of scale—are indeed natural monopolies—the argument is not affected: a rival group in a contestable market can still bid away the members of the interest group with a lower price.

There is evidence in support of Stigler's challenge. A particularly striking

53. Ibid.; M. Olson, *The Rise and Decline of Nations* (New Haven: Yale University Press, 1982).

54. Olson, *Rise and Decline.*

55. Stigler, "Free Riders and Collective Action."

example is the experience of the American Automobile Association (AAA) which provides a number of selective incentives to attract funding for its lobbying activities. One such service is the provision of carefully designed route maps for members who request such assistance. The larger gasoline companies determined that they could provide route maps at a lower average price than the AAA, because they diverted no part of the revenues for collective action. Thus, AAA suffered a considerable financial reverse and loss of membership. It is now much less active in political lobbying and focuses its activities much more specifically on its members' direct car needs.

Olson, perhaps in response to Stigler-type criticisms, suggests that there is often a symbiotic relationship between the political power of a lobbying organization and the business institutions associated with it.[56] This relationship often yields tax or other advantages for the business institutions. Moreover, the publicity and other information flowing out of the political arm of a movement often generates patterns of preference or trust that make business activities of the movement more remunerative. If so, the surpluses obtained indeed would provide positive selective incentives that recruit participants for the lobbying efforts. Olson offers no examples of such symbiosis. Evidently, the difference of opinion between Stigler and Olson concerns a matter of fact and must be resolved by sound empirical and institutional analysis.

Small groups, or occasionally large federal groups that are made up of many small groups, have an additional source of both negative and positive selective incentives. Most individuals value the companionship and respect of those with whom they socially interact. The censure or even the ostracism of those who fail to bear a share of the burdens of collective action sometimes can be an important selective incentive. Olson cites the example of British trade unionists who refuse to speak to unco-operative colleagues, that is, "send them to Coventry."[57] Equally, members of an interest group may offer special honours to those who distinguish themselves by their lobbying efforts, thus providing positive selective incentives for such sacrifices.

As Olson recognizes, the availability of social selective benefits is limited by the social heterogeneity of some interest groups that could benefit from effective collective action. Even in the case of small groups, such social heterogeneity may prohibit the kinds of social interaction needed for social se-

56. Olson, *Rise and Decline.*

57. Ibid.

lective incentives to become meaningful. Many individuals resist extensive social interactions with those that they deem to have higher or lower intellectual or social status or greatly different tastes. Even non-conformist groups typically are composed of individuals who are more similar to each other than they are to the rest of society.

Moreover, socially heterogeneous groups, even when they can be brought together at all, often will not agree on the exact nature of whatever collective good is at issue or on how much of it is worth buying. If collective action occurs under such circumstances, it does so at extra cost, especially for the leaders of whatever organization is involved. The American Bar Association (ABA) is an interesting example of this phenomenon. It holds most of its membership by the act of lobbying for licensing entry restrictions and cartel arrangements for the legal profession. Yet, its pursuit of other political agendas, notably the filling of federal judgeships with left-leaning judges and its endorsement of the pro-choice abortion stance, costs its leaders support among conservative and Catholic attorneys, even extending to membership losses. Such behaviour ultimately could provoke a membership revolt and the removal of the politicized oligarchy that controls the ABA.[58] Alternatively, the ABA might segment into separate components, each reflective of its membership's collective action preferences.

If large interest groups must resort to selective incentives in order to pursue political lobbying, the environment is more promising for small interest groups, especially if they are composed of socially homogeneous members. In small groups, individuals can avoid the free-riding prisoners' dilemma by behaving strategically, that is in ways that take account of the effect of their own choices on the behaviour of others. Although group-optimal outcomes may not be achievable, small interest groups often are able to engage in collective action without selective benefits. Olson refers to such groups as privileged groups. Privileged groups predictably will be disproportionately successful in political markets and will shift political outcomes away from median voters in favour of decisive minorities characterized by high preferences for specific policies.

Olson's logic of collective action, which I essentially endorse, is sharply different from that of Gary Becker. It focuses attention on the problem of asymmetric access to political markets, whereas Becker tends to emphasize

58. C. K. Rowley, *The Right to Justice: The Political Economy of Legal Services in the United States* (Brookfield, Vt., and Aldershot, England: Edward Elgar, 1992).

equal access. It emphasizes problems of free-riding, whereas Becker emphasizes deadweight social losses as the principal reason for collective action failures. It stresses, much more than Becker, the importance of small size as a determinant of lobbying impact. It highlights the cost of organizing interest groups and the difficulty of holding them together, whereas Becker tends to emphasize the ease of organization and the attraction of the gross returns to collective action.[59] In my view, the preponderance of the evidence is in favour of Olson, though further testing of both theories is desirable.[60]

Let me now return to the relevance of my own rent-seeking insight to this debate over the role of interest groups. Writing in 1965, Olson could not be aware of the concept, and indeed he developed a theory of interest group behaviour that did not focus attention on the potentially high resource losses associated with lobbying competition. In 1982, however, although he did not discuss rent seeking as such, Olson clearly recognized the resource destruction implicit in bargaining over wealth transfers.[61] He also recognized that the imposition of such public bads might be rational policy for small, well-organized interest groups. In his 1982 book, Olson endeavours to show that the social losses associated with government regulations can sometimes be colossal and that they are often the direct result of special-interest lobbying. I thoroughly agree with this assessment.

In contrast, Becker more or less explicitly plays down the cost of rent seeking in his theory of pressure group competition. His 1983 article incorporates the normal costs of organization into the theory of pressure group organization. Except for this, however, the paper centres attention exclusively on Harberger triangles as a source of social loss and ignores Tullock rectangles. His 1985 paper notes that aggregate efficiency "should be defined not only net of dead weight costs and benefits of taxes and subsidies, but also net of expenditures on the production of political pressure . . . since these expenditures are only rent-seeking inputs into the determination of policies." Becker does not follow through on this insight, but lamely concludes that

59. M. A. Crew and C. K. Rowley, "Toward a Public Choice Theory of Monopoly Regulation," *Public Choice* 57 (1988): 49–68.

60. See W. C. Mitchell and M. C. Munger, "Economic Models of Interest Groups: An Introductory Survey," *American Journal of Political Science* 35 (1991): 512–46, for an excellent survey.

61. Olson, *Rise and Decline*, 43.

"little is known about the success of different kinds of political systems in reducing the waste from competition among pressure groups" (335).[62]

Neither Olson nor Becker recognizes that a principal determinant of the volume of resources dedicated to rent seeking is the magnitude of the rents available from the political market. This lacuna is especially important for Becker, since such an interaction would significantly affect the nature of the Cournot-Nash equilibria that his model generates. I shall return to this issue of efficient rent seeking in a later chapter.[63]

In a way, it is fortunate that rent seeking is subject to the free-rider problem, since this undoubtedly reduces the total amount of rent-seeking activity and mitigates the resource cost to society. Unfortunately, Olson's logic of collective action impacts much more sharply upon the large numbers of heterogeneous individuals who wish to protect their property rights from the scavenging of rent-seekers, but who cannot organize effectively because of the free-rider problem. Rent-seekers typically exert disproportionate political influence, because, if large, they can coerce their members or by-product their collective actions by the provision of selective incentives. If they are small and socially cohesive, they overcome the free-rider problem by strategic bargaining. In this perspective, interest group competition over transfers, contrary to Becker's theory, tends to be high cost both in terms of Harberger triangles and Tullock rectangles and constitutes a major ongoing threat to economic freedom.

I shall suggest, in the concluding chapter of this book, that constitutional constraints and institutional reforms can mitigate the extent of rent seeking on the part of interest groups.[64] However, as Wagner has argued, the parchment of the Constitution itself is vulnerable to the guns of the special interests unless the Constitution itself can be protected by those general interests that find it so difficult to engage in democratic politics.[65]

62. Becker, "Theory of Competition"; Becker, "Public Policies."

63. See Rowley, Shughart, and Tollison, "Interest Groups and Deficits," for an empirical analysis of this issue.

64. J. M. Buchanan, "Rent Seeking and Profit Seeking," in Buchanan, Tollison, and Tullock, *Toward a Theory*, 3–15; J. M. Buchanan, "Reform in the Rent-Seeking Society," in Buchanan, Tollison, and Tullock, *Toward a Theory*, 359–67.

65. R. E. Wagner, "Parchment, Guns and the Maintenance of Constitutional Contract," in *Democracy and Public Choice: Essays in Honor of Gordon Tullock*, ed. C. K. Rowley (Oxford: Basil

THE BUREAUCRATS

Olson has been criticized for treating interest group lobbying as a pure demand phenomenon and for leaving out a powerful role for government.[66] In my view, this criticism is misplaced, since interest groups are located on both the demand and the supply sides of the political market, and government serves primarily as a broker of the pressures that they can bring to bear. I am not convinced by North's suggestion that the state should be accorded a pre-eminent role in the formation and administration of property rules and rights, just as I am not convinced that it should be modelled as a revenue-maximizing Leviathan.[67] Ultimately, empirical testing will determine which of the two models is correct, or whether indeed some other model is superior.

Nevertheless, I strongly endorse the view advanced by Niskanen, building on earlier work by myself and by Downs, that bureaucrats play a significant role in political markets not just as implementers of brokered policies but also on the demand side of the market.[68] As such, they make a significant contribution to rent seeking and to the dissipation of wealth in society, taking full advantage of their status as small, privileged, homogeneous special-interest groups empowered by their ability to coerce members and, thus, to overcome the free-rider effect.

In most democracies, including the United States, the bureaucracy carries a considerable political clout simply because its members make up a sizeable minority of the electorate. In the United States, government bureaucrats, federal, state, and local combined, make up some 20 per cent of the total electorate, with a direct interest in expanding the scope of government. Even if their vote strength alone is recognized, as well-informed voters on issues central to their bureaux they would present a serious threat to the cause of lim-

Blackwell, 1987), 105–21; R. E. Wagner, "Agency, Economic Calculation and Constitutional Construction," in Rowley, Tollison, and Tullock, *Political Economy of Rent-Seeking*, 423–46.

66. Mitchell and Munger, "Economic Models."

67. D. C. North, *Institutions, Institutional Change and Economic Performance* (New York: Cambridge University Press, 1990); H. G. Brennan and J. M. Buchanan, *The Power to Tax: Analytical Foundations of a Fiscal Constitution* (London and New York: Cambridge University Press, 1980).

68. W. A. Niskanen, *Bureaucracy and Representative Government* (Chicago: Aldine Press, 1971); W. A. Niskanen, "Bureaucrats and Politicians," *Journal of Law and Economics* 18 (1975): 617–44; G. Tullock, *The Politics of Bureaucracy* (New York: University Press of America, 1965); A. Downs, *Inside Bureaucracy* (Boston: Little, Brown, 1967).

ited government. For this reason, a case can be made for disenfranchising all government bureaucrats with respect to elections at their respective levels of the federal system. Of course, such a recommendation is not likely to survive log-rolling pressures in any pluralistic vote mechanism.

In any event, despite attempts by the Hatch Act in the United States to prohibit the use by bureaucrats of taxpayer monies to lobby the legislature, the bureaucrats exert an influence on the legislature significantly in excess of their vote power alone, in order to secure special-interest benefits. Such benefits take the form of tenured employment, privileged health-care packages, contribution-free inflation-proof pension arrangements, and the like, well beyond the expectations of private-sector employees. They also take the form of income- and employment-augmenting special-interest legislation initiated by senior bureaucrats working within the so-called "iron-triangles" composed of private interest groups, congressional committees, and civil servants that log-roll among themselves to secure self-serving legislation financed by rationally ignorant and rationally casually ignorant voters. Such behaviour extends well beyond the federal bureaucracy and is evident, for example, in the success of the U.S. Post Office in protecting the letter mail from private competition and in securing for itself an overmanned and over-paid workforce financed by excessively high prices and public subsidies.

Let me focus on the rent-seeking potential of the federal bureaucracy through the formal lens provided by Niskanen, where bureaux are defined as non-profit organizations financed, at least in part, by a periodic appropriation or grant, and where the rational behaviour of senior bureaucrats, responsible for the budgets and outputs of their bureaux, is subjected to careful institutional analysis. Niskanen's model, basic though it now may seem, provides a useful foundation for assessing the rent-seeking capabilities of government bureaux.[69]

Niskanen uses the term *bureaucrat* to define the senior official of any bureau with a separate identifiable budget. These bureaucrats may be either career officials or individuals appointed directly by the elected executive. In his view, each bureaucrat seeks to maximize a utility function made up of the following variables: perquisites of the office, public reputation, power, patronage, output of the bureau, ease of making changes, and ease of managing the bureau. All of these variables save the last two, in his view, are a positive monotonic function of the total budget of the bureau. Although the problems

69. Niskanen, *Bureaucracy and Representative Government.*

of making changes and the personal burdens of managing a bureau are often higher at higher budget levels, both tend to be reduced by increases in the total budget. Niskanen concludes, therefore, that budget maximization should be an adequate proxy even for bureaucrats with a relatively low pecuniary motivation and a relatively high motivation for making changes in the "public interest." Evidence strongly supports the hypothesis that most distinguished civil servants substantially increase the budgets of the bureaux for which they are responsible.

Given that bureaucrats seek to maximize the size of their budgets, the constraint that ultimately limits the size of bureaux is the requirement that a bureau, on the average, must supply that output expected by the sponsor on its approval of the bureau's budget. The necessary condition for achieving the expected output is that the budget must be equal to or greater than the minimum total expected costs of supplying this level of output. This constraint is a critical element from which Niskanen develops a theory of supply by bureaux as outlined in Figure 4.

In Figure 4, a one-period relationship is outlined between a bureau, considered to be a monopoly supplier of the service but a competitive purchaser of factor inputs, and a legislative committee sponsor that is assumed not to exercise its potential monopoly power as a single buyer of the service, because of either lack of incentive or lack of opportunity. The total potential budget available to the bureau is represented by the budget-output function:

$$B = aQ - bQ^2, \quad 0 < Q < \frac{a}{2b} \tag{3}$$

The minimal total cost is represented by the cost-output function:

$$TC = cQ + dQ^2, \quad 0 \leq Q \tag{4}$$

The budget constraint is represented as:

$$B \geq TC \tag{5}$$

In Figure 4, V_1 represents lower demand conditions for the bureau's services, given by the marginal valuation function of the sponsoring legislative committee. The marginal cost function of the bureau is given by cC. The equilibrium output of the bureau, in this case, is *budget-constrained* at output $a_1 - c/b + d$, where the area of the polygon ea_1gh is equal to the area of the polygon ecfh. At this output, the bureau must be X-efficient, since its total budget just equals its minimum total costs. The output of the bureau, however, is higher than optimum, assuming that the legislative committee's mar-

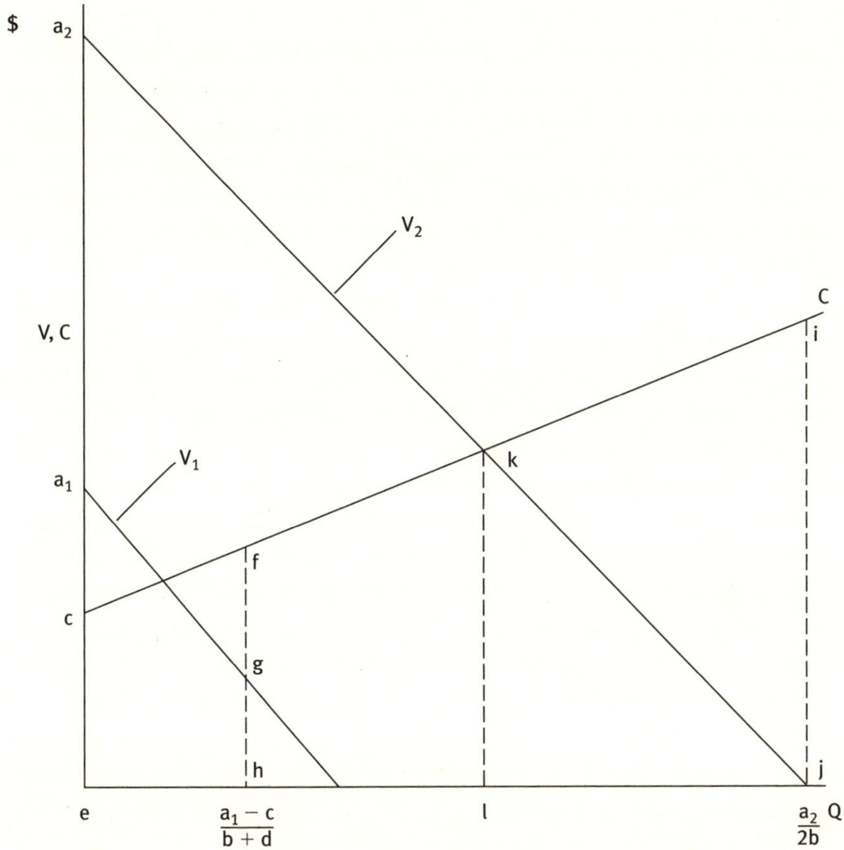

FIGURE 4
Budget-constrained and demand-constrained bureaux

ginal valuation function somehow reflects aggregated voters' preferences. This is evidenced by the fact that marginal cost, hf, exceeds marginal value, hg, at equilibrium output.

For higher demand conditions represented by the marginal valuation function V_2, however, the equilibrium output of the bureau is *demand-constrained*, with the marginal value of output equal to zero. The total budget, given by the area of the triangle ea_2j, exceeds minimum total costs given by the polygon ecij. At the equilibrium output, the bureau is X-inefficient. Output is also higher than the "optimal" level, with marginal cost at ji and with the marginal value of the service equal to zero.

Niskanen assumes that the bureau typically operates like a price discriminating monopolist securing for itself the maximum available surplus by offering a total output in return for a total budget appropriation. Bureaux are also assumed to benefit from better information regarding production costs than that available to congressional committees, thus protecting themselves from X-inefficiency challenges in the high-demand situation. There is a great deal of evidence that X-inefficiency permeates the federal bureaucracy, manifesting itself in overmanning, excessive on-the-job leisure, gold-plating of offices, and cost ineffective input purchases, despite periodic investigations that draw the attention of casually informed voters to the horror stories that not infrequently emerge.

Bureaux are adept at responding to threatened budget cuts with promises to eliminate services most valued by voters, thus marshalling the vote motive in favour of their bloated budgets. Politicians often lend credence to such defences, responding to special interests that rent-seek for the bureaucratic services that are under review. This interaction between bureaucrats, politicians, and interest groups is referred to as the *iron triangle* by *cognoscenti* of Washington politics.

Two frequently cited examples demonstrate the nature of this dangerous rent-seeking relationship. The first concerns the unjustifiable farm subsidy programme that I have already referred to in this book. Bureaucrats in the Department of Agriculture work closely with the farmers' lobbies and with congressmen on the agriculture committees of the U.S. Congress to maintain inefficient farms, to grow and then to destroy uneconomic crops, and to provide already affluent farmers with per-capita income subsidies several times higher than the annual earnings of the average U.S. worker. Their own return is to be found in bureau budgets significantly higher than would be attainable if the U.S. farming industry was to be returned to capitalist enterprise.

The second example concerns the military. The major armament manufacturers together with individuals who live around and service military installations ally themselves with congressmen dependent on defence industry contracts for their constituents and with bureaucrats from the Department of Defense whose budgets are dependent on high military appropriations from the U.S. Congress. Such iron triangles are very resistant to voter attacks even in circumstances that clearly call for budgetary retrenchment.

The iron-triangle hypothesis runs counter to recent theories advanced by Weingast and Moran and by Rowley and Elgin that suggest that the legislature itself monitors the behaviour of federal bureaux and periodically forces such bureaux to constrain their budget maximization objectives.[70] If the congressional committees are controlled by high-demand congressmen, highly responsive to interest group pressures, they are highly unlikely to rein in the services of bureaux that feed those same interests. I am aware that some of the empirical evidence suggests that federal bureaux do adjust behaviour in response to changes in the composition of oversight and appropriations committees.

All such adjustments, however, are at the margin, and often are reflective of changes in the preferences or relative strengths of the interest groups that determine the political equilibrium. More sophisticated testing is necessary to determine whether Congress ever moves directly against the interest groups to weaken the base of the iron triangles and to lower bureau budgets in some public-interested spirit. I doubt that much evidence of this sort will be uncovered, or that congressmen given to such flights of public interest would survive in politics.

One modification of Niskanen's theory that does merit attention is the notion advanced by Migué and Bélanger that bureaucrats may place less value on maximizing the size of their budgets than on maximizing the size of their *discretionary* budgets.[71] If this is correct, then bureaucrats would select output i in Figure 4, where marginal cost equals marginal value, thus choosing to operate at the "optimal" rate of output. Of course, the discretionary budget typically would be utilized to indulge the private preferences of bureaucrats, providing opportunities for luxurious office accommodation, for conferences and training sessions in exotic locations, for expensive business travel, support facilities, and the like. As I have demonstrated in my own writings on income redistribution, such bureaucratic budget diversions are important reasons why poverty programmes fail to redistribute income to the poor.[72]

A second modification is the notion that bureaucrats may be lazy and evi-

70. B. R. Weingast and M. J. Moran, "Bureaucratic Discretion or Congressional Control: Regulatory Policy Making by the Federal Trade Commission," *Journal of Political Economy* 91 (1983): 765–800; C. K. Rowley and R. S. Elgin, "Toward a Theory of Bureaucratic Behaviour," in *Public Choice, Public Finance and Public Policy*, ed. D. Greenaway and G. K. Shaw (Oxford: Basil Blackwell, 1985), 31–50.

71. J. L. Migué and G. Bélanger, "Toward a General Theory of Managerial Discretion," *Public Choice* 17 (1974): 27–42.

72. G. Tullock, *The Economics of Income Redistribution* (Hingham, Mass.: Kluwer-Nijhoff, 1983).

dence a high preference for work-avoiding activities.[73] In the limit, they may prove to be so lazy that they do not actually produce any real output at all, hiding their ineptitude by bureaucratic obfuscation in areas where interest groups do not counter rational voter ignorance. An excellent example of such a bureau was the American Spruce Woods Corporation.

During World War I, airplanes were made of wood, and the American Spruce Woods Corporation, with a director, four clerks, and a chauffeur was set up in 1918 to expedite the movement of wood into the aircraft industry. Thereafter, the bureau did nothing. After World War II, Congress required that the Bureau of the Budget list all government corporations in its budget presentation. A vigilant congressman then queried the role of the Corporation and it was quietly disbanded. By that time, 28 years had elapsed, and its six long-term employees had all qualified for federal government pensions.

In conclusion, bureaucrats themselves actively rent-seek through the political process, often conspiring with powerful interest groups and relevant congressional committees. In some cases, this rent seeking results in excessive rates of output, in others in bloated budgets, and in yet others in manifest laziness and ineptitude. It should be kept in mind, however, that bureaucrats are often manipulated by other rent-seekers, and that they certainly could not rent-seek as effectively as they do without the widespread compliance of politicians and the rational ignorance of much of the electorate.

THE PRESIDENT AND THE COURTS

The U.S. Constitution was devised to create a federal government whose powers would be checked by the separation of powers with no one of the three branches—legislative, executive, or judicial—deemed to be superior to any of the others. In various ways, each branch technically has influence over each other branch and can use this influence to retaliate against unwarranted interference. In practice, as the Founding Fathers predicted, the legislature has proved to be the dominant branch, able to secure the deference of the Supreme Court on most matters and able to dominate the President over budgetary policy in the absence of a line item veto. For this reason, my rent-seeking analysis largely focuses on the legislative market-place. Of course, this focus is even more justified in the case of parliamentary democracies such as the United Kingdom where the legislature is constitutionally supreme.

73. A. T. Peacock, "Public X-Inefficiency: International and Institutional Constraints," in *Anatomy of Government Deficiencies*, ed. H. Hanusch (Heidelberg: Springer Verlag, 1983).

In the case of the United States, however, the potential influence of the courts and the President over the rent-seeking market should not be ignored as completely as it often is in the public choice literature. Let me briefly deal with each in turn, starting with the Supreme Court, which, in principle, is supposed to be an ultimate custodian of the Constitution, protected from political interference by the lifetime tenure and security of nominal income enjoyed by the justices.

In one view, advanced by Landes and Posner, the independent judiciary plays an active role in promoting rent seeking in the legislature by promoting durable legislation. Indeed, the judiciary helps current legislators to raise the rents available to successful interest groups by ensuring that the work of one legislature is not overturned by the next legislature. Landes and Posner argue that the courts tend to resolve legal disputes by reference to the actual intent of the propounding legislature. By so doing, their own budgets and the salaries of their judges and of their staffs tend to rise more rapidly than would be the case if they adopted a less accommodating stance. In my view, this theory of the independent judiciary ignores important political pressures that are applicable to the market for judgeships. Moreover, the econometric results obtained by Landes and Posner scarcely support their hypothesis. However, there may be something in the basic argument.[74]

An alternative view sees the Supreme Court justices as pursuing their own individual agendas that made them attractive to the Presidents who appointed them at the time of their appointment.[75] Where the Senate majority and the President are of the same political party at the time of appointment, this prediction seems to be particularly persuasive. Where they are not, ideological preferences predictably will be more muted and less unambiguous. Only if a sequence of like-minded Presidents is able to appoint a majority of like-thinking justices (notably Reagan and Bush in recent years) is anything resembling a cohesive Supreme Court agenda likely to emerge. Rowley has traced the reversal of Supreme Court judgements on takings cases since 1986, which, if sustained, will slow the pace of development of rent seeking

74. W. M. Landes and R. A. Posner, "The Independent Judiciary in an Interest-Group Perspective," *Journal of Law and Economics* 18 (1975): 875–901.

75. C. K. Rowley, "The Supreme Court and Takings Judgements: Constitutional Political Economy versus Public Choice," in *Taking Property and Just Compensation: Law and Economics Perspectives of the Takings Issue*, ed. N. Mercuro (Boston: Kluwer Academic Publishers, 1992), 79–124.

through the U.S. legislature. Evidently, such an agenda could fade in an unfavourable political climate or in the wake of new appointments to the High Court following the election of a left-leaning Democrat to the presidency. Of course, if a left-leaning majority dominates the Supreme Court (the Warren Court) and defers to a Democratic majority legislature, then the Landes and Posner hypothesis becomes extremely plausible.

The impact of the President on the rent-seeking equilibrium brokered by the legislature is similarly ambiguous. Following the idea of Landes and Posner, Crain and Tollison hypothesized that the veto powers exercisable by a President, designed to force the legislature into supra-majority voting on new legislation, itself extended the perceived durability of existing legislation. In this view, the legislature and the President are seen as *de facto* colluders, purveying long-term legislation to the dominant interest groups. Econometric results offer some support for their hypothesis. Once again, this theory seems to me to over-generalize. Surely much depends on whether the President and the legislature share the same political perspective and, if not, the particular time-sequence in which new legislation is presented to the President for his signature.[76]

In the alternative view, which may be especially relevant when the President's party does not control the legislature, the President may intervene to destabilize the existing political equilibrium, either by log-rolling or by direct challenges to the legislative process.[77] Furthermore, the President may appoint bureaucrats whose specific purpose is to make use of available bureaucratic discretion to effect policies that are not fully endorsed by the legislative majority. The outcomes of such intervention for rent-seeking equilibria are not unambiguous. If my judgement is correct, that the electoral college constituency is less dominated by special interests than the constituencies of senatorial congressmen, then presidential interventions, where effective, will typically mitigate rent seeking, most especially during the first term of any given President's incumbency.

For the most part, I am inclined to focus attention on the legislature, where the rent-seeking process is basically centred, and to view the courts and the President as side-players, who, occasionally, become more important.

76. Landes and Posner, "Independent Judiciary"; W. M. Crain and R. D. Tollison, "The Executive Branch in an Interest-Group Perspective," *Journal of Legal Studies* 8 (1979): 555–67.

77. Rowley, *Right to Justice.*

Efficient Rent Seeking

If a given rent is available from the legislature, how much rent seeking will this given rent attract? This question is extremely important, given my insight that a great deal of rent-seeking behaviour may be wasteful of scarce resources. It is instructive to answer this question within the framework of specific rent-seeking games, given that most rents are competed for, often in circumstances where the highest bidder receives at least a large part of the available rent.[78]

An early illustration of a rent-seeking game in which the total amount of the rent-seeking outlay exactly equals the available rent (the exact dissipation outcome) was provided by Posner in his widely cited paper on the social costs of monopoly and regulation. Posner posited a situation in which ten firms vie for a government monopoly which carries with it a present value rent of one million dollars. He asserts that each firm has an equal probability (.1) of obtaining the rent, that each firm is risk neutral, and that constant costs hold universally.[79] In such circumstances, each firm will spend resources on rent seeking equal to one hundred thousand dollars, the expected present value of the prize, in an attempt to obtain the monopoly. Only one firm will succeed, and its costs will be much smaller than the monopoly profits; but the total costs of obtaining the monopoly—counting losers' expenditures as well as winners'—will be the same as under certainty. Most of the costs in fact are made in unsuccessful attempts to seek rents—and not surprisingly these may be overlooked in empirical studies of the cost of rent seeking to society.

Posner's exact dissipation hypothesis is popular among the small group of scholars who attempt to calculate rent-seeking costs (including Posner himself), no doubt because it facilitates empirical work. If the entire Tullock rectangle is to be wasted, this is an area which can be reasonably approximated, given basic information on costs and demand elasticities, and then be measured, if necessary, nationwide. Moreover, even if Posner's theory is generalized, to take account of free entry into the bidding mechanism, the underlying exact dissipation holds in the equilibrium solution. Although the winner receives ever more of the available rent as a super-normal return on its own rent-seeking investment, the equilibrium will not provoke subsequent

78. Peltzman, "Toward a More General Theory."

79. Posner, "Social Costs of Monopoly."

rent seeking by others as long as durability is fundamental to the initial rent-seeking game.[80]

Somewhat ironically, the exact dissipation outcome, which is not at all attractive from the perspective of Paretian welfare economics, has become known in the literature as the *efficient rent-seeking* outcome following my 1980 article on that topic, which questioned the likelihood of such an outcome in the real world. In that paper I outlined a range of rent-seeking models, in which the competitive process leads either to under- or to over-dissipation of the available rents, and in which rent seeking does not take place under the constant cost conditions specified by Posner. This paper has generated a considerable volume of articles, none of which has succeeded in resolving the problem that I posed, although in many ways the important parameters have now been identified.[81] Issues such as risk aversion, arbitrary limits on the number of bidders, imperfect information, and decreasing and increasing returns turn out to be very important.[82]

Although I can easily generate over-dissipation outcomes, it might seem that this solution is unlikely to hold, at least in respect to games where competitors become aware that they are engaged in a game *ex ante* which lowers their expected net wealth. If over-dissipation occurs, and the rent-seeking

80. But see M. A. Crew and C. K. Rowley, "Dispelling the Disinterest in Deregulation," in Rowley, Tollison, and Tullock, *Political Economy of Rent-Seeking*, 163–78, when durability is not anticipated.

81. G. Tullock, "Efficient Rent Seeking," in Buchanan, Tollison, and Tullock, *Toward a Theory*, 97–112; Posner, "Social Costs of Monopoly"; Rowley, Tollison, Tullock, *Political Economy of Rent-Seeking.*

82. W. J. Corcoran, "Long-run Equilibrium and Total Expenditures in Rent-Seeking," *Public Choice* 43 (1984): 89–94; W. J. Corcoran and G. V. Karels, "Rent-Seeking Behavior in the Long-Run," *Public Choice* 46 (1985): 227–46; R. S. Higgins, W. F. Shughart, and R. D. Tollison, "Free Entry and Efficient Rent-Seeking," *Public Choice* 46 (1985): 247–58; A. L. Hillman and E. Katz, "Risk-Averse Rent-Seekers and the Social Cost of Monopoly Power," *Economic Journal* 94 (1984): 104–10; W. P. Rogerson, "The Social Costs of Monopoly and Regulation: A Game-Theoretic Analysis," *Bell Journal of Economics and Management Science* 13 (1982): 391–401; Tullock, "Efficient Rent Seeking"; G. Tullock, "Back to the Bog," *Public Choice* 46 (1985): 259–63; G. Tullock, "Another Part of the Swamp," *Public Choice* 54 (1987): 83–84; G. Tullock, "Rents and Rent-Seeking," in Rowley, Tollison, and Tullock, *Political Economy of Rent-Seeking*, 51–62; G. Tullock, "Future Directions for Rent-Seeking Research," in Rowley, Tollison, and Tullock, *Political Economy of Rent-Seeking*, 465–80; Tullock, *Economics of Special Privilege.*

outlays are wasted, a society which tolerates the creation of rents by government may end up impoverished. In the extreme case depicted by Magee, Brock, and Young, for example, 100 per cent of the economy may end up devoted to lobbying. As I note in my 1989 book, the rent-seeking industry appears to be too small, at least in the United States, to give credibility to the over-dissipation hypothesis.[83]

Under-dissipation where rent-seekers, as a whole, outlay less than the total value of the rent available is a much more likely outcome. Hillman and Katz have demonstrated that risk aversion among the rent-seekers will generate such an outcome. Rogerson has shown that comparative advantage among monopolizing inputs also causes under-dissipation. I have shown that game-specific factors plausibly will produce such an outcome. In my view, increasing and decreasing returns to scale are potentially very important factors.[84]

Suppose that diseconomies of scale dominate the rent-seeking game. Under such circumstances, the smaller the enterprise, the more profitable it is, and even with free entry and perfect competition, super-normal returns persist. In the limit, an infinite number of disappearingly small enterprises would outlay only a small proportion of the total rents provided by the competition. In reality, there are practical limits to such a process. A large number of individuals can write letters to their congressmen; but each must attach a 29-cent stamp to his letter. This lower bound will limit the number of competitors, although evidence of abnormally high returns may stimulate additional socially wasteful outlays.

Suppose instead that there are economies of scale. Over-dissipation is then highly likely unless one rent-seeker makes a preclusive bid to keep other rent-seekers out before the active competition commences. There are dangers that such bids will be ill thought out because they must be made in haste and will turn out to be misguided. For example, Sony recently outlaid 1.5 million dollars to buy a movie script and added to this an outlay of 45 million dollars to make the movie. On completion, they showed the movie to trial audiences

83. S. P. Magee, W. A. Brock, and L. Young, *Black Hole Tariffs and Endogenous Policy Theory* (Cambridge: Cambridge University Press, 1989); Tullock, *Economics of Special Privilege*; G. Tullock, "Efficient Rent-Seeking Revisited," in Rowley, Tollison, and Tullock, *Political Economy of Rent-Seeking*, 91–94.

84. Hillman and Katz, "Risk-Averse Rent-Seekers"; Rogerson, "Social Costs of Monopoly"; Tullock, "Efficient Rent Seeking"; Tullock, "Back to the Bog."

and realized that it was so poor that it could not be released. Explaining this error, a senior executive of a rival company remarked that "this business is so unscrupulous and so cut throat that there is no time to think about anything." This is very much the environment in which preclusive bid calculations must be effected. Any social pay-offs to available scale economies may well be squandered in a sequence of risky gambles.

The most desirable rent-seeking outcome is that in which rent-seeking costs are zero and in which rent seeking results in wealth transfers rather than in the dissipation of wealth. The Chicago School tends to promulgate transfer models with such characteristics, emphasizing the endogeneity of transfers and the incentives for interest groups to avoid dissipation.[85] There is no evident competitive mechanism that ensures such socially desirable outcomes. If scarce resources are dedicated to rent seeking, clearly they cannot be used elsewhere to create producers' and/or consumers' surplus over cost. In my view, the zero dissipation result is a figment of neoclassical theorists' imaginations. Such evidence as is available offers no support for any such hypothesis, at least in economies like the United States where expensive election campaigns typically waste whatever initial transfers individual congressmen manage to accrue.

The Transitional Gains Trap

One of the major activities of modern government is the granting of special privileges to various groups of politically influential people. On the whole, the profit record of such protected organizations does not seem to differ systematically from that of the unprotected sections of the economy. This simple observation led me to raise questions that culminated in my theory of the *transitional gains trap.* My thesis is that there are only transitional gains to be made when the government establishes privileges for a group of people. The successors to the original beneficiaries will not normally make exceptional profits. Unfortunately, they will usually be injured by any cancellation of the original gift.[86] It would seem, as David Friedman has put it, that "the government cannot even give anything away."

Let as consider a very simple example of government monopoly creation,

85. Becker, "Theory of Competition"; Becker, "Public Policies."

86. Tullock, "Competing for Aid."

namely the taxi medallion system basically as it operates in New York City. In the absence of entry restrictions, the taxicab market is extremely competitive, with price equal to marginal cost, and with only normal returns available to taxicab operators. By artificially restricting supply, the freely distributed medallions raise price above marginal cost, transferring some consumers' surplus to the taxicab owners and imposing a deadweight social loss on some would-be consumers who now find themselves displaced from the market. Ignoring any rent-seeking costs that initially induce the government to monopolize the taxicab industry, taxicab owners fortunate enough to obtain medallions clearly gain a great deal.

Now revisit the taxicab market after a number of years have elapsed. The capital value of the monopoly profit has been fully taken into account throughout the industry. New taxicab firms enter only by purchasing the requisite number of medallions on the open market. With the monopoly profit fully capitalized, they obtain only normal profits. The surviving original owners now have opportunity costs equivalent to the value of the medallions that they hold. On these costs, they also receive only normal returns. The customers remain worse off because the price remains higher than competitive cost.

The medallion holders will lobby vigorously against any attempt to withdraw the medallion scheme, many of them arguing with justice that they have paid out capital, investing in medallions as a prerequisite for entering the taxicab market. In a very real sense they have established property rights in a system that is the creation of the New York City government. The public choice pressures against deregulation in such circumstances predictably will be well nigh insurmountable, to say nothing of arguments based on property rights and even social justice.

The trap may be even tighter where government subsidies are concerned. Suppose that the government decides to pay manufacturers a subsidy on each chocolate bar sold. Initially, this enables the manufacturers of chocolate bars to make super-normal profits. These profits, in the long run, attract other companies into the industry, render the chocolate bar industry uneconomically large, and lower profits once again to the competitive norm. The economy as a whole is smaller and less efficient than in the pre-subsidy situation, and no manufacturer is making any gains.

Now suppose that a proposal emerges to terminate the subsidy. The chocolate bar manufacturers predictably will fight hard to retain the arrangement, recognizing that its termination must impose sharp short-run losses on existing manufacturers until total capacity falls to that capable of supporting the sale of unsubsidized chocolate bars. In addition, the subsidies benefit specifically and perhaps significantly those individuals who purchase chocolate bars. If they can overcome the logic of collective action, such individuals will join the manufacturers in the pro-subsidy lobby. At least, the manufacturers can target the chocolate bar consumers and dispel their casual ignorance as they decide whether or not to vote, and for whom, in upcoming elections.

The problem posed by the transitional gains trap is the ratchetlike nature of rent seeking. Once a rent has been successfully sought out through government lobbying, it is very difficult to remove even after it has ceased to produce positive profits for its rent-seeking beneficiaries. Its elimination almost always implies losses for those who now exercise the privilege. To avoid such losses, they will rent-seek yet again to retain the privileges. Politicians are rightly reluctant to inflict direct losses on specific sections of the electorate—inevitably a vote-losing strategy.

The general interest, if it can overcome the logic of collective action, may occasionally convince the median voter that the rent-seekers in question are entirely undeserving of their rents and that economic well-being would increase if they were stripped of their privileges. It is even possible that the U.S. deregulation process of the 1980s was facilitated by electing Ronald Reagan to the presidency on just such propaganda as this. Experience indicates, however, that it is much easier to attack the property rights of those who have succeeded in private competitive markets than it is to restore such rights to those who have had them seized. The rent-seekers, after all, are specialized in manipulating propaganda and public relations for self-seeking ends.

More realistically, government privileges may be vulnerable when they no longer serve the purpose for which they were originally designed. The New York taxicab medallion usefully illustrates this possibility. The number of taxicab medallions in New York has remained unchanged for a very long period of time. It is somewhat unlikely that the demand and cost conditions in the taxicab market have continuously been such that an unchanged number of cabs has maximized monopoly gains. It is more than likely that the monopolists are unable fully to exploit the consumer, because the number of medallions is no longer optimal. The medallion holders may be reluctant to lobby to change the number of medallions for fear of provoking voter reaction. In such circumstances, a feeble push for deregulation may encounter little resistance.

The regulated sector is likely to fall behind generally, because the protection from competition reduces incentives to cut costs, to innovate, and to pay close attention to changing consumer preferences. In such circumstances, the original rents slowly disappear, leaving the sector vulnerable to internal reform. The Soviet empire, by 1989, was in just such a situation. Internal reforms are occurring there despite the 30 million card-carrying communist party "medallion holders" whose livelihoods have been jeopardized by the bonfire of privileges.

In general, however, the transitional gains trap is a warning and not an opportunity. It is very costly to facilitate successful rent seeking because it is very difficult indeed to deregulate under conditions of democracy.[87]

Rent Protection, Rent Extraction, and Rent Creation

Consideration of transitional gains leads naturally to the subject of rent protection—the problem of retaining rents once they have been secured from the political market. Not only do individuals deploy scarce resources to seek out rents, they also deploy scarce resources to protect their rents from other rent-seekers and from rent-avoiders. Rowley and Tollison set out the key issues that govern any rent-seeking, rent-protection game in their study of trade protection.[88]

They assume, following Stigler and Peltzman, that the market in regulation responds even-handedly to the precise balance of dollar-votes expended in the battle over an available privilege.[89] They further assume, for the sake of argument, that the consumer interest is not entirely eroded by free-riding. In such circumstances, the durable privilege defined by the regulation market will not secure maximum available rents for a successful rent-seeker. Equilibrium will confirm output in excess of, and price less than, the full monopoly potential, reflecting the marginal impact of consumer outlays in the political market. Figure 5 illustrates such an outcome.

In Figure 5, producers rent-seek a full monopoly right, at price OA and output OQ_m. Consumers defend the competitive solution, at price OE and

87. M. A. Crew, "Rent-Seeking Is Here to Stay," in Rowley, *Democracy and Public Choice*, 158–62.

88. C. K. Rowley and R. D. Tollison, "Rent Seeking and Trade Protection," *Swiss Journal of International Economic Relations* 41 (September 1986): 141–66.

89. G. J. Stigler, "The Theory of Economic Regulation," *Bell Journal of Economics and Management Science* 2 (1971): 3–21; Peltzman, "Toward a More General Theory."

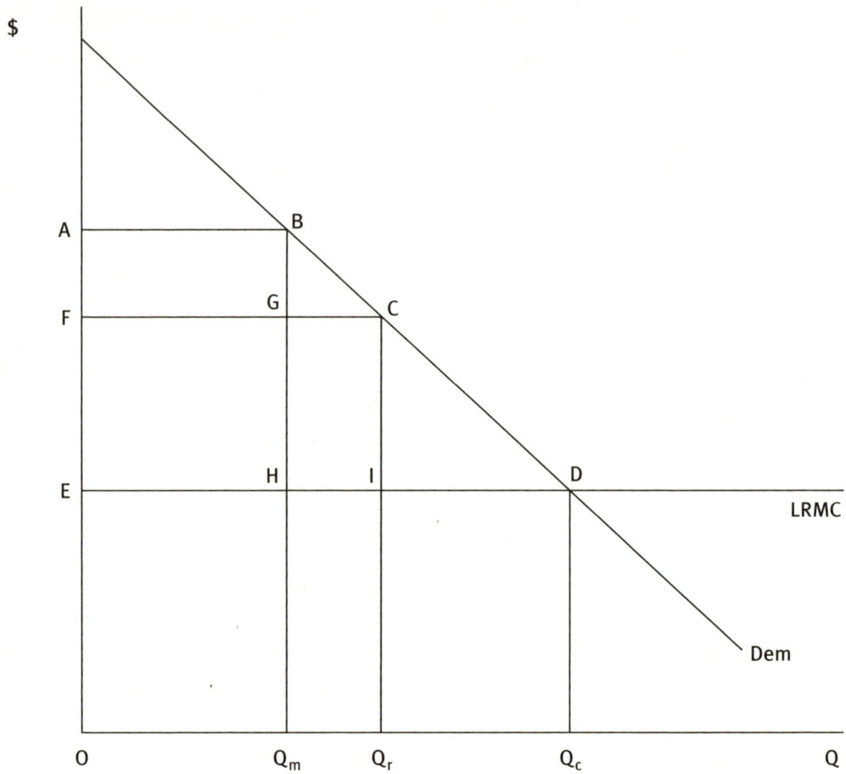

FIGURE 5
The Rowley–Tollison model of rent-seeking and rent protection

output OQ_c. All such expenditures represent social waste. The political market brokers an equilibrium at price at OF, somewhere between OA and OE, weighting equally the dollar votes of producers and consumers. In their example, the political price, OF is established slightly above the midpoint OA − OE, reflecting differentially heavy lobbying by the producers. Specifically, the producers outlay the present value of the rectangle FCIE to lift price from OE to OF. Consumers outlay the present value of the trapezoid ABCF to hold price below the monopoly level OA. Since FCIE exceeds ABCF, the political price OF reflects the producers' lobbying advantage.

In Rowley's and Tollison's example, the social cost of the partial monopoly outcome, assuming that all outlays are dissipated as social waste, is identical to that of the full monopoly outcome in the absence of rent avoidance by consumers. The area ABCF + FCIE + CID is exactly equivalent to the area ABDE. This result is particular to the assumptions employed but illustrates the general nature of rent-seeking, rent-protection battles under conditions of rational expectations. Once a particular rent has been extracted, the threat of rent-protection outlays predictably dampens reform initiatives, as the transitional gains trap insight clearly implies. Viewed dispassionately, the fact that rent-protection outlays waste scarce resources dampens the social welfare argument in favour of deregulation at least where time rates of discount are high. Of course, social welfare arguments have little impact on political markets, which typically respond to the redistributionist forces identified by public choice theory.[90]

In 1987, McChesney advanced this analysis significantly by integrating the role of the politician into the basic rent-seeking, rent-protection model. McChesney modelled politicians not as mere brokers redistributing wealth in response to competing private demands, but as independent actors making their own demands to which private actors respond.[91] This conceptual reversal of roles, in turn, forces consideration of the ways other than rent creation whereby politicians can gain from private parties.

Political office confers a "property right," not just to legislate rents, but to impose costs. A politician can gain by forbearing from exercising his right to impose burdensome restrictions on private actions. For example, the passage of sharply focused taxes and regulations will reduce the returns that private capital-owners receive from their skills and investments. In order to protect these returns, private owners have an incentive to strike bargains with legislators, to pay extortion, as long as such extortion outlays are lower than the expected losses from compliance with the threatened law. Such transfers create incentives for private actors to invest in specific capital, since such investments render them especially vulnerable to the politicians' protection racket. Figure 6 illustrates McChesney's theory.

Figure 6 depicts an industry in which producers have differing amounts of entrepreneurial capacity or some firm-specific, fixed-cost asset. The industry supply curve in the absence of regulation (S_0) thus is upward sloping. Re-

90. Crew and Rowley, "Dispelling the Disinterest."

91. F. S. McChesney, "Rent Extraction and Rent Creation in the Theory of Economic Regulation," *Journal of Legal Studies* 16 (1987): 101–18; F. S. McChesney, "Rent Extraction and Interest-Group Organization in a Coasean Model of Regulation," *Journal of Legal Studies* 20 (1991): 73–90.

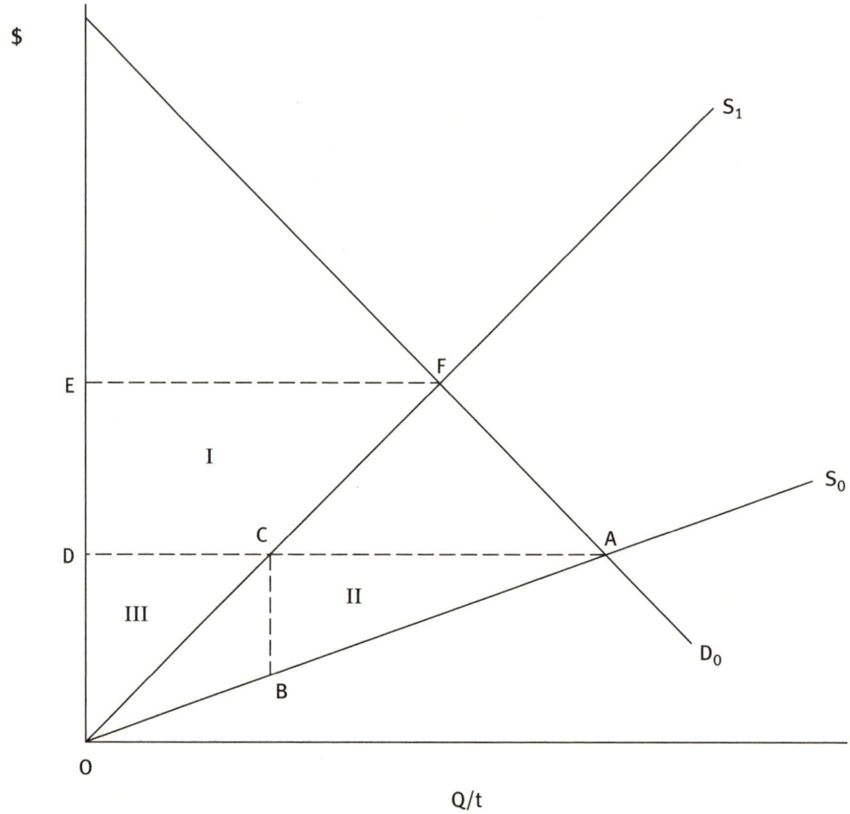

FIGURE 6
The McChesney model of rent extraction

turns to entrepreneurship and specific assets come as rents out of producers' surplus, OAD. Regulatory measures could be identified that would increase costs for all firms, but more for marginal firms, rotating the industry supply curve to S_1. To inframarginal producers, regulation is advantageous as long as there is a net increase in rents. In Figure 6, area I is greater than area II (CDEF > ABC); thus the gains from higher prices exceed the losses due to fewer sales.

However, rent creation by a government-mandated shift from S_0 to S_1 is not the only option open to politicians. *Existing* private rents rewarding specific assets are greater than the rents that can be created by regulation (OAD > CDEF). Regulatory measures can be identified that would expropriate this producers' surplus. Once such regulation is threatened, the price that producers would pay politicians in return for governmental inaction would exceed any payment for rent-creating regulations:

> "Milker bills" is one term used by politicians to describe legislative proposals intended only to squeeze private producers for payments not to pass the rent-extracting legislation. "Early on in my association with the California legislature, I came across the concept of milker-bills—proposed legislation which had nothing to do with milk to drink and much to do with money, the mother's milk of politics" . . . Representative Sam, in need of campaign contributions, has a bill introduced which excites some constituency to urge Sam to work hard for its defeat (easily achieved), pouring funds into his campaign coffers and "forever" endearing Sam to his constituency for his effectiveness. Milked victims describe the process simply as blackmail and extortion. The threats are made quite openly. One reads, for example, that "House Republican leaders are sending a vaguely threatening message to business political action committees: Give us more, or we may do something rash."[92]

Rent extraction can succeed only to the extent that threats to expropriate private rents are credible. To this end, politicians may sometimes have to enact legislation extracting private rents from owners who do not pay up, just as the *Cosa Nostra* occasionally burns down the buildings of those who fail to pay its protection levies. Evidently, as McChesney concludes, there is no such thing as a free market, at least in countries like the United States that have abandoned all constitutional protection for economic rights and have allowed free rein to majoritarian politics.

The Cost of Rent Seeking

The measurement of rent-seeking costs is a treacherous business even in Western economies that are relatively open and well endowed with statistical sources. The concept itself is nebulous, even when rent seeking is restricted to government-targeted outlays, for all the reasons outlined in this book. Not surprisingly, empirical estimates of the social cost of rent seeking fluctuate widely from study to study both for the United States and elsewhere. I shall

92. McChesney, "Rent Extraction," 108.

not attempt to survey the growing literature in detail, but rather will sample the results to indicate the lack of any general consensus on this issue.

The first attempt at measurement was that by Krueger, whose crude estimates suggested that the value of rents in India in 1964 amounted to 7.3 per cent of India's national income and that rents from import licences alone in Turkey in 1968 approximated 15 per cent of Turkey's gross national product.[93] Estimates of this order, even for Third World countries, certainly helped to put the rent-seeking problem on the economics map. Of course, questions remain as to what proportion of these rents was actually wasted and what proportion changed hands as undiluted transfers of wealth. The continuing impoverished state of both countries lends credibility to the social waste hypothesis.

In 1975, Posner used the concept of the Tullock rectangle to raise Harberger's calculation that the social cost of monopoly in the United States was a mere 0.1 per cent of gross national product to the much more significant figure of 3.4 per cent. He also noted that the regulated sector of the U.S. economy, unjustifiably, had been omitted from Harberger's estimations. Since then, the studies have mounted rapidly and with them, generally, the estimated costs of rent-seeking behaviour. Ross, for example, estimated that trade-related rent seeking in Kenya accounted for some 38 per cent of that country's gross domestic product.[94]

Recently, work by Laband and Sophocleus; Magee, Brock, and Young; and Murphy, Schleifer, and Vishny have attempted to use attorneys as a proxy for rent-seeking waste, and have suggested through regression analysis that attorneys in the United States reduce income by as much as 45 per cent. Laband, in a more speculative study that includes locks, insurance, and police expenditures as proxies for rent-seeking waste, estimates that some 50 per cent of United States gross national product was wasted in rent seeking in 1985. I am sceptical of these measures, given the almost metaphysical nature of the rent-seeking concept itself at the present time.[95]

93. Krueger, "Rent-Seeking Society."

94. Posner, "Social Costs of Monopoly," but see F. M. Fisher, "The Social Costs of Monopoly and Regulation: Posner Reconsidered," *Journal of Political Economy* 93 (1985): 410–16; V. B. Ross, *Rent-Seeking in LDC Import Regimes: The Case of Kenya*, Papers in International Economics, no. 8408 (Geneva: Graduate Institute of International Studies, 1984).

95. D. N. Laband and J. P. Sophocleus, "The Social Cost of Rent-Seeking: First Estimates," *Public Choice* 58 (1988): 269–75; Magee, Brock, and Young, *Black Hole Tariffs*; K. M.

In my book, *The Economics of Special Privilege and Rent Seeking*, I attempt to explain the apparently small size of the rent-seeking industry, given the magnitude of the rents available through the political process. If one visits Washington, D.C., or indeed any other national or state capital, one is immediately impressed by the number of fancy restaurants and night-clubs that are frequented by the lobbyists for private corporations and other special interests to entertain high-ranking government officials.

However, the outlays on lobbying appear to be trivial in comparison with the government largesse that is handed out. Not all of the difference can be made up in the form of bribes and illicit campaign contributions, although these are far from trivial even in the United States where corruption may be less pronounced than in most Third World countries. Although legitimate campaign contributions attract a great deal of publicity, these also amount to only a small percentage of the value of the special privileges that are routinely dispensed by government.

Let me conclude by emphasizing that we do not actually have good measures of rent-seeking cost at the present time for reasons both theoretical and empirical. We do have sound theoretical reasons for believing that rent-seeking costs are relatively high and for suspecting that many are hidden, taking the form of failed bids, aborted enterprise, uncharted waste, and threatened but never activated public policies. We also know that most senior executives of large companies and trade associates now spend a fair amount of time in Washington. In 1890, they never went there at all.

Feasible Political Reform to Protect Property Rights

Vincent Ostrom has explained clearly that the use of government authority involves a difficult Faustian bargain. Government involves the use of an instrument of evil, force and compulsion in human affairs, because of the good that it is hoped will come out of that evil. We can hope that the good that comes from this evil instrument will be great, and equally we can hope

---

Murphy, A. Schleifer, and R. W. Vishny, "The Allocation of Talent: Implications for Growth" (manuscript, University of Chicago, 1990); D. N. Laband, "An Estimate of Resource Expenditures on Transfer Activity in the United States," *Quarterly Journal of Economics* 58 (forthcoming).

that the evil that results will be small. What I have been discussing to this point is the evil that results because of government's ability to use force. The evil that has been done is, I fear, gigantic. In any event it is far removed from being small.[96]

The relevant question, of course, is whether there is anything better. We need government to protect us from each other and to secure us from foreign threats. To be sure, those foreign threats might seem weaker these days. And doubtlessly they are at this time. But one of the great certainties of history is that things change. Francis Fukuyama argues that whatever changes the future may bring, the chaos and bloodshed of the past are unlikely to be part of it. He may be right. We will have to wait and see. I am not so confident that the end of history is at hand. More likely is the possibility that we are at some plateau or resting point, with further threats to come.[97]

Even if we set aside external threats, the Faustian bargain still characterizes internal politics. The major justification for government is to secure our rights from violation from our fellows and to provide those public goods that cannot be well provided through ordinary market processes. The ability of government to use its monopoly of legitimate force is central to the fulfilment of these tasks. But monopoly is never used for good only. The temptation to commit evil will often prove irresistible. Rather than protecting rights from violation, government power will often be used as an instrument of violation, as much of the literature on rent seeking notes. And rather than providing genuine public goods, government will often use its authority and its taxing power to provide private goods desired by particular politically influential people at public expense.

The Faustian dilemma is intrinsic in the nature of government. We cannot hope to abolish it. All we can hope for is to be able to mitigate the evil consequences through reducing the frequency and vigour with which rent-seeking activities are pursued. But how can this be done? There is no simple, magic recipe to be followed. I can say this with assurance, having spent the bulk of my professional career thinking of such matters. All we can hope for is to secure modest improvements when the opportunity arises. I have no

96. V. Ostrom, "Why Governments Fail: An Inquiry into the Use of Instruments of Evil to Do Good," in *Theory of Public Choice—II*, ed. J. M. Buchanan and R. D. Tollison (Ann Arbor: University of Michigan Press, 1984), 422–35.

97. F. Fukuyama, *The End of History and the Last Man* (New York: Free Press, 1992).

utopian plan to offer, only a few suggestions for modest improvement. But we must not forget that even the longest journey must begin with the first step.[98]

What I shall do in this closing chapter is review five modest steps towards political reform that would better protect property rights: qualified majority voting, greater use of referenda, required balanced budgets, limits on the size and extent of government, and better constitutional enforcement. In describing these steps as modest, I do not mean to imply that I think any of them is feasible politically. All I mean is that they are simple, easily understandable reforms that would improve matters. How much improvement is hard to say, but the change would be in the right direction in any case. Moreover, I am confident other people will have other good ideas that they can add, with the result that we might be able to come up with a list of quite substantial improvements after all.[99]

In "Problems of Majority Voting," I described how simple majority voting led to a wasteful expansion in the size of government. Essentially this was because the members of winning majority coalitions were able to secure personal price reductions because of their ability to force part of the cost of their desired programmes on to others.[100] This expansion in the size of government is a simple proposition of elementary demand theory. Someone who likes to go to movies will go to more movies if the price is cut in half. Majority voting essentially allows this to happen. The members of a winning coalition get price cuts to the extent that the taxes to finance the programmes are paid for by outsiders.[101]

To be sure, people who are in winning coalitions on one issue can be in losing coalitions on another issue. It might seem as though things would even out in the long run. But this is not so, even ignoring Keynes's point that we would be dead by then anyhow. Let me give you an example. Suppose meals are eaten and paid for in common. The population is roughly equally

98. C. K. Rowley, "Rent-Seeking in Constitutional Perspective," in Rowley, Tollison, and Tullock, *Political Economy of Rent-Seeking*, 447–64.

99. C. K. Rowley, *Democracy and Public Choice: Essays in Honor of Gordon Tullock* (Oxford: Basil Blackwell, 1987).

100. G. Tullock, "Problems of Majority Voting," *Journal of Political Economy* 67 (1959): 571–79.

101. J. M. Buchanan, C. K. Rowley, and R. D. Tollison, eds., *Deficits* (Oxford: Basil Blackwell, 1987).

divided between those who prefer meat and those who prefer fish. Further, within each category there are cheap meals and expensive meals. Depending on their tastes, people would eat the kind of food they prefer, and in their preferred mix of cheap and expensive portions. Suppose the population consists of people who would eat cheaply five days a week.

Now suppose the supply of meals is to become a collective budgetary choice, and first the meat preferrers are on the winning side. Since roughly half of the cost is placed on to the fish preferrers, it is unlikely that the meat preferrers would choose expensive meals on only two days. How many expensive meals they would choose would depend on their demand for expensive meals in relation to the lower price that the winning coalition secures. Should the relationship be reversed and the fish preferrers be the winning coalition, they too will increase the frequency with which they eat expensive meals. Throughout the entire society the costliness of meals rises because of majority voting. Yet everyone is worse off; they are eating expensive meals five days a week, say, and paying for them, whereas they would prefer to eat expensive meals only two days a week.

Qualified majority voting mitigates these damages imposed by simple majority voting. The extreme case of qualified majority voting is unanimity, which was examined in *The Calculus of Consent.*[102] But any increase in the voting rule above a simple majority increases the share of the cost that the members of a winning coalition must bear. A rule of three-quarters majority, for instance, would tend to mean that members of a winning coalition would bear three-quarters of the cost of their choices, and so would support lesser, inefficient increases in government than they would under simple majority voting.

Another voting change that would generally reduce rent seeking is to allow greater use of referenda. Switzerland, which permits referenda on an immense number of things, has the smallest government of any European nation. The Swiss government is also highly decentralized, with Cantonal and Communal activities being a major portion of a governmental activity. To be sure, the referendum does not eliminate rent seeking, but only restricts it. In the United States perhaps only California even remotely approaches the extensive Swiss usage, and California clearly has a great deal of rent seeking. But do not forget that California's pioneering effort at tax limitation was the outcome of a referendum.

102. Buchanan and Tullock, *Calculus of Consent.*

Referenda work best to restrict rent seeking when they are restricted to a single issue. With such a restriction, a measure will pass only if it benefits a majority of voters. This still leaves plenty of scope for transfers from losing minorities to winning majorities, along with the inefficient expansion in government that this allows. But it does cut out the log-rolling packages where each component offers large benefits to intense minorities at general expense. A legislature can vote on a project to aid farmers, with the representatives of, say, the inner cities being promised something in another bill in exchange for their support. Such trades are difficult in referenda, though, unfortunately, they are not impossible. In Tucson, where I live, we recently had a referendum on a large collection of street repair and school building projects that were arranged as a gigantic log-roll to secure sufficient support for the package, when no single item would be likely to pass.

Another simple change that would protect property rights would be to require the federal government to operate with a balanced budget. Many state governments already operate with such a requirement, and they get their business done. Just as surely, state governments are full of rent seeking, so a balanced budget requirement will not eliminate rent seeking. But it can reduce it. Without a balanced budget requirement, politicians can promise favours to constituents without having to impose taxes sufficient to pay for those favours. Deficit finance makes it possible to postpone part of the cost into the future. A balanced budget requirement would force politicians more fully to assess the opposition to higher taxation that would accompany proposals for increased spending.[103]

Direct limits on the size and growth of government would also be a simple device that would help to restrict rent seeking. I have already mentioned the tax limitation referendum in California. There is no reason that something similar could not be imposed on the central government. A government that was tax-limited to 20 per cent of national output would be a much smaller government than we now have, though I am confident a great deal of rent-seeking activity would still be going on. It has always struck me as a little curious that proposals for tax limitation typically seek to freeze the relative size of government where it currently is. This might seem to be a reasonable and expedient compromise with existing political interests, though I see no rea-

103. J. M. Buchanan, *Public Principles of Public Debt* (Homewood, Ill.: Irwin, 1958); J. M. Buchanan and R. E. Wagner, *Democracy in Deficit: The Political Legacy of Lord Keynes* (New York: Academic Press, 1977).

son why some provision could not be allowed for relative shrinkages in government over time. Why must we always see governments asking for tax increases? Why not have political parties competing to offer tax reductions?

To this point, I have advanced some rather traditional proposals that are easily implementable and would restrict rent seeking, though would not eliminate it. Let me now offer some more speculative remarks. Surely, one way to reduce the amount of rent seeking dramatically would be to require members of Congress to read the bills that they pass. It would be nice to be able to get the members of Congress actually to think about those bills, but even getting them to read them would be a great improvement. We could also hope that when legislation provides for regulations being issued by, say, the Secretary of the Interior, that the Secretary of the Interior would also read those regulations.

A friend of mine in Connecticut once became part of a group that would read all proposed legislation before the Connecticut legislature, in order to advise a recently elected legislator. The members of the group, however, soon stopped their reading. It was a lot of work, the material was as dull as it was prolix, and the representative paid little or no attention to the group because she was too busy making trades and deals with the other members of the legislature.

I know of no practical method of implementing such an idea, but merely to articulate it makes the point: there is far too much legislation, most of which is written by special-interest groups, and about which even the most conscientious members of a legislature could not keep informed.

Televising Congressional proceedings is, however, an activity about which something can be done. At the moment, Congressional rules prohibit the television camera from moving away from the speaker. As a result it is impossible for viewers to tell that the only members in the chamber are those designated by their parties to sit in at all times and see to it that nothing untoward happens. Usually, three of four of these watchmen are present, and sometimes a few more individuals are present. Suppose the television cameras were free regularly to scan the benches of the House and Senate, thus permitting people at home to witness the empty chambers. Such a change would doubtlessly lead to some revision in Congressional proceedings, or possibly even the elimination of television, save for limited, special occasions where good attendance can be assured. Yet this, too, would be a minor reform, because the bulk of the damage is done before a bill gets to the floor of Congress.

Finally, I should like to close by re-examining some ideas on "constitutional mythology" that I published in 1965.[104] We continually hear statements to the effect that the Supreme Court is the ultimate arbiter of what the Constitution means. This is pure myth. While myths can be entertaining and even illuminating so long as they are treated as literature, they can be dangerous if they are believed and acted upon. This is true for the myth that holds that the Constitution means what the Supreme Court says it means. Precisely what the Constitution sought to avoid by its system of checks and balances was a situation where one of the branches of government became dominant over the other two. Rather what the Constitution sought to create was a situation where all the branches of government were subservient to the Constitution. Constitutionality, in other words, would be tested by a concordance among the three branches of government, and most surely would *not* be tested by one branch dictating to the other two.

This understanding held sway until recent times. This meant that the Supreme Court would refuse to issue orders enforcing what it regarded as unconstitutional acts by Congress or the President. In like manner, the President would refuse to enforce what he regarded as unconstitutional rulings by Congress or the Supreme Court. For instance, President Andrew Jackson responded to a ruling of Chief Justice John Marshall in the *Cherokee Indian Cases* with the remark: "John Marshall has made his decision, now let him enforce it."[105] In other words, a proper understanding of our system of checks and balances, an understanding which has disappeared during the postwar period along with the eruption of rent seeking, would regard all three branches of government as independently charged to uphold the Constitution, and with no one branch being superior to the other two branches.

Such a system of concordant authority would be similar to the framework within the Western legal tradition developed until the past two centuries or so.[106] The Western legal tradition began in the 11th century, with the joint autonomy of ecclesiastical and secular authorities. To be sure, there were continual conflicts along the boundaries. But, for the most part, both authorities were autonomous, and most people owed partial allegiance to both authori-

104. G. Tullock, "Constitutional Mythology," *New Individualist Review* 3 (1965): 13–17.

105. C. Warren, *The Supreme Court in United States History*, vol. 1 (Boston: Little, Brown, 1922).

106. H. Berman, *Law and Revolution: The Formation of the Western Legal Tradition* (Cambridge: Harvard University Press, 1983).

ties. The sentiment commonly voiced that law transcends politics was a reflection of this situation, for both monarch and church were bound by law, as evidenced by the need for concordance between the two. Our Founders recognized that religious authority had lost its transcendent position in society, to be sure, but they also recognized that the existence of competing authorities for constitutionality were central to the maintenance of free institutions. For to the extent governance requires a concordance among independent sources of authority, that governance will tend to reflect the common or general interests of those being governed.[107] That was the promise of the American Founding; it is a promise that we dearly need to relearn today.

107. Wagner, "Parchment Guns"; Wagner, "Agency, Economic Calculation."

PART 2

MORE ON EFFICIENT RENT SEEKING

EFFICIENT RENT-SEEKING REVISITED

In *Toward a Theory of the Rent-Seeking Society*, there is an article entitled "Efficient Rent Seeking," which among other things presents a rather difficult mathematical problem. The next five articles in this collection are devoted to the essentially mathematical discussions set off by this problem. In order not to keep the reader in suspense, I should say that it is still a problem and, indeed, one of the points of publishing this exchange is the hope that it will inspire mathematically inclined readers to solve the matter.

In my initial paper, "The Welfare Costs of Tariffs, Monopolies, and Theft," I said rent-seeking had aspects of a lottery. For example, if a number of people made efforts to obtain tariff protection, only some of them will succeed. This is of course realistic, but a little hard to deal with in its full institutional complexity. In "Efficient Rent Seeking" I formalized the problem into a true lottery. Specifically, it is a special form of lottery intended to closely approximate the nature of rent-seeking activity under conditions of risk and/or uncertainty. Assume that some number of rent seekers are permitted to buy tickets in the lottery. Each of the rent seekers is permitted to buy as many tickets as he or she wants, and write his or her name on each one. They are then put in a hat. One of them is drawn out, and the person whose name is on it gets the rent. For the purpose of this illustration, let us assume that the rent is a prize of $100.

What is the appropriate number of tickets to purchase? If there is a correct answer to this question, then any individual rent seeker would have to assume that not only he but other players would figure it out. He does not have a monopoly on information. This means, more or less, that each individual should assume that if there is a correct strategy, others will also follow it. The mathematical problem is that there may or may not be an equilibrium in this case, and where there is an equilibrium it is sometimes most peculiar.

There is one further complication. We do not know the production function for influence in lobbying. There could be economies of scale or dis-

Reprinted, with kind permission of Kluwer Academic Publishers, from *The Political Economy of Rent-Seeking*, ed. Charles K. Rowley, Robert D. Tollison, and Gordon Tullock (Boston/Dordrecht/Lancaster: Kluwer Academic Publishers, 1988), 91–94.

TABLE 1. ***Individual investments (N-person, no bias, with exponent)***

	NUMBER OF PLAYERS				
EXPONENT	2	4	10		15
1/3	8.33	6.25	3.00		2.07
1/2	12.50	9.37	4.50	I	3.11
1	25.00	18.75	9.00		6.22
2	50.00	37.50	18.00		12.44
3	75.00	56.25	27.00		18.67
5	125.00	93.75	45.00	II	31.11
8	200.00	150.00	72.00		49.78
12	300.00	225.00	108.00		74.67
		III			

economies of scale. It is even possible that there are neither.[1] In table 1, we have indicated increasing or decreasing returns to scale by the exponent. In other words, it is assumed that when you put in a given amount of money on the first line, you get the cube root of that number of tickets. This is rising marginal cost with a vengeance. On the second line the rent seeker gets a number of tickets equal to the square root of his investment, and on the third he gets one ticket for each dollar. On the fourth line we show economies of scale by giving him the square of the amount he invested. Even greater economies of scale are shown by the lower rows.

For simplicity of exposition, the table shows the "equilibrium" investment for specific numbers of rent seekers, but general equations which can be found both in the original article and in the following chapter permit solutions with any number of potential rent seekers. Table 2 shows the sum of all of the investments made by the rent seekers with varying combinations of rising or falling marginal costs and numbers of rent seekers.

The problem is that except for an infinite number of players and constant marginal costs, the market does not clear. With two players and constant marginal costs, for example, each will invest $25 for a 50-50 chance of $100. This seems absurd, but if the reader will experiment with his pocket calculator he will quickly discover that if he invests more, he increases the likelihood that he will win but with the winnings less than the value of the investment.

1. The reader who finds this discussion too compressed is advised to turn to the original article in *Toward a Theory of the Rent-Seeking Society*.

TABLE 2. ***Sum of investments (N-person, no bias, with exponent)***

	NUMBER OF PLAYERS					
EXPONENT	2	4	10	15		LIMIT
1/3	16.66	25.00	30.00	31.05		33.30
1/2	25.00	37.40	45.00	46.65	I	50.00
1	50.00	75.00	90.00	93.30		100.00
2	100.00	150.00	80.00	186.60		200.00
3	150.00	225.00	270.00	280.05		300.00
5	250.00	375.00	450.00	465.65	II	500.00
8	400.00	600.00	720.00	746.70		800.00
12	600.00	900.00	1,080.00	1,120.05		1,200.00
			III			

To take a converse case, the exponent-of-three row shows pronounced economies of scale. In this case, the two parties in "equilibrium" would each put in $75 for a 50-50 chance on $100. Once again it seems absurd, but your trusty pocket calculator will show that this is the only point where neither player can gain by changing his investment. Dropping out of the game might be better than playing, but this guarantees a profit for the other player.

The reader will note that the tables are divided into three regions, I, II, and III. Region I is the area where the total amount invested in the "equilibrium" condition is equal to or less than the prize. In other words it is sensible to play such games. In region II the sum of all of the investments is greater than the prize. In region III the individual investments are greater than the prize. In most of region I the total investment is sharply lower than the prize. In other words, the market does not really clear. Regions II and III would appear to be games that no one would play, but they have the interesting characteristic that if no one else is playing you should play. In other words, the paradox of the liar is involved. For the mathematically inclined, it perhaps should be pointed out that there is no Nash equilibrium in this game because there is a pronounced discontinuity at zero.

This then is the puzzle to which the following five articles are devoted. They do not reach a solution, although I think they clarify the problem. It is our hope that one of our readers can find the solution. Good hunting!

BACK TO THE BOG

My role in connection with the efficient rent-seeking model is, I think, a rather ill-omened one. I began the discussion by inventing a model with an apparent paradox. The market doesn't clear even with free entry and competition. There have been a number of efforts to deal with this problem.[1]

It is my unfortunate role, having discovered this particular intellectual swamp, to frustrate efforts to get out by pushing people back in. I first invent a difficult problem, and then when people try to solve it, I say that their solutions are either wrong or at least incomplete. I should therefore say that I do think that the work of Corcoran and Karels (1985) and Higgins, Shughart, and Tollison (1985) has indeed made progress toward a solution even if they have not finally solved the problem.

Corcoran and Karels come close to solving the original problem, provided we keep the framework of efficient rent-seeking rigid and unchanging. The problem is that there is one assumption in that initial framework which I now realize was unduly restrictive.

It is a usual practice among economists, when we observe a number of people engaging in the same kind of competitive activity, to assume that they all behave the same. The reason for this is partly that they face the same problem, and we would assume they reach the same conclusion, but I think even more important, that an assumption that they do not behave in the same manner means that you have to explain why some of them carry out one policy and some another.[2] In the particular case of efficient rent-seeking, it is, in

Reprinted, with kind permission of Kluwer Academic Publishers, from *Public Choice* 46 (1985): 259–64.

1. G. Tullock, "Efficient Rent Seeking," in *Toward a Theory of the Rent-Seeking Society*, ed. J. M. Buchanan, R. D. Tollison, and G. Tullock (College Station: Texas A&M University Press, 1980); W. J. Corcoran, "Long-Run Equilibrium and Total Expenditures in Rent-Seeking," *Public Choice* 43 (1984): 89–94; G. Tullock, comment on Corcoran, "Long-Run Equilibrium," *Public Choice* 43 (1984): 95–98; W. J. Corcoran and G. V. Karels, "Rent-Seeking Behavior in the Long-Run," *Public Choice* 46 (1985): 227–46; R. S. Higgins, W. F. Shughart II, and R. D. Tollison, "Free Entry and Efficient Rent-Seeking," *Public Choice* 46 (1985): 247–58.

2. The so called Hawk-Dove literature helps to provide an explanation for this kind of behavior under some circumstances. Unfortunately, it is not applicable to the subject of this comment.

general, more profitable to violate this rule. You will make more money if you do not make the same bid as your colleagues.

Before going further, I should frankly confess that I have no solution to this problem. It appears once again to be a case of the paradox of the liar. If one deviates from the pattern, he makes a profit; if all follow his example, they lose. The sensible behavior for an individual is not sensible unless the other people are doing something else. If this gives the reader a headache, I can only recommend Tylenol.

Let me take an obvious example from Corcoran and Karels, Table 3.[3] Suppose that we are in the area of increasing marginal efficiency, specifically the exponent, or *r*, value is 1.5. If seven people are playing, one player puts the minimum preclusive bid at $14.29. Suppose that one of the players instead of putting in $14.29 puts in $14.39, while the other six stick to the $14.29. As a result, he acquires an expectancy equivalent to $14.41. The $.10 additional investment has paid off with $.12. Each other player loses $.02.

The reason that this would occur is, I suppose, fairly obvious whenever *r* is greater than 1. This is the area of increasing marginal returns, and hence the return on additional marginal units will always be greater. Many equilibria in which all of the people are assumed to make the same investment will be subject to this problem. Indeed, in many cases, a complete outsider entering and making a large bid can gain. For example, consider eight people playing with *r* 1.3, and each putting in $12.50. This is, of course, spending $12.50 to buy an expectancy of $12.50. Suppose that a ninth party arrives and puts in $25.00. His expectancy is $26.14. The expectancy of the original eight has of course gone down sharply.

I realize the problems that this will generate. Once again, we seem to be in a situation in which there is no rational way of playing the game. If nine players each put in $25.00, the result is disastrous.

One way of dealing with this problem, of course, is for individuals to attempt to put in individually preclusive bets before anyone else enters. The outcome of such preclusive bets is shown in the left column of Table 5 of Corcoran and Karels.[4] The problems here are, first, the one that I mentioned

3. Corcoran and Karels, "Rent-Seeking Behavior," 243f. This involves rounding. There are seven players and 7 × 14.29 is, of course, slightly more than $100, but the matter is unimportant for the example.

4. Ibid., 239.

in my original article, which is that it leads to a previous game to be first.[5] There is, however, a second problem here, which is that if we look at real-life rent-seeking activity, it is a little hard to see what the equivalent of making that single large initial investment is. A lobbyist can hardly simultaneously provide a Congressman with twenty-two dinners and five blondes. In corrupt societies where cash is used, this problem, of course, is less severe.

When we have an exponent less than 1, i.e., when there are declining returns to scale, Corcoran and Karels essentially depend on the fact that there will, in practice, be a least feasible bid. I have no quarrel with this, but I should point out that there is here a problem analogous to the problem we have discussed above which makes calculation at least difficult. Look at their Table 1, and consider the first line.[6] Suppose that one of the two people who are placing a bet, instead of placing a bet of $12.50, places one of $12.00. He of course does not have an even chance of winning, so his expected return is not $50.00, but $49.49. His expected profit is $37.49, instead of $37.50. But his percent return on capital is better. If he had put in $12.50, he would have received a profit three times his initial capital. If he puts in $12.00, he receives a profit 3.12 times his original capital. Of course the other player, the one who still put in his $12.50, does better than he would had the first player also put in $12.50. Specifically, he makes an additional expected $.51. This is, however, only a return of 3.04 times his capital. The explanation, of course, is that here we are in an area of declining marginal returns.

Naturally I am not claiming that I have solved the problem. What I have done is make it more difficult. Let us now turn to Higgins, Shughart, and Tollison. The first thing to be said is that all of the problems mentioned above apply here also. When playing one of their stochastic strategies, it will normally not be rational to play the same amount as the others are doing.[7] It is also subject to the problem that a single large preclusive bet normally dominates their stochastic procedure. But once again, the high profitability of such a preclusive bet means that there would be a previous game to obtain such preclusion.

The basic point of the Higgins, Shughart, and Tollison paper is to arrange

5. Tullock, "Efficient Rent Seeking."

6. Corcoran and Karels, "Rent-Seeking Behavior," 230.

7. I recently saw a propaganda movie about the Chinese communes. It was made several years ago, and would not be permitted in present-day China, but I saw it in Philadelphia. In one sequence each of the commune children was encouraged to work faster than the others.

through stochastic methods that all of the players receive a normal return on their capital (as most economic work, this is shown as in zero profit) by stochastic means. There are occasional situations in which the number of players for the zero-profit condition is an integer. More commonly, however, it is not, and their stochastic model is designed to deal with this much more numerous category. Unfortunately, there is here a defect. The mathematical expression that they use has the ingenious characteristic that the same (zero as usual) profit is made by playing every time, by playing their stochastic procedure, or by transferring one's capital to some other normally profitable activity. If, however, one of their players, instead of playing stochastically, chooses to play every time, he will achieve a normal return on his strategy; the other players will suffer losses.

The reason is clear, although a little involved. When I put my bid in, whether I do it because Higgins, Shughart, and Tollison's stochastic process tells me I should at this time, or for some other reason, that stochastic process followed by the other players gives me an expectancy of exactly normal profits. If I play continuously, I will get normal profits. But since I am not playing the stochastic model, I am entering more often than I should and am inflicting a negative cost on others. Every time that I play when by the stochastic model I shouldn't, I lower the profits of the other players.

In general, in this kind of efficient rent-seeking model, an individual player imposes external costs on others. The Higgins, Shughart, and Tollison model guarantees that these external costs are evenly distributed and balanced by profits. A single player who deviates by playing more often injures the other players.

Now it should be pointed out that there's no strong motive for a player to do this. It is true he will be able to invest more capital in an activity which gives a normal return, and he might drive some of the other players out, in which event he would begin making positive profits. The latter possibility of course brings us into the extremely complex area of predatory competition and I don't want to go through that very lengthy argument. I do presume my readers are already familiar with it. Suffice it to say that it does not seem as if this would be a long-run way of obtaining profits.

The other problem here is not that once the Higgins, Shughart, and Tollison equilibrium stochastic process has reached equilibrium someone may deviate, but that it is very hard to see how you would get there to begin with. Clearly they are not talking about a carefully calculated conspiracy among all the players; because if there is such a conspiracy, there are far more profitable strategies to play. Their equilibrium would have to be obtained by players who simply find out over time that this is the appropriate strategy. Unfortunately, there seems no path by which they can do so.

As an example illustrating the problem, suppose that we have a situation in which seven players, if they all made the same and optimal bid regularly, would make a positive profit; whereas eight players, if they all made the same and equal bid, would lose. We start with eight players. All of them are losing, but one of them who has read Higgins, Shughart, and Tollison calculates the efficient stochastic strategy and begins following it.

There will now be two different kinds of games. First, those games in which this player, after consulting his table of random numbers, plays. In those games there will be eight players, and all of them will lose. The second set are the ones in which he does not play; there are seven players, and all of them gain or at least lose less. By his behavior, he has benefitted the others for at least some of the games, while in all the games in which he plays, he loses as much as before. If a second player began following the same policy, once again the players who were not playing stochastically would do better than those who were.

Note, there's nothing in this which indicates that anybody will actually make a positive profit. It is just that the non-stochastic players will more often have a profit in a particular play than the stochastic players, and these profits will, on the average, be larger. Thus there is no way for the players by simply experimenting with different stochastic procedures to reach the Higgins, Shughart, and Tollison equilibrium.

As I said before, my role in this controversy is to watch people trying to get out of the swamp and then to push them back in. Clearly, my role is not a constructive one, but nevertheless, I feel it is necessary. On the other hand, it seems to me that if the work of Corcoran, Karels, Higgins, Shughart, and Tollison has not gotten us out of the swamp, it has at least moved us to a place where the mud is less deep. I don't know much more about the geography of the swamp, but the prospect that we can find a bit of dry land somewhere has improved.

ANOTHER PART OF THE SWAMP

Suppose that I am engaged in a game with nine other people in which the prize for each round is $100. I think that they will use the Hillman strategy. Instead of taking the trouble to compute the strategy, I simply play 95 regularly.[1] I should receive the same return as if I had been playing the Hillman strategy. I would win most games, but I'd make only $5 when I won, and when his strategy put somebody in the range above $95, I'd lose; the two would balance.

Although this would be true for me, for other people the world would have changed radically. They would lose almost all the money that they bet. Following the Hillman rules, any one of them could expect to win less than once in every two hundred plays, and they would net less than $5 on that victory. This would not even come close to compensate them for their losses on their less than $95 bets.[2]

My strategy provides another change in their world. Since I am not going to play above 95, returns to plays above 95 are now somewhat higher than they would be if I were following the Hillman rules. One of my opponents by playing 96 could guarantee himself a positive profit even if a very small one. Under the circumstances, it seems extremely unlikely that they would continue playing the Hillman rules. They could simply drop out of the game, which would mean that I begin making positive profits, or they could recalculate their strategy. For any such recalculation there is a pure strategy for me which does as well as their strategy but imposes losses on them or (sometimes "and") a pure strategy which gives me a profit while imposing costs on them.[3]

Hillman's equilibrium is an equilibrium which attracts people simply because it is an equilibrium. A maximizing player who, among other things, has the right to stop playing right after a coup, can certainly do better in the sense

Reprinted, with kind permission of Kluwer Academic Publishers, from *Public Choice* 54 (1987): 83–84. Copyright 1987 Martinus Nijhoff.

1. And I have not bothered to compute it in writing this note.

2. The situation is even worse. Sometimes two of my opponents would simultaneously bet more than $95, and then one would lose.

3. For those to whom this proposition is not intuitively obvious, I offer a challenge. Send me a recalculated strategy together with a $10 check. If I can't produce a pure strategy which does as well or better while imposing costs on other players, I will return the check and send one of my own with it. Otherwise, I cash the check.

that he doesn't have to bother to calculate. Further, if he plays a reasonably well selected pure strategy, his opponents have the choice of losing very large sums of money, dropping out of the game, which improves our basic player's net profits, or recalculating their strategy. If they recalculate the strategy, and our stratigizing player duplicates their calculations, he certainly will have at least short-term opportunities for profits. Once again there is no true equilibrium if we assume that the parties are all attempting to maximize their return.

STILL SOMEWHAT MUDDY

A COMMENT

Perez-Castrillo and Verdier seem to have solved the bulk of the first-level mathematical puzzles in my "Efficient Rent Seeking."[1] There still remains the second order of puzzle mentioned in my first article, the question of which "agent" (to use their terminology) will be the one or more who buys tickets in this lottery. This, I am happy to say, is somewhat easier than the original problem, but until it is solved we can't claim to understand the issue in general.

Let me begin with a case where *r* is less than 1. In these declining marginal efficiency cases Perez-Castrillo and Verdier follow the conventional approach and point out that there usually is some minimum cost, postage for example. Hence there is a restriction on the minimum bid.

This is of course true, but it raises another problem. Suppose that in the lottery for $100, *r* is 1/3. Further suppose that it costs $3 in actual resource expenditures to get your lottery ticket. According to Table 6.2 in "Efficient Rent-Seeking," we see that 10 people are the right number for this amount. Each of these 10 would be investing $3 to get a 1-in-10 chance of $100, and this is obviously not equilibrium.[2]

The procedure investigated in "Efficient Rent Seeking" when *r* is less than 1 is that as more people invest, the average amount invested by each person goes down, and there is no true equilibrium. With a minimum effective bid of $3.00, however, we would anticipate that not 10 but 33 people would invest their $3, which is the minimum resource cost of a ticket. This is an equilibrium, but a peculiar one.[3]

This particular set of circumstances, i.e., when *r* is less than 1, is one in which preclusive bidding is not possible. Indeed, the person proposing to get

Reprinted, with kind permission of Kluwer Academic Publishers, from *Public Choice* 76 (1993): 365–70. Copyright 1993 Kluwer Academic Publishers.

1. J. D. Perez-Castrillo and T. Verdier, "A General Analysis of Rent-Seeking Games," *Public Choice* 73, no. 3 (April 1992): 335–50.

2. J. M. Buchanan, R. D. Tollison, G. Tullock, eds., *Toward a Theory of the Rent-Seeking Society* (College Station: Texas A&M University Press, 1980), 97–112.

3. They mention in passing the possibility that *r* would turn up somewhere. This seems to me to be a dubious solution to the problem, but they don't analyze it, and I will follow their example.

in with a large sum should break his investment up into a lot of small pieces, as small as possible, and make a lot of small bids. The reader will recall that not very long ago an Australian syndicate bought 5 million $1 tickets in the Virginia State Lottery and collected $27 million dollars.[4] Of course, in this case there is no evidence it was equilibrium.

Since the Virginia State Lottery Commission has changed the rules to make this harder in the future, the lottery may never reach an equilibrium of this sort. In essence, they raised the private cost of buying a lottery ticket, and perhaps the normal private purchase of 2 or 3 million tickets is in equilibrium under those circumstances. Strictly speaking, of course, where there is an effective minimum bid, r is 1 at that bid.

If r is greater than 1, then we have two distinct areas. When r is between 1 and 2, N* can be quite a large number. In cases where r is 2 or above, N* is always 1. Incidentally, they talk to some extent about the symmetry or asymmetry of the investments here, and it's a little hard to see what that terminology means if r is above 2.

From the standpoint of the agents wondering whether to buy tickets in the lottery, there are three different types of game. In the first you can buy a certain number of tickets and then either increase your holdings or cash them in and take back your money right up to the time the drum is spun and the number is withdrawn. In the second, you can buy any number of tickets you wish and increase the number at any time, again up to the time the drum is spun, but you can't cash them in and withdraw. In the third, you must make a single purchase, and that's it.

The first of these would correspond to many speculative markets where you can get in and out very easily.[5] The second is what I think most people thinking of rent-seeking regard as normal. Once you give a congressman an expensive evening's entertainment, there is no way you can get the money back. The third would be the case of the sealed bid. It's apparently little used in rent-seeking, and, hence, I shall give it relatively little attention.

Let us begin with the case in which you can withdraw your investment at any time and assume that this is costless. Further, I'd like to use a particular game which is easy to think about, specifically one where there are only two agents, and r is equal to 3.

4. "Despite Violation, Virginia to Pay a Lottery Jackpot of $27 Million," *New York Times*, 11 March 1992, A13.

5. Usually with a small cost.

Let me assume as a starting point that both of them have already bought $50 worth of tickets for a $100 prize. Agent A now goes up to $75. In doing so, he increases his probability of winning so that his expected value goes up by $27 so, per se, that is a sensible investment. Agent B now has a choice. He can match agent A's bid by going up to $75, which will increase the value of his expectancy from the $23, which it is after agent A went up to $75, to $50, which, looked at by itself, once again is a sensible investment, or he can get out.

Assume that he goes up to $75, and then both of the players begin making strong statements about how they are going to stick regardless. In fact, there is no reason to try to cash in their chips and get out until the very last minute, since there is always some chance that the other party will do so first.

The question there is whether it is sensible to cash in at the last minute. Note both of the parties face this problem, and neither one can wait until after the last minute to cash in his own lottery tickets and get out. The last minute is, after all, the last minute.

If agent A thinks that agent B will withdraw with exactly 50% probability, and agent B thinks that agent A will withdraw with exactly 50% probability, they each own a right with a present discounted value of $75, but if they both stick they have an expectancy of −$25. If either one thinks that the chance that the other will check out is greater than 50% he should stay in, and if he thinks it is less than 50% he should get out.[6]

We have here an example of the paradox of the liar. The situation in which, if there is a correct strategy, and it can be computed by A, B can then compute what A's correct strategy is. He can then use whatever his best strategy is in return, and in general that will mean that A's strategy is not really the best; i.e., there is no optimal strategy. This is the problem that led Pascal to give up on games of strategy. They lead to an infinite regress.

Now in this particular case there is, as it happens, a mixed strategy.[7] The problem is that if I think my opponent in this game in which we both put in $75 is going to actually have an exactly 50% chance of staying in or leaving

6. There is an alternative to getting out, which is to go down to a low number. For example, A might go down to 1 on the theory that if B goes down to 0 you get the money at a low price, and if he doesn't he will lose only a little bit. The problem with this is, again, it's symmetrical—the same strategy is open to both.

7. For my general criticism of mixed strategies, briefly summarized in the following few sentences of text, see G. Tullock, "Games and Preference," *Rationality and Society* 4, no.1 (January 1992): 24–32.

(let us say I saw him flip a coin) I am now free to do anything, depending on extrinsic matters. I may, for example, be risk averse. Or I may dislike him and want to make sure that he doesn't win. The strategies provided by those two different preferences are both costless in expectancy terms, and hence, the sensible thing is to ignore the expectancy and make up my mind. Unfortunately, once again, this is true for both agents, and there is no true solution to the game.

What about the situation in which you can buy a certain number of tickets and then can buy more but cannot take money out of the game? The first thing to be said is that if *r* is much above 1, whoever gets in first can lay a preclusive bid. For example, $99 by A would keep B from making any purchase at all and, hence, is pretty much a guarantee of $1 profit.

Of course, $99 is not the most profitable way of precluding your opponent. You would want the lowest possible amount. Unfortunately, this is a difficult problem. It is particularly difficult in the area of *r* between 1 and 2, because in this case there are apt to be a considerable number of people investing unless you preclude all of them. If they do invest there is no guarantee of any profit for anyone.

Let us return to our simple case where there are only two agents, and *r* is 3. Assume temporarily that A is thinking of a preclusive bid and is attempting to calculate the appropriate one. Unfortunately this is not an easy problem if he wants to make the minimum preclusive bid.

Depending on what he thinks the other party will do and what he thinks he will do in response to the other party and what he thinks the other party will think he will do in response, etc., it can be any number from about 30 to about 60. If A goes too low, B can dash in with, let us say, 75 and preclude A from raising his bid. If he bids too high he is investing money unnecessarily. Unfortunately, if he stops to carefully work out this problem he will probably be beaten by B, who dashes in with some large number, perhaps 75, without thinking about the matter.

Of course it's not essential that any party make a preclusive bid. If, however, an individual party does not make a preclusive bid, then almost anything can happen. It's easy to develop scenarios in which a preclusive bid is made by nobody and in which almost any outcome that you want to specify occurs. Unfortunately, for reasons we will discuss later, making a preclusive bid is a very risky strategy also.

In the real world, this is not the only calculating problem. A high Hollywood executive explaining (anonymously) to the *New York Times* how Sony lost $45 million on a single film said: "This business is so competitive, so cynical, so absolutely cutthroat that before you have a chance to digest information you start moving."[8] Putting it differently, a preclusive bid is necessarily highly risky. You can't afford to stop and think the matter over, because if you do somebody will get in ahead of you.

Of course you can put in a small amount of money and then go up. Indeed, rent-seeking works just that way. You invite the congressman out to dinner and make up your mind at that point whether you will have more dinners or more resources invested in that particular issue. You take into account what other people are doing. Unfortunately, if r is above 1, and you get into this kind of a game, costs are generally sunk, and the odds are that the total amount invested by all of the rent-seekers will be greater than the prize. The only really good motive for small initial investments would be as a strategic investment in finding out what your rivals are going to do.

There is a possible solution, but before we deal with it let us turn to our third category, the case in which you are permitted to make only one bid. As far as I know this is not common in rent-seeking activities, but for completeness we should at least mention it and point out that it raises the same problem. Once again, what you want to do is get your bid in first and have a preclusive one. Of course if some kind of sealed-bid technique is used you can't even do that.

Consider the situation if there are a number of problems of either our second or third type coming up. The case of Hollywood firms deciding what movies to produce is, of course, a clear-cut example, but so is the situation in Washington in which the highly paid lobbyists of the various industries and labor unions must decide how much they will put into lobbying different congressmen.

There is in biology a solution to this kind of problem which is called the hawk-dove equilibrium.[9] What we would expect is that there would be a large number of agents who would decide to stay out of business completely and another large number of agents who would make a profession of attempting preclusive bids for various opportunities. Note I say attempt, because it is clear that they would miscalculate; they don't have time to calculate

8. "Tracking the Tailspin of 'Radio Flyer,'" *New York Times*, 9 March 1992, B1.

9. For an explanation and an application to other economic problems, see G. Tullock, "Hawks, Doves and Free Riders," *Kyklos* 45 fasc. 1 (1992): 25–36. German translated excerpts were published in *Wirtschafts Woche*, 8 November 1991, 132–34.

accurately. The miscalculation would frequently mean that more than one agent put his money down, and only one won the lottery.

The hawk-dove equilibrium in this case would be that there would be enough people who are engaging in the strategy of making quick investments in the rent-seeking lottery so that the return that they had over time would be roughly the same as that of those who made no such investments. In other words, any potential profit would be competed away, but competed away not in the individual lottery but over the universe of all lotteries and all agents.

Note that this leaves us with no solution for any individual lottery. All we know about it is that there is a preclusive bid which somebody can make first, but he will not know exactly how big it is, and further, he won't actually know the value of the lottery, because the agents have to make their bids without careful calculation. If they spend time carefully calculating, somebody else will get in ahead of them.

The business would appear to be a nerve-wracking one, and as far as we can tell that is indeed true. Back in the days when stomach ulcers were a major disease we would have predicted many of them among Hollywood producers and lobbyists in Washington. Those people, of course, with the specialized talents which make it possible to make these calculations quickly and with a somewhat lower error rate than other people have, would be very highly rewarded.

Once again, note that here there is no social gain from this activity. We would anticipate that enough bids would be made so that any potential profits would be more or less eroded away. It would not be true that for any particular agent making bid for any particular lottery the expectancy would be a normal profit. Sometimes they would make a lot of money, and sometimes they would lose a lot of money, e.g., Sony's $45 million.

In both the case where r is below 1 and r is above 1, we have situations where although we can predict the outcome, mainly as a result of the work of Perez-Castrillo and Verdier, the outcome is inefficient. Resources are wasted in investments which simply transfer rents from one group of potential rent-seekers to another. There is an equilibrium, but it's not a nice equilibrium.

PART 3

THE ENVIRONMENTS OF RENT SEEKING

RENT SEEKING AS A NEGATIVE-SUM GAME

I have just sold one house and bought another. As it happened, the transaction was completed very quickly, taking less than seventy-two hours, and, during that time, the real estate agent who managed both of these transactions spent something under four hours talking to me and to the person who bought my old house and showing us around. For this rather short period of time, he collected commissions totaling about $5,000. If we regard this as a return on the time he spent on this specific transaction, it represents $1,250 an hour, which gives him an hourly rate similar to that of the president of a large corporation.

Obviously, this is not the proper way to explain his income. In addition to the actual sales effort, he has many other expenses. He maintains a well-equipped office complete with a radio beeper that makes it possible for him to be reached anywhere within fifteen miles of Blacksburg. He is very well informed about the local real estate market; indeed, it was this very fine information, together with his ability quickly to discern people's needs for housing from rather brief conversations, that led to the extreme speed with which this transaction was completed. There are also advertising costs, time involved in creating the impression on his clients of great efficiency and helpfulness, and simple "waiting" time involved in his business.

If we consider all these factors, it is doubtful that he makes an excessively high return on his investments. Note, however, that the bulk of his costs occurs before, and is not directly related to, any given individual transaction. He invests over a long period of time in acquiring information, specialized abilities to deal with clients, and a good reputation; the payoff comes in the form of relatively rare but lucrative commission payments.

To take one (probably fairly small) example, I have seen him and his partner selling to farmers, to a group of hippies, and to university professors. They must maintain a sizable wardrobe right in the office to change clothes between these various activities, because they certainly look like farmers, college professors, or hippies at the appropriate time. All this is perfectly nor-

Reprinted, with permission, from *Toward a Theory of the Rent-Seeking Society*, ed. James M. Buchanan, Robert D. Tollison, and Gordon Tullock (College Station: Texas A&M University Press, 1980), 16–36.

mal, and I presume all of us would agree that the agent is probably earning only a normal return on these resources, his personal talents counted among them.

There is, however, one more preliminary investment in the sale of real estate I have not mentioned: it is necessary for him to take an examination before he can sell real estate. Although the subjects covered in the examination are not totally irrelevant to his business, they are not so closely connected that the resources he invests in studying for the examination can be said to have a direct return at the same rate as those shown above. He earns a return on his complicated wardrobe by continuously using it. He earns a return on the resources he invested in passing the examination because the existence of the examination means that the real estate business is not quite as competitive as it otherwise would be.[1] Hence, his income is slightly higher.

For the purpose of this paper, I am going to call income derived from *this* kind of resource investment a "rent," and "rent seeking" is the effort to obtain such income. Thus, an individual who invests in something that will not actually improve productivity, or will actually lower it, but that does raise his income because it gives him some special position or monopoly power, is "rent seeking," and the "rent" is the income derived. Note that this is different from the normal economic meaning of rent seeking, but not so radically different that we must seek out a new word.

Let us now turn to a somewhat similar situation. In imperial China the highest status and wealth positions, other than that of the imperial family itself, were occupied by high officials in the bureaucracy. Entrance into the bureaucracy was by way of a very, very difficult competitive examination. Its difficulty can be seen by the fact that only about a hundred people a year in all of China passed. Further, of those who passed the examination, only a minority—those who finished very near the top—really had much chance for high government office.

The returns to those people who *did* rise to high position by becoming a grand secretary, viceroy, and so forth, were very great indeed. The imperial government did not believe in saving money on the compensation of its high-level executives, although as a matter of fact a good deal of this compensation came in the form of fees for specific services rather than salaries. There was substantially no other occupation in China that could lead to anywhere

1. The exam is actually fairly easy, and hence, the effect is small, but it does go in this direction.

near the same type of income, power, and prestige possessed by the high official. It is fairly certain that high officials of equivalent talent could have been hired at lower salaries had there been some method of determining their suitability.

As a result of this institution, there were immense investments of resources all over China in preparation for the examinations. The examinations have had bad press because they contained sections on poetry and good handwriting. Nevertheless, to a considerable extent they were devoted to the kind of problems that might actually affect governmental performance. Hydraulic engineering, a critical view of history, and a good knowledge of the basic philosophy that was supposed to guide the Chinese government were clearly important in passing the examination.

Here again, the return, once one became a high official, was to a large extent a return on talents and work invested long before. Further, there was an immense gamble here. The number of people who spent a great deal of time and energy preparing for the examination was a very high multiple of those who finally reached the top rank. Of those who did invest large amounts of time in an attempt to pass the examination, the overwhelming majority were eliminated in the first stage, which meant that they actually got no return at all on their educational efforts, except insofar as there may have been a direct consumption return. The remainder would receive a relatively small return, except for those few who became very high-ranking officials.[2]

Presumably, the individuals investing resources in preparation (or, more commonly, in the preparation of their children) for the examination invested these resources only to the point where the marginal expected return matched that on other possible resource investments. In practice, it was like a lottery in which a large number of people buy tickets and only a few win. Of course, in this case the winners were not selected by luck—or at least not primarily by luck. There is, I take it, little doubt that the people who passed the examination with high scores were in fact geniuses. Still, when the formal education of a child who was preparing for the examination began, no one could tell whether he was going to pass or not; hence, the initial investment was made under conditions of stochastic risk.

The situation, looked at economically, is unusual. Individuals were entering into a high-risk activity and investing resources in a way that discounted

2. This is to some extent an oversimplification, but I think it is basically correct. For a more detailed account, see almost any history of China.

both the probability of failure and the extremely high rate of return if success was achieved. Nevertheless, it is hard to avoid the impression that the system was economically wasteful. The education given to the students preparing for the exam was of little or no use in any walk of life other than government. Further, most of the people who passed the examination and received minor government jobs would make only modest use of their highly intensive and expensive educational backgrounds. It was not necessary that a Hsien magistrate at the bottom of the official system be deeply learned in Chinese philosophy and history and be well up into what psychologists would call the "genius" category. In the great days of the British Empire, the district commissioners who held somewhat similar jobs were selected essentially for personality traits rather than for learning and high intelligence. They seem to have done about as good a job as the Chinese Hsien magistrates.

Even at higher levels, it is not obvious that China gained a great deal from the extremely high qualifications of her senior officials. They may have invested the bulk of their superior knowledge and intelligence in maneuvers and intrigue rather than in actual governmental efficiency. Still, most visitors to China before about 1800, when the system was functioning well, admired it.

It will be seen that this system raised the same problems that modern education does with respect to the capital investment–screening problem. It is not clear whether the examination impelled people to acquire valuable capital or simply screened out the inherently brightest people. Probably it did both. In any event, it is clear that the bulk of the people who participated in the process did not gain from it, regardless of its social effect. They entered into a gambling game, in which they lost.

From the standpoint of individual parties, it is not clear whether this game is a positive-sum, zero-sum, or negative-sum game.[3] To anticipate, and put simply what is really a quite complicated line of reasoning, the game can be positive, zero-sum, or negative-sum from the individual's standpoint, depending on certain parameters. Unfortunately, the empirical work necessary to determine the real-world parameters has not been done and will be extremely difficult.

From the social standpoint, however, it is clear that this was a negative-sum game. Assuming, as I think we can assume, that the very large amount

3. See chapter 6 of this volume for a mildly mathematical preliminary investigation of this type of game.

of learning undertaken by the candidates for the examination was partially screening and partially capital investment, and that the capital investment failed for those people who did not complete the examination, it is clear that the total social cost must have been much greater than the social benefit, regardless of the rationality or irrationality of the individual resource investments.

The problem is that the individual invests resources in a form in which they are not readily transferable to other uses. If, for example, the imperial Chinese government had sold government positions at auction, it would have obtained a quite different type of candidate, but the funds invested would have been useful for something else. When the individual candidate invested the same amount of resources in learning to write Tang dynasty poetry of a somewhat stuffy nature, it was just as rational from his standpoint, but society has lost these resources, except insofar as having one more producer of rather stuffy Tang dynasty poetry may have a positive value.

If we assume that the type of officials obtained by the examination were a great asset to China, that their value exceeded the cost of generating them, counting the cost of having all those people study Confucian classics all over China, and that there was no other less expensive way of obtaining the result, then the society would have gained from the institution. The situation would be rather similar to what we see in retail trade. People are always opening new restaurants, some of which go bust. Resources invested in the restaurant are wasted,[4] but we regard that as a necessary cost for maintaining an efficient restaurant industry. The imperial Chinese examination may have been an example of the same kind of thing. I have no doubt that it did produce a superior civil service, but I suspect that the cost was greater than the benefit.

If the benefit was greater than the cost, then this activity would not meet our definition of rent seeking, although it would clearly resemble the rent-seeking situation. Even so, we would prefer to select the same quality of candidate without expenditure of all these resources. This "waste" of resources does not occur if the investment takes the form of paying a fee that may then be used. The same reasoning applies if it is invested in some resource, human or otherwise, that pays a positive and continuing return at the existing marginal rate of interest. The student who had invested a great deal of time and effort in preparing for the imperial examination and failed had invested a great deal of resources and produced no personal or social gain. Similarly,

4. It may have resale value.

those very numerous people in India or Kenya, for example, who go to the local equivalent of a university and then remain "unemployed" for many years while they maneuver for government jobs are making a large investment that may have no return at all. The situation resembles the potlatches of the Pacific Northwest, where prestige and power were obtained by physically destroying valuable objects. The one who destroyed the most in the way of valuable products "won" the game and increased his prestige and influence.[5]

The situation may be contrasted with the custom of buying government jobs for cash, until recently quite common on the continent of Europe. The French government is a particularly good example, and most of the jobs held by French civil servants under the *ancien régime* were obtained by purchase. It should be emphasized that not just anyone could purchase a job and that after someone had purchased it he was subject to a good deal of control and supervision (mainly by people who had purchased their supervisory jobs), but the fact remains that one had to put up a large sum of money for the job. This money was then regarded as ordinary government income and spent. Once again, the person buying the right to collect a particular tax in Orléans was making an investment in much the same way that the restaurant proprietor did. In this case, although he created no capital assets, the money he paid was at least used for government expenditures, such as extending Versailles.

Another outstanding example of a somewhat similar institution was the officer corps of the British Army prior to about 1860. Almost all officers of the rank of colonel or below had purchased their commissions and then purchased their promotions. They were compelled to spend time in each rank (at least one day), but they could buy a lieutenant's commission, spend a day as a lieutenant, sell that commission and buy a captain's commission, and so on. Many wealthy men who wanted to be colonels went through exactly that process. Generals were not appointed by this method.

It is notable that, although this system has been very widely criticized, there seems to be no obvious evidence that it worked badly. The British Army, staffed in this manner, undeniably had the best infantry in Europe. Further, it is notable that their very long record of military success was obtained without anything very outstanding in the way of higher command. Essentially, these "purchasing" officers appear to have been superb trainers and leaders of men. Why this is so, I do not know.

5. I have always been doubtful about the anthropological discussion of these potlatches, and hence I would not like to certify the statement above as true. Nevertheless, this is what the anthropologists say happened.

If we turn to the French example, although many people have criticized the *ancien régime*, the fact remains that during the period of two hundred years before the French Revolution (the period in which this system operated), France was usually accepted as the most powerful and progressive state on the continent of Europe. Certainly it would be hard to argue that its government was worse than its contemporaries.

William Niskanen has offered an argument for this type of government, an argument that is not intended to be conclusive but that does have some interest. If one bought an office under these circumstances and was later found guilty of bad performance, he could be removed from the office, and the purchase price would *not* be refunded. Thus, in essence, the individual was posting a large bond for good performance. Bad performance would lead to forfeiture of the bond, but good performance would mean that he could either eventually sell the job to someone else—like a British Army officer's commission—or leave it to his heirs. As a third possibility, it would terminate with his death. In the latter case, of course, the price paid for the office was actuarially discounted for the life span of the individual who would hold it. Further, in the latter case, the amount forfeited in case of bad behavior would fall progressively as the incumbent aged.

Thus, we have several different types of "investment" that will produce a rent. In the first, an ordinary capitalist investment is made with the object of obtaining rent in the future. Granted there is a speculative element, it is quite possible the rent will not be obtained; however, real assets are created by the investment, and therefore society is better off, although perhaps not as well off as it would have been had the investment been successful. The second type is the case in which the rent is obtained by actually purchasing the right to collect it, as in the case of the young man who purchased the job of lieutenant in the Light Brigade in 1853. In this case, no social assets are produced, but at least there is no waste, since the payment goes to someone who gains from it. It is a pure transfer operation.

People who object to the second kind of rent seeking characteristically object only if the income source that is purchased is some kind of government employment. If I purchase an income stream by buying government bonds, they do not object. But if I buy the right to be customs inspector, they do. The objection to my purchase of the right to be customs inspector is apparently based on two distinct arguments. The first is that the person who can afford to buy the job may not be the best qualified man for it. In a perfect capital market, of course, this would not be true, but capital markets are certainly not perfect. The second objection is that the individual will use his job to repay himself for his "investment" and obtain further gains if he can. Whether this is an objection or not depends entirely upon the type of supervision the individual faces. If the supervision is of good enough quality that he maximizes his return by efficient service, then the argument would fall to the ground. Presumably, in most cases the performance is not that well supervised, but still it is not obvious that supervision in such cases would be worse than supervision for people who have obtained jobs in other ways. Hence, it is not obvious that this system would lead to poorer performance than other systems. The question of good or bad performance depends on rewards and penalties as they are administered during the course of the job, not on how one got the job.[6] If supervision is known to be very good, one would anticipate that the amount bid for the job, or the rent of the job, would be lower than if the supervision of the job were bad and it was possible to steal.

Our final case, and the one to which this paper is primarily devoted, concerns obtaining a rent by competition in what I suppose we may call a potlatch—in wasting resources. This is a situation in which a job will be given to one of a group of people, all of whom have invested a great many resources in seeking the job, with these resources useless for any other purpose. There is, therefore, a loss to society on those resources invested by the unsuccessful job-seekers and a good deal of loss on those resources invested by the successful job-seekers as well if the resource investment does not improve their efficiency in the job they seek out.

As we shall see below, the "rent-seeking economy" leads to further waste, but let us temporarily consider only this one particular waste—the waste of resources used in obtaining employment. Anne Krueger has looked into the issue of the returns to those engaged in organizing foreign exchange regulations in India and Turkey. She showed that the gain obtained by these people was about 7 percent of the gross national product in one case and about 15 percent in the other.[7] If we assume that the people who obtained these jobs were not simply selected at random, that they had maneuvered for the job, and that the people maneuvering for each customs inspectorship invested resources that totalled about the present value of that inspectorship, this would mean that a capital value, perhaps 70 to 150 percent of the gross national product, was dissipated in obtaining these jobs.

6. This ignores temporarily our previous comment about the quality of the job-seeker.

7. Anne O. Krueger, "The Political Economy of the Rent-Seeking Society," chapter 4 in this volume.

Note that the fact that the individual customs inspector may be compelled to kick back to his superiors does not change this conclusion. His superiors will have had to maneuver for their jobs, and their superiors, and so on. What happens is that a very large quantity of resources is transferred from the productive sector to an activity that pays off for the individual participant but does not increase the consumer surplus for other citizens. Indeed, from my own experience in Asia, it seems to me that this cost is one of the basic reasons for Asia's backwardness. Asian countries have been doing this for a very long time.

It should be noted in this connection that Krueger's numbers apply to only one aspect of the centralized economic control maintained in both India and Turkey. When we consider that there is very much more in the way of such rent-seeking activity, it is clear that the economic waste must be extremely high.

So far we have been discussing what we might call a mature system of government rent seeking, one that has been in existence a long time and in which resources have adjusted to their long-run best use. In practice, probably most rent-seeking economies in the world today have many large incomes that are windfalls rather than the result of investment.[8]

This situation occurs because many of these governments are newly established, and it seems very doubtful that anyone anticipated that these large gains would be available at the time the individual young intellectual first turned his attention to political matters. For example, presumably many of the district commissioners in Ghana actually made quite modest investments in political maneuvering in the British colonial period, and then, when the Nkrumah dictatorship was established, found themselves in very high paying jobs. In general, this would be true throughout the former colonial world. The previous colonial governments were not completely free of bribery and corruption, but there was less than there has been since then. Further, the people who collected these payments previously are now gone, and the new holders of these sinecures (in the technical sense of the word) generally got them much more easily than their successors will.

In another context, we may contrast the career of Thomas Corcoran ("Tommy the Cork") with that of a present-day graduate of Harvard Law School who is considering entrance into the Washington legal business. It

8. See Donald L. Huddle, "An Estimate of Import Surplus under a Disequilibrium System," *Public Choice* 5 (Fall, 1968): 113–120.

seems very dubious that Corcoran, at the time he was going through law school, or even when in the early Depression years he was recommended for a job in Washington by one of his former professors, thought seriously about a permanent career negotiating with government agencies that at the time did not even exist. He got in early, however, and through great natural talents, application, and good connections became an extremely wealthy man.

In contrast, the present-day lawyer coming out of Harvard has had this idea in mind for a long time. He works on it in order to get into Harvard Law School (which in Corcoran's day was fairly easy), and then he quite deliberately takes a job in Washington at comparatively low pay for the purpose of developing the appropriate capital. Further, since he faces much competition in Washington, it is most unlikely that he will be able to achieve what Corcoran achieved so easily.

This is not an example of rent seeking but of rent avoidance (to be discussed below); however, the time structure is the same as in many existing governments where rent seeking is important. The resource cost of the high income of the present district commissioner in Ghana did not occur at the time he was maneuvering for the position, because in those days it was a relatively low cost operation. It occurs in the present day when many citizens of Ghana, observing his success and large income, are devoting themselves to the attempt to get such jobs in the future.

Now let us consider a few additional costs of the rent-seeking economy. Note that these costs will depend to a considerable extent on the assumption that the rent is obtained by soliciting bribes for performance or nonperformance of duties. I think that this is normal in most of the countries we think of as rent seeking, although when I turn to American applications, this particular problem will be relatively small.

Suppose that an individual wanting to start a factory in Ghana contemplates the situation. First, he must obtain the necessary customs import license to import his equipment. This may or may not involve foreign exchange controls as well, depending on whether the person is a foreigner who is making a new commitment in Ghana or someone who is using funds that have been derived from Ghana at some time in the past. Once the equipment is in the country, he must move it to the potential investment site and begin construction. This will normally involve him with a set of officials totally different than those involved in passing the entrance of the equipment. Further, the district commissioner in the area where he is establishing his plant must be pacified. There are also other officials. There may be lawsuits, in which case judges will be involved. The use of public utilities may require special side payments, and so on.

The problem with these very large sets of payments is that they are not coordinated. The fee to the government that would maximize government revenue would be a single fee on the whole transaction. The fee to the customs inspector that will maximize his revenue, plus the fee to whoever arranges transportation, plus the fee to the district commissioner, and so forth, is likely to total much more than the revenue-maximizing fee for the government as a whole. The reason for this is the usual rule that when there are a number of stages in production and a monopoly on each one, the output (unless all monopolies can reach an agreement) is apt to be low and monopoly payments per unit high.

We usually face such a monopoly situation in this kind of government activity. The result is that the total fees are markedly larger than those which would optimize the revenue of the government, even if we assume the government had no other objective. In consequence, the investments that are made pay very high fees, but a great many desirable investments are not made at all.

One may ask here why the government itself does not aim at maximizing its income and deal with this matter by having a single payment. The explanation appears to be mostly simple inefficiency, in that the government does not recognize the situation that exists, but it is partly an innate characteristic of the use of illegal payments for the activity. These illegal payments are, almost of necessity, not appropriately recorded, and therefore no one knows exactly what the total is. Further, it is not necessarily obvious to a high-level official whether some particular delay he observes at a lower level is genuinely technical (as his inferior tells him) or is an effort to hold out for some additional payments.

The inefficiency is complicated by the fact that normally all the different agencies dealt with by the person attempting to establish a new factory are not even parts of the same ministry; hence, coordination is very difficult. The result of all of this is a set of payments markedly higher than would be desirable, even if we assume simply that the government's sole objective is to maximize its own revenue. This means that the rate of growth, living standards, and the like, are markedly lower than they would be if the purely exploitative but efficient government were in charge of matters.

I have discussed this process in terms of establishing a new manufacturing enterprise, but it is obvious that it fits many other situations. Simply living in the country may involve fairly high payments, particularly if the person who is living in the country has a higher-than-average living standard. The officials are rather apt to follow a policy Ludwig von Mises called "egalitarianism," but which I think would better be described as "private egalitarianism." They do not attempt to equalize incomes throughout society, since that would involve a reduction in their own incomes, but they do tend to equalize incomes in the private sector. It seems likely that the reason for this is not a desire for equality, although the officials may well rationalize it in that sense, but simply that this is the easiest way to collect their fees.

Plucking $10,000 from one wealthy man is much easier than plucking $100 from a hundred poor men. Thus, people who are in the private sector face what amounts to a very highly graduated income tax, and one that may effectively penalize productive labor much more severely than the type of progressive income tax with which we are familiar in Western countries. This is particularly so, since the wealthy man whose assets are relatively immobile and hard to conceal (for example, the builder of a steel plant) is an obvious target, whereas a wealthy man whose wealth is largely in Switzerland, who lives in comparative moderation while he is in Ghana, and spends large amounts only when he is elsewhere, is much harder to tax. Thus, the system not only penalizes progress by lowering the incentives for hard work and intelligent investment, but in particular it penalizes those kinds of activities which tend to produce conspicuous assets.

There is another, very large cost imposed by the rent-seeking society of the type we are discussing, and this one is becoming important in the United States, too, although I think the previous ones I have mentioned are not yet significant. Let me begin by telling a story about Korea. In the years after the Korean war, President Rhee drove around the streets of Seoul in an old Packard automobile originally imported into Korea as the personal car of the American ambassador; it was sold to Rhee when the American ambassador got a newer car. The most important single businessman in Korea visited the United States and then returned to Korea, not by air or by passenger ship, but on a freighter. The freighter docked at Inchon, about twenty miles from Seoul, and there were on the deck of the freighter two Buicks, one green and one blue. Also, in the hold of the freighter there was a very large quantity of various things the businessman wanted to bring into Korea. When he arrived at Inchon, the customs inspectors promptly informed him that substantially everything he had with him was illegal for import.

The businessman, however, was a very good businessman, and he had planned for this contingency in advance. There was no reason why *he* could not land, and he went from the ship directly to the Kyung mu Dai (the Korean White House). There he told President Rhee that he had been concerned about the Korean president's driving around in an elderly car and had brought back a Buick for the president. In fact, he said that he had brought back two Buicks, so that the president could have his choice; he himself would use whichever one the president did not want. President Rhee was pleased and asked where the Buicks were. The businessman said, "Well, all my personal effects are currently being held up in customs in Inchon, but if you would like to see them immediately, I'm sure that you can arrange to get them released." President Rhee accordingly ordered that the businessman's personal luggage, including large items, be released. The businessman arrived the following day at Kyung mu Dai with two Buicks, and President Rhee chose the blue one.

Note that this very ingenious operation resulted in the businessman's getting a very large amount of material into Korea for payment of only about $5,000 or $6,000 in the prices of the time. Surely, if he had negotiated with the customs inspectors, the cost would have been on the order of $75,000 to $100,000. This is what I call rent-avoidance activity, and it is a major source of inefficiency in rent-seeking economies.

In these societies, a very major cost, and clearly a cost that varies a good deal from enterprise to enterprise, is the interference of the government. In most of the rent-seeking societies government officials want bribes, but in the United States the government makes specific administrative rules. Minimizing the cost of these bribes or regulations is a major activity of the higher management and, indeed, may become the *sole* activity. Some friends of mine visiting a factory on the outskirts of Seoul began their visit by talking to the president of the company. They asked whether his equipment was mainly Japanese or imported from Europe. He replied that it was mostly imported from Europe. They then went to visit the plant and discovered that almost every machine in it was in fact Japanese.

This issue is unimportant on its face; there was no reason why the plant should have one type of machinery rather than another, although it was true that it was during Rhee's tenure as president and that President Rhee was violently anti-Japanese. The impressive feature, however, is that the president of the company did not know enough about his own capital stock even to realize where it had been originated. He could not possibly have been engaging in a deliberate lie, because he knew that the visitors were going to go look at the machinery. He had to have been in ignorance.

This does not imply in any sense that he was inefficient. He had been devoting his time and attention to the area where he had the highest comparative advantage and the area with the highest payoff—greasing the wheels of government. He was asked a question about what, from his standpoint, was clearly a minor aspect of the company (production) and answered to the best of his ability. He normally left such matters to inferiors, who probably did at least a moderately good job, just as most American corporate presidents really pay very little attention to the janitorial staff in their factories.

The activity to which this corporate president was devoting himself is what I would like to call "rent avoidance." He was attempting to minimize the total rents that would be imposed on his company by direct bribe solicitation by higher officials and/or unfortunate administrative decision. The job is a difficult one. From the cost-benefit standpoint, is it better to invite the provincial governor to an elaborate dinner with *kisang* girls than to make a direct payment to the local magistrate? Perhaps the corporate president should visit the capital and spend several months there in general socializing.[9]

Further, many of these decisions are long-term investments. The careful cultivation over a period of years of individual officials develops a very real type of human capital in the form of friendly relations that can be utilized. In the American context, Tommy the Cork, Clark Clifford, and Abe Fortas are all examples of people whose main stock-in-trade is this kind of connection.

No doubt such people are in fact invaluable to their companies or, for that matter, their branches of government, if it is a government enterprise. In the socialist economy, a man who has good contacts in the planning bureau is probably of more use to his particular enterprise than a good engineer. Probably also his personal income is a good deal higher than that of a good engineer.

The problem with this, although it is efficient from the standpoint of the

9. The refugees from Communist China sometimes involve reasonably high-level officials. One of them has revealed that the governor of the province of Shantung characteristically spends nine of the twelve months of the year in Peking rather than in Shantung. This was no doubt sensible from his standpoint and may even be sensible from the standpoint of Shantung, but it surely does not lead to what Niskanen would call "process efficiency" in the Shantung government.

individual enterprises, is that it involves a tremendous waste from the standpoint of the society as a whole. Large resources in terms of human capacity are diverted to the rent-seeking part of the government and the rent-avoidance activity in the private sector. In a way, the two activities tend to cancel each other. In these rent-seeking societies—such as traditional (or Communist) China, Korea, or India—they are, in a real sense, the major sources of income and wealth. In a way, there is a vast negative-sum game in which people with high natural talents who are willing to work hard can get very large returns while generating a social loss.

This illustrates a very old point in economics. Competition is not always a good thing. In a well-organized market, the individuals aiming solely at benefiting themselves end up benefiting other people. In a sufficiently badly organized market, and the market I am now describing is an example, they simply generate waste. Further, in most of the rent-seeking societies, the sum total of the activities of the rent seekers and the specialists in rent avoidance is not really zero-sum. They do not simply waste their own talents; in the course of their maneuvering, they impose costs on the rest of society that retard development.

The provincial governor who promulgates a new regulation with the intent of increasing the number of fees he gets for permitting people to avoid it not only increases his own income and the potential income of the specialists in rent avoidance, but he also imposes a real burden on society, for the regulation, in at least some areas, will be enforced. Further, he may, as a result of concentrating on this kind of activity, have this time distracted from such necessary functions of government as maintaining public order. He may not be supervising his junior officials, with the result that the kind of multiple exaction I have described above occurs. Altogether, one would expect poverty from this system, and, if we turn to the parts of the world where it is dominant, that is what we see.

If we examine the United States and most modern European countries, we find relatively little direct bribing of government officials. Note that I say relatively little, not zero, and I should also add that in my opinion the amount is increasing; unless changes are made, it will become quite a large amount in a generation or so. Still, in a direct sense the phenomenon of rent seeking does not exist.

In an indirect sense, rent seeking does exist to some extent, and the bureaucrats tend to be paid a good deal more than is actually necessary for the performance of their services, although the very highest officials are normally paid less than would be needed in order to attract people capable of managing these immense organizations. This conflict between fairly high pay for the lower officials and fairly low pay for the higher officials may be one of the reasons why in most Western countries the lower-level bureaucracy tends to be relatively uncontrolled from the top. The salaries offered to the upper administrators simply cannot attract people who have the personal ability necessary to control such a large apparatus.[10]

The bureaucrats and other government officials, however, if they do not do very much in the way of soliciting bribes, do in fact issue a very large number of regulations and laws that directly affect many private businessmen. Further, the actual administration of these laws is invariably subject to a good deal of discretion. I should say in passing that the highest level of discretion of this sort is in fact exercised not by what we think of as bureaucrats, but by an older bureaucracy, that is, the courts. The judges are far more likely to make decisions on their own without being deeply bound by the law than are the regular bureaucrats. This is concealed from view to some extent by the fact that the judge's decision is defined as the law, and we do not generally notice how little it is controlled by the law that existed before he pronounced it.

This matter aside, what we observe is the development of very large-scale rent-avoidance activities. The DuPont Corporation for many generations was headed by chemical engineers. In the early days, these engineers were members of the DuPont family, but after two generations in which the president was a young man who had married the daughter of the previous president, rather than a direct DuPont, it slipped into the control of people who are not members of the family. It is notable that the current president, Irving S. Shapiro, is not a chemical engineer but an attorney who is a specialist on public relations and government influence. I do not wish to criticize DuPont for this decision, which I think under the circumstances was very sensible, and I certainly do not wish to criticize Shapiro, who I think is an extremely competent, intelligent, and well-motivated man. However, I do criticize the social order that made it necessary for this company to switch to a manipulator for its chief executive. Surely our medicines and plastics will be poorer in the future than they would be had the company retained its concentration on essentially technological matters.

Note that all this is a sharp change in emphasis, not an absolute change in

10. This assumes that there are people with this kind of ability. No private company is anywhere near as large as, let us say, the Department of Health, Education, and Welfare.

nature of the world. Private businessmen do a good deal of rent seeking and rent avoidance, too, but it is a relatively minor factor. As a bachelor, I normally spend Christmas with my sister and brother-in-law. About nine years ago, my brother-in-law went to a small town in Iowa to take over the management of a very small company founded by his father. It had been operated until that time by a very pleasant man who was essentially a salesman with little interest in the formal details of management. I well remember the first Christmas and the deluge of expensive gifts my brother-in-law received from the suppliers of various raw materials used by the company. My brother-in-law, as head of the company, was intensely interested in the quality and price of the products he bought and less interested in the personal relations with the companies that generated them. As a result, although the company today purchases something like ten times as much in the way of raw materials, he now gets Christmas cards.

It will be seen from this example that the sales vice-presidents of the various companies with which he dealt made the same kind of calculations to which I have been referring in my rent-avoidance discussion. What happened when my brother-in-law replaced his predecessor was simply that the relative cost-benefit calculations of an expensive gift, compared with very slight reduction in price, changed. Therefore, these vice-presidents switched their approach. This is characteristic of the market. Salesmen, like the one from whom I bought my house, do cultivate the personal arts that would characterize the rent-avoidance expert in a rent-seeking economy. There is a payoff to it, but it is a relatively modest payoff, and this particular type of personality and type of activity have a reasonable but not gigantic return.

As we move to more and more government activity, however, and as this government activity becomes more and more a matter that various individual officials can change at their discretion, we move to higher and higher investments in rent avoidance on the part of private individuals and companies. This is not inefficient from their standpoint. They are, indeed, behaving in an appropriate manner. From the standpoint of society as a whole, however, this activity is almost total waste. Today the small company of which my brother-in-law is president invests a fair amount of executive time in worrying about, and in some cases attempting to influence, government regulations. When he first took over ten years ago, this was a very small-scale activity. Now it is quite significant. Surely this use of time means (1) that the executive staff is larger than it was before and (2) that it devotes less attention to problems of production, product design, and distribution. The economy as a whole is less efficient, even though the adjustment by this little company to the present reality is an efficient one.

When I first went into the diplomatic service, there were two of us from the University of Chicago Law School in the same class. I ran into the second again about twenty years later. Like me, he had left the diplomatic service, but he had gone into rent avoidance and jointly writing novels. Specifically, he was vice-president of the Bank of America in Washington, although the Bank of America at that time had no branches east of the Mississippi. The job, which left him enough leisure so that he could write novels, involved serving on several government commissions, acting as a representative to some of the international banking organizations with headquarters in Washington, and, of course, developing friends. He was also much interested in public relations activities and apparently passed on almost all press releases by the Bank of America, although I am not sure that is so. I am sure that Bank of America was getting its money's worth from his activities, but it is very doubtful that the United States was.

He was only one representative of a very widespread phenomenon. I would anticipate that, with time, the problems of New York will be complicated by more and more companies moving to the Washington area. As the principal economic activity of high officials becomes more and more concentrated on rent avoidance, we can anticipate steady growth of the Virginia and Maryland suburbs.

However, in the United States rent avoidance is not the only thing that absorbs resources. Private companies may be interested in influencing the government not to reduce their costs, but to increase the costs of their competitors or, perhaps, in getting a government-sponsored cartel organized. This would be a case of rent seeking by government activity. Further, the civil servants frequently feel that promotion can be achieved through expanding the scope of their bureau. This, again, involves rent seeking. It is likely, however, that under present circumstances in the United States and in most western European countries, this rent seeking is of much lower importance than rent avoidance. Once again, I doubt that this will continue to be true in the future.

Thus, the problem in the United States, although real and growing, is very modest compared with what we observe in the less developed parts of the world. Indeed, it seems to me that this difference is, to a large extent, the explanation for the backwardness of these areas or, perhaps more accurately, the advance of the West. The situation in which there was a relatively open economy and governments that had relatively little influence over the details of economic life was, historically, highly exceptional. The rent-seeking, rent-avoiding economy had been the historic norm and is today the world norm. The exceptions to it have been rare. In a way, what has been happening here in the United States and in Europe is a return to a more normal form of government from an extraordinarily unusual form. This more normal form of government apparently carries with it that other phenomenon that has been normal both in history and in the world today—poverty.

If we look around the world, then, the United States still seems to be a rather favorable place to live, both from the standpoint of existing capital assets and the prospect of producing more. Perhaps the Common Market in Europe, where individual governments are highly interventionist but where freedom of trade in the Common Market as a whole puts severe limits on their powers, may, with time, overtake and surpass the United States in real wealth. Still, we are well off. We have far less rent seeking and rent avoidance than most countries. We have far more rent seeking and rent avoidance, however, than we had a hundred years ago, and I fear that in another hundred years we will be a relatively normal country in this regard.

INDUSTRIAL ORGANIZATION AND RENT SEEKING IN DICTATORSHIPS

The dominant form of government in the world today is dictatorship. Further, throughout history, dictatorship has been the commonest form of government, indeed, for much of history the only form of government in the world. This fact is somewhat obscured by our language. When the dictator is hereditary, we call him a king or an emperor. His position, however, is very much the same as a dictator's. The basic difference from the standpoint of the government is that a king is apt to feel less fear of being overthrown than the dictator is. This is to a large extent offset by the fact that the accidents of heredity can lead to some fairly stupid people becoming kings, while dictators, no matter whatever else we think about them, are almost uniformly intelligent, aggressive people.

If we look at the typical dictatorship or monarchy, we find a great deal of rent seeking activity. The granting of monopolies of one sort or another to friends of the ruler is very common, and one of the major forms of enterprise is to "court" the ruler in hopes of getting such special privileges. To a considerable extent, the tendency of such governments to provide rent seeking opportunities to various of their citizens is concealed under ideologies. Whether this ideology is mercantilism, socialism, or in a few modern cases, a misunderstood capitalism, to a large extent it simply covers the distributing of rents to friends of the ruler. Normally, the dictator himself shares, indeed, frequently has the lion's share, in these rents. Usually, but not always, the rent involves a government-created monopoly.

Looking at these three "cover stories" one at a time, we begin with mercantilism.[1] Adam Smith, that great opponent of mercantilism, knew that the ideology was merely a disguise.

> It cannot be very difficult to determine who have been the contrivers of this whole mercantile system; not the consumers, whose interests have been entirely neglected; but the producers, whose interests have been so

Reprinted, with permission, from *Journal of Institutional and Theoretical Economics* 142 (March 1986): 4–15.

1. The following is largely based on R. B. Ekelund Jr. and R. D. Tollison, *Mercantilism as a Rent-Seeking Society* (College Station, 1981).

> carefully attended to; and among this latter class our merchants and manufacturers have been by far the principal architects.[2]

In fact, of course, Smith was talking about England, which was well on the way to democracy, and it is unlikely that the control of the executive branch over these rents was anywhere near as good as in a true dictatorship. Usually in a true dictatorship it is the government's and, in particular, the ruler's interests that are carefully protected, and the merchants and other people who receive these privileges are expected to pay for them.

But in either event, there is ideological cover, and that ideological cover alleges an effort to benefit the country by providing an inflow of gold, etc. Further, in many cases, simply improving the quality of production will be used as the excuse for giving, let us say, soap manufacturers a monopoly.

Mercantilism as a formal theory has vanished, but it is still true that balance of payment problems are frequently offered as an excuse for protection against foreign competition. Indeed, Mitterand in France, after having failed in his initial experiment with socialism, has gone back to traditional mercantilism although he doesn't use the word.

Today, however, socialism is a commoner cover story. The socialist philosophy leads to a great deal of government ownership and control of industry under that rubric. The people engaging in this, even genuine believers in socialism, may divert a good deal of the profit to themselves or to politically influential groups.

Normally, this socialist activity, unlike the mercantilist, involves direct and blatant violations of the actual law, whereas mercantilism doesn't necessarily do so. This is because the operators of socialist industries are civil servants, and there normally is a specified wage, etc., for them. Needless to say, they are rarely satisfied with it. Further, there is no reason to believe that the dictator is in any way surprised if he finds out that they are padding this amount. Indeed, they may regularly be passing 90% on to him and keeping only a commission.

Lastly, some modern governments have decided that they will be capitalistic and, as a step in that direction, have created various local monopolies. It would appear that they learned their definition of capitalism from Karl Marx rather than from Adam Smith. Nevertheless, this is not particularly uncommon in the present-day world. President Rhee of Korea, for example, dis-

2. A. Smith, *The Wealth of Nations*, edited by E. Cannan (New York, 1937), 626.

tributed all of the confiscated Japanese factories to his friends, and then gave them effective monopolies. A life-long socialist, he took this action in order to get support from the Eisenhower administration. Clearly he thought it was true capitalism, and the Eisenhower officials did not know enough about the details of his actions to object.

In all three of these cases, what you actually have is an ideological cover for a system of rent seeking. It is not even in accord with mercantilism, because it does not, in practice, make any great effort to develop the domestic economy.

This has been a discussion of the camouflage over rent seeking. It is important for two reasons. Firstly, it is indeed true that a certain number of western observers are normally taken in. They may honestly believe that a proposal to denationalize a given government industry is simply an effort to enrich foreign capitalists which will injure the common man. Similarly, a proposal to eliminate a protective tariff may be seen by western observers as something which generally will spread unemployment. The last is of course particularly likely to be believed because in a number of cases there would indeed be a temporary burst of unemployment.

The capitalists frequently are people who believe that protective tariffs are part of capitalism. An American steel magnate who is working hard to keep Japanese and Brazilian steel out of the United States is unlikely to feel that some South American country's effort to protect an automobile industry is other than the true essence of capitalism.

Further, the egalitarian trend of much modern intellectual activity is apt to be helpful in disguising the actual inefficiency of the socialist system. I have currently been reading a series of articles in *The Washington Post* in which a communist official in Vietnam is quoted as saying that their society is stabler than other South East Asian countries' because although it is extremely poor, the poverty is evenly spread. The reporter clearly thought this was a significant argument.[3]

Further, he didn't seem to notice that the poverty was not evenly spread. The higher officials, of course, do not live like the common people, although in communist countries this difference is usually carefully concealed.[4] There is, however, one area of great inequality which a foreign visitor of necessity must see, and that is the radically different way in which foreigners in the

3. *Washington Post*, 21–27 April 1985.

4. Apparently this is not so of Nicaragua.

country are treated. It is unlikely that a system in which a visiting foreign reporter is openly provided with a living standard perhaps thirty times as high as that of the average person with whom he comes in contact would be one where there is a high degree of social solidarity and lack of objection to the system.

But, all of this has to do with reasons why the rent seeking attitude of many of these societies tends not to get much play in the foreign press. It has to be admitted that these disguises may also influence the officials of the government in question. This is, of course, particularly true in the case of the capitalist cover because most people who have not studied economics think that the very essence of capitalism is that there are some very wealthy people.

Thus, giving a factory to a friend of the president free and then guaranteeing that factory a monopoly will impress them as a most perfect example of capitalism. The individual owner of the new enterprise regards his wealth as simply an indication that the economy is now organized in the efficient capitalist way. He could quite honestly feel that the withdrawal of tariff protection and the resulting sharp fall in his own wealth was not only an injury to him, but an injury to "capitalism."

It is not quite so easy to justify this kind of rent in either a mercantilist or a socialist society, although probably, it's a bit easier in mercantilism. Nevertheless, here once again, simply a lack of strong critical feeling will conceal the distinction. An individual who is a high official in Moscow and who lives the way high officials in Moscow do live probably has never heard any significant criticism of the system. He honestly believes that it is a good thing and that his relatively high position in it is part of that system. He will defend any rents that his particular status gives him without a bad conscience as long as he doesn't engage in careful introspective reasoning. Since such careful introspective reasoning would be (a) hard and (b) unpleasant, he is not likely to do it.

This is no personal criticism of such officials. All of us tend to accept whatever general philosophy exists in our society without very much thought. We are apt to use that general philosophy to defend the status quo, and we would be deeply surprised and perhaps offended at anyone who questions it. Since most of my hearers here are academics, I suggest you consider your own attitude or that of your colleagues towards tenure. I'm sure if you give this idea any serious thought, which you rarely do, the immediate reaction will be the invention of a number of further arguments for it. One cannot be particularly surprised if a Russian who is currently a Deputy Minister of something or other would respond similarly at a proposal that that particular whole industrial ministry be abolished and the plants be, let us say, incorporated and the stock be distributed to their current workers.

All of this has been merely introductory. The main theme of this paper is the costs of the creation of these monopolies in dictatorships. It is an unmistakable historical fact that such monopolies are frequently set up in dictatorships. Whether they are more frequent on the average than they are in democracies, I don't know for certain. It would, I think, be very difficult to collect reliable data on this subject, and I am not at all positive that it is worth the trouble. In both cases, the contribution to inefficiency is quite considerable.

There are two contrasting trends in the establishment of these monopolies in dictatorships, and it is perhaps easiest to describe them by taking pure examples. In practice, of course, the two will be mixed. First I consider the kind of monopoly which we find in traditional mercantilism;[5] we frequently see what appears to be essentially a bidding process. A number of courtiers or a number of different guilds apply to the king for a particular monopoly. In their applications, they normally point out that they are loyal, skilled workers and that they're willing to make payments to the king in some given amount. The whole process looks very much like an auction. Let's begin our analysis by assuming that it is indeed an auction; the monopoly or whatever it is goes to the highest bidder, and if the bidder in fact finds he can't make enough to make payments out of the monopoly, he will lose it.

Looked at in this way, the procedure is simply a revenue-raising device for the state. Almost any economist would argue that it is a less efficient revenue-maximizing policy than would be permitting free competition and then imposing a tax, but still looking at it in the narrow terms I have given above, it is a revenue device.

In some cases, particularly in Tudor times in England, the monopoly was given for a period of years to someone who either had a new process of some sort, or who proposed to import some foreign technology. The argument for it could, then, be much like the argument normally given for patents. It may well have been efficient. The question of why these early monarchs used the monopoly rather than the tax method is not an easy one. It is sometimes argued that granted the inefficiency of their state, this was basically simply a better method of collecting revenue. It was easier to get a single payment

5. Ekelund and Tollison, *Mercantilism.*

from a single monopolist than it would have been to set up a tax procedure for dealing with a lot of countries, and actual collections might have been higher, granted the inefficiency of the tax systems at that time. The tax collectors, for example, might have put a very heavy tax on the producers and transferred relatively little of it to the king.

I find it difficult to believe that anything quite this simple is the explanation for the widespread use of this kind of monopoly revenue device. One can see inefficiency and corruption in many governments, but it would seem that the inefficiency and corruption would be almost as great in enforcing the monopoly as in collecting the tax. A bidding process can as easily be used for tax collecting. In fact the *ancien régime* in France relied on tax farmers who bid for their "farm" in collecting taxes.

Thus, it seems to me, a more likely explanation for the use of these methods of revenue raising is simple economic ignorance on the part of the government concerned. During the period in which they were most highly developed in England, bleeding was the commonest medical treatment. I see no reason to believe that the kings were more sophisticated in their choice of revenue methods than in their choice of doctors.

If we look at the underdeveloped world today, we will also find this kind of thing to some extent. Once again, it seems to me that we have to concede corruption and inefficiency in the revenue-raising branch of government, but that a sizeable amount of economic ignorance on the part of the dictator is both a correct statement of the nature of the world and necessary to explain this phenomenon.

This is one model; the second is even less efficient. If we visit Kenya today, we will find that the current dictator is in the process of removing Kikuyu managers of most enterprises, because economic and political appointments were made by the previous dictator, who was a member of that tribe. He is replacing them by his own fellow Kalenjin tribesmen. There seems to be absolutely no reason to believe that either tribe contains an exceptional concentration of efficient managers. The reason they are being given these positions is because they can be trusted by the dictator. The dictator likes trustworthy people more than efficient people. Of course, he would prefer to get managers who are both trustworthy and efficient, but such paragons are rare.

Let me discuss this in terms of an American example. Trujillo, when he was dictator of the Dominican Republic, appointed various of his relatives as heads of particular industrial enterprises. We shall take a sugar refinery as our example, because the Trujillo cousin who ran the largest sugar refinery in the

Dominican Republic was by no means the most efficient manager of a sugar refinery. Clearly, the refinery made relatively modest profits. The principal advantage from Trujillo's standpoint was that this provided a reason for his cousin to remain loyal to him. The same thing would have applied if it were not his cousin, but some military man whom he really feared.

The problem with this is that it is fairly ferociously inefficient from the standpoint of Trujillo and his cousin. If Trujillo had hired the most efficient manager he could find for the sugar refinery, then taxed away the profit, it would have been possible for him both to pay his cousin more than the cousin made as an inefficient manager and probably have something left for himself.

Why then do we find all over the dictatorial world people whose only qualification for industrial management is that they are, politically, supporters or, equally likely, people who might become politically dangerous if not bribed? The Argentine military, when it took over Argentina, appointed various high officers as managers of almost all of the state industry in Argentina. The same thing happened in Brazil. Why not instead simply tax these industries heavily, maintaining, of course, efficient management, and then pay the amount to the military officers?

I have been bothered by this question for some time, and recently two of my students have proposed a solution. In essence, their explanation depends on the fact that the individual, cousin, military officer, etc., is apt to exaggerate his own managerial capacity.[6] Suppose we have, once again, our sugar refinery, and if you imported an American expert to run it, he would charge $75,000 a year. For that price, he would generate a profit of $250,000 a year. Trujillo gives $125,000 to his worthless cousin and pockets the other $125,000. This is the efficient arrangement.

The problem with this is that the cousin, or military officer if this is Argentina, mistakenly thinks he could manage it as well as or better than the imported expert. He, therefore, contrasts his $125,000 pension not with the $75,000 that is being paid to the current expert, but with $200,000, which is what he would get if he worked on the plant as efficiently as the person who is now running it, and continued to receive his pension. In practice, he is put in charge, and turns out not to be very competent, and is able to skim $50,000 for himself and passes little or nothing on to Trujillo. He, however,

6. W. Brough and K. Mwangi, "On the Inefficient Extraction of Rents by Dictators," *Public Choice* 48 (1985): 37–48.

evaluates the situation erroneously. He puts down the low profits to various factors beyond his control that make it impossible to make more money in the plant. He is convinced he would do just as well as any imported manager.

In the private market, when this kind of thing happens, for example, when the incompetent son inherits his father's business, he is not simply removed from control; he is bought out by somebody who pays the appropriate capital value of the enterprise. This, however, is impossible in this kind of dictatorial scheme, because there is no way in which the dictator can, in fact, give a secure, transferable title to a new purchaser. Since there is no way to get the cousin, or once again, the Argentine Colonel, to voluntarily remove himself, under the circumstances, the economy is apt to be run inefficiently by a set of rather inept managers who have political importance.[7]

I am not sure that this is the correct solution to the problem, but I have no other. I find it difficult to think of a way of formally testing the hypothesis.

Of course, if we look at the actual world we see mixes of these two pure types. Usually the dictator or king does check among his courtiers and people whom he has to worry about, both in terms of the political benefit of getting their support, or at least their non-opposition, and in terms of the revenue benefit. Which is more important depends on the particular circumstances of the case. It is likely that even if promises of fairly high cash payments have been made at the beginning, a failure to operate the enterprise at that profit, or indeed any profit at all, will not automatically lead to the removal of the manager. At that time he has established a sort of quasi-property right, and his removal might annoy not only him, but a lot of other managers, which may be dangerous.

In many of these countries, Argentina of course is a good example, these military officer managers are actually running their enterprises at substantial losses. They themselves are obtaining rents, and normally they have succeeded in getting monopoly power by arguing that the losses would be even greater if they did not have the monopoly.[8] It is necessary to subsidize them

7. This phenomenon is an example of what psychologists call "self-serving attribution." Research on this subject seems to have started with F. Hieder, *The Psychology of Interpersonal Relations* (New York, 1958). It has been subject to a good deal of research since then. D. T. Miller and M. Ross, in "Self-serving Biases in the Attribution of Causality: Fact or Fiction?" *Psychological Bulletin* 82 (1975): 213–25, review the literature and provide a reasonably complete bibliography.

8. In many cases, of course, even the best management could not produce a profit, because Peru is, let us say, not a good place to produce automobiles.

out of regular tax money. One of the reasons that the underdeveloped countries have consistent difficulties in their finances is that once they get into this kind of trap it is very hard to get out.

It should be pointed out in this case that you don't have to have corrupt government officials to get into this mess. The Israeli official body is not markedly corrupt, although I would not like to argue that it is totally free from corruption. Nevertheless, they have succeeded in messing up their economy by much the same mechanism. In their case, the rents of the monopolies, and they are probably quite sizeable, come partly from government subsidies, and partly from monopoly prices made possible by import controls. They are normally absorbed, not by the higher management, but by the ordinary employees. Of course, this is not an example of a dictatorship.

All of this, when dealing with dictatorships, turns on the problems of the dictator in holding his office. In a democracy, the same is true. The dictator of Sudan has just been overthrown because he raised the subsidized food prices. Premiers of Israel and, indeed, other democracies have felt that they too would be removed for the same reason even though the removal process would take the form of losing an election rather than a coup d'etat.

The normal life of a dictator is as tied up with preventing his overthrow as is that of the democratic politician with preventing the loss of an election. Indeed, the problem is more severe. The democratic politician normally can feel confident that he will remain in office for at least some specified period of time. Most elections come at regular intervals, and in those cases where they do not, the prime minister currently in office can decide what time the election will be held, which is clearly a major advantage.

For the dictator, however, there is no such even temporary stability. The coup may occur at any time. Indeed, it is almost a requirement for the success of the coup that it catch the dictator by surprise. On the whole, also, the effects of a successful coup on the dictator who is replaced are much more severe than the effects of losing elections are on a democratic politician.

The dictator is continuously concerned about this problem, and there doesn't really seem to be much he can do to permanently protect himself from it. Some dictators have ruled for very long periods of time, and indeed, there is a long-run tendency for dictatorships gradually to develop into hereditary monarchies. Nevertheless, overthrows are always possible. To take the history of England, there are practically no cases in which the throne was passed on peacefully for three generations until the kings became mere figureheads.

The reason this is so can be put in formal mathematical terms.[9] The dictator himself, as Hume pointed out, cannot truthfully rule by pure terror. He must sleep, and at most he must be able to trust his own guard not to kill him. Thus, he rules by what Hume called "opinion." This "opinion" may only be held by his own guard and secret police, but nevertheless, it has to be the "opinion" of a number of people. Hume thought that this "opinion" was one of legitimacy or virtue on the part of the ruler, but more accurately, it is simply the view that if it comes to a fight, he will win. As long as everyone thinks this, he will be successful in preventing the coup. The problem is that it is hard for him to keep all of his higher officials together with his personal guard convinced that that is true.

Let's look at the matter formally. The dictator is continuously surrounded by a group of high officials, guards, policemen, etc., who could all benefit if he were removed, simply because his salary and perks would all be distributed among them. The Prime Minister becomes the dictator, the Minister of War becomes the Prime Minister, etc. Further, when the change comes, the winners could no doubt remove a number of his other officials with the result that there will be even more boodle to pass around. Thus, the motive for a coup is always present.

Any attempted coup will involve a group of officials who attempt to throw out the dictator and another group who are on his side. Either the group attempting to throw him out is successful or they lose. If they do lose, it is obvious that if some of his supporters had joined the attack on him, he would have lost. Thus, there is always a proto-coalition if not a real coalition which can remove the dictator from office.

It will be noted that this proof is very close to Arrow's paradox of voting. The principal difference is that Arrow's mathematical technique takes the form of proving that if his other conditions are met, there must be a dictator. His dictator is a mathematical abstraction. But if we turn to a real-world dictator, we face the same mathematical instability conditions as do distributional coalitions in a voting mechanism.[10] The problem of the dictator is to deal with this danger. He knows that among his supporters there are innu-

9. The following is a condensation of "A Generalization of the General Impossibility Theorem," by G. Tullock, forthcoming.

10. When there is more than one candidate to overthrow the dictator, which is by no means unlikely, a dictatorial analogue of the "lack of independence of irrelevant alternatives" also exists.

merable theoretically available coalitions, all of which would gain from throwing him out, and all of which are capable of doing so. His problem is to prevent them from changing from proto-coalition status to genuine coalition status. This is not easy, but it is also not completely impossible.[11] Distribution of the various rents that I have been describing are part, indeed an important part, of this process. We note in this he is not too different from a democratic politician. The distribution of political favors is important for a woman who wants to remain Prime Minister of England as well as for a typical African dictator. Rewards for loyalty and bribes for people whom you suspect of potential disloyalty are the main motivating factors in both cases. The major difference is that the dictator has means for dealing with people whom he suspects of conspiring against him that are not available to a democratic politician.

The procedure for getting rents under a dictatorship are much the same in theory as those in a democracy. In both cases, there is an implied promise of at least temporary political support. In the dictatorship case, there may also be a promise of diverting the rents directly into the pocket of the dictator. I would not like to argue that this kind of thing never happens in a democracy, but it certainly is not as common. Nevertheless, diversion of the rents to various ways of purchasing additional support for the politician in power is certainly as common or more common in a democracy than in a dictatorship.

Both major parties in Israel, for example, set up schemes for transferring major rents to their political supporters: Histradut, in the case of labor, and a rather diverse collection of minor groups, particularly including the religious parties in the case of Likud.

Insofar as the dictatorial rents accrue actually to the dictator or are used to support regular government functions as they frequently were in Tudor days, it might seem that there was less rent seeking cost in the case of dictatorships than in the case of democracies. This is, however, largely an illusion. In one sense, the rents that are derived by governments from the establishment of these various monopolies may simply replace other revenues and, hence, produce no rent seeking costs. Let us suppose that Henry VIII sold somebody a monopoly on playing cards and used the entire revenue so derived to build up his Navy. There would be an excess burden from the monopoly,

11. I am currently writing a book, *Autocracy*, which will deal with dictatorships and in particular with this problem.

which would presumably be greater than the excess burden from a well-designed tax raising the same revenue, but there would be no real rent seeking costs.

The same is true under some circumstances in a democracy. Suppose that a highly talented businessman, whose normal salary is $250,000 a year, takes a job as a Cabinet Secretary at very much less than that salary because he thinks that will give him an opportunity to give favors to certain companies which will be reimbursed after he ceases to be a Secretary, so that he actually makes somewhat more as a Secretary than he would as a businessman. Note that since these jobs are distributed among a number of competitors, there's no obvious reason that the person who takes a government job for this motive should make more than a normal profit on it. If the government obtains superior executive talent by this method, once again, it is not markedly different from having somewhat higher taxes and paying him the amount in cash. The rent seeking cost is not important.

Unfortunately, in the case of the average dictatorship, or for that matter, the average democracy and certainly in the case of Henry VIII, this kind of thing is decidedly an exception although it does happen.

In dictatorships and for that matter in hereditary monarchies, a large part of these rents are diverted to the personal account of the ruler. Someone who has visited Versailles, or better yet, the complex of Imperial palaces in Peking, will realize that this is not a totally trivial amount.[12] Insofar as these rulers use government revenue derived from taxes or, more commonly, from rents, this increases the value of the office itself, and hence increases the rent seeking expenditures of potential candidates for dictator or for king. Thus this rent seeking cost is still there, but at one remove.

The same can of course be said about democratic politicans, but in general we do not offer them such a large reward. Thus, for instance, the President of the United States knows that not only will he be well paid as President, but he receives a reasonably good pension when he ceases to be President and can make a very large sum of money by writing books. Just how much this contributes to the desire to be President, I do not know. Nelson Rockefeller, for whom all of this would be a mere bagatelle, certainly tried hard enough to become President.

12. It should be said, however, that I am always astonished at how little absolute monarchs take for their own expenditure. The absolute cost of Versailles or the Imperial palace complex in Peking was very large, but as a share of GNP it was quite small.

At a more significant level, however, rents distributed to lower-level supporters of the dictator or democratic politician are presumably a much greater drag on the state. I have pointed out that if you are simply purchasing efficient management, and all the remaining rents are simply expended by the ruler, then the only rent seeking cost would be the efforts to become ruler. If, however, the rents are, to a considerable extent, distributed in terms of purchasing political support, this ceases to be true. From the standpoint of the society as a whole, the political support is simply an irrelevancy.[13] We may have preferences as to which dictator or democratic politician rules over us, but these preferences are normally not affected at all by how much support he has purchased.

Empirically, the only evidence I know on this point suggests that in dictatorships the total number of people receiving such rents is lower than in democracies, but that the individual rents are higher. This is not surprising since the ruling elite can afford to be smaller in a dictatorship.[14] It is not at all obvious that this difference is a relevant one.

Presumably, with this higher income, the average rent recipient in a dictatorship is of somewhat greater personal capacity than in a democracy. Since there is no real reason to believe that this capacity is used for the public benefit, once again, it is not obvious that it is very relevant.

In sum then, the difference between rent seeking in a democracy and in a dictatorship is not great. The dictatorship is apt to have a rather smaller collection of officials, but they are highly paid. Indeed, some of them may be very highly paid indeed. A democracy is apt to have a lot of officials who, even if they're not paid very much, are still overpaid.

When we leave officialdom and look at monopolies and special regulatory restrictions, in the dictatorship they're more likely once again to benefit a rather restricted group of people whose income is quite high. In a democracy, they may benefit a lot of people whose income is not so high, although it is

13. I should perhaps add here that most people would tend to regard the personal consumption of the king, dictator, or their friends, as a net bad rather than a net good for society. We economists tend to treat all transfers as having no net social cost, and we are no doubt technically right. The average person, however, dislikes transferring funds to certain people.

14. R. J. Cao Garcia, *Explorations Toward an Economic Theory of Political Systems*, dissertation presented to the Center for Study of Public Choice, Virginia Polytechnic Institute and State University, 1979. It is no criticism of this dissertation to say that the data base was rather weak, and hence, Cao Garcia's conclusion cannot be regarded as apodictically certain.

normally above average. The tendency of most democracies to provide favors to their farmers, with the result that everyone else pays too much for their food, can be contrasted with the tendency of most dictatorships to arrange things under which their farmers are exploited for the benefit of various minorities. The most important of these minorities is, of course, the officials managing the farm program.

The methods of obtaining the special privileges differ in appearance, but not in essence. In both cases, manipulation of opinion and offers of support to the dominant political structure are the basic techniques. It seems likely that these are at least as costly in a dictatorship as in a democracy.

All of this is both rather discouraging and not very certain. We just don't have very much detailed statistical data on dictatorial governments. Nevertheless, in one way, it is encouraging. There is a myth in our society that dictatorships are more efficient than democracies. I am delighted to be able to say that it is a myth.

TRANSITIONAL GAINS AND TRANSFERS

Information Costs and Transitional Gains from Oil

I recently visited Alaska, which had an unusual problem, a problem in fact that it shared only with such places as Saudi Arabia and the Trucial States. The problem was government revenue far above any conceivable direct government expenditures. In all three cases this revenue came from oil reserves, which were confiscated in the case of Saudi Arabia, and in the case of Alaska subjected to a high fee.

When Alaska began to consider this windfall, the state first decided simply to distribute it in cash to Alaskans. It then occurred to them that since any American has a perfect right to move to Alaska, the net effect would be a large in-migration. If the state had gone through with this procedure, there would have been a period of time in which Alaskan natives were receiving large sums of money, and people would have been pouring into Alaska.[1] As the people poured into Alaska the per capita payments would have gone down, and the return from labor invested in productive activity in Alaska would have fallen sharply because the people who had moved in expecting this payment would be willing to supplement their income by working at very low wages.[2]

At the same time, of course, the returns on rental real estate in Alaska would rise very sharply, and various industries that received this influx of cheap labor would probably become extremely profitable. Adjustment to all of this might take many years. Indeed, if people contemplating moving to Alaska thought that the cash payments would not continue indefinitely into the future, and hence discounted the prospect of the payments terminating against the quality of life in what is, after all, not the most pleasant of American states, it is likely that the original inhabitants would have a permanent net transfer to them, equivalent roughly to this risk premium plus the cost of moving for citizens of the other forty-nine. Still, the really big gains would have been in the early days and would have been only transitional. In prac-

Reprinted, with permission, from *Cato Journal* 6 (Spring–Summer 1986): 143–54.

1. I think the proposal was sensible, even if it would have the in-migration effect. Alaskans do, in fact, receive a small annual payment, but very much less than the value of the windfall.

2. Of course, the deterioration of the cartel would have had the same effect.

tice, and I shall return to this below, it was decided to use the money for purposes that on the whole were a good deal less valuable.

Saudi Arabia and other Arab participants in the oil cartel did not have this problem, since they are not required to permit noncitizens to immigrate. Various American Indian tribes[3] were likewise permitted under U.S. law to particularize the entire benefits of oil revenues to their own members. A given tribe that decided to enter into a contract with an oil company for the exploitation of its tribal area or that was compensated by either the U.S. government or the state of Alaska for land taken over could have simply distributed the money among its members. There does not seem to be any evidence that they even contemplated this particular simple and efficient solution.

I have an acquaintance who was an ambassador in Arab areas and who speaks excellent Arabic. He was discussing with me the economic situation in one of the minor Arab states and remarked that they had a revenue so large that there was no conceivable way of making use of it. Actually there are many ways, but the one I suggested to him was simply paying it out to the subjects of the sheikh.[4] It was clear that he had not previously thought about this, and certainly none of these governments seems to have contemplated it. The Alaskan government did give some thought to the matter, as mentioned, but decided against it.

It seems to me that direct payments out would have been a sensible thing to do, but because the profits of the oil would come as an income stream over time, and this income stream in the future was of necessity rather uncertain, the distribution of a current property right to some particular share of future incomes would no doubt have been preferred by the citizens of Saudi Arabia or Alaska to the direct cash payment. Further, by making this distribution immediately, the prospect of in-migration to Alaska would have been sharply reduced. Thus each Alaskan citizen could have been given a transferable certificate permitting its owner to receive one one-hundred and fifty-seventh thousandth, or whatever is the correct number of the future oil royalties received by the state of Alaska. In the case of the Arab countries, it would have been even simpler to incorporate the new nationalized oil companies and give shares to their citizens. Some arrangement to make certain that the cartel remained intact would of course be desirable. It seems likely that a private

3. Sometimes called original Americans, although, as a matter of fact, they seem to have arrived after Folsom man, and to have killed him off.

4. In practice, it was very largely paid out to the family of the sheikh.

corporation owned by the citizens of the various Arab countries would have been a more efficient way of handling this problem than the OPEC cartel.

In all of these cases, it would have been possible to arrange so that the transitional gain made by the beneficiaries of these very large transfers was indeed the whole potential value of the OPEC cartel.[5] But that is not what happened. In fact, the gains received by the average citizen of Alaska, or the average member of an American Indian tribe in Alaska, are much lower than the potential profits. The same is true with respect to the Arab states, although in this case the ruling classes have done very well. Nevertheless, the amounts they have received are very much less than the present value of the cartel at the time it was organized. There have been immense wastes.

Further, it seems likely that in all of these areas, by now, no one is actually making any gains. The Arab prince is probably now making about the same return on his rights in Saudi Arabia as he is on his investments in South Carolina farm land, if we discount properly for the relative riskiness of these two investments. He received very large gains originally, and the bulk of these he has kept in the form of investments, whether in the form of bank accounts in Zurich or retaining his rights in Saudi Arabia which he could have unloaded, albeit, they were not subject to ordinary sale transactions. Disposing of them in return for further investments in, say, Portugal, would have involved a political rather than a purely commercial transaction. Nevertheless, it was possible.

Thus, very large potential gains were in fact sacrificed by the "owners" of these potential transfers. The reason seems to have been largely *information difficulties* that prevented them from realizing just how wealthy they were. They turned to expert advisors like my friend, the American ambassador. These expert advisors were, first, not very expert and, second, heavily biased toward spending the money in some way other than simply enriching the Arabs or the citizens of Alaska.

Winners and Losers under Alternative Transfer Schemes

In general, the experts developed systems under which the money would go to some kind of "development" in the area. In some cases, this "develop-

5. The Alaskans would, of course, have made something out of their oil even without the organization of OPEC, but much less.

ment" went into direct investments in nonoil resources, which at least in theory were going to be around after the oil was exhausted. My guess is that the investments are not very good, and hence the returns will not be great. There is, for example, a building in downtown Juneau that is the headquarters of the corporation of one of the Indian tribes. The corporation exists to invest the tribe's ill-gotten gains. I am sure the executives of the corporation will do reasonably well, but it is not obvious that anyone else will.[6]

This is characteristic of most of the redistribution methods that I have described. The "technical" personnel who are involved in advising and making use of the funds have normally obtained for themselves an increase in income. In the case of the Saudi Arabian example this increase in income has been very great indeed. In Alaska it is probably quite modest, with civil servants being paid more and there being more of them than there were before, but no giant gains.

Practically no one, when asked how this money should be spent, suggests simply distributing it to the citizenry. Another possibility, of course, would be distributing it only to the poor. Alaska does not have very many, but there is no constitutional barrier preventing the state from distributing its money to poor people outside Alaska. One would think that the average left-wing intellectual would be in favor of such a distribution, but so far as I know, it has never been suggested. The end product of all of this is that most of the funds available from these particular large transfers were wasted, and many of the potential beneficiaries are probably not even aware that they are being mulcted.

Why is this money then used either to simply expand what we might call normal state activities or to cut taxes, and not directly paid to the citizenry? Clearly the citizens would be better off. Further, the king of Saudi Arabia would be better off if he had not decided that, in addition to paying off his family and various friends, he would undertake a fairly major development project in an area that is probably as resistant to development as any in the world. Clearly, if the development money had simply been paid out to the tribesmen, they would have done much better in terms of personal security and avoiding revolution than under the present arrangement. One would think that expenditures on secret police and armies also would be highly attractive, but only a small part of the oil revenue has been invested in such matters.

6. Since writing the above, I have seen reports of the financial problems of the corporation. It just proves that social scientists can predict.

Note in particular that the expenditures in, say, Alaska for improving state services and reducing regular taxation are in general ultramarginal. That is, the services now provided would not be provided by the citizens if they had to pay for them in a more direct way. They were willing to pay only their previous tax rate for the previous services.[7] Thus, the money is being spent on things that are of less value than the money itself. Of course, the citizens now have a somewhat different income position than they had before, but in fact, the effect has been fairly minor granted the way the money is being spent.

The gains were transitional rather than permanent. If the expenditures have any benefit, they will attract immigrants into Alaska to share in the gains until such time as migration to Alaska and life in Seattle are equivalent. Of course cash would bring in many more people, but there is no obvious reason why the current citizens of Alaska would be deeply distressed by that. The state is so large that those who want privacy can easily find it even if the population goes up by several million.

If we consider the problem from the standpoint of the civil servants who are called on to advise, the transitional gains may be quite substantial. Their wages are raised, and as civil servants they can hardly be fired even if more civil servants are brought in at the new wage rate. Thus, bringing the whole matter into true equilibrium might take a full generation, and they would achieve transitional gains during that entire period.

If we consider the intellectuals who, generally speaking, tend to favor this kind of thing, it is hard to avoid the impression that they are simply making a mistake. That would not be true, of course, of intellectuals living in Chicago who would not gain from anything going on in Alaska. But one would think that newspaper reporters on Alaskan newspapers would prefer direct payment of cash to increases in the state services. It may be in this case, however, that the intellectual community was so small that they were completely dominated by intellectuals elsewhere. The intellectuals elsewhere would not I presume be terribly happy about direct payments to citizens of Alaska, whereas they might be strongly in favor of, say, government-sponsored housing there.

The latter explanation also might apply in Saudi Arabia, which had practically no intellectuals with any economic background. Intellectuals from the outside, like my friend the ambassador, would not have gained from any direct cash payment, and in the United States tend to be vaguely in favor of various government projects. They can transfer that vague preference to the Trucial States by way of bad advice at no cost to themselves.

7. Insofar as the voting process measures these two factors.

So far, I have discussed this particular, very pleasant transfer entirely from the standpoint of the beneficiaries. It is notable that most of the losers did not seem to think there was anything much they could do about it. Further, they had a strong tendency to blame the wrong people.[8] That there were very real and very large effects on the victims is of course true, and it is also true that these effects were larger than the benefits that the recipients would have received if they had taken it in straightforward cash.

This is of course characteristic of most transfers by government. In this case, successful efforts on the part of the oil consumers in the United States to reduce the transitional cost of the organization of OPEC increased its total cost over time to those same consumers. Indeed, it is not positive that OPEC would have been able to remain in existence if the price control had not been slammed on retail gas expenditures at the beginning. Peculiar circumstances in which wealthy Texas oil men were compelled to subsidize the import of OPEC oil provided an additional market for the cartel, which may have been necessary for its stability.[9]

But these are what we might call pleasant transfers. The beneficiaries of the transfers did not have to impose any cost on anyone who was politically relevant to them. They could simply take the money. In the case of Alaska, they

8. In 1973, I spent some time in Pittsburgh and read the local Pittsburgh paper. Almost every day, the paper had two leading stories. One story was invariably an account of OPEC meetings and OPEC ministers' decisions about prices, production, etc., and the other an attack on American oil companies for raising oil prices. The probable reason for this was not entirely muddle. The voters could do something nasty to the American oil companies without violating their own moral code. A naval expedition up the Persian Gulf, although a trivial military activity, would have appeared to them to be imperialistic and wicked, and hence they were not going to think about it. For another account of somewhat the same phenomenon, see A. L. Olmstead and P. Rhode, "Rationing without Government," *American Economic Review* 75 (December 1985):1044–55.

9. Public misunderstanding was extreme. Edward Byers and Thomas B. Fitzpatrick, "Americans and the Oil Companies: Tentative Tolerance in a Time of Plenty," *Public Opinion* 8 (December/January 1986): 43–46, say, "Throughout the protracted energy problems of the 1970s, Americans doubted there was a real oil and gasoline shortage stemming from a genuine depletion of natural resources. They believed that the oil shortages were contrived—a conspiracy manufactured by large oil companies." Notably, Byers and Fitzpatrick also do not seem to be aware of OPEC's role. The long delay imposed by the environmental movement on the trans-Alaskan pipeline was almost certainly also important. If it had come into production at its originally planned capacity and date (1973), it is dubious that the Arabs would have even tried to organize the cartel. Possibly those environmental lawsuits were the most expensive that have ever been filed anywhere in the world.

were not called on to do anything that imposed costs on anyone. Selling their petroleum at the highest price was indeed the course of action that benefited the rest of the world more than any alternative.[10]

The Arabs organized a cartel, but it seems to have been an accidental by-product of the 1973 war. The strengthening of the cartel in 1979 was also a by-product, in this case of the Iran-Iraq war. In any event, the people injured by the cartel were entirely outside of the Arabs' direct political jurisdiction. Thus, it is quite different from the average cartel. Indeed, it closely resembles such things as the piratical expeditions of Drake.

Transitional Gains from Higher Education

Let us consider then some more normal transfers. The obvious one, of course, is the transfer of money from the average citizen to people who have more than average talent and hence would normally have higher than average incomes, by way of the university system. The first thing to be said here is that it is not really obvious that there is any true transfer here except for inframarginal individuals. Those of us who are inside the margin, either as employees of universities or as students, may be making a gain in the form of a rent, but as usual in economics, it is not very obvious that there are inframarginal individuals or that the gains are very great.

Leaving this possibility aside, employees of the university system are being compensated at their opportunity cost. It may be that many of them have relatively little talent to do anything else so that the mere existence of the university system pushes their total income up, but this once again is not obvious. In any event, I propose to ignore the employees for a while and concentrate on the theoretical beneficiaries, the students.

If we go back to the early days when these universities were first founded, there clearly was a transitional gain. The first state university in the United States was in South Carolina, and there can be no doubt that the students who went there in the first few years made a gain even though the subjects they studied would, we would think today, have had no commercial value. They came out knowing Latin and Greek, but also certified as upper class. At first, there were relatively few such people in South Carolina. Thus, there was considerable scarcity value in the degree. With time, of course, and with

10. The federal government's refusal to permit exploration for oil in most of Alaska or the export of the oil is another matter.

more people entering the university until such time as the present discounted income stream of going to the university was the same as going to work, this gain vanished. At this later stage, the university cost the state money but conferred no benefit on students. Government agencies are hard to terminate, however, and those students who were in residence at any given time would have lost from the termination of the university.[11] In this case, and I think this is very nearly unique, there would have been a transitional gain, however, from discontinuing the university. If it had been stopped, those people who had already graduated would with time have begun to get positive gains on their degrees because the number of university graduates would decline. The gain would be a distant one, however, since death and retirement are very slow processes.

Every expansion of the university would create a somewhat similar transitional gain for students who had not previously been eligible. Further, changes in the university, such as teaching subjects with more immediate commercial value, would be a distinct advantage to the students who took these courses in the early days. When the modernized university, with its new business and accounting courses, had been in existence for some time, once again, students would make their decisions in such a way that the marginal student had an income the same as that of what he would have had had he chosen not to go to school.

As far as I can see, that is indeed what the present statistical studies of return to education show. There have been times in which it seemed to be positive, mainly after large expansions of the university, and then periods in which it seemed to be negative, but I suspect the latter was purely transitional.

I have given very little discussion to the alternative theory of higher education, which is that it is simply a certification process rather than an educational process. That is, the possession of a degree indicates that you have a certain level of intelligence and willingness to work hard, rather than that you have learned certain things. This theory has always been disliked by academics because it implies that we really are not teaching people very much, and that the students who choose easy courses and forget what they have learned right after the exam may well be wiser than we.

I am going to continue paying relatively little attention to the certification aspect of the school. Clearly, if that is what it does, then it does it in a very inefficient way, and very large resources could be saved by switching to a more

11. The university was stopped and then restarted after a number of years as a result of post–Civil War developments.

efficient way of measuring intelligence and willingness to work. I shall also pay little attention to the possible rents of faculty members.

The outstanding characteristics of this very large activity is that, insofar as it subsidizes anybody, it subsidizes people who would do well in life anyway. It is not obvious, however, that any subsidy is derived. It may be pure waste, and there is certainly a large element of waste. The beneficiaries were mainly people who achieved a transitional gain when the organization was set up and the running costs were quite high.

Note that in all of these cases there is the excess burden that is normally discussed in connection with any tax or monopoly. There is also another excess burden because recipients of the funds also change their behavior. There is then the rent-seeking cost, the cost of arranging all of this by lobbying or whatever methods are used, and in some cases a rent-avoidance cost of people who are trying to avoid paying these rents. Lastly, there is the pure waste through the inefficiency with which the funds are in fact transferred. It is to this last cost that I now wish to turn.

The Rationale for Inefficient Transfers

Consider the current educational system and assume that the money raised from the taxpayer to pay for higher education was simply given as a cash gift to those people who have the capacities to get through whatever the requirements of the university are. They could then use this amount of money to pay tuition in a school that charged its full costs, which might be much lower than those that our present universities charge, or they could invest it in some other way. If you do not trust young people, you might insist that they invest it rather than spend it, although it is by no means obvious that time spent in the university is actually an investment rather than a consumption good.

Clearly, the excess burden to the taxpayer would be the same, but the excess burden on the recipients would be less than with our present arrangement. It is not obvious what would happen to the rent-seeking cost because this large sum of money would probably be worth more to the recipients, so they would be willing to invest more in rent seeking. Producers of things that the potential students would choose not to buy would suffer to some extent, although presumably not a great deal, and those who are providing things the students would choose to buy would gain. Again, probably not a great deal. Except for one group of factor producers, nobody seems to be injured by the change, but it should be said that the factor producers would be the ones to whom the legislature and the average citizen would normally turn for advice on reorganization of the educational system.

In Alaska somewhat the same situation pertains. Simply paying the money out in cash to the citizens of Alaska, preferably in the form of transferable certificates for future income, would be better from their standpoint and would injure no one except a certain number of factor producers, in this case primarily civil servants or potential civil servants. Again the loss would be small, and the gain to other factor producers would also be small. It is hard to see what the effect on rent-seeking activity would be in this case, because it would be very important that this be done quickly so that a large number of people would not pour into Alaska to share the gift.

Why do we not observe these efficient methods of transfer instead of the inefficient methods? I think the answer is ignorance. If we look at the learned literature, we find the only kinds of transfer that are ever advocated are transfers to the poor, a real but not very large part of our transfer economy. Most people are willing to make at least some gifts to the poor, and doing so is actually a productive activity that makes both the giver and the recipient better off.

Transfers back and forth in the middle class, however, which is what we actually observe, are discussed only by people who argue that they should stop. You can search the literature in great detail without finding anyone who actually is arguing for an efficient method of making them. People who talk about them invariably talk about them as undesirable.

There is an old chestnut which I heard when I was at the University of Chicago before World War II and which still is occasionally repeated by Chicago types. It is that we could make the farmers of the United States much better off than they are now while saving the taxpayer money by simply giving them cash instead of maintaining our present programs. This was not offered as a real suggestion, but as a criticism of our present programs.

Indeed, in this case, the statement about transfers is normally made in a very casual and careless way with the result that Gary Becker was able to demonstrate that it was not obviously correct.[12] It might be quite difficult to distribute cash to the farmers in exactly the same amounts as they now receive.

12. Gary S. Becker, "A Theory of Competition among Pressure Groups for Political Influence," *Quarterly Journal of Economics* 98 (August 1983): 371–400.

None of the people who offered this typically Chicagoan criticism ever gave any attention to it, and hence it is easy for Becker to demonstrate that their specific proposals would not distribute the money in exactly the same way as the present program.[13]

In all of this, the proposal is typical. We find in the literature occasional references to this kind of transfer, which is after all the dominant one in our society, as being inefficient in contrast to a cash transfer. We never find discussion of how *efficient* transfers from badly organized middle-class voters to well-organized groups should be organized.

Under the circumstances, it would not be surprising if the average voter or the average politician were ignorant of how to do it. I do not think that very many economists have given any thought to the matter. The reason that economists have not given any thought to this, and for that matter are not likely to, is first, it is obviously a bad thing to do. Second, politically no one is going to follow their advice, because a certain element of concealment and confusion is necessary to get the voters to favor such programs. Open cash transfers, which appear to be the efficient way, are just too blatant and could not get through in a democracy.

Thus, we have a combination of an absence of any technical discussion of this subject in the technical literature, and strong reasons why people in favor of such transfers would not be willing to talk in clear-cut efficiency terms. Thus, that people would behave in a rather inefficient way is not at all surprising.

Another problem is that other groups who might conceivably offer technical advice in these areas—government employees and potential government employees who will eventually administer the programs—are, on the whole, not in favor of efficient transfers. Their salaries depend to a considerable extent on the existence of fairly large and complex structures which may be eliminated in the name of efficiency. The academics who are hired by these people to engage in research on these programs also normally know on which side their bread is buttered.

Further, the people who are professionally engaged in urging this kind of transfer normally are aware that simple efficient transfers would not get through the democratic process. Hence, one of their major talents is in inventing complicated procedures that conceal the nature of the transfer and which almost by definition are apt to be inefficient.

13. There is no reason to believe that the politicians have selected the optimal redistribution money from the standpoint of political gain.

The result is inefficient transfers—transfers so inefficient that normally only the transitional gain is real. The transitional gain, of course, tends to be devoured by rent-seeking costs. The result is what I call the "Chinese-type economy" and what my old friend Alex Kafka referred to as "South Americanization," in which government is engaged in a very large number of activities that are normally a sort of distant result of rent seeking sometime in the past. There is usually strong opposition by various well-organized special interests to terminating the program.

More efficient transfers could, of course, if we only go this far, lead to a higher national income. Unfortunately, these more efficient transfers would inevitably lead to more rent seeking. If there is more money to be obtained, more resources will be put into seeking it.

Conclusion

The general picture that emerges is not a very pleasant one. No one looking at real-world governments can doubt that they do to some extent generate genuine public goods. No one observing them can doubt they also engage in a lot of transfers, mostly the result of rent seeking. Indeed, Dwight Lee has argued that what public goods they do generate are normally a by-product of rent seeking by the factor suppliers in those areas.[14]

In the 19th century, England deliberately and consciously moved away from a very well developed, rent-seeking society to one of the most open economies known to history. I can think of few more important research topics than a careful examination of how they did it. By this I do not mean what bills they passed, but how the political support was developed for those bills. Lacking the magic formula which might conceivably come out of that research, all we can do today is to argue against rent-seeking activity. Whether our arguments will have any impact is an open question.

14. Dwight R. Lee, "Public Goods and Politics: The Usefulness of Inefficiency," working paper, Department of Economics, University of Georgia, 1986.

RENTS AND RENT-SEEKING

Rents are a perfectly good economic category, and there is absolutely nothing in general against seeking them. If I were to invent and patent a cure for cancer and then became extremely wealthy by claiming rents on the patent, most people would regard me as a public benefactor. Nevertheless, "rent-seeking" is regarded as an unadulterated evil. The reason of course is the type of rent. The rents that attract rent-seeking, waste resources in static models. In dynamic settings, their injury to society is even greater. The purpose of this essay is to clearly distinguish between what we may call "good rents" and "bad rent-seeking."

But before we turn to this issue, let us look more carefully into the traditional theory of rents. For this purpose we will adopt the simplifying assumptions that there are no transactions costs and that everybody has the kind of perfect information which is customary in economics articles. Figure 1 shows Ricardo's pure land rent. There is a demand for wheat, shown by DD, and six tracts of land of varying fertility. The opportunity cost of producing wheat on each of them (assuming that appropriate technical decisions are made on all other factors) is shown by the line CC. The equilibrium price is P, and there is further land of even worse quality to the right of Q. It is, of course, not farmed. In each case the rent is the area above CC and below P, and the six owners, A, B, C, D, E, and F, are collecting that rent.

Suppose now that technical innovators G and H appear and produce new land, possibly by draining the sea, or discovering America. Their land is somewhat superior to the existing land, although not very much. As a result, we rearrange our diagram so that G's and H's land is to the left, and the land of Mr. A, now rechristened A′, moves over two spaces to the right. He is still going to produce at the same cost as before, as are Messrs. B, C, and D, who also have been rechristened B′, C′, and D′. F will go out of production and E, now E′, will be able to use only half of his land. The new cost curve is C′C′ which is identical to CC on the original plots of land which have been moved

Reprinted, with kind permission of Kluwer Academic Publishers, from *The Political Economy of Rent-Seeking*, ed. Charles K. Rowley, Robert D. Tollison, and Gordon Tullock (Boston/Dordrecht/Lancaster: Kluwer Academic Publishers, 1988), 51–62. Copyright 1988 Kluwer Academic Publishers.

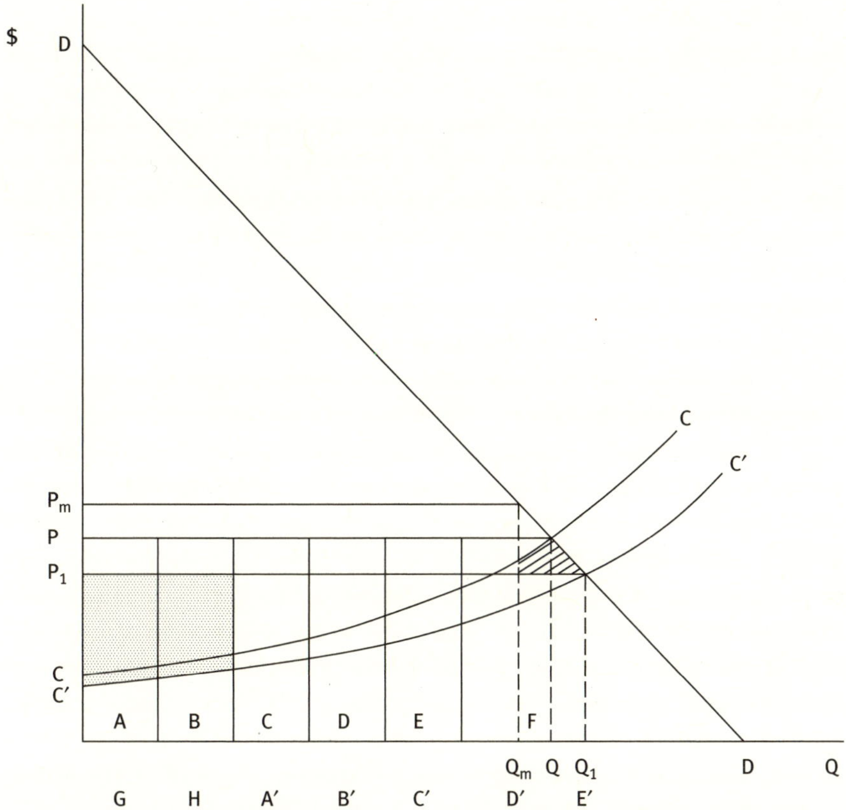

FIGURE 1

to the right. The new plots, G and H, have been added at the left, and have a lower cost than A and B.

With this new land in production, the new equilibrium is at the point where line C′C′ intersects the demand curve, and the price is P_1. Consumers have gained from the fall of the price from P to P_1. All of the previous farmers have lost, since the value of their land has gone down. Perhaps they will organize to restrict G and H, but we will leave that for later.

But do G and H net the rent shown by the dotted area? Probably not. The production of this new land, whether it involved draining the sea or getting into a boat and running the danger of falling off the edge of the world, was costly. People would on the average invest the present discounted value of the rent to be derived, i.e., the dotted area. Resources were invested in the search for rent, and we would anticipate that these resources would in the average case approximate the present discounted value of the rent to be derived.

Resources have been invested up to the value of the rent on plots G and H, and the net social gain from all of this is only the small shaded area on the right. This includes both the traditional welfare triangle and some costs previously incurred in producing wheat at higher than the new price on Mr. F's land. The most important effect of this technical innovation is a sizeable transfer from the owners of the previous farm land to the consumers.

But suppose, guided by Professor Ronald Coase, we had insisted on full compensation. With no transactions cost such compensation would, of course, be possible. It is obvious that transactions costs would be extremely high in the real world. Different consumers would be charged different amounts, and the landholders would also have to be differentially compensated. It is, to say the least, dubious that the transactions costs could be overcome in any realistic setting.

In the real world any compensation for the owners of the former farm land would almost of necessity have to come out of the profits of the redeveloped land. It is clear that if such compensation were attempted, the total resources to be invested in actually creating the new land would be very small indeed. This matter will be taken up later in connection with conflict between different lobbying groups.

The usual solution to this problem, one held by most economists, although rarely clearly expressed, is that the innovators be permitted to drive the owners of pre-existing capital out of business and that the owners of pre-existing capital not be compensated. The Western Sizzlin' Steak House opened in Blacksburg and drove Rustlers into bankruptcy. No one suggested that the very prosperous franchisee of the Western Sizzlin' Steak House should compensate the bankrupt franchisee of the Rustler.

In essence, we have a system in which any investment is to some extent risky because of the possibility that innovations, new inventions, change in social climate, etc., will make it worthless or sharply reduce its value. This of course means that the return on any capital investment includes an implicit risk premium. Note that this would be true of the capital invested for production of the new land as well as the capital already invested in the old land. In both cases, there would be an implicit risk premium with the result that the total market rate of return on capital invested in either of these activities would be somewhat higher than that on a riskless investment.

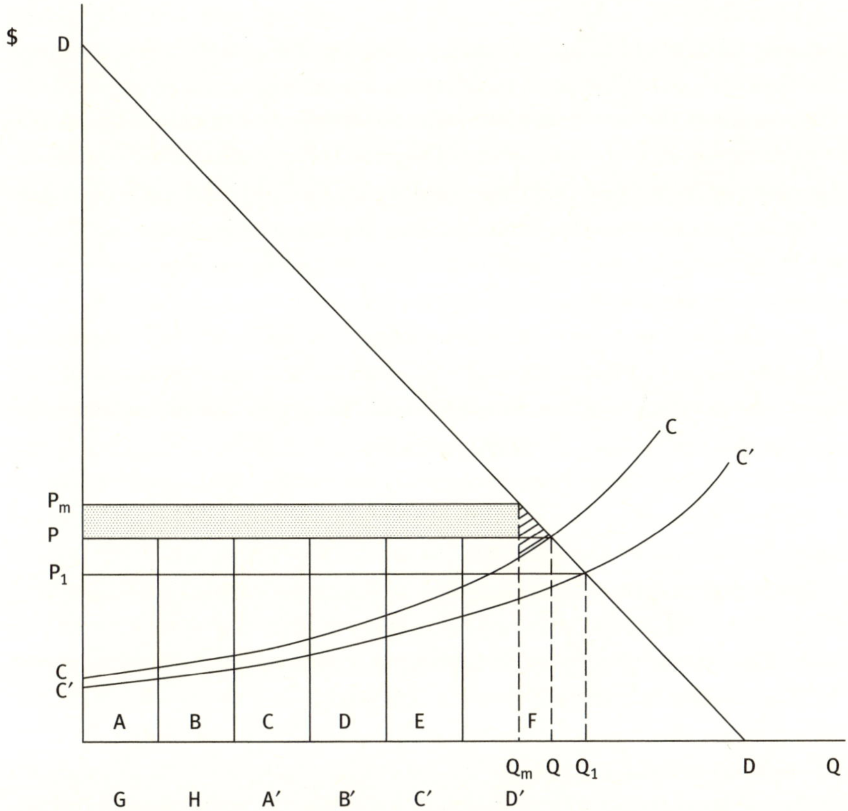

FIGURE 2

Traditionally this risk premium was visible in the difference in the dividends on common stock and the interest on government bonds. Today the prospect of inflation makes a government bond far from riskless, and the income tax makes capital gains more attractive than dividends. Thus we have no simple market measure of this implicit risk premium.

In figure 2 we have taken the same land and assumed the organization of a monopoly by the original landholders. This leads to the price P_m and quantity Q_m. Until the discovery of rent-seeking, the loss here would have been measured by the small triangle above line P, below P_m, and to the right of Q_m. The contribution of the rent-seeking literature from the time of "The Welfare Effects of Monopolies, Tariffs and Theft" has been that the actual cost should include the dotted rectangle which represents the resources invested in obtaining the monopoly. The traditional literature tended to ignore the possibility of true Ricardian rents in production and hence did not consider the loss of rents on land which is taken out of production as a result of the creation of the monopoly. We have shown this by extending the shaded triangle below P down to the line of the cost. Thus, part of the cost of organizing the monopoly from the standpoint of society as a whole is the removal of part of F's land from production. The same effect would be felt from the loss of quasi-rents on fixed factors of production in almost any newly organized monopoly.

Even in the traditional, pre-rent-seeking vein, however, both the shaded triangles in figures 1 and 2 should be counted as the social cost of creating the monopoly as opposed to the new land. This alone would be about four times as great as the Harberger triangle.

Earlier we remarked that there is an implicit risk premium in capital values. Although it will be analyzed with some care later, let us for the moment ignore it. Looked at from the standpoint of an entrepreneur who contemplated either of these investments, the monopolizing one or the creation of the new land, the situation is more or less even. In both cases, he invests the same resources, and receives only a normal return on them. In the first case, the efficiency improvement case, the largest effect is a massive transfer from the old landholders to the consumers.

If, on the other hand, he invests his resources in obtaining the monopoly, once again he obtains a normal return on his investment, but that return comes straight out of the pockets of the consumers. There is also the traditional welfare loss shown by the shaded triangle at the right above line P in figure 2. If we compare the two situations it is obvious that both of these shaded areas should be included as being in the advantage for society of the innovation over the monopoly, and the usual rent-seeking arguments for including the dotted area as cost are real also. What we have done so far is to slightly increase the welfare costs given in the traditional rent-seeking literature.

The inventor or the producer of any new efficiency improvement and the lobbyist receive the fair market value of their efforts, but the value to society of their activities is radically different. In one case, they produce an externality which benefits the consumers as well as improving pure efficiency enough to cover all their costs. In the other case, they reduce efficiency while extracting their entire cost from the consumers.

We have by no means finished our analysis here. In at least one way of looking at the matter, the landholders who suffered a reduction in their rent did not actually bear a cost. I earlier mentioned that any return on investment in the modern society carries with it an implicit risk premium because the investment itself may be made obsolete by further development. Schumpeter referred to this as the "perpetual gale," and von Mises also was fond of that phrase. It is surely true in the modern world that unexpected improvements in some other person's enterprise or in some other part of the economy can make your investment much less valuable. Presumably investors take this into account.

If this is so, then what happened when the value of this land fell sharply was that the landholders in essence were forced to absorb the value of the additional payments they had previously been receiving on their investment because it was risky. They made choices between saving and expenditure in full knowledge that there was a risk on the savings. They might not get their money back, and the risk has now eventuated. There is no reason to regard this as any worse from their standpoint than the requirement on the insurance company to pay out when one of its customers' houses burns down. In both cases, no doubt, the landholder and the insurance company would rather not make the payment, but it is part of their business.

Note that the same kind of risk argument can be made with respect to the monopoly. Indeed, if we look at the real world, monopolies are probably among the least secure types of investment. Monopolies which are created by simple entrepreneurial activity in the market almost always are eliminated in time by market forces. Monopolies provided by obtaining government action, strenuous lobbying, etc., normally also are eroded over time, partly by political forces and partly by market forces. If looked at in this way, the fall in price stimulated by the technical innovation is actually a net benefit to society with no real cost. The landowners were in essence insurers of themselves, in that they were taking a larger return as a sort of premium on the prospects that their capital would fall in value.

Note that consumers here probably have the same general anticipations as the producers; i.e., they anticipate that there will be technical developments which will make them better off. It is for them, however, almost a pure gift. They do nothing to achieve this benefit. Indeed, economic growth to a very, very large extent consists of just this. The actual product rises by an amount which is much larger than the return on capital invested and we as consumers all benefit.

It is, by the way, possible that this phenomenon means that we will save more money. This is not because the return on investments is higher, but because the general rate of progress means that a dollar next year will purchase somewhat more than a dollar this year. It will be possible to buy new products or the same products at lower prices.

Although we have now a good measure of the well-being of society, particularly the consumers, being obtained from these two different kinds of investments, it is not necessarily a good measure of the well-being of individuals with resources to invest. From their standpoint, investment in attempting to obtain rents through manipulating the government or creating monopolies (or, for that matter, burning down their competitor's factory) has about the same potential return as the productive activities.

We mentioned earlier that the existing landholders who are going to have their rents reduced by the introduction of the new land might attempt to organize to prevent it from being brought into production. There is no reason that this could not be, from their standpoint, a wise investment of resources, regardless of what we think of it from the social standpoint.

Let us assume therefore that the landholders do indeed organize. In this particular case we will assume that the organization takes the form of hiring lobbyists to pressure the government to get the new land banned. Clearly, this to some extent reduces the likelihood that the new land will be brought into production. It could mean that the entrepreneurs who were bringing the new land into production (G and H in our case) would be well advised to hire their own lobbyist.

The first thing to be said about this is that if the innovators know that there is a realistic possibility that they will have to hire a lobbyist in order to protect themselves against possible restrictions, then the innovation itself becomes somewhat less desirable. Suppose, for example, that the income to be expected from the new land (discounted to the present) was $1 million. The estimated cost of bringing the new land into production, including normal profit, is one dollar less than $1 million. On the other hand, the cost of the lobbyist will be $100,000. For simplicity we temporarily assume that if the lobbyist is sent there will be no restrictions.

Under these circumstances the innovation would not be attempted because its total cost would be $1,100,000 and its value $1 million. Only those innovations which could be made for $900,000 (including normal profit) and which would bring in $1 million would be attempted, with the result that society would be worse off.

However, the above assumption contains the unrealistic statement that the entrepreneurs know for certain that their lobbyist will be successful. In fact, all they could have would be some kind of probability distribution. As a result, innovations would be attempted only if the cost of obtaining one worth \$1 million was, say, \$450,000.

In practice the effect is apt to be considerably stronger. The landholders and the potential innovators would have to invest resources in lobbying in Washington to the point where the present discounted value of each, including the risks of success or failure, was equivalent to their net return. Since from the standpoint of the holders of existing land the cost of the innovation is very great, they are obviously motivated to invest in lobbying if there is any significant chance of success. Further, it should be pointed out that the existence of an organization of professional lobbyists in Washington designed to defend the existing landholders would be a warning to potential entrants that they would have to not only produce the new land, but also run a fairly large lobbying cost and have a fairly large risk of not getting any return on their investment. Under the circumstances, the net effect of an institution which permits this kind of lobbying would be a very sharp retardation in investment in improved production methods.

So far, we have developed an argument that the cost of rent-seeking is actually twice as large as even the rent-seeking literature has normally counted it. Of course this argument could easily be extended to quality improvements or to a new product rather than to cost saving. There is, however, a technical difficulty having to do with the implicit risk premium on any investment. Clearly, this involves some cost to society. People do find themselves facing risks, and presumably even wide diversification cannot totally eliminate it.

It is not obvious whether this kind of risk would increase or decrease the total amount of savings in society. People buy insurance for which they pay more than the present discounted value of the income they will receive because they want to guarantee at least some return. This might well be true here. If the risk here did not reduce the total investment, then there would be no cost to society other than a certain amount of nervous tension.

On the other hand, the social gains from institutions which permit people simply to wipe out other persons' investments by being more efficient are obviously very great. Note that this is not truthfully a Paretian argument. Strictly speaking, persons who are injured should be compensated for their injury. It is clear that our existing landholders would think they had been injured and demand a compensation. This has been avoided in traditional literature by referring to the problem as "merely a pecuniary externality." I think that this phrase can be taken as implying an externality which we will not count or at least not require compensation for. Clearly that is my attitude toward it.

So far, we have mentioned only briefly rent-seeking aimed not at creating a monopoly but at simply protecting existing rents. It is a fairly obvious characteristic of our political process that protecting what you have is somewhat easier than acquiring a new income source or wealth. That some business will be driven out of existence if the Japanese are permitted to import something or other is far more likely to be accepted by Congress as an argument for protection than the converse, which is that the business can expand if it is protected from competition.

This being so, we do have the possibility that the existing landholders would organize to prevent the introduction of the new invention. Unfortunately, this might well lead to organization of a general cartel. It is therefore sensible before we begin talking about the conflict between the existing landholders and the potential entrant to talk about the monopolistic side of the matter. Suppose then that a monopoly has been already organized and is charging the price P_m for quantity Q_m, making a nice profit on the existing land. It is suggested that this monopoly invest resources in order to search for new plots of land which will be owned by the monopolists. Would they be interested in investing the same amount of resources as our original example, in which new land is brought in by outsiders? Unfortunately, it all depends on the details of the case.

There is a good deal of literature which indicates that monopolies always select the lowest-cost method of production, the best product, etc., but there is little on how much research they should do on producing new devices or cutting costs.

It is clear in our case that there will be very considerable gains to the monopoly by pushing the cost curve down from CC to C′C′. It is also clear that if they did push the cost curve down, the monopoly optimizing price would be somewhat lower than it is with the CC cost curve. Once again, the consumers would gain a sort of externality from technical progress. Both the monopolists and the consumers would gain, but would the monopolist be motivated to put as much resources into the search for new land as G and H in our previous example? The answer to this question unfortunately is that it all depends on the specific parameters of the problem. It is fairly easy to produce a set of cost prices and cost savings, in which the monopolist makes sizeable investments. Unfortunately it is just as easy to produce a set in which the monopolist will invest much less than competitive entrepreneurs.

Still, there does not seem to be any strong argument that monopoly would be particularly slow in innovating. It might be slower than the competitive market, or it might be faster. What we can say for certain is that the price would be higher and the quantity sold lower than in a competitive market, but the rate of change in those two quantities might be as high in a monopoly as in the competitive market.

Let us return to the potential conflict between current landowners. The mere existence of the potential for conflict means that innovation almost automatically has to have a higher payoff per unit of invested capital (other than that invested in fighting your way through the regulations) than otherwise. Further, the existing well-organized groups always have an advantage.

Let us take a very brief history of the cable television industry as an example. At the very beginning of television Dumont attempted a fee-for-viewing television using a combination of over-the-air broadcast and the telephone lines. This failed, but, almost immediately thereafter, people began talking about connecting television by cables which would of course permit at least some direct fee collection from the viewers.

The well-organized television companies who, in the early days, frequently had congressmen on their boards of directors, were able to fight off this menace. They had no particular objection to cables being laid out in areas with very poor visibility, i.e., in marginal reception areas. Thus a number of small companies developed in these marginal areas. The big television companies confined their lobbying activity to compelling these stations to carry signals of the nearest regular television stations. In essence the cable people thus raised the advertising revenue of the regular stations slightly.

With time, the number of such cable television systems increased. They formed an association and began lobbying in Washington and gradually were able to force back the restrictions which were imposed on them by the over-the-air TV people. This led to the present situation in which a very large part of the country is wired for cable, and organizations like HBO directly transmit to the receivers. There is no doubt, however, that the development of cable was immensely impeded for a long time not by technical considerations, but by the lobbying power of the entrenched special interest.

There is, however, another aspect of this story which is even more interesting. As part of the payment for their political privileges, both the over-the-air television and the cable networks are forced to carry a good deal of material that nobody wants to watch. For example, in the cable business, there is the "rent-a-citizen" part of the expenditures of the average cable network. They characteristically devote a contractually agreed upon portion (usually fifteen percent) of their total capacity to carrying programs of local political or cultural interests. It is likely that the only people watching these programs are the families of those who happen to be featured.

They are, in essence, entertainment, and very expensive entertainment, though valuable for the people who are appearing on them. It is likely that this particular element of waste is larger in total cost to society than all the direct lobbying. This is by no means exceptional. In almost all cases in which we see active lobbying, the lobbyists not only put pressure on Congress, etc., but Congress, etc., puts pressure on them and through them on their principals. The product has changed in various ways to make it more politically acceptable. "Rent-a-citizen" programs are merely a particularly clear example of this phenomenon.

The regular over-the-air television faces a very large number of regulatory restraints on its programming. Defense industries place their factories in the district of influential members of the Armed Services Committee. They may even redesign their aircraft in order to purchase components from the district of an influential congressman.

But all of this is simply a statement of how the competition goes on, not a statement about the competition between lobbying groups themselves. The diversion of resources into lobbying is, as pointed out in the early rent-seeking literature, a cost. The cost of the other improvements in our society that we do not receive as a result of this malinvestment is also real. Turning to figures 1 and 2, the customers in figure 2 are worse off, not solely by the rent-seeking cost and the welfare triangles, but also by the cost of the innovation forgone. If the resources put into an innovation must in part take the form of rent protection, this latter gain will be smaller.

Suppose, for example, that although there was no possibility of talking the government into giving the current producers a formal monopoly, it would be fairly easy to talk the government into preventing G and H from coming in and depriving them of a large part of their rent. Under these circumstances, the traditional rent-seeking losses would not occur, but the gains from the innovation would also vanish. Indeed, we might go further. It might be that the current owners are compelled to maintain a significant lobbying organization simply to protect themselves. In this case, there would be a direct wasteful outlay as well as the cost of no innovation. The cost of this protective lobbying then would not only be preventing the innovation, but also its own direct cost.

If we are to become wealthier than we are now, we must have continuous innovations. Whether these innovations take the form of new inventions or simply the opening of a Western Sizzlin' Steak House is unimportant from this standpoint. In both cases we need a property law in which the innovator is not hampered in introducing his innovation by the fact that his competitors will be injured. A situation in which the government may restrict innovations because they damage competitors is highly undesirable.

We also want a property system in which there is little to be gained from going to the government and lobbying for special privileges of any sort. Note the emphasis on little to be gained. The government will no doubt behave more efficiently if the people concerned with various measures inform it of their concerns. After all, it has to have some information about cost and benefit. We would like this information cost to be modest and in fact simply to improve the structure of government.

When investments, in influencing the government, are capable of doing more than simply improving the efficiency of the government, then those resources will be invested. The cost will not be merely the Harberger Welfare Triangle, plus the additional welfare triangle we have added on here, plus the total cost of the resources invested in influencing the government, but also the cost of the benefit which we would have received if those resources had been invested elsewhere. It is important that the government provide us with a secure property system, but it is equally important that it only be secure in certain ways. The legal system of Mr. Gladstone's England, or of the United States in most of the 19th century, met this test. We are still better off in this respect than most of the world, but that is weak praise.

Further, although the property system of much of the 19th century and of the English-speaking world did tend to meet the test given above, it surely could be improved upon. Whether such improvements are in fact possible, granted the nature of the political process, is an open question. The rent-seeking literature points to problems in the market process, but these problems are very largely the product of problems in the political process. A cure must proceed in both areas simultaneously.

WHY DID THE INDUSTRIAL REVOLUTION OCCUR IN ENGLAND?

Like most economists, I am a great admirer of Adam Smith and feel, again like most economists, that the application of his ideas had much to do with the efflorescence of British civilization in the 19th century. The industrial revolution, however, got its basic start, and indeed according to some historians was completely accomplished, before *The Wealth of Nations* had significant influence on government policy. The Savery steam engine was built in England in 1698, the Newcomen in 1721, and by 1763 Watt had created the modern steam engine. Hargreaves' spinning jenny was invented in 1765, and Arkwright's water frame in 1769. Crompton introduced his "mule" in 1774. *The Wealth of Nations*, of course, was published in 1776, but it is hard to argue that the introduction of the power loom by Cartwright, in 1785, was the result of policies based on Adam Smith's work. In fact, Smith had little or no effect on English governmental policies before 1815.

Thus, the industrial revolution was well under way before Adam Smith wrote. Basically, it was in place before the Smithian Revolution in government policy even began. Indeed, England was widely regarded as the most technically advanced country in Europe as early as 1725 or thereabouts. In a way, the whole point of the French revolution was to transfer to France certain English institutions which people like Voltaire thought were the explanations of England's success. Voltaire visited England before Adam Smith's book was published.

What then was the reason for this great economic development in England before Adam Smith produced the theory and policies which led to its even greater prosperity in the latter 19th century? I propose to argue that it was an accidental by-product of certain political changes arising out of what I would like to call "the English revolution," i.e., the series of events in the 17th century beginning with Charles I's difficulties with Parliament.

In most of the world, throughout most of history, rent-seeking has been a major activity for the more talented and aggressive members of society. This

Reprinted, with kind permission of Kluwer Academic Publishing, from *The Political Economy of Rent-Seeking*, ed. Charles K. Rowley, Robert D. Tollison, and Gordon Tullock (Boston/Dordrecht/Lancaster: Kluwer Academic Publishers, 1988), 409–19.

is one of the reasons, albeit not the only one, why progress in general has been slow. If a large number of the most talented people in society spend almost all their efforts in the attempt to obtain special privileges for themselves, they first generate no social surplus for others; secondly, they actually reduce the total output by at least sometimes obtaining their monopoly, special privilege, etc. England, like most of the rest of the world, was a society dominated by rent-seeking in 1600. By 1750 rent-seeking was relatively unimportant. A combination of the sharp reduction in the number of monopolies, restrictive practices, etc., together with the fact that the most talented and aggressive people in society turned from rent-seeking to more productive activities, jointly constitute, in my opinion, the principal cause of the industrial revolution. Of course there were, as I shall point out below, other major causes.

The problem obviously is why the industrial revolution occurred in England and not in France, Italy, or Germany. Firstly, it must be said that it would be very hard to argue that in 1600 or, for that matter, in 1750 science was more advanced in England than in those three other countries, or the Netherlands, Sweden, etc. Further, it is clear that the general state of civilization was at least as high in, say, France, as in England. Indeed, most people in those days would have said it was higher. There were far more Englishmen studying in continental universities than there were continentals studying in English universities. Indeed, the state of the universities in England (well described by Adam Smith) was such that it is very dubious that anyone would have studied there for intellectual reasons. The Scotch universities were, of course, different, but even they did not deserve anything like the reputation of Paris, Heidelberg, or Leyden.

The general standard of civilization in England was no higher and probably somewhat lower than that on the continent. It should also be said that the general standard of public morals was probably worse in England. It is no great compliment to the French government of that date to say that on the whole it was a more honest government than that of England. The British government ran on corruption.[1] The king quite literally bought approval of laws in Parliament. Further, a very large number of the seats in the Lower House were owned in fee simple by someone, usually someone who personally sat in the House of Lords. The House of Pitt, for example, owned six seats in Commons.

1. See almost any one of the books of Sir Phillip Namier on 18th-century English politics.

This corruption of government, together with the fact that it depended on handing out special favors, surely was an atmosphere where one would anticipate large-scale rent-seeking. Indeed, the government itself ran almost entirely by rent-seeking. Individuals would invest resources in obtaining appointment as collector of customs or promotion to captain in the Navy.[2]

But if this is the way the government operated internally, the rest of society was remarkably free of rent-seeking, granted the date and the world in which England lived. It could not be said that there was none. Occasionally, Parliament granted some group of businessmen special monopolies, but it was rare, and in most cases there was at least a colorable argument of public interest, as in the famous case of the Honorable East India Company's special privileges on the import of tea. It should be pointed out, of course, that the special privilege in this case was a low tax rather than tariff protection.[3]

There were, of course, a large number of regulations still on the books which had been enacted mainly before 1620 or so and which had originally given people various important and valuable privileges. Gradually, however, these regulations had become largely obsolete. They were, as Adam Smith pointed out, a burden on trade, albeit not too much of a burden because people had worked out ways of getting around them. The bulk of English manufacturing, for example, was located outside of incorporated towns and hence avoided the guild regulations. The competition of this extramural industry meant that the guilds in town had to recognize they faced competition and hence could not be as extortionate as they were in France, for example.[4]

This development can hardly be regarded as the result of conscious policy. Indeed, there is practically no evidence of anybody having consciously thought about these issues before Adam Smith. Those people who did think about them, normally felt that what was needed was improved regulations rather than letting the old regulations gradually disintegrate. Smith then in-

2. Nelson was captain at 21. In his case, he no doubt deserved it. His rapid promotion, however, depended not on his merits but on the fact that he had a close relative in the Admiralty.

3. The Boston Tea Party is a particularly good example of a democracy getting hopelessly muddled. Although a number of New England merchants who had expensive smuggled tea in their warehouses were about to lose money, the average American would clearly benefit from the much lower prices on tea.

4. R. B. Ekelund, Jr., and Robert D. Tollison, "Economic Regulation in Mercantile England: Heckscher Revisited," *Economic Inquiry*, forthcoming, 1980, and "A Rent-Seeking Theory of French Mercantilism," unpublished manuscript, 1980.

spired the intellectual revolution which later had great effect on British policy, but by 1776 England had already moved a very long way from the rent-seeking society.

Why did this happen? It is the thesis of this paper that the basic cause was the English revolution of the 17th century, and that it was essentially a by-product of decisions of a political nature taken for other reasons.

If we consider English history, the first thing we note is that England had in many ways the most disturbed political history of any European country that actually succeeded in achieving central government. Germany and Italy, of course, had more disturbed histories and ended up divided into small countries instead of single countries. Spain, France, the Netherlands, and Sweden, all, like England, achieved a central government and unification, but did so with much less in the way of civil wars and turnovers of dynasty than did England. From the time of the Norman conquest to the time of the American revolution there were few examples of the throne of England passing peacefully from father to son to grandson. George III was in this way, as in many other ways, an exception to the general rule of the English history. Still, with the accession of Henry VII, who in fact had practically no claim to the throne of England beyond his victory at Bosworth field, things became at least temporarily stable. Henry, a cold-blooded, unscrupulous, and extremely clever man, felt that he must protect his dynasty first by killing anyone who had even any faint claim to the throne, and secondly by weakening the power of the great nobles. In achieving the latter objective, he turned to a number of expedients, one of which was the strengthening of the power of Parliament. This was intended to and indeed did reduce the power of the great nobles, but it should be pointed out it was also intended to increase the power of the king, and did so as well.

If we move forward to Henry VII's granddaughter, Elizabeth,[5] we then see a government in which the Queen had more power than any English king had had for a long time. The greater nobility had pretty generally been brought to heel and the commons were in general obedient. There was, however, no professional army, which clearly meant that the Queen was not as powerful as the king of France or Spain. Elizabeth, like the two other children of Henry VIII who sat on the throne of England, had no children of her own, and the throne passed to a rather distant relative, the king of Scotland.

5. Her killing of Mary, Queen of Scots, was a continuation of the policy founded by her grandfather of killing all the people that had any, even remote claim to the throne of England.

James I, having been impressed by his current contemporaries in France and Spain, wished to improve the power of the throne even more, but he was one of the most tactless men who has ever sat on the throne of England, and it is likely that his reign actually weakened the crown.

Before discussing the events of the reign of his son, Charles I, however, it is sensible to pause briefly and explain the rent-seeking situation then in England. It was the policy of the Tudor kings in England to make use of royal monopolies for various private citizens to a considerable extent as a revenue-raising device for the king.[6]

Nevertheless, these monopolies were a product of rent-seeking activity, and there was much other rent-seeking activity in the economy as a whole. Robert Tollison has suggested that the basic cause of the Civil War was the desire of the House of Commons to take over the profits of this rent-seeking activity from the king.[7]

The monopolies, however, had to be enforced. At that time there were a number of courts in England. First, there were the Courts of Chancery, which will not be dealt with again here, because of their rather special jurisdiction. They in fact played little role in the events that followed. Secondly, there were the common law courts. These had developed into a system in which judges appointed for life administered jury trials, although the basic decisions as to guilt or innocence in any criminal charge were made by the jury. Lastly, there was the court which we now refer to as the "Court of the Star Chamber," which was simply an appointed commission set up by the king for the purpose of carrying out such laws as he wished. The latter was primarily used to enforce the various monopolies and the special privilege grants which the king made. The "Court of the Star Chamber" was used among other things to impose certain taxes on the English upper classes, particularly ship money, and as a general rule annoyed the non-royal part of the British society.

We now proceed to the unpleasantness between king and Parliament, which I think is normally badly described as a revolt against the king. As a matter of fact it was a revolt by the king against Parliament. The king found it necessary to leave London in order to raise his standard. The only professional part of the military apparatus, the Navy, remained loyal to Parliament. The Parliament, throughout the war, also had access to a more regular rev-

6. Ekelund and Tollison.

7. Ekelund and Tollison.

enue than did the king, with the result that their army was characteristically larger, better equipped, and better paid. In the early part of the Civil War, nevertheless, the king won a number of battles. Eventually, however, the Parliamentary forces were brought under the control of Cromwell who was capable of winning if he had numerical superiority. In a way it was rather like the Army of the Potomac, which was regularly beaten by Lee in spite of numerical superiority until it came under the control of Grant, who was capable of winning if he had numerical superiority.

The war, of course, ended with the complete defeat of the royal forces and the execution of the king, but it also ended with Pride's purge and Parliament being brought completely under the control of Cromwell. The result in essence was merely another and stronger king. Indeed, Cromwell probably had more power than any king of England had ever had.

The incidents of the struggle, however, are of more interest to us than this specific outcome, particularly since Cromwell's government was swept away after his death.

First, there was the statute of monopolies passed by Parliament. This prohibited royal monopolies except for patent monopolies. Note the accidental characteristic of this development. Parliament passed a bill prohibiting the king from establishing monopolies but made an exception. Gradually over the next century the issuing of monopolies for new inventions switched from being a matter of royal favor to being a bureaucratic step carried on at the lower level of government. This made it possible for people to invest sizeable resources in attempting to develop new devices, i.e., it opened up a new area of research. This certainly had much to do with the development of new inventions in England. I shall, however, argue below that although it was certainly important, there were other steps which were at least of equal or perhaps of greater importance.

It seems likely that, as Ekelund and Tollison pointed out,[8] Parliament's motive in passing the statute of monopolies was not to eliminate monopoly rents or rent-seeking, but simply to transfer these rents to their own hands. As it turned out, Parliament was unable to get very much profit from this rent for a number of reasons. One, a fairly obvious one, is that the transactions cost of fixing a large body of men like Parliament was much higher than that of dealing with the king. This would certainly have reduced the amount of rent-seeking activities. There are however other reasons.

8. Op. cit.

The first problem encountered by Parliament in its desire for rents is that Charles I in the early part of his long dispute with Parliament dealt with Parliamentary opposition in a simple, straightforward way. He did not call Parliament into session for twenty years. This certainly eliminated any possibility of rent-seeking by Parliament during that period. Further, when Parliament finally did come into session, the developments very rapidly moved into Civil War, and Parliament in general had little time to devote to such matters. At the end of the war, Cromwell purged Parliament of everyone who he thought could not be trusted to vote exactly as he thought was desirable, and hence there was another period of time in which Parliament was unable to capture any significant rents from the granting of monopolies. Functioning of Parliament was eventually reestablished in the second half of Cromwell's reign, but the people who had passed the statute of monopoly were long gone.

But that does not explain why the new Parliaments—and for that matter the kings—did not revive rent-seeking at this point. Charles II was certainly not the type of person to shy away from establishing monopolies for his friends. The explanation, I think, comes from another by-product of the disturbances. As I have said, the "Court of the Star Chamber" enforced the various rent-seeking activities, i.e., the monopolies and special grants privileges. It did not, of course, enforce the payment of government officials who had obtained their jobs by rent-seeking activity, and it is notable that rent-seeking in that form continued to be very active and important in England right up to the 19th century.

The "Court of the Star Chamber," however, had been used to collect taxes from the upper class in England, who to a large extent were responsible for the revolution and had therefore acquired a very negative image. As a part of the revolutionary development it was abolished. This left the judiciary of England almost entirely[9] in the hands of the common law courts, where decisions basically were made by juries. To put it briefly, juries cannot be depended upon to put people in jail for having violated the monopoly privilege of some rent seeker. Under the circumstances rent-seeking ceased to be very valuable because the rent could not be protected.

A little more discussion of the jury is called for at this point. Juries in general are rather erratic in their performance, as I suppose we would expect from a group of people drafted into a service for which they are not in any

9. Once again exempting Chancery.

way specially trained and then manipulated by two specialists in such manipulation, one for each side. There are certain characteristics of their behavior which can be predicted, however. They are, for example, generally speaking, prejudiced against large corporations and, for that matter, the government. More particularly, however, they generally do not enforce laws that they disapprove of. A maximum price is the kind of thing that they are apt to approve of, but a minimum price is not.

Not very long ago the Interstate Commerce Commission, becoming upset at the violation of its rules, arranged for a roundup of independent truckers in the vicinity of Chicago who were violating regulations by charging too low rates and breaking into the monopolies that had been granted to larger companies. As we will explain below, under modern circumstances enforcement of this kind of special privilege is dealt with not by a jury but by a judge sitting alone. Hence the truckers were in fact fined and ordered not to continue. Now imagine the situation if the only way of dealing with them had been to call them before a jury. No district attorney in his right mind would have brought a poor, black truck owner[10] before a jury and accused him of having unfairly competed with a large trucking monopoly, offering as evidence the fact that he was charging lower prices than the monopoly. If the district attorney was so foolish to do this, he would be lucky not to have the jury find him guilty.

The same problem would occur in most other areas where monopoly rents can be obtained. The jury would tend to feel that the person who violated this rent was either a person to be congratulated or in any event somebody who had done nothing particularly awful. U.S. experience in the early 19th century, when private persons competed with the Federal Mail Service and efforts to convict them were almost totally nugatory because the juries refused to do so, would be repeated.

In 17th- and 18th-century England the reluctance of juries to convict in rent cases was reinforced by the fact that the jury was not drawn from the citizenry at large, but almost exclusively from the gentry and minor gentry classes. The basic source of revenue of such people was land rent. Typically a person who was accused of violating, say, the monopoly on soap by producing soap, would be tried in the area where he had his establishment. Finding him guilty would, to some very slight extent, lower land rents in that area. Hence there was a positive (if minor) material motive for not convicting.

10. Subject to a 95% mortgage.

Indeed, in general, the result of the Civil War was to put the government of England for a long period of time in the hands of the land-owning classes, whether these classes were the great nobles with the great estates or the local gentry with their smaller properties. These landholders, who were without access to tax money and any real prospect of obtaining monopoly rents (because on the whole it was not possible to establish a monopoly on farm products under the conditions of England at that time), were primarily interested in increasing the total land rent of England. Expanding commerce and industry in general would have moved in that direction, albeit very modestly. These members of the gentry and great Lords were very anxious to obtain what privileges they could out of a state and were frequently quite ingenious in achieving such privileges. They found themselves in a situation in which the presence of the jury trial as the only way of enforcing any government regulation meant that, outside of securing government jobs for their nephews, there was very little they could do. They did what they could, but it was not very much.

Of course, the use of the jury was not the only factor, although before the adoption of "liberal" policies in England in the early 19th century, it was probably the most important factor. After 1815, as a result of Smith's and Ricardo's influence, there was actually conscious planning for growth. The switch to free trade, which has been so much and so correctly extolled by economists, not only improved efficiency in and of itself, but made rent-seeking particularly difficult. There was little or no advantage in being given special privileges for the manufacture of anything in England if foreigners could always import it. Further, the very restricted size of the total government during the 19th-century heyday of *laissez-faire* in England not only lowered the tax burden, but also reduced the possibility of rent-seeking in other areas. I have mentioned above that the English government in the 18th century was the most corrupt in Europe, with government jobs being the principal source of corruption. There just were not very many government jobs in 19th-century England, and hence the development of a non-corrupt civil service involved very little sacrifice for anyone.

In the 18th century the requirement of juries was much more important. Still it should be said that although economists can claim credit for the 19th-century English reforms, the United States did as well without consciously adopting good economic policies, simply because of the internal free trade provision in the Constitution. The combination of the federal system, internal free trade, and a very small and relatively inactive central government (which was characteristic of the United States, certainly up to the end of the

19th century) also made rent-seeking difficult. Once again there is no evidence that the American government personnel were opposed to rent-seeking, or did not actively engage in what rent-seeking they could. Indeed, the way the tariff was manipulated by the federal government, land grants in the West, and the introduction of the spoils system in the government's personnel policies all were good examples of rent-seeking activity. Further, if we look at the states we find that they almost continuously attempted to provide monopolies to special groups or to bend their budgets in such ways as to benefit particular areas.

The states found this behavior generally non-paying because of free trade within the United States. The national government was just too small to have any great impact on anything except perhaps such specialized areas as the arms industry. Even here, however, the early development of a significant export market meant that the importance of rent-seeking was small. Thus, the general absence of rent-seeking in 19th-century England and in the United States was not solely the product of the requirement that juries be used to put people in jail. Still, economists can claim credit for the 19th-century English Reforms, although the United States did as well without consciously adopting good policies.

Reestablishment of rent-seeking as a major activity both in England and in the United States in this century has depended on the removal of the jury in these areas. In England the jury has very sharply been downgraded in all areas and to all intents and purposes is not available in civil cases. Nevertheless, the enforcement of rents depends in England as it does in the United States on a specific technique of evading the normal requirements that people must be convicted by a jury before they are put in jail. I am not sure exactly what the history of the development was, but in any event during the latter part of the 19th century it occurred to a number of people that a law of this sort could be enforced, not by accusing people of violating it and giving them a trial, but by getting a judge to order the person to obey the law and then holding him in contempt if he violated this order. People accused of this kind of contempt have no right to a jury trial, and since the judge who would decide whether they had committed contempt or not was the judge who had issued the order, it was unlikely that they could escape punishment. Under the circumstances the enforcement of the rules became technically possible because of the denial of the right of jury trial for violations of this kind of regulation. The development of extensive rent-seeking activity, beginning with the Interstate Commerce Commission, was, I suppose, the inevitable outcome.

Those who have read my books on the law[11] know that I am opposed to the jury system. This is because it is erratic, inaccurate, and cannot be depended upon to enforce the law. When we have a law that I prefer not to have enforced and which I can predict the jury will be biased against, I favor the jury. In a way what we now have from my standpoint is the worst of all possible worlds. People charged with murder, theft, rape, etc., are brought before this inaccurate, frequently biased, decision-making body, while people charged with violating an ICC-granted monopoly on trucking and with charging too low prices are dealt with by a judge. This is the exact opposite of the arrangement I would favor.

In sum, I have argued that the development of the industrial revolution in England was essentially the result of a series of changes in the British political order that occurred during the period of the English revolution. These changes were not implemented as part of a plan for the industrial revolution, but as a by-product of the political struggle. Disestablishing the "Star Chamber" was primarily motivated by the desire not to be subject to future impositions like ship money. That the abolition would to a large extent abolish rent-seeking activity was probably totally unanticipated by either its proponents or its opponents. It did in fact have that effect.

11. *The Logic of the Law*, New York: Basic Books, Inc., 1971, and *Trials on Trial: The Pure Theory of Legal Procedure*, New York: Columbia University Press, 1980.

RENT SEEKING AND TAX REFORM

I. Introduction

As some readers may know, I once was a Chinese expert, and rectifying terms was a main preoccupation of Confucian scholars. Let me begin, therefore, by briefly discussing the meaning of both "tax reform" and "rent seeking." My personal definition of rent seeking essentially is using resources to obtain rents for people where the rents themselves come from something with negative social value. For example, if the automobile industry invests resources to get a tariff on Korean cars, then this makes Canadian citizens worse off. Hence, even though the automobile companies will gain, such investment of resources is rent seeking.

If, on the other hand, the automobile companies invest resources in developing a mechanical improvement on their automobiles, then I would not call it rent seeking. The cars would in fact be better. Note, however, that the benefit obtained from the mechanical improvement may in fact be less than its cost. Businessmen try to avoid such malinvestment, but it does happen. A rather crude distinction exists here. I would not call it rent seeking, even though society on the whole would have been better off had the investment not been undertaken.

Resorting to such a crude distinction is unfortunate, but it is the best we can do. We would prefer a general continuous function that includes both the benefit (or harm) and the costs of the activity. Unfortunately, because I have not yet been able to develop such a function, I am stuck with a crude distinction.

II. Advertising

Many cases exist in which expenditures that are privately beneficial have little or possibly no benefit for society as a whole, but at least they do no harm. As an obvious example, advertising often simply shifts customers back and forth among competing companies but has little other effect. The cur-

Reprinted, by permission of Oxford University Press, from *Contemporary Policy Issues* 6 (October 1988), 37–47.

rent arrangement of installing small signs directly on the shoulders of interstate highways is cheaper than, and presumably about as effective as, constructing large billboards.

Over the long term, the existence of competing advertising means that the product quality is subject to considerable improvement. Nevertheless, at any given point in time, cutting each company's advertising budget by 90 percent would save money and probably have no other significant effect. I do not think that such advertising should be called rent seeking. The same applies to research laboratories' investing in duplicative research in their efforts to win the patent race.

III. Tax Reform

The second term that must be rectified is "tax reform." The common technical meaning of tax reform is rearranging the tax code so as to meet some criterion—frequently a rather vague one—of efficiency. No implication of an increase or a reduction is necessary.

But that is the technical definition. I think that most ordinary citizens are not particularly interested in efficiency, and that they view tax reform as having two other characteristics. The first characteristic is that taxes go down, and the second—rather paradoxically—is that taxes on the very wealthy go up.

A sort of alliance exists here between the economic specialist and the ordinary unwashed citizen in that both oppose "loopholes." The common citizen thinks that the rich benefit greatly from loopholes and that if these loopholes were closed, then his own taxes would go down. The economic expert may also think that the rich have too many loopholes. However, the expert basically views the loopholes not as particularly favoring the rich but as distorting resource allocation.

IV. Loopholes

This, of course, raises the question of what exactly is a "loophole." The most common single definition of a loophole is a legal provision under which someone does not pay taxes when I think he should. Tax codes are immense bodies of rules with immense numbers of both taxes and arrangements for non-taxes, i.e., provisions for not collecting taxes. Classifying as loopholes and "non-loopholes" the various provisions that permit the private citizen to keep at least some of his money is inherently rather arbitrary.

As an obvious example, most income taxes are at least moderately progressive. That people in lower tax brackets are not required to pay as high a percentage of their incomes as are people in the upper brackets is not classified as a loophole. This is, of course, a clear case in which one category of taxpayers is treated differently from another.

The usual assumption is that some kind of a general tax exists and that special interest groups have secured arrangements under which one of their particular activities is exempted from taxation, or one of their particular expenditures is regarded as a business expense and hence not part of income. I should point out that loopholes also exist in revenue measures other than income tax. The U.S. Supreme Court, for example, once had to determine whether a tomato was a fruit or a vegetable since tariffs were different on the two categories of food products.[1]

Let us turn to income tax under which most of these problems arise. First, people listing the loopholes normally treat the deduction of interest on a home mortgage in a rather bizarre way. They include it in the data on the absolute size of the total loopholes in the tax code. Indeed, this deduction makes up more than half of total loopholes. On the other hand, when these people get around to listing loopholes and considering their elimination, this deduction rarely is mentioned. Some have suggested, however, that the deduction be withdrawn for second or third homes.

I suppose that the political reasons for this treatment are fairly easy to understand. Nevertheless, it clearly is an arbitrary distinction. Another arbitrary distinction is that many economists feel an expenditure tax would be better than an income tax since it would encourage investment. I have never heard any of these economists refer to this idea as a loophole for savings.

Nevertheless, I now introduce a rather artificial definition of loopholes that reflects the viewpoint of what one may call traditional public finance. I call a loophole any provision in a quite general tax rate that will exempt some particular matter. The reason for this is simply that such loopholes tend to lower economic efficiency. General taxes that are hard to evade—the true income tax, sales tax, value-added tax, real estate tax, etc.—do not much change

1. A distant relative of mine who was a scientist specializing in brewing techniques once spent much time and energy developing something that tasted like wine but technically was beer. The advantage, of course, was in the tax.

resource allocation among different uses except insofar as they remove resources from the private sector. They may, of course, reduce the work incentive or savings incentive. (If the money is spent on genuine public goods, then the result of the whole package may be to increase such incentives.) The depletion allowance loophole in the U.S. income tax, however, did lead to an overinvestment in oil exploration. Most special provisions have similar characteristics.

V. Desirable Loopholes

Note that loopholes that switch resources may have a constructive purpose. For example, our maintaining—for military reasons—some particular industry that could not support itself without a subsidy may be desirable. As another wide example, the U.S. tax code grants exemptions for money contributed to a large variety of charitable organizations. Apparently, the American people feel that these institutions should be subsidized but mistrust Congress's ability to decide which particular charity should receive which particular subsidy. This system permits individual citizens, rather than Congress, to allocate the subsidies. This is not an ideally efficient system, but clearly one may argue that it is desirable.

Aside from these cases, the bulk of such special provisions result from lobbying by special interest groups. Indeed, that probably is also true of the charitable exemptions—at least in the U.S. Most special interest groups would argue that the production of milk, gloves, etc., should be subsidized by the government—and hence that the exemption is desirable. I was particularly intrigued by the lengthy treatment of racehorse breeding in the former U.S. income tax law.

VI. Lobbying

Suppose, then, that a well-organized lobby proposes to get the taxes lowered on some special industry. According to our earlier definition of rent seeking, whether or not this is rent seeking depends on both the tax side and the expenditure side.

The first consideration, of course, is whether reducing this particular tax will lead to a shift of resources that results in the economy as a whole being worse off. To keep this particular case pure, suppose the result of the loophole is not only that some particular industry—e.g., glove manufacturing—is exempted from tax, but that the rest of the tax structure is raised so that all other industries have a slightly higher tax. Clearly, this would make society as a whole worse off.

But suppose that when this loophole is generated, the government cuts back expenditures instead of raising other taxes. Then the question of whether or not this is desirable turns on where the money is saved. Some distortion in the manufacturing industry still will occur, but it easily could be a minor factor compared with the impact of the expenditure cut. Suppose, for example, that the necessary saving is made by abolishing the British Columbia Egg Board. (The Egg Board is self-supporting, but the amounts that it now charges egg producers could be retained for some other purpose while the Egg Board itself were terminated.) The distortion of the economy caused by exempting the glove industry from taxation would not likely be as great as the distortion relieved by abolishing the Egg Board.

As an equally extreme example on the other side, suppose that the expenditures reduction cut Environmental Protection Agency funding so that the amount of air pollution rose considerably. In this case, the damage that the loophole causes could be quite considerable. First, it would distort the manufacturing industry, and second, it would increase air pollution. I clearly would classify this act as rent seeking.

Note that from the standpoint of those organizing the lobby, this distinction simply is irrelevant. They are trying to make money by manipulating the government. They don't care about the secondary consequences, and yet I am classifying their activity as either rent seeking or non-rent-seeking solely in terms of those secondary consequences.

Lobbyists sometimes lobby for things of general benefit. Some years ago, I read an article in the *Washington Post* dealing with what that newspaper called the "Christmas tree" committee of Congress. To the indignation of the *Washington Post*, the committee with jurisdiction over tariffs was listening to various industry representatives and then doing what they asked. But the intellectual climate of opinion had changed since the 1920s, and these industries now were asking for reductions in tariffs. Generally, they wanted to eliminate the tariffs on their raw materials or components.

The *Washington Post* was correct in identifying this as perfectly ordinary lobbying activity by special interest groups—indeed, the lobbyists were standard industrial lobbyists. But even if the net effect of these tax cuts was less

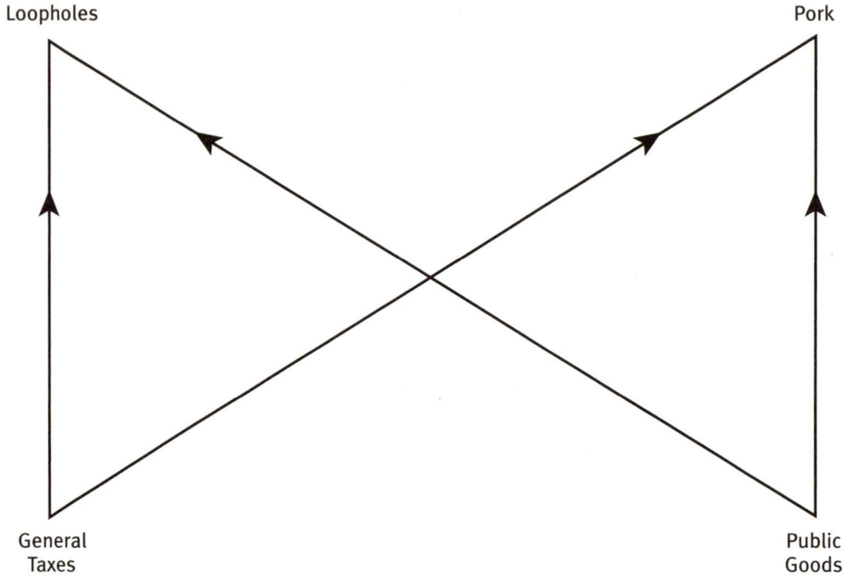

FIGURE 1

desirable than simply abolishing the protective tariff as a whole, the net effect still was desirable. Loopholes in a bad tax code may be better than no loopholes in a bad tax code. That is particularly so in this case since practically no revenue effect was involved. Of the tariffs about which they complained, most had been set so high that nothing was being imported under them anyway.

VII. Special Interests

When I wrote "Problems of Majority Voting"—the tiny acorn from which *The Calculus of Consent* sprang—I ended by pointing out not only that special interest expenditures are funded by general taxation but that special interest loopholes could be funded by reducing general interest expenditures.[2] The model that I presented can best be seen by considering figure 1.

2. G. Tullock, "Problems of Majority Voting," *Journal of Political Economy* (December 1959): 571–79; J. M. Buchanan and G. Tullock, *The Calculus of Consent: Logical Foundations of Constitutional Democracy* (Ann Arbor: University of Michigan Press, 1962).

A continuous tendency exists to use revenues from general taxation for special interest expenditures and to relieve special interest groups of their taxes, i.e., to "fund loopholes." Similarly, the general interest type of government expenditure is continuously attrited by transferring funds to expenditures that benefit special interests and to tax loopholes that reduce the total amount of money available.

Of course, not all special interest tax exemptions are undesirable on general grounds (e.g., charitable exemptions maybe), and not all special interest expenditures cost much more than they are worth. But virtually all special expenditures for limited groups of people and virtually all tax loopholes affecting special interests result from lobbying. In some cases, however, this lobbying conveys a positive benefit—or at least does no harm—to the citizenry. Therefore, following my crude distinction between rent-seeking and non-rent-seeking activities, I can identify rent seeking in only some of these cases.

Like most economists, I would like the government to shift to a general tax system with no loopholes except possibly for industries in which special subsidies genuinely are desirable. Even then, I would prefer that the subsidies be direct rather than indirect. I also would like the government to discontinue the large range of activities—the British Columbia Egg Board is a clear-cut example—that actually lower the efficiency of the economy. This not only would abolish the present tax loopholes and a great many government expenditures, but would result in a much lower but quite general tax level.

Clearly, most representatives of special interests would be delighted with such reform, provided that it would not affect their particular special interests. They want reform to affect all others. The special interest groups that object to true reform—and they are quite numerous—generally are engaging in straightforward rent seeking. Unfortunately, these groups also are engaging in what is likely to be politically successful activity.

VIII. General Agreements

For a long time, Public Choice scholars have pointed out that getting rid of individual loopholes or individual pork-barrel government expenditures is very difficult. However, because on the whole such loopholes and pork-barrel expenditures hurt everyone, a general agreement to abolish all of them not only would be in the public interest but also might pass. Problems are twofold. First, because the public simply is not well informed on this or any other matter, dealing with a single all-or-none reduction—as opposed to a series of small steps—is politically difficult. Second, the special interest groups all are well informed and will fight intensely for their own particular special interests.

If the automobile industry could get repealed all tariffs and quotas on everything except automobiles, then this would serve its interest greatly. The industry would be even better off if all tariffs, together with all pork-barrel legislation, were repealed. But here we have the classic prisoner's dilemma. The automobile industry's best possible strategy is to get everything else repealed and to retain its own special privilege. If everybody tries that, then we likely will end up in the less than socially optimal lower right-hand corner (rational action without collusion) instead of in the socially optimal upper left-hand corner (rational action with collusion) of the prisoner's dilemma matrix.

That President Reagan was able to get through a rather general change in the U.S. tax code, in the direction that I have discussed above, is encouraging. As enacted, of course, the bill was a long way from perfect, and various special interests indeed were protected. One reason the bill went through may be that because the U.S. currently is depending so heavily on deficit financing, no lobbies favoring particular expenditures were worried about taxes to support those expenditures.

That the 1984 Democratic presidential candidate campaigned in favor of increasing taxes probably was not entirely a coincidence. Although favoring a tax increase was a very un-Democratic view, it perhaps was intended to rally all of the pork-barrel lobbies on the candidate's side. But it failed.

We are approaching a situation in which those people who want to cut taxes—either the economists seeking general reductions or the special interest groups seeking loopholes—are being thrown into a fairly direct conflict with those who want expenditures increased or at least held constant. On the expenditure increase side, once again, are the pork-barrel expenditures and the more general expenditures.

The tendency that I have described above—for things to go from the general to the particular—would seem to indicate that expenditures for items such as improving the U.S. military machine are apt to be dropped in favor of expenditures for special interest groups. I should emphasize, by the way, that a very important special interest group is the officer corps and the civil servants of the Department of Defense. The U.S. has one officer—mainly field-grade and up—for every seven enlisted men, and one admiral on service in Washington for every single deep-draft vessel that the U.S. owns. Firing three-quarters of all field-grade and flag officers surely would improve the U.S. military establishment while simultaneously saving money. Unfortunately, this is one case where well-organized special interest groups will not only fight but no doubt win.

IX. Charitable Expenditures

One area where an interest group exists, but where it seems ineffective, is in aid to the poor. Clearly, the poor are interested in this and tend to use whatever political assets they have to get such aid. In practice, however, they do rather badly. As one example, people in the second decile from the bottom receive larger transfers than do those in the bottom decile.[3] As another example, the poor were doing relatively as well during the middle of the 19th century as they are doing now, according to Lebergott's study.[4]

The apparent explanation for this is that the poor are poor because they are not very competent people. In some cases, their lack of competence comes from perfectly genuine organic illness. In any event, this lack of competence apparently carries over into the political sphere. They are relatively inept as special interest groups, and I think that the money they do receive largely reflects charitable impulses of the upper-income groups. In any event, whether the poor engage in any significant amount of lobbying is not clear. Of course, various middle-class civil servants and social workers lobby in the name of the poor, but little money actually gets to the poor.

X. Ideal Taxes

Perhaps I should deviate a bit here and discuss what one might call the economist's ideal of taxation. First, in a new country—and I should point out that large parts of British Columbia still are unsettled—confiscatory taxation of land site values has much to commend it. One wants the land value to be confiscated by the state since no excess burden exists there. Also, one wants the land speculator to retain full return on his investment of talent.

3. See G. Tullock, *Economics of Income Redistribution* (Boston: Kluwer, 1983), 94.
4. S. Lebergott, *The American Economy* (Princeton: Princeton University Press, 1976), 57.

This is hard to do in areas that already are settled. But in areas that have not yet been occupied, selling land at auction—while including some kind of agreement as to what type of land taxes will be collected in the future—suits these conditions.

Second, most economists favor taxing things that, if left to themselves, would be overproduced. Air pollution is an obvious example. In this case, provided the tax is calculated properly, there is not only no excess burden but actually an excess benefit.

Unfortunately, in both of the above cases, resources may be invested to create inefficient institutions. For example, people may wish to receive the land free since from their personal standpoint, the land's highest value is as a place where they may occasionally go on camping trips. Similarly, people may invest resources to establish pollution taxes that are either too high or too low.[5]

Such nearly costless taxes, unfortunately, are insufficient to support most modern governments. This leaves two other types of taxes—one of them very general—that comprise the classical areas in which loopholes occur and to which economists refer when they discuss tax reform.

XI. User Taxes

Before turning to those areas, however, I must mention one other very important area. The impact of many government activities is quite widespread—but not spread over the entire population. In such cases, the obvious solution is a user tax. But arranging such a tax may be difficult. For example, the weather bureau is far more important for people proposing to fly and for farmers than it is for office workers. However, taxing the beneficiary groups without taxing others would be difficult if not impossible.

In this area, one first should examine the possibility of taxing the users. In the U.S., the road system is paid for partly by gasoline taxes and partly by real estate taxes that local governments impose. As a rough rule of thumb, the major highways are paid for by gas taxes and the local feeder roads are paid for

5. J. H. Dales, *Pollution, Property and Price* (Toronto: University of Toronto Press, 1968), has suggested tradeable pollution rights, i.e., certificates permitting certain amounts of pollution, which would be issued probably by sale to individual companies and which could then be resold. They would have less susceptibility to rent-seeking activity than do pollution taxes.

by real estate taxes. This arrangement may not even approximate an ideal allocation, but it clearly is far from pathological.

However, for those services for which this type of funding is difficult to implement, relying on general taxes may prove economically desirable. After all, over their lifetimes, most people benefit about as much from these things as they would be harmed if the whole bundle of such services were taken away.

But this is an economic judgment and not a political one. If special services for special groups are funded out of general taxation, then rent seeking by those special groups will likely lead to overexpenditure. Many years ago, James Buchanan suggested a solution: The U.S. could select—perhaps at random—some other group of people about the same size as the benefitted group and could put the tax on them. Thus, two lobbying groups would be opposing each other and the outcome presumably would be improved.

XII. Budget Reform

One way to implement this solution would be to change the present budget procedures to those of a more traditional system. If we go back in history, we usually find that no such thing as a government budget existed. Individual government services were paid for by allocating specific taxes or parts of specific taxes to fund those services. The Lord High Admiral of Spain, for example, collected one gold guinea from every ship that called at a Spanish port. The only way to increase his revenue was either to encourage more shipping to call into Spanish ports or to fight it out with other government bureaus for a share of their taxes.

One can easily imagine similar arrangements, under present circumstances. Taxes could be allocated to individual bureaus, and the large tax sources could be broken up. The Department of Defense, for example, might receive, say, 75 percent of the personal income taxes or, possibly, all income taxes collected from people whose income is in the top one-third of the distribution pyramid.

This means that individual bureaucracies and the rent-seeking groups would, in essence, find their success dependent on dealing with somewhat similar-sized opposing groups. I think that this would lead to a more efficient allocation of resources than does our present method, but I certainly would not argue that it would be optimal in any theoretical sense. The objective would be to set lobbyists and special interest groups against each other. I should note that whether or not the lobbyists would be considered rent seekers would depend, more or less, on which side they were on and possibly would vary from budget year to budget year.

Suppose, for example, that in the middle of a major war, the upper-income taxpayers—who, by our proposed system, are paying the entire cost of the armed forces—were lobbying for reduced expenditures while the military suppliers, including the officer corps, were lobbying for increased expenditures. One might well argue that the upper-income people are the rent seekers in this case. As soon as the war is over, and assuming that the U.S. wins, cutting back sharply the size of the army would become desirable. Then the U.S. would begin listing the defense suppliers and the officer corps as rent seekers and would stop calling the wealthy taxpayers rent seekers. This is the result of the crude distinction given above. Again, I hope that somebody can improve the distinction.

All of this has been a digression on optimal taxation. Optimal taxation will not likely exist, of course. When contemplating tax legislation, one usually sees a good deal of effort to make the tax system less efficient and to spend whatever money is derived in wasteful ways. Obviously, this is clear-cut rent seeking.

If the U.S. attempts to put a special tax on the beneficiaries of some services—for which the externality is genuine—but not on the entire population, then one may expect defensive rent seeking. One may expect rent-seeking activity to open holes in general taxes for special groups and to divert the revenues of special and general taxes to special expenditures. Only when the rent seekers desire a loophole and the revenue lost by that loophole is compensated by a wasteful expenditure's being discontinued can one regard lobbyists' activity as other than rent seeking. Mainly, rent seeking in tax reform is as undesirable as it is in other areas.

Indeed, when lobbyists engage in an effort to create loopholes, whether or not their effort is rent seeking depends on how the money would have been spent had they not created the loopholes. We favor special interest groups that seek to save themselves from taxation by reducing government expenditures if such reduction itself is desirable. When this is not so, we call it rent seeking and condemn it. To reiterate a theme underlying the bulk of this paper, the concept of rent seeking is a crude one. At the moment, however, it is the best that we have.

XIII. Conclusion

In summary, tax reform is very difficult. If successful, however, it can reduce greatly rent seeking and other kinds of government waste. Unfortunately, rent seekers have motives to prevent this type of "reform." Fortunately, their opposition is not necessarily decisive. A general bargain in which everyone loses special privileges is apt to benefit everyone. With sufficient political ingenuity and work, this sometimes is possible.

RENT-SEEKING AND THE LAW

Suppose I want something or other from the government, I hire a lobbyist, and he goes to work. Let us also assume that what I want will inflict a concentrated injury on someone else, and they hire a lobbyist to fight against it. After some time there is either a decision by Congress that I shall get my privilege, or a decision that I will not. We all accept this straightforwardly as an example of rent-seeking behavior on my part and rent-avoidance behavior on the part of my opponents.

Let us change the situation a little bit. Let us assume that it is a court and that I hire a lawyer in order to sue some person, and that person hires a lawyer to defend himself. We don't usually refer to this as rent-seeking, but I am prepared to argue that it has a very strong resemblance to the kind of rent-seeking we normally talk about. To discuss both the resemblance and the difference is the purpose of this paper.

Let me begin by pointing out that both lobbying and legal proceedings do have, at least possibly, a positive social value. It is not true that all lobbyists are arguing for something which has a negative social payoff. I recall some time ago reading an article in *The Washington Post* (economically muddled as usual), in which they talked about the lobbyists who were engaged in lobbying for changes in the tariff. The *Post* referred to the committee they were lobbying before as the "Christmas Tree Committee."

This all does sound very much like Schattschneider's study of the lobbying for the Smoot-Hawley tariff years ago.[1] As a matter of fact, if you read further in the article you found that what all these lobbyists wanted was a tariff reduction, and the committee was giving it to them. They were all manufacturers who were asking for a reduction on the tariffs for raw materials or intermediate goods that they used in their product.

We have no difficulty in distinguishing between the case in which you are asking for a protective tariff as clear-cut rent-seeking and the case in which you are asking for a reduction in tariff, which I would say is not rent-seeking because the ultimate outcome will be socially beneficial. I realize in this case

Reprinted, with permission, from *Current Issues in Public Choice*, ed. José Casas Pardo and Friedrich Schneider (Cheltenham, U.K.: Edward Elgar, 1996), 179–88.

1. E. E. Schattschneider (1985), *Politics, Pressures and the Tariff: A Study of Free Private Enterprise in Pressure Politics, as Shown in the 1929–1930 Revision of the Tariff.*

my usage of the term "rent-seeking" is a little unusual, but I think it is better than the more normal use. In other words, I use rent-seeking only when resources are invested to do something for which the net effect will actually lower the national product, rather than, as in this case, raise it.

If we look at the lobbying industry of Washington, we do indeed find that a good many people are urging Congress to do something which is socially beneficial. I regret to say that they are heavily outnumbered by the people on the other side. Still, we can't complain about their activities.

Suppose we have a situation where Congress in its usual sloth is not proposing to do anything at all. It is pushed into action either by a lobbyist for a special interest of the type we normally talk about, or those other lobbyists for special interests, the bureaucrats who normally want to expand their bureau. There may be active objectors. This may not be the ideally efficient way of getting laws enacted, but we can't maintain that it is a totally inefficient process. It works for good laws as well as bad.

Hearing the arguments for both sides in some particular policy issue presented by skilled advocates, and I can assure you from what little personal experience I have had that the lobbyists in Washington are indeed highly skilled and intelligent people, may be a necessary way of getting the best policies. We would all prefer that our elected representatives know the truth, and proceed to enact it without being pushed. In practice, we don't have that much confidence in them, and are not surprised that their policies are to a large extent the result of pressures that are brought to bear on them.

We would prefer that we didn't spend all of this money on lobbying, but when the lobbying leads, as it sometimes does, to changes in the law which are beneficial, we are happy about it.

We can go a little further. If we were convinced that this procedure leads on the whole to better outcomes than would be obtained by having Congress totally ignore special interests on either side, then we could say that these people are engaged in productive activity. This would even be true for those lobbyists who are lobbying for something undesirable, because we believe that the discussion process is a reasonably good way of reaching the truth.

What does all of this have to do with the law? The answer is that the legal proceedings are almost exactly the same as the proceedings that involve a fight between two lobbyists. The basic difference is that legal proceedings have been the subject of fairly stringent rules for a long time. The whole thing is more formal, but, basically, it is similar. I sue you and obtain a lawyer for that purpose, and you hire a defense lawyer, resources are expended and there is an outcome.

I should deviate here, since this address is in Europe, to explain that the Anglo-Saxon and specifically American legal system is a good deal less efficient and more expensive than that which you are accustomed to in Europe. As you may or may not know, I am opposed to the Anglo-Saxon procedure, and would prefer a procedure based on Roman law. This is not because I think it is ideal, it is because I think it is better than the Anglo-Saxon system.

Having said that I don't like the Anglo-Saxon system, I am going to have to talk primarily about the American system. This is partly because I was originally trained in American law, but even more importantly because most of the empirical information we have is produced by various research organizations in the United States.[2] Apparently, the Europeans are not so interested in this and have not collected much data. I have written two books on this general subject[3] and the work in them has been largely summarized and brought up to date in an article, "Court Errors," in the *European Journal of Law and Economics*.[4]

The first thing to be said about the American procedure is that it is extremely costly. If you take the fees of the attorneys on both sides, together with, in some cases, some very expensive expert witnesses[5] and the government's expenditures in maintaining the court,[6] the costs of the trial normally are about as large as whatever is at issue. Suppose that I sue you for $30,000;[7] there would normally be about $10,000 in fees for the attorney on each side, which adds up to $20,000, and there would be a social cost of

2. England has produced some very good work, but unfortunately only in a small quantity.

3. *The Logic of the Law*, New York: Basic Books, 1971; and *Trials on Trial*, New York: Columbia University Press, 1980.

4. 1, 1994, pp. 9–21.

5. Some of these witnesses are experts only in the sense that they are specialists in looking sincere and honest while producing ridiculous testimony. On the whole, they are an honest body of men, but it is usually possible for both sides to get their own expert.

6. Actually these figures are underestimated in the empirical work. American courts frequently involve juries, and they are conscripted and paid a small sum of money much below their actual opportunity costs. If we adjusted the figures to include real costs to the jury, the costs would be much higher. I feel strongly about this because recently I wasted two whole mornings in the Federal Court as a conscripted candidate for a juror but was never called.

7. I would normally ask for more than $30,000, but we will assume that $30,000 is what both your attorney and my attorney think I will get if I win.

$10,000 to maintain the court. This is a simple summary of a lot of rather tedious data. If you are curious about the details, the Rand Foundation has an immense project which produces such data on a continuing basis.

The American courts are in error in at least one case in eight. In other words, they go wrong in about 12 per cent of all cases. Further, this is over the whole body of cases: in more difficult cases they clearly go wrong more than that, but the one in eight is a lower boundary, and they must go wrong at least this often.[8]

It is interesting that I am the only person who has made these calculations, although they were based on data collected by other scholars, many of them very intelligent people. Apparently it is thought to be dangerous actually to consider seriously the error term. The normal study will point out that there are defects in the process, but as far as I know I am the only person who has made use of the data to calculate the number of errors.

I should explain that I believe that European courts are less prone to error than American courts, but this is more a matter of feeling that their procedure is more likely to reach the truth than a decision based on actual statistical knowledge. Certainly it is not true that when the European courts put somebody in jail for ten years, they are always right. They must be often wrong, but I can't say how often. To repeat, I think they are more likely to be correct than American courts, but this is not an estimate based on real data.

No doubt Congress's error term is higher than that, but note the situation: in both cases people are attempting to push a decision-maker into action in their favor. In the case of the American court system we actually have a measure of this cost, and we find that it is high enough totally to exhaust, or more than exhaust, the so-called "Tullock rectangle"[9] if we think of it in rent-seeking terms. My guess would be that in Europe it is considerably smaller. As in rent-seeking, the party which wins makes a net profit from the activity, but from the social standpoint this is more than offset by a cost inflicted on other people. This is the similarity between the legal process and lobbying.

Let us consider somewhat more carefully the situation in the law and put aside for the time being lobbying Congress. First, we can ask what is the

8. My basic method of calculation of these errors is in both of my books previously cited, and is brought up to date in the article in the *European Journal of Law and Economics*, also cited previously.

9. The amount which in early work was thought to be the profit derived by the rent-seekers.

point of this process? Let me confine my discussion to Contract Law, and let us also assume that we are dealing with contracts which are not against public policy and hence can be enforced by the courts.

The first thing to be said is that it is clear that people should be permitted to make enforceable contracts. We know this, among other things, because such contracts are completely voluntary. There is no reason why people who want to make an unenforceable agreement can't do so. Thus the choice of enforceable contract methods is a clear-cut case of people voluntarily agreeing that under some circumstances they may go to court.

I should say here that in the United States there is a relatively new and a rather muddled branch of the law which deals with the question of whether two parties who are negotiating about something, have or have not actually reached the stage at which they have a contract. You perhaps have heard of the Pennzoil case in which a decision of some ten billion dollars was brought in against the company as a result of this rule. Of three parties that were one way or another involved in this complex set of negotiations, two thought there was no contract, and the third thought there was. The court held that the negotiations had proceeded far enough along so that there was the contract, but the fact that highly skilled and intelligent attorneys were on the other side makes it clear that this is not a translucent piece of law.[10]

The economic advantage of enforceable contracts is obvious even if we ignore the fact that people enter into them voluntarily. The possibility of credit arrangements or agreements under which things will be done in the future depends upon the possibility of making a binding contract. If it is to be binding, there must be some mechanism for enforcing it. The mechanism that we normally use is a court[11] which will investigate the matter and make a decision. Whether there shall be lawyers on both sides is not an absolutely clear-cut matter. In general, we favor permitting the two parties to present arguments for their side. We also permit them to hire a specialist advocate to make these arguments.

In the European procedure these specialized advocates are pretty clearly simply people who assist the court with the bulk of the actual investigation carried out by the court. In the Anglo-Saxon procedure, the court, if there is a judge, is very nearly a neutral judge of a duel between two highly skilled

10. For myself, I wish we were back in the olden days in which the agreement was not a contract until a little ceremony had been gone through. The ceremonies were not obviously of great social significance, but they eliminated doubt as to whether there was a contract or not.

11. The "court" may be a non-governmental body, as in arbitration.

advocates. If there is a jury, then the judge is sort of in the situation of a referee in a game played by the two attorneys. The actual decision is made by the jury.

A lot of rules have developed which restrict what can be done in court and the type of evidence allowed. The set of rules I am most familiar with is the one used in American courts. I would say that generally they are counterproductive, even though some individual rules are desirable.[12] I am under the impression that the European courts are less hampered.

It is obvious that if, whenever one party claimed that the other had broken a contract, there was a quick and costless method of correctly deciding the issue, the law of contracts would be a highly desirable institution. Unfortunately, without divine intervention it does not seem likely that we can produce such a system.

In practice there are several things to be said about the law of contracts. The first is that if the two parties are permitted to make the decision as to what resources to invest, the situation is similar to that I discussed in "Efficient Rent Seeking"[13] in which each party increases his chance of winning and reduces the chance of the other, by each dollar he invests.

In the American court the situation is worse because a party can impose a substantial part of the costs on his opponent. If I am suing someone, I can subpoena his records and interrogate his officials before the trial. Further, I can engage in lengthy cross-examination of the officials before the trial without compensating them. Thus it is possible for me to run up significant costs on the budget of my opponent. Needless to say, if these costs make even a very modest increase in the likelihood that I will win, I will do it. It is these pre-trial interrogations that have run the cost of American suits up so far in modern years,

In sum, then, this is a desirable social institution, that is, enforceable contracts. Unfortunately the enforcement proceeding is structurally rather similar to rent-seeking by lobbying Congress in those cases where there are lobbyists on both sides. It looks very much like the ordinary rent-seeking case, except for the specific fact that in a lawsuit there is normally a specific person who is opposed to whatever is being asked for by the first attorney. In other

12. The Supreme Court made some drastic changes in these rules when drafting the current rules of federal procedure. The new rules are certainly much less counterproductive than the old.

13. *Toward a Theory of the Rent-Seeking Society*, James M. Buchanan, Robert Tollison and Gordon Tullock (eds) (1980), College Station: Texas A&M University Press, pp. 97–112.

words, it differs from those cases which are common, in which Congress is lobbied for something or other, and there really isn't anyone on the other side. In court, both sides are normally fully represented.

It should be said that this system, if we count only the outcome and the costs of the suit and if we assume that it has an accuracy of something in the order of seven out of eight, could still be highly socially productive. Note that even the fact that it is inaccurate to some extent does not make this impossible. In a way it is like medieval "trial by ordeal" in which people would go to considerable lengths to avoid even being suspected.

If we assume that there is a retrogression and we begin deciding whether contracts are breached by one of the classical ordeals which has roughly a 50–50 chance of reaching the correct conclusion, we can feel confident that most people would try to avoid anything which looked like a breach, or a false claim of a breach, simply because the results of the ordeal going against them would be so expensive that it is not sensible to run a 50–50 chance.

The same argument, in fact, may be much more strongly applied if the court is assumed to be right seven out of eight times. Although in these cases the person who is either in breach of the contract or is falsely claiming a breach of the contract realizes that he has some chance of winning, he should also realize that he has a more significant chance of losing. Even if the cost of losing were only his legal fees, this would still be a major detriment. Add on the possibility of damages, and a desire to stay out of court would be expected.

To sum up where we are at the moment, the lawsuit has a considerable structural resemblance to ordinary rent-seeking. In those cases in which the laws are desirable, as the laws enforcing contracts are, the outcome should be positive, but the reason that they will be positive is not that the court proceeding itself has a positive outcome—it has a negative one—but because the threat of such a court proceeding leads people to keep their contracts and not make false claims of breach on the part of the other party.

Even if we contemplate such a ghastly miscarriage of justice as the Pennzoil case (you should keep in mind that this is only one example), there must be immense numbers of other cases in which people have decided to keep their contracts because of the risk of an unfavorable decision if they go to court, together with the certainty of a lot of expense.[14]

14. In the United States the plaintiff frequently does not pay his expenses. His lawyer has taken the case on a contingent fee basis, and will be paid only if he wins. In this case, it is the

We have not completed our discussion of the effects of the court on laws of contract, and rent-seeking activity. The threat of legal proceedings is obviously real, and this means that the contract should be drawn up with this in mind. It is likely that in the United States far more attorneys are engaged in drawing up contracts than actually litigating them.

Whether this drawing up of contracts by attorneys is a productive activity, ignoring its possibility of reducing a number of lawsuits, is unclear. A number of people, Douglass North, for example,[15] have stated that this activity on the part of the attorneys facilitates contracts, and hence improves the functioning of the economy.

In order to consider this in a pure sense let us assume that we have a perfect court system which at no cost always determines whether there has been a breach of contract, and enforces the law if there has. Under these circumstances, we expect to have specialists who actually draw up the agreement. It is clear that such specialists could produce a positive social value. They would be aware of various things that could go wrong, which were not known to the ordinary businessman. The businessman, after all, normally knows only his own business, and not the business of whomever he is dealing with. The attorneys could, by making certain that clauses are put into the contract to cover contingencies which the two parties might well face, but which did not immediately come to their minds, perform a valid social function.

It should be pointed out here that there is another way of dealing with this same problem. If a contract turns out not to cover the contingency that in fact has happened, today the courts will in essence impose a solution of some sort on the parties. Of course, the legal system itself provides a large number of such imposed decisions. It is obvious that the cost of negotiation and foreseeing all of these possibilities is greater than the cost of having something imposed at the time the contingency arises.

If then the point of the attorneys who are engaged in negotiating the actual contract is simply to clarify terms and call the attention of the parties to things that might happen in future which they haven't thought about themselves, we could certainly say that they perform a valid function. Whether the function would be worth their fees is another matter, but I don't see how we

lawyer who pays the costs and makes the calculations that I have mentioned above. But, as a matter of fact, contingency fees are rare in contract actions.

15. *Structure and Change in Economic History*, Douglass North (1987), New York: Norton, pp. 188–91.

can get any empirical evidence on this because, as a matter of fact, our attorneys are mainly involved in something else.

The main duty of attorneys when drawing up a contract is to make sure the contract is drawn up in such a way that a very complex set of previous legal decisions and court decisions are complied with. In other words, they don't seek out the best alternative which works for the two parties, but the alternative which can be pushed through in court. This can be the same thing, but there is no requirement that it be so. It may be that the optimal agreement between the two parties is, due to a decision made in the Court of Errors in Massachusetts in 1877, banned from an inclusion in a contract. It should be said that attorneys are very good at getting around this kind of thing, but they normally do so with very complex, lengthy and expensive clauses.

Here again I am not saying that attorneys are useless, but there is a rent-seeking aspect. If I am attempting to get into a contract with you, and I spend more money to hire a better attorney, he may know of some obscure legal decisions that your attorney doesn't, and take advantage of them to write a contract which, unknown to you, is very much to my advantage.

Under these circumstances, there is a sort of contest between the two parties to have the best attorney. To some extent my attorney has been hired to prevent me from getting into trouble over some contingency that I had not thought about, but to a considerable extent he has also been hired to try to sneak something into the contract which will disadvantage you, without your knowing the real meaning of the obscure paragraph 77 in the contract. Your attorney will attempt to do the same thing.

Once again we have something here that is structurally similar to rent-seeking. Resources are invested which, for each individual party, increase his chance of success. The work of my attorneys to some extent cancels out the value of yours, and yours to some extent cancels out the value of mine. It is like my buying an additional ticket in the lottery, and your buying another to make up for it. To repeat, I have no idea how much of the work of attorneys is of this sort. It can be very tricky. The obvious example is the one that I referred to above, the Pennzoil suit in which highly skilled attorneys on both sides were in disagreement as to what the law was.[16]

It is an unfortunate characteristic of Anglo-Saxon law that it is particularly

16. The ten-billion-dollar award was later reduced by an out-of-court negotiation to "only" two billion.

subject to erroneous interpretations. My impression is that the much briefer law of Europe is not so much subject to misinterpretation, but that is largely because there is less of it.

As an illustrative example, my first book on the law [*The Logic of the Law*] [17] uses a number of exemplary lawsuits in which a Mr Right and Mr Wrong are involved. This book did not exactly take the legal profession by storm. In fact, more or less, I have been thrown into the outer darkness where there is wailing and gnashing of teeth by the law and economics people. This particular part of it, however, led almost every single lawyer who had read the book, and talked about it, to make a comment which I think is of interest. They all said, you do not know who Mr Right or Mr Wrong is until after the lawsuit is over. In other words, our legal system is so vague that you can't tell in advance what the law is.

As a matter of fact they were exaggerating greatly. They were accustomed to dealing with difficult cases, and the fact that many cases are easy had sort of passed out of their thoughts. Nevertheless, the fact that they thought this was a problem is of interest.

Thus drawing up of the contract by a specialist in drawing up contracts obviously has some social product, but it is likely to lead to rent-seeking activity. In this respect, it is similar to the actual enforcement of the contract about which the same two things can be said. To repeat what we have said very often, it is also true with respect to lobbying in Congress, which has a genuine social product, but is apt to degenerate into almost pure rent-seeking.

If we had a method of reaching the truth without using debate between adversaries on both sides, or if we had a method of drawing up a good contract without adversaries on both sides, we could avoid these things. Unfortunately, we don't have such a mechanism.

This does raise the possibility that the rent-seeking costs may be greater than the social product in these cases. I know no way of measuring this, but let me at least speculate on what we could do if it were indeed true.

Suppose that having the two attorneys and the process of enforcing the contract increase the accuracy of the outcome by some amount, and that this amount is less than the actual cost of these services. We could then change to a rule, which in fact has been used by many courts throughout history, which is that you may not have an attorney. Courts that are purely investigative, that is, which simply go and investigate the matter themselves, will nor-

17. *Op. cit.*

mally question the parties, but not necessarily permit the parties to make speeches on their own behalf, and certainly not permit them to have a professional make speeches.

This proposal will impress many of you as shocking, and perhaps reactionary. Still, that is the way traditional Islamic courts operate. Athenian courts also operated that way for a long time.

In order to avoid being referred to as a pure reactionary, I should point out that one of the reforms that Communist Russia intended to put into effect was the abolition of all attorneys, appeals and so on. They thought the Islamic rules were ideal. Needless to say they gave this up rather quickly, but it should be said that advanced social thought in most of the rest of Europe thought that they were right. Lawyers and appellate courts are, generally speaking, unpopular with everybody except themselves.

Thus the argument for permitting lawyers and, for that matter, permitting an adversary process of any sort, must be that the increase in accuracy is greater than its costs. Granted the large costs, this means that the improvement must be very great. For all I know maybe it is. My methods of calculating the accuracy of courts work only when the data are available, and so far it is only available for American and British adversary process courts.

The specialist in drawing up contracts also performs a social service, but once again the question of whether the social service he produces is greater than its costs is an open one. In all of these cases, the individual party gets his money's worth by hiring an attorney, just as the person who buys tickets in the lottery of the original rent-seeking game gets his money's worth, but socially there is a net loss.

Note here that although I am arguing that I don't know for certain that having lawyers is a good idea, I should emphasize I am not arguing that they are paid more than their value to the person who hires them. I am saying that socially it may be that they cost society more than they contribute. This could be particularly true, granted the fact that high-quality lawyers are among the brightest, most energetic and strongly motivated people in our society. In some other activity they presumably would do a good deal of good. They may be doing a great deal of good in their present activity. My theme has been that we don't know.

To return to pure rent-seeking. What I have been saying here could also be said about the lobbyists who deal with Congress. I don't think anybody looking at the output of modern governments could argue that they have a high degree of accuracy or efficiency. It may still be so that this efficiency is higher and their ability to adjust to the desires of the people is higher than if they did not have this elaborate rent-seeking going on.

As you no doubt can guess, I don't think this is so. Indeed, I am convinced that it is not so, but I have to concede that the information upon which we make these decisions is not really decisive. Insofar as I know there has never been democratic or dictatorial government which has not had something similar to lobbying and other kinds of rent-seeking going on within it. Further, I can't think of any legal way of preventing it from happening.

Under the circumstances, the speculation that perhaps attorneys produce a positive value is just that: speculation. The basic problem here, as in war, is that when you have opposed interests, and resources can be invested to the benefit of each one, the value of the process depends on the production function.[18]

All of this is part of the human condition and is not specifically limited to what we think of as conventional seeking of favors from government, legal practice or many other things. The prospects of limiting it may not be strong, but we should certainly investigate them as thoroughly as we can.

18. Once again I refer to "efficient rent-seeking." It is an open question as to whether the resources invested will end up being worth more or less than the benefit derived from them. It is not even certain that it will be better for the winner of the contest, although in general he will gain.

EXCISE TAXATION IN THE RENT-SEEKING SOCIETY

Long ago when I took my first and only course of economics from Henry Simons, he discussed what in those days were called "luxury taxes." This was long before anybody realized that cigarettes could cause lung cancer. The fundamental luxury taxes of the U.S. government, and indeed most other governments in those days, were taxes on cigarettes and alcohol. The taxes on cigarettes were particularly heavy.

Simons pointed out that the real reason for these taxes was that the people who consumed cigarettes did not regard them as a luxury. He pointed out that if you put a tax on potatoes, people will reduce their consumption of potatoes considerably, so the revenue derived from the tax might not be very great. If you put a tax on cigarettes, on the other hand, people will reduce their consumption of cigarettes only slightly. Hence, the net incidence of a tax on "luxuries" was a reduction in the production of "necessities," because the people consuming them had a different attitude toward what was necessary, and what was not, than did the legislators.

Simons thought that the legislators knew all of this, and that the basic reason they were using taxes on cigarettes, alcohol, and the like for raising revenue was simply that they knew the demand for them was very inelastic and, in fact, that consumption would be reduced only slightly. A tobacco tax might not even actually reduce the revenues of tobacco farmers, about which more will be said later. These taxes were very widely dispersed, the incidence in reduction of consumption of other things was very hard to trace, and the likelihood of various difficulties in the legislatures was low.

It should be pointed out that this was long ago, when taxes were generally much lighter than they are now, and various religious influences were also stronger, so taxes on alcohol certainly were backed by a number of clergymen. There were even some who thought that smoking was sinful.

It seems likely that the elasticity of demand for cigarettes, alcohol, marijuana, cocaine, and so on still is quite low. Taxes on them, if left to themselves, would not reduce their consumption very much, but would reduce

Reprinted, with permission, from *Taxing Choice: The Predatory Politics of Fiscal Discrimination*, ed. William F. Shughart II (New Brunswick, N.J., and London: Transaction Publishers, 1997), 369–73.

the consumption of other goods perhaps considerably. I think this is probably one of the reasons why such taxes are still favored by politicians, but there are others. That it is actually undesirable to have people smoking, drinking, and using illicit drugs is now quite widely believed. Except for the particular people who smoke or engage in other politically incorrect behaviors, there is no significant demand for lowering existing taxes or for refraining from raising them.

There have been other developments, though, so it seems likely that there will be little revenue gained from raising excise taxes on cigarettes. It should be said that the tax increases that are being recommended are much lower than the ordinary taxes on cigarettes that one finds in most European countries.

The prospective revenue gains from taxes on cigarettes right now are low. The consumers of cigarettes not only are being bombarded with propaganda about the dangers of the cigarettes, but also are being seriously harassed in various ways. They are frequently compelled to spend considerable periods of time without smoking, which is likely to reduce addiction.

I recently took a nonstop airline trip from Hong Kong to Los Angeles, thirteen hours in the air on Cathay Pacific Airlines. Cathay Pacific is effectively, if not legally, completely free from any regulations since it dominates policy in Hong Kong, its home base. This flight was nonsmoking for the whole of the MD11 aircraft.

Further, most airports have restrictions under which smoking is permitted only in certain places, and on the average, the places where they permit smoking are rather unpleasant. The one in Tucson is a good example, but I have seen it elsewhere.

The combination of a campaign to reduce smoking by propaganda and a program of harassment of people who do smoke seems likely to move the demand curve for smoking sharply to the left. Even if the demand stays relatively inelastic in the price dimension, these other factors may sharply reduce total sales.

The tax increase might be taken by smokers as evidence that they will eventually be forced to stop, and that they may as well get it over with immediately. It is not at all unlikely that revenue from cigarette taxes will fall sharply whether the tax is increased or not, but surely increasing the tax is risky at the moment from the revenue standpoint.

From the revenue standpoint, there is another problem here. The price of tobacco has been held up for the benefit of tobacco farmers for many years.

The system, like most agricultural price supports, involves restricting total production by reducing the amount of land that can be cultivated for that purpose. In fact, tobacco farmers regard their allotments—which are freely transferable within counties—as highly valuable pieces of capital. Any reduction in demand will hit them hard.

It seems fairly certain that a rise in the price of cigarettes as a result of the tax would sharply reduce the revenues that tobacco farmers can get—in essence, it would confiscate rents on their allotments. Thus, the effect on the final price of cigarettes would be less than one might expect if one ignored this aspect of the matter.

Since such a large part of the costs of raising tobacco is the capital value of the allotments, it is likely that the supply of tobacco, as opposed to tobacco products, is extremely inelastic over a considerable range of prices. This is the reason why the tobacco farmers, a well-organized political pressure group, are so much opposed to the tax.

But to return to the harassment of smokers, it is not by any means confined to governmental bodies.[1] Much private harassment is by people who claim they don't like smoke. These claims are, I assume, correct, but it used to be that people who didn't like smoke simply kept their mouths shut.

In essence, as has been said a number of times, the ownership of the air has changed from people who want to smoke to people who do not want to smell smoke. The federal government has taken steps to "prove" that secondhand smoke is a dangerous carcinogen. But even if you accept the bizarre statistical study supposedly demonstrating this, the calculated risk of death from cancer is utterly trivial. Further research may indicate that there is a greater risk, but it may also indicate that there is even less.

An amusing twist on this matter is that recent demographic studies have begun to indicate that smoking may prevent Alzheimer's disease. The studies currently are not conclusive. Indeed, they are rather like the studies linking cigarettes with cancer back in the early days, but it is intriguing that the people interested in public health are not immediately calling for larger studies. As a matter of fact, they are offering criticisms of these studies using exactly the same arguments that the tobacco lobby offered against the early studies supposedly showing that cancer is caused by smoking. But this is merely an amusing phenomenon; it doesn't prove anything.

As mentioned above, there is the problem of ownership of the air, which

1. Cathay Pacific Airlines is not, of course, a governmental body, although it has great influence on the Hong Kong government.

apparently once belonged to smokers and now belongs to nonsmokers. This is a very difficult problem, a type of externality that raises very broad issues. When I was in Taipei recently, I acquired what was either a mild case of flu or a very bad cold. It didn't immobilize me, and I went on to Hong Kong and the Pacific Rim meeting of the Western Economic Association. I attended panels, appeared on some, had meals with other members, and so on. It was almost certain that I was breathing out the virus of my illness, mild though it was. The health risk of my breath was much greater than the health risk that would have occurred had I been smoking.[2]

It could be argued that I should have been compelled to remain in some safe area. This could not have been my hotel room, because I would have left the virus for future occupants, but the hotel could maintain a set of special rooms for people who have diseases, just as they have smoking rooms. Needless to say, this is not what we do, but it is not very obvious that we shouldn't.

My personal opinion is that any mild externality, which my virus was, and which, in my opinion, secondhand smoke also is, should largely be ignored. But that is a personal opinion, and there is no strong argument one way or the other on the issue. I would recommend further research on the point, except that I can't think of any way of undertaking the research.

It appears to be an area where we must depend on political decisions, and where the political decision of necessity has a very large element of error. What we should have is further research. It is astonishing that some forty-five years after the association between lung cancer and smoking was first discovered, we still do not know what the physiological mechanism is.

It might be that there is some single constituent of smoke that can be removed, eliminating this problem. It is also possible that there is a single constituent of smoke that is a specific against Alzheimer's disease and could be given to people in the form of pills. It is also quite possible that the initial studies indicating that smoking protects against Alzheimer's disease are defective, as in 1950 it was possible that the studies showing a relationship between smoking and cancer were defective.

The propaganda and harassment of people who smoke, combined with the requirement that a good many of them spend considerable periods of time without smoking at all because of being in a no-smoking area,[3] are likely

2. I have never smoked at any time in my life.

3. The new building in which I teach at the University of Arizona, McClelland Hall, is a smoke-free building. However, there are some open porches, and you are permitted to go outside and smoke if you wish. Very few of our staff take advantage of the privilege.

to reduce the demand for cigarettes. This will produce a lower demand, even if it remains inelastic.

In dealing with the fiscal aspects of a tax on smoking, you should pay attention to the expenses that smoking either imposes on or saves for the government. To begin with, consider the current, by no means certain, evidence that smoking is a specific against Alzheimer's disease. This is a very expensive illness, because a person who has it is not likely to die soon, but requires expensive custodial care.

The diseases caused by smoking, however, are cheap diseases. When you get lung cancer, the odds are very good that you will die and that the treatment given to you, while you are waiting to die, will be relatively inexpensive. On the other hand, if you do not get lung cancer and you live longer, the odds are that you will draw at length on Social Security funds, and that you will become eligible for very, very expensive treatments for one or more of the large number of ailments that afflict the elderly. The same can be said about the various heart problems that can be caused by smoking.

From the fiscal standpoint, then, it would appear that we would be wise to encourage smoking. Obviously, I realize that there are other arguments. After all, executing everybody at the age of sixty-five would also reduce the fiscal burden. Simply repealing the pension system and not paying for medical care of older people would do the same.

All of these examples show that fiscal arguments are not decisive in such matters; indeed, most people don't even like to think about them. If we do think about fiscal matters, it is clear that reducing the amount of smoking is hard on the government. It can increase expenses and reduce tax revenues.

Of course, we don't know whether the amount of smoking would fall solely from the propaganda and harassment even without a tax increase. If it would, then a tax increase might well generate additional revenue, because there would still be elements of inelasticity in the demand.

People do not think of the problem of tobacco smoking in terms of revenue. Indeed, the introduction of this consideration in the Clinton health care reform program changed the general discussion considerably. The basic issue nowadays is that a great many people want to try to help other people by forcing them to stop smoking, along with the issue of who owns the air, which involves a mild genuine externality.

Both of these questions are ones in which the economist can offer some help, but where the answers have to be based on noneconomic criteria. Thus I hope this chapter may be of some help in clarifying thinking about them, but I refrain from telling you what I think your answers should be.

PART 4

THE COST OF RENT SEEKING

THE COSTS OF RENT SEEKING

A METAPHYSICAL PROBLEM

It is well known that one of the reasons that Congressmen vote for such things as protective tariffs and the farm subsidy program is that they think it will attract votes. Economists are almost always opposed to these items because they think that they injure the voters. Technically speaking, what happens is that the voters specialize their vote, i.e., concentrate their entire preference function on one particular issue (or a few issues) which has considerable importance to them. Other voters, concentrating their voting decision on other special issues, ignore the well-being of the first voter.

Economists would argue that all of the voters are worse off than if they had not so specialized their votes. On the other hand democracy is supposed to give the voter his choice, not what some economists think that they should choose. The voters vote for such things. Can we count this as a cost?

There is another problem here, which is that voters are apt to be very badly informed. Indeed any *Public Choice* scholar worth his salt at sometime during his teaching proves to his students that the rational voter who gives thought to the matter will decide not to be well informed about politics unless he happens to regard politics as a hobby.

As an example of the difficulties here, consider the following from the former Chairman of the President's Council of Economic Advisors Herbert Stein: "The 'problem' of the deficit is to make the decisions as well informed and as responsive to the desires of the public as possible."[1] The problem, of course, is that if the public is systematically poorly informed, then the two criteria are inconsistent. And the public *is* systematically ill-informed.

The problem raised by individuals making choices, which from the outside seems to be unwise, is a real one. Do such choices impose a cost on the chooser? Note that in the market and in politics, this is a hard question to answer, but fortunately in the market, it is rarely, if ever, an important question. If we are trying to measure the cost of rent seeking, it may be very important,

Reprinted, with kind permission of Kluwer Academic Publishers, from *Public Choice* 57 (1988): 15–24.

1. H. Stein, "Balancing the Budget—Compared with What?" *AEI Economist* (February 1987): 3.

indeed, because it may be the principal payoff to a Congressman for votes for, let's say, the farm program, come his reelection by voters who are voting because of the farm program. Is this a cost?

Let us digress a little bit and talk about costs in the private market in cases where information is poor. Two hundred years ago someone who was ill would go to a doctor and ask to be bled. Suppose the doctor bleeds him, using a knife which he has earlier that day used to bleed eight or ten people with assorted diseases. He has never sterilized the knife, because he has never heard of germs. Ignoring the germ problem, bleeding is a treatment which will make the person worse almost regardless of what disease he has. Is there a cost in this? With our present scientific knowledge, this was clearly an erroneous decision by the purchaser of medical services.

To make the problem a little more difficult, let us assume it is not 200 years ago, but 130 years ago and that most doctors and most patients have realized that bleeding is not a good treatment. Suppose, however, that an old-fashioned patient and an old-fashioned doctor reach a mutually agreeable bargain under which the doctor bled the patient once again, using an unsterilized knife. Does this impose a "cost" on the patient?

These questions are not very important for a student of the market, but, once again, when we turn to rent seeking, they are significant. Let us take an example where the people are well informed but where there are externalities. Suppose a car driver is polluting the air, and this is in the early 1950s, where there are no regulations on it. He would be aware of the fact that if he stopped polluting the air, it would have almost no effect on him although everyone else in the society and, for the matter, he himself would be trivially better off. Since the cost would fall entirely on him, and the benefit to him would be trivial, he would choose not to do so. This would be so even if the benefit from that act, summed over the entire society, was very considerably greater than the cost to him. Economists normally say that, in this case, he would be imposing a cost on the society, and they would favor social institutions to compel him either to stop imposing his pollution on the society or at least to pay its full costs.

Let us go to another case which is a closer fit to what we have in mind. Suppose that the society is proposing to restrict air pollutants and that the dry-cleaning establishments organized for the purpose of being exempted from the act. They make deals with various other pressure groups agreeing to vote for Congressmen who favor restricting the import of Japanese automobiles, favor the farm program, etc. As a result they get their exemption built into the act with the result that the level of air pollution is very considerably higher than it otherwise would be. Is this a cost?

The last is particularly important because it seems very largely true that rent seeking depends on just exactly that kind of maneuvering, and the question of whether it is a cost or not is important in attempting to measure the cost of rent seeking. Suppose, for example, that we have perfect information and are able to investigate all of the influences which led to, let us say, the farm program getting through. We found that misinformation about the farm program on the part of non-farmers was important. As a result of their ignorance they did not push against it, and the farmers used their influence to get it. These two factors between them are, let us say, 90% of the "causal" factors, which led to its going through. There were, in addition to this, some campaign contributions, spectacular dinners with feminine companionship, and possibly bribes, but these things added up to less than 10% of the "causal" factors. Would we include the 90% in the cost of rent seeking or would we not?

Suppose that we have a political system like that which is sometimes seen in high school civics texts, in which the voters vote in terms of what they think is good for the country. These texts imply, probably not too inaccurately, that what is good for the country is also good for the individual voter. The voter, being systematically uninformed, would make a very bad choice of policies to benefit the country. If we turn to a realistic situation, in which at least a great many voters vote specifically to benefit themselves by such things as the farm program, the outcome would certainly be different than if they were voting in terms of the "public interest," but it's not obvious that it will be inferior.

As a former Foreign Service Officer and a man much interested in foreign policy, I have paid careful attention to the development of American policies in this area. No doubt, some of them are motivated by fairly selfish drives on the part of the voters. At one time, for example, the aid program was keeping the American locomotive industry alive. On the other hand, there is equally no doubt that a number of the policies do not have any particular selfish group in the United States pushing them.

Our generally vague desire that foreign countries be democracies is an example. In this case, a great many Americans will maintain, without showing any signs of realizing how absurd it is, that such democratic governments are in the interest of the United States as well as something we think is ethically good. This is, however, pretty clearly a rationalization. Schumpeter described

American policy as "ethical imperialism," i.e., an effort to impose the American ethical system throughout the world.[2] This is something that most Americans want, although most of them refuse to admit that it is their objective. It doesn't have very much in the way of selfish benefit for the average American.

The point, however, of this discussion is that, having studied the situation for a considerable number of years, it is my impression that the common good of the United States in foreign affairs is, on the whole, damaged more by the policies which aim (ignorantly) at the general public good rather than by the policies which are the result of rent seeking.

This is of course merely a subjective option, and in any event, even granted the reader agrees with me about foreign policy, it would not prove the same relative damage was done by the two different criteria in domestic affairs. What we have here is a case of voters who, if they get involved in attempting to deal with the public good would do so in a very badly informed way. If the rent seekers are pushing for some special benefit for themselves, they also will not be very well informed and not engage in a great deal of thought about the problem. But the odds are that the policy will be more likely to serve their selfish interests than "publicly interested" policy is to serve the public good.

It is not at all obvious, even if we look at this from the standpoint of an abstract external observer who knows all, that we would object to the voters specializing their interests. It may not do as much damage as attempting to implement the public good.

Another problem is that in some cases we want the special interest to be implemented. My first article in this general area dealt with the situation in which road repairing, up to a point, benefitted people who lived on the road to be repaired more than the cost imposed on society as a whole.[3] There are many cases of this sort, i.e., situations in which for some reason or another it is hard for a small group to provide something which is of interest to them, but where providing it would cost society less than the benefit to the small group. In these circumstances we would suggest that society provide it on the assumption that all of us will from time to time be in the same small group situation.

The problem is, of course, that the small group may push for things where

2. A. Schumpeter, *Capitalism, Socialism and Democracy* (New York: Harper, 1942).

3. G. Tullock, "Problems of Majority Voting," *Journal of Political Economy* 67 (December 1959): 571–79.

the benefit to them is smaller, indeed in many cases immensely smaller, than the injury inflicted on other people. Unfortunately, these rent seekers may get their way.

Of course, our desire to impose our ethical system on other people may also have very negative effects. William Jennings Bryan was Secretary of State in the early part of the Wilson Administration. His policy towards China, which was an active one, aimed at the objective of not interfering with the rapid conversion of China to Christianity which he believed was taking place at that time. Indeed, he not only refrained from interfering with it, he was in favor of pushing it ahead. This was an ethically driven policy intended to do good, and the most one can say for it is that quite possibly it did no positive harm.

In a way, the Chinese Revolution was brought on by President William Howard Taft who was making a very ill-advised[4] effort to obtain special privileges for American bankers.[5] In doing so he delayed the construction of some important railroads. The delay, through a set of devious channels, was the initiating cause of the revolution in the same sense that the assassination of Archduke Franz Ferdinand was the initiating cost of World War I.

All of this has been simply a general discussion. Let's try and do a little formal reasoning. For this purpose, let me assume someone has produced a computer which knows everybody's utility and is able to calculate those private and public decisions which will maximize that utility.[6]

Let us begin with private purchases and assume that this computer is in charge of somebody's purchases and buys the things for that person which will maximize his or her lifetime utility. In 1776 this would not have ordered a bleeding, for example. Compare this with the decision that would have been made by that person himself, assuming that he also had perfect knowledge about that nature of all products and services on the market, but not perfect knowledge about his own utility production function. The last seems a little absurd, but you do buy things which you think you'll enjoy and then discover that you don't. The computer would not make this kind of error.

Thus, the computer would do better than the purchaser would even if the

4. The advice came from the Department of State which simply misunderstood economics.

5. The bankers didn't want them.

6. We need not worry about the problem of comparing utility between persons. Science fiction, after all, is science fiction.

purchaser devoted an infinite amount of time studying before each purchase.[7] It would, in fact, do better than any human instrumentality because it would know things that have not yet been discovered. In reality, of course, the individual does not know very much about most of the products and services he buys. Further, he in essence depends on other people to make a lot of the preliminary decisions for him.

I buy clothes from stores that specialize in producing clothing for people who, like myself, are in the upper- but a long way from the top-income brackets. In doing so, I am assuming, first that my fellow consumers from this store do at least a reasonably good job in judging price and quality and secondly, that the store owners who want to make money by pleasing their customers do a reasonably good job at meeting those standards. I am to some extent free riding on the other customers, and each of them is free riding on me. If turned to such subjects as medicine, electronic devices, etc., my state of knowledge differs even farther from that of our super computer.

Bentham, as mentioned above, dealt with this problem by saying that we should let the individual make decisions not because those decisions would necessarily be right, but because they were more in accord with his utility than would be any other mechanism we could design. In other words, he denied the existence of my super computer. Since it is only an imaginary construct, I naturally would not disagree with him. Thus, it is probably sensible to let people make decisions of this sort, and indeed we can refer to a society in which such decisions control almost everything as being optimal in what is not a nonsensical use of the word "optimal." Those critics of the market system who point out that customers are frequently ill-informed are quite right. But once we get out of the market, the information problem is much more severe.

It's not widely known, but one of the things that the market provides to the private citizens is an opportunity to benefit other people. They may contribute money to the American Cancer Society, George Mason University, or simply give money to a beggar on the street. In all of these cases, you would say that they are purchasing a feeling of satisfaction gained by benefitting other people, although, once again, information can be bad.[8] Indeed, in this case the information is far more likely to be bad than in the straightforward

7. With the infinite time somehow having zero cost to him.

8. G. Tullock, "Information without Profit," *Papers on Non-Market Decision Making* (Charlottesville, Va.: Thomas Jefferson Center for Political Economy, 1966).

purchase, because the individual who is purchasing a feeling of satisfaction from having made the gift will not himself directly benefit or be injured as a result of what the gift actually provides.

Once again, Bentham would say, and I do not disagree, that the individual should make this decision, seeking out whatever advice he thinks is sensible.[9]

So far we have been comparing the computer with decisions made by individuals in the market environment. Further, we have totally ignored externalities. We must now deal with externalities because we are going to turn now to talking about government, specifically democratic government. After all, externalities are the basic reason that we have governments. Hence it is sensible to leave them aside in discussing the market. The government should deal with them, although anyone who looks at actual governments realizes that they're almost as likely to generate externalities as to eliminate them.

Let us then turn, once again, to our perfect computer and assume that it is dealing with some decision which, due to externalities, must be made collectively. The computer, knowing all and making no calculating mistakes, determines whether some particular government activity should be undertaken and its scale. Of course, our perfect computer could also allocate the entire cost of the activity among the taxpayers in such a way that the cost was proportional to the benefit, but we will assume that it does not do that; it uses ordinary taxes. Thus, there will be probably some people gaining and some people losing. What the computer does is to make certain that the total gain in utility is greater than the total loss. Once again, I would like to emphasize that the machine is a piece of science fiction designed for this article.

The actual behavior of the voters is apt to deviate sharply from this ideal pattern of behavior for two reasons, one of which is they're not perfectly informed nor perfect calculators. The other is that individuals will favor things that benefit themselves, even if the total cost is greater than the total benefit. Let us take these two problems up, one at a time, beginning with information.

As mentioned above, there is a very elderly and respectable proof in the Public Choice literature which demonstrates that individuals are normally badly informed in politics, and this is particularly true with respect to what we might call public interest types of matters. These individual decisions are

9. I knew a wealthy man whose foundation provided financial support for tournaments between professional bridge players. I thought this was a total waste of money, but he didn't. The Internal Revenue Service ruled that it was a charitable contribution.

apt to deviate from the decisions of our computer in a fairly extreme way simply because of poor information.

This poor information is not just poor information in the sense of lack of calculation, however. Our computer not only makes all perfect computations, but knows what other people's utilities are. The average voter will not know other people's utility.

When it comes to matters directly affecting the voter, he is apt to be better informed than in matters of general interest. To say that he is apt to be better informed is quite different from saying he is apt to be very well informed. Here too, public good consideration means that the single person who is one of a group of one hundred thousand who will be benefitted by something or other will devote not too much time to becoming well informed about it. In fact, if he is well informed it is more likely to be for other reasons. He reads farming journals for technical help in running his farm and gets political information as a by-product.

When we turn to individual's knowledge of other people's utility, the situation becomes even worse. Firstly, he may not be interested in whether they are gaining or not, but, secondly, if he is interested in helping them, and most of us are to some extent interested in helping others, he has very little information as to what actually will help them. In particular, if we look at the programs to help the poor, it is obvious that the people who design them think that the poor's judgement of what will benefit them is bad. Payments in kind are very common under such circumstances, and detailed efforts to regulate the lives of the people who are being aided are also very common. In a way, the charitably inclined person is like our giant computer attempting to give people what is good for them and not what they, ill-informedly, want.

There is an area where possibly bad information benefits society when looked at in the whole matter on a large scale. The individual probably has an ill-thought-out set of principles of public behavior and morality which will affect his voting behavior when he hears that something has gone on in government which he objects to. Scandals such as misappropriation of funds are an obvious example, but there are a whole collection of others. In particular, transfers or special regulations that benefit small groups have to be to some extent presented in deceptive ways which makes them much less efficient than they otherwise would be. This lack of efficiency, however, has the positive benefit that it reduces the profit from these activities and hence reduces the amount of energy that rent seekers will put into attempting to get them.

On the other hand, there is no doubt that the fact that these are ill thought out has a major disadvantage. Anyone who is attempting to sell a significant government reform knows the normal immediate reaction of simple objection with nothing very well thought out in the way of reasons for that objection and an unwillingness to devote much time and thought to the matter. The standard approach of the average voter is moralistic, and he will accept moral criticism of the government and, in fact, suggest the government become more moral. But any attempt to convince him that the structure is somehow badly designed is normally resisted, and the resistance is not based upon serious thought or good information.

The second problem is that the individual, unlike our machine, is interested in himself more than in other people. To repeat, he probably has, as most of us do, at least some interest in helping the country, the poor, the people who are suffering from cancer, etc. But this is usually less intense than his desire to help himself and his family.

If it were not for the externalities problem, and in politics the externality frequently takes the form of a tax on somebody else, we could ignore that matter. We could let individuals all make their decisions in terms of what benefitted them, and assume that those issues which passed by majority vote, be it directly or by logrolling, on the average will be beneficial. They would not be quite as good as our machine's calculation, but they wouldn't be very much inferior.

Unfortunately, of course, governmental activities are externality laden, and the decision of the textile workers, for example, to push for a tariff on textiles[10] will generate very decided external costs.

Suppose then that we observe a set of protective tariffs which were voted through democratically. We sometimes say they are costly, because they differ from what would have been passed if the voters had all been simply interested in maximizing the public interest. But are they really costly? This is the problem that I have been leading up to in this article.

It seems possible that the principal payment that politicians in the United States receive from rent-seeking groups comes not in the form of elaborate dinners or direct cash payments, but in the form of specialized votes. The special interest group which makes it clear that it has a sizeable number of voters who will ignore all other considerations and vote solely in terms of whether

10. I've just been informed that a senior professor in one of the states which produces textiles is in the process of being driven from his university because he wrote a paper in which he said that textile tariffs were a bad idea.

their Congressman has or has not backed, let us say, a cotton textile tariff inflicts an injury on the economy as a whole, but can we say that these votes are in fact costly?

In a democracy, the government is supposed to be controlled by the votes cast. If the voters vote for something which economists think is not in fact desirable, can we call it a cost? Can we follow the Benthamite assumption that their judgement is better than any other judgement here? Note that, once again, Bentham's judgement did not turn on any argument that they were right, but on the argument that individuals knew more about their own utility than anyone else. It should of course also be pointed out that Bentham would be horrified by a cotton textile tariff.

This whole problem turns on deep metaphysical views as to what the government is supposedly doing. Most economists think of government as an organization for internalizing externalities. It makes it possible for us to reach a higher level of satisfaction than we could without it. From that standpoint the cotton textile tariff clearly is undesirable. We might argue that the government as a whole is highly desirable even if it does enact tariffs on cotton textiles, but still, we can say that the cotton textile tariff is simply wrong.

If on the other hand we, and once again as most economists do, believe that the people should get what they choose, the cotton textile tariff is right and desirable. Add on the prospect that if the voters stop voting in terms of their special interest and began voting in terms of the public interest, their motives for becoming well informed would be extremely weak, and hence their decisions would have almost a random relationship to that public interest. Then the problem becomes even more difficult.

Let me add on a final item of difficulty and then resign the problem to my readers. The final item concerns the fact that pressure groups very commonly deliberately spread misinformation among the voters. Thus, a regulation may be so designed that it benefits some participants in a given industry but not in others, but it would be sold on the theory that it benefits "the industry." To take an example, when the AAA was introduced in the 1930s it benefitted the owners of agricultural land a great deal and injured hired labor in agriculture a great deal. I suspect that most hired laborers would have favored Congressmen who voted for this bill, because they thought it was good for "agriculture." Certainly they were encouraged to do so by the farm groups' propaganda.

This, however, is within the group; outside you also have this kind of misinformation. The widespread view among the citizenry that protective tariffs are beneficial not just to the industry that is protected, but to everybody, is an example. Suppose that someone votes for something which he mistakenly thinks will benefit him because he is a member of a special interest group, but it will not. Is this a "cost"? Suppose that a citizen whose only connection with the cotton textile industry is to buy clothes is convinced that at the very least a Congressman voting for a protective tariff on textiles is doing nothing which injures him and perhaps doing something that benefits him. Once again, is this a cost?

The problem here is how much weight we should give to people's ill-considered views as to what should be done. The argument for giving them overwhelming weight in private decisions is not only Benthamite, but favored by practically all other economists. For public decisions the argument is not nearly as strong.

There is another problem. We have no objection to people making their market decisions in terms of their own selfish well-being. Once again, in the case of the government it is not so obvious that we should feel that way. On the other hand, it is not at all obvious that we shouldn't.

I subtitled this article "A Metaphysical Question." Metaphysics, in this case, is not meant in strict technical terms, but in the sense of a rather confusing problem. Further, it is a problem of great importance, particularly for the analysis of rent seeking. This essay certainly does not solve it. Can the readers do better?

RENTS, IGNORANCE, AND IDEOLOGY

This chapter will begin my substantive efforts to explain the small size of the rent-seeking industry. In it I will make some modifications in the theory which are intended to make it fit the world better. The change will not appear gigantic, and indeed I do not think it is, but it is a movement toward greater realism. Furthermore, it does not in any way reduce the waste that has normally been blamed on rent seeking. In my "Rents and Rent Seeking,"[1] I greatly expanded this waste, and this chapter leaves that expansion intact. In essence, the quantity of waste is left unchanged, but the form of that waste is altered.

I have already pointed out that the size of the rent-seeking industry seems too small. Let me elaborate the point by a brief discussion of some observational problems with the present-day rent-seeking theory. First, the rents do not seem to be large enough. Congressman Biaggi, for example, saved a gigantic dockyard in Brooklyn from bankruptcy by intervention with the federal government. He was tried and convicted of having accepted three vacations in Florida at a total value of $3,000 from the management of the dockyard.[2] This appears to be utterly trivial compared with the amount of money in question.

As another example, the formal lobbyists hired by the Chrysler Corporation for the Chrysler bail-out were paid a total of $390,000.[3] Once again, this amount seems trivial. In both cases it is likely that there are some payments that were not publicized. If they were ten times as much as the payments that are known publicly, however, this would still be insignificant compared with the government action.

Campaign contributions also seem too small. If we assume that the total

Reprinted, with kind permission of Kluwer Academic Publishers, from *The Economics of Special Privilege and Rent Seeking* (Boston/Dordrecht/London: Kluwer Academic Publishers, 1989), 11–27. Copyright 1989 Kluwer Academic Publishers.

1. *The Political Economy of Rent-Seeking*, Charles K. Rowley, Robert D. Tollison, and Gordon Tullock (eds.) (Boston: Kluwer Academic Publishers, 1988), pp. 51–62.

2. The congressman has been convicted in another much larger scam. In this case, the amount he allegedly was paid was several million dollars but the cost to the federal government was many times that much.

3. *New Deals, The Chrysler Revival and the American System*, Robert B. Reich and John D. Donahue (New York: Penguin Books, 1986), pp. 204–5.

in the average election is a billion dollars (probably an overestimate),[4] it is still small compared with the economic size of the various restrictions imposed on the economy to the benefit of particular groups. Direct budgetary cost, not counting the increase in prices, of our agricultural program runs between $15 billion and $30 billion a year. Total campaign contributions from farmers are a small part of that.

Further evidence is indicated by the lifestyle of American politicians. Unlike presidents of Mexico, these Americans do not retire as vastly wealthy men. They are no doubt well off, but their style of life indicates that they are far from being extremely wealthy. Given the total social cost of the distortions which they have imposed on the economy for the benefit of special interest groups, this seems odd.[5]

To take a specific example, the members of the Texas Railroad Commission conferred benefits worth many billions of dollars on the oil industry. They were elected officials, and their lifestyles, both when on the commission and when retired (one served for 33 years), indicate that they mainly lived on their modest salaries. This was, of course, frequently supplemented by elaborate dinners and visits to expensive resorts, but their returns were trivial compared with the effect of their decisions.[6] These casual observations are not the kind of measures that we would like, but they are unlikely to be off by ten orders of magnitude.

If the observed size of the rent-seeking industry seems to contradict existing rent-seeking theory, it is not alone. There is a second observation to supplement it; simply that the rents are normally transferred by extremely inefficient means. Giving someone a monopoly in something is a socially inefficient way of transferring to him whatever profit he makes. Further, in most

4. *One Billion Dollars of Influence: The Direct Marketing of Politics*, R. Kenneth Godwin (Chatham House, Chatham, N.J., 1989). Provides a large body of data on the use of money in politics, basically money raised by direct mailing. For individual elections the amounts are way under a billion dollars in spite of the title.

5. For an amusing example of the triviality of these things, see "Policy Making in Washington: Some Personal Observations," by James C. Miller III, *Southern Economic Journal* (1984), p. 395. Incidentally, Dr. Miller kindly read an earlier draft of this paper and gave strong general approval to its theme. Given his combination of economic expertise and governmental experience, I regard this as a strong endorsement.

6. For a detailed account of the matter, see Gary D. Libecap's "Political Economy of Fuel Oil Cartelization by the Texas Railroad Commission 1933–1972" (August 1977), as yet unpublished.

cases where valuable production controls are provided, they are not awarded to a single person or organization but to a considerable group of producers who find themselves facing a higher price than would be obtained from the unhampered market, but who increase production competitively in order to take advantage of that price. Libecap demonstrates that the Texas Railroad Commission did not even come close to maximizing the profits of the Texas oil producers.[7]

"The CAB [Civil Aeronautics Board] controlled price competition, but allowed airlines to compete for customers by offering non-price frills like free drinks, movies, and half empty planes. The airlines competed away, through additional costs, the rents granted them by the prices the CAB set."[8] In the later days of the regulations one of the transcontinental airlines actually had a piano bar on its flights. This was simply an extreme indication of the half-empty nature of the aircraft which was in competition with others for passengers at the CAB price. The airlines were, in fact, not making markedly higher profits than they do today when the seats are closer together, more fully occupied, and less expensive.

Why, then, do we observe both of these phenomena? Note that I have given no extended citations, because I presume the reader can simply look around. As a possible answer there is an argument by Becker (partially supported by Peltzman) implying that there is no inefficiency in the system. I do not believe it, but will defer answering it until I have presented a theory of wasteful rent seeking.

In figure 1, I show a situation in which rent seekers confront technical difficulties: specifically, that they can only get their rents by choosing an inappropriate technology of production. We defer discussing why they would be forced to choose such an inappropriate technology until the basic theory has been explained.

In figure 1 we have the usual demand and supply curves. The supply (CC) in this case is variable cost. The triangle between line CC and the price P_0 is the rent derived by the owners of fixed resources in this industry. We can consider it as wheat land, and this is a Ricardian rent. The producers now orga-

7. Libecap, unpublished.

8. Dennis Mueller, *Public Choice II* (draft of second edition), chapter 15, p. 13. He cites Douglas and Miller, but this is a draft, and the citation is incomplete. See also *The Politics of Deregulation*, Martha Derthick and Paul J. Quirk (Washington, D.C.: Brookings, 1985), pp. 152–53.

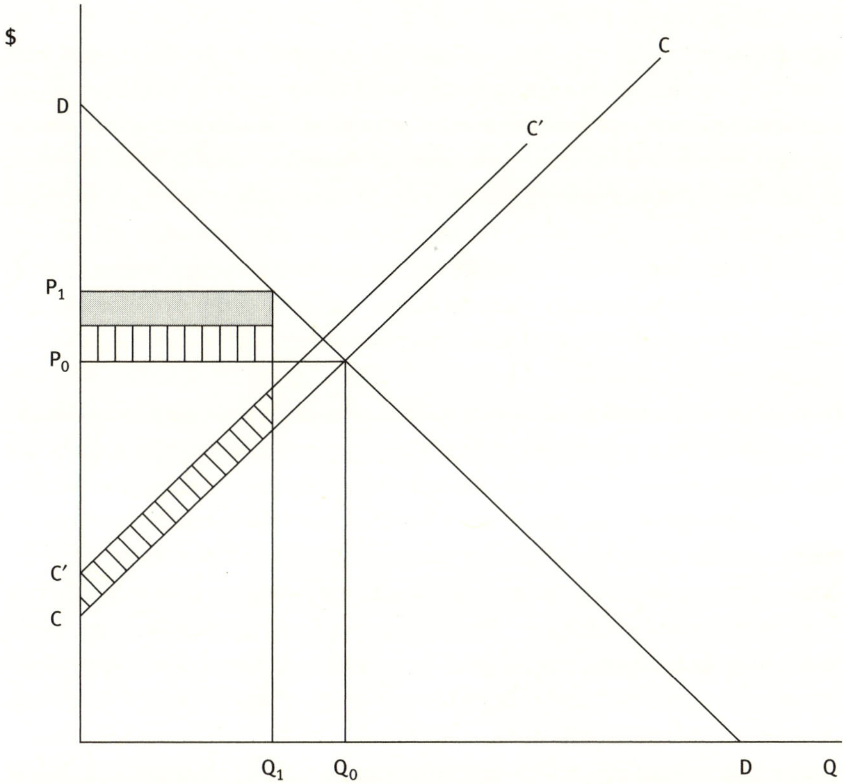

FIGURE 1
Hampered rent seeking

nize and obtain government restrictions.[9] The specific details of the restrictions would be determined by political considerations which are outside the scope of this chapter.

Assume here, however, that the trade restriction carries with it adoption of a less efficient production method shown by the increase of cost to C′C′. The price rises to P_1 and quantity falls to Q_1. The standard rent-seeking rectangle is shown to the left of Q_1 between P_0 and P_1. I have broken

9. A private monopoly would be just as conformable for our analysis, and perhaps in 1890 would have been a better subject. Today, however, most trade restrictions are government sponsored.

the rectangle into two categories in the figure for reasons that will become obvious later.[10]

Let us consider the occurrence of Luddism in early-nineteenth-century England. Workers, apparently paid by competing manufacturers,[11] broke the knitting frames used to make stockings. If the workers were working, they would have produced something for society. When they simply stop working, society loses that product. Of course, the principal sufferers are the idle workers themselves. When they occupy their time breaking machines, however, society loses not only their positive product but the machines, too.[12] Society does not have its product but does have a lot of broken knitting frames.

Traditional rent-seeking literature has counted only the equivalent of the broken machines and has ignored the loss of positive product. Thus, the real cost is greater than previous scholars (including Tullock) have realized. The workers not only created illth[13] in the form of machine breaking, but they refrained from creating wealth. Both are costs.

We are here assuming that the rent-seeking activity has carried with it not only a restriction but a requirement that inefficient technology be used. Thus, the cost line goes up to C′C′, and there is a net loss from the inefficient technology shown by the area with slanting lines. Since the people still remaining in the industry, i.e., those that are not eliminated by the restriction, have to use this technology, and it raises their costs, I have transferred this area up to the rent-seeking rectangle, where it is shown by the vertically lined sub-rectangle. The actual return on the rent seeking from the standpoint of the people who organized it, then, is the vertically lined sub-rectangle, much smaller than the total increase in price. This, of course, is a consequence of the need to use an inefficient method.

Returning to our Luddite example, the frames broken were the property

10. The standard Harberger triangle and the larger area just below it are not specially shaded. This is to improve the clarity of the diagram. I presume the reader can recognize them on his own.

11. See "Luddism as Cartel Support," Robert D. Tollison and Gary Anderson, *Journal of Institutional and Theoretical Economics* (December 1986), pp. 727–38.

12. Since in this case they were being paid by rival manufacturers (Tollison and Anderson, 1986), the whole cost fell on the customers through higher prices.

13. "Illth," a word traditionally ascribed to John Stuart Mill, although I do not know of a specific citation, is the opposite of wealth. Unfortunately, a great deal of economic activity generates illth instead of wealth.

of efficient cutthroat competitors. The manufacturers who had hired the Luddites were more conservative in both their technology and their merchandising. Their gain would not be the entire increase in price shown by the whole rectangle but only a portion of it. Part of the increase in price would be eaten up by the necessity of using more expensive manufacturing techniques, shown by the shaded sub-rectangle. Their return on hiring the frame breakers would be only the dotted sub-rectangle. Presumably the amount they spent in hiring Luddites, the rent-seeking cost would not exceed this sub-rectangle.

But even this does not show the total loss. The workers imposed a positive loss on society by breaking the machines. The machine owners' loss when the frames were broken is not directly on our diagram. More importantly, the machine breakers presumably earned only a normal return on their labor when they engaged in this destructive activity. If they had been hired at the same wages to do something constructive, society would have been better off by both their product and the absence of the destruction. The positive product that they could have produced is not on our figure. Thus, the real rent-seeking loss is even greater than the classical literature implies.

While we are examining this construction, let me point out that empirically it immediately explains the low resource investment in rent seeking. The reason that the apparent payoffs to people who arrange the rents are so low in our society is that the actual "profit" to the beneficiaries of the rents is much lower than the traditional measure of the value of rent seeking (in this case, the tradition being only about 20 years). Thus, Congressman Biaggi may, in fact, have obtained the full value of his intervention.

It is not only the airlines and the Brooklyn dockyard where this problem comes up. Consider agriculture. The government program, in general, has taken the form of restricting the amount of real estate that may be used in producing crops. This has led farmers to change their production technology so that it uses less land and more fertilizer and other resources (at a higher cost because they could have used that technology before).

The current program has been modified to prevent such costs from becoming infinite, but the use of historic levels means that much of the previous technology is retained. Further, the present system prevents certain technological changes that might improve efficiency. More on this later. The long-run gain to the farmers is much less than the subsidy plus the increase in price.

Most government restriction programs will turn out to have this particular characteristic. They are cartels without any binding restriction on the quantity of resources invested. Farmers, for example, for many years faced a restriction on the amount of land they could use, but not on other resources. People can and do invest resources and change their technology as a result of the restrictive arrangement; hence, the profit to the producers is considerably less than the cost to the purchasers. This is in addition to the deadweight loss shown by the Harberger triangle. The situation should be described as "handicapped competition" rather than monopoly or oligopoly.

Thus, for true rent seeking, the total cost is not only the dotted rectangle, or even the dotted rectangle plus the vertically lined area that is the traditional rent-seeking cost, but as in the machine-breaking example discussed above, there is also the loss of what would have been produced if the same resources had been used productively.[14] Thus, the resources that are used for the purpose of creating rents, i.e., lobbying the government for some restriction, not only are wasted, but they are positively detrimental, as in the case of the workers who devoted their energies to destroying machines. The cost is the sum of the positive damage and the simple waste of those resources.

But what about the use of the inefficient technology in this case? The arguments so far appear to apply only to the dotted rectangle, or possibly the dotted rectangle minus the loss of standard Ricardian rents shown by the lower small triangle. Resources used in producing under the technological inefficiency would appear to be simply wasted. We have here what amounts to a metaphysical problem that has to do with the meaning of waste and the meaning of injury. Since we are assuming that government requires this particular wasteful method of technology as a "payoff" for the restriction, the resources involved in producing it are also part of the resources used to reduce production.

The skilled professional lobbyist hired by the farm lobby tells them that if they really want to get a subsidy out of the government, it is essential that they take the subsidy in a form that lowers the technological efficiency of the agricultural sector. They must use less land and more fertilizer. The change in technology is as much an effort to get the reduction in total product and the general lowering of our GNP as was the money directly spent on (or by) the lobbyist.

14. See my "Rents and Rent-Seeking," *The Political Economy of Rent-Seeking*, Charles K. Rowley, Robert D. Tollison, and Gordon Tullock (eds.)(Boston: Kluwer Academic Publishers, 1988), pp. 51–62, for a more complete explanation.

Returning to our Luddite example, they did not break all knitting frames but only those of the most efficient manufacturers.[15] The additional cost of inefficient manufacturing would also be a cost of the rent seeking. The additional costs imposed by those guidelines which the lobbyist thinks are necessary in order to get the restriction would also be social costs of the farm program. Clearly the waste here is both the loss of the work the farmer could have accomplished and the additional costs of using these resources in a destructive way.

When we turn to the necessary adoption of an inefficient method of production as part of the rent-earning activity, we have the problem that its total cost may be quite hard to measure. This is because such inefficient technologies may generate external effects on people who are not even in the industry in question. The arrangement under which the airlines flew aircraft half empty across the continent was, among other things, supposed to increase the demand for aircraft, and it quite possibly did.[16]

What we can say is that the industry itself will only fight for a system under which the costs of the inefficient technology for that industry are less than the benefit it obtains from the restriction. Further, it will use resources in the usual rent-seeking method—for example, lobbying—up to the point where the surplus above the cost of production under the inefficient technology and the price that can be derived under the restriction are fully absorbed by the rent-seeking activity.

As the reader will know if he or she has seen my "Efficient Rent Seeking"[17] and the various articles that have come out of it, I am not sure that this is true. (The reader who is not familiar with this material will find a reprise in chapter 4.) Leaving this problem temporarily aside, the standard approach to the cost of rent seeking, from the time of "The Welfare Costs of Tariffs, Monopolies, and Theft"[18] to the present, has been to assume that there is no reason for the return on investment in lobbying and other rent-seeking activity to be any different from the return on the investment in, say, building a steel

15. See Tollison and Anderson, 1986.

16. This is a subject of dispute.

17. In *Toward a Theory of the Rent-Seeking Society*, James M. Buchanan, Robert D. Tollison, and Gordon Tullock (eds.) (College Station: Texas A&M University Press, 1980), pp. 97–112. This article set off a fairly lengthy series of comments mainly published in *Public Choice*. The whole exchange is contained in *The Political Economy of Rent-Seeking* (1988).

18. *Western Economic Journal*, Vol. 5 (Fall 1967), pp. 224–32.

mill. If that is so, then the present discounted value of the restriction would always be fully absorbed in equilibrium by the rent-seeking cost.

The manufacturer planning on making money would be indifferent between improving his own steel mill or going to Congress and trying to get a quota on imports of Japanese steel. In spite of the doubts raised in "Efficient Rent Seeking," I am going to use that assumption throughout this chapter. I sincerely hope that the present state of the efficient rent-seeking debate in which we are mired in paradox is simply a transitional stage. With luck, someone will solve the problem in the not-too-distant future.

So far in this chapter, I have discussed the costs of rent seeking under the assumption that it normally requires not only that prices be increased but that inefficient technologies be adopted. I have so far offered no explanation as to why the latter should be so, although I have pointed out that it is quite common in the real world. Let us then return to why it is so, and at that point we pick up "ignorance and ideology" from the chapter title.

Consider an efficient transfer scheme. For the purpose of illustration, let us use the Tullock Economic Development Program. This involves placing a dollar of additional tax on each income tax form in the United States and paying the resulting funds to Tullock, whose economy would develop rapidly. Most would agree that politically this measure, regardless of its desirability, has not the slightest chance of going through.

Let us compare the Tullock Economic Development Plan with the Tucson Air Pollution Reduction Program. Tucson is like many cities in that it does have an air pollution problem, not very serious, but still real. While it is an issue that has excited a lot of people, no one wants to engage in the expenditures and suffer the inconvenience that would be necessary to seriously reduce the pollution. This is normal. A number of gestures that have a minor effect on pollution but make people feel good while not being too expensive are all that can be expected.

The Tucson Air Pollution Reduction Program fits. In order to understand it, we must realize that Tucson has a heavily subsidized bus line. Part of the subsidy comes from the federal government, part from the City of Tucson. Since the busses are much underused—I have in all my time here never seen a full bus—the cost of transportation in terms of passenger mile must be extremely high. The busses also in all probability increase total pollution, because they run empty much of the time or with a scattering of passengers, generating more pollution than I believe would have been generated by cars carrying the same (small) number of passengers. They are, however, supported by three pressure groups: the drivers of the busses, the small population that actually does use them, and the environmentalists who like noble gestures of this sort.

The Tucson Air Pollution Reduction Program consists of doubling the size of the bus line, and at the same time a research project will be put in hand. It will be naturally allocated to the University of Arizona economics department with arrangements that two friends of mine, one an engineer and the other a locational geographer, share. The grant for Tullock in this program is $30,000. Of course, a research grant is not the same as $30,000 in cash, but not too much different. Each of my friends would get a similar $30,000, and there would be additional funds for hiring research assistants and other staff because we would actually do some research. Basically, the bulk of the money would simply go into buying and subsidizing the operation of more busses.

Given my choice between the Tullock Economic Development Plan and the Tucson Air Pollution Reduction Program, I obviously would favor the first. But given my choice as to which one I should put $10,000 of my own resources into in the form of lobbying effort, I would choose the Tucson Air Pollution Reduction Program. I estimate that I would have about a 50–50 chance of getting my $30,000 as a return on the $10,000 in this program. My chances of getting many millions for putting $10,000 into lobbying the other are so small that the present discounted value is much below the $15,000 of the Tucson development program.

Economically, the Tullock Economic Development Plan, if one ignores the rent-seeking costs, is an efficient transfer. Economically, the Tucson Air Quality Improvement Program—which we will assume has exactly the same cost—is a ghastly mistake. Nevertheless, I would predict more things are passed by any democratic legislature that are like the Tucson Air Quality Improvement Program than are like the Tullock Economic Development Plan.

We see the same thing in the farm program. From the beginning and right up to the present, the farm lobby has fought vigorously against any proposal to directly pay farmers cash.[19] We clearly could give farmers as a whole the same benefits they now receive with much less cost to the rest of us by direct cash payments equal to the discounted value of the program, but with no restrictions. This is superficially a little puzzling.

19. Recently, disguises have become harder and harder to devise. As a result, some of the present programs impress most economists as direct payments. Fortunately for farmers, most voters are not economists.

The explanation is simple and straightforward. The farmers realize that such a program would be just too raw. The voters would not buy it. In another paper, I referred to the "public image"[20] as a problem for rent seekers. Citizens do not think of government tasks as just anything. There has to be some cover over any transfers to the well-to-do which the government undertakes. Changing the technology with which something is produced can frequently conceal the real objective as, say, improving total production or helping people without directly paying them. Direct payments would not work.

To take one example, from the organization of the Civil Aeronautics Board (CAB) until almost its end, no trunk-line carrier was permitted to enter the industry. Suppose instead of this provision the government had simply enacted a tax on all trunk-line airplane tickets and paid the resulting cash to those particular companies that were operating trunk lines at the time the CAB legislation was enacted. It is fairly obvious that this procedure, from the standpoint of both the airlines and the air travelers, would have been superior to the system that was in fact adopted. Like the Tullock Economic Development Plan, though, it would have failed passage through Congress. It was necessary to use the inefficient method that was adopted if any aid at all were offered to those risk-prone entrepreneurs who had entered the airline business in the thirties.

Something a bit like this applies also to private monopolies. When we look at the history of such monopolies, and it is a long one, we note that almost never do the monopoly organizers openly avow raising prices and increasing their profits as their motive. They are concerned with stabilizing the price, improving the quality, guaranteeing a reserve of production for possible use in war, and so on. It is true that these slogans have less effect on private monopolies than the similar slogans do on government-sponsored monopolies, but even there, overt choice of purely exploitative methods is rare.

But when we turn to the government and government restrictions, the cover of public interest becomes much thicker and much more expensive both to the rent seekers and to society as a whole. Thus, turning back to figure 1, if this were a private monopoly, the rent-seeking rectangle to the left would have very little in the way of adoption of inefficient technologies. The lined area would be very small, and the dotted area showing the resources invested in obtaining the monopoly would be very large. When we deal with the government, the reverse situation is likely to be true.

20. Rowley, Tollison, and Tullock (1988).

Public misunderstanding of the actual situation is almost a logical necessity for the average rent-seeking activity. Total losses are greater than the total gains; hence, there is a superior strategy available to people who are fully informed. Furthermore, as a normal rule, the number of people who gain is much smaller than the number who lose.

Logrolling is one method of getting through that benefit a minority at a dispersed cost to the majority. It is easier to do this, however, if you are able to deceive the majority so that their opposition is minimized; hence, in a democratic system straightforward transfer from the poor to the wealthy producers of wheat would certainly lose. There are, then, two ways in which such a device can be gotten through. People can be deceived, or the information can simply be kept from their knowledge. Minor revisions benefiting small groups are frequently implemented by the latter strategy.

The average citizen cannot possibly know all of the clauses even in one major bill. Under the circumstances, the prospect of something simply slipping through is always there. The decided risk inherent in this technique is that scandals attract newspaper attention, and the citizenry is likely to become indignant.

At the time I drafted this chapter, Senator Hart had just withdrawn from the Presidential race. In addition, an immense, long series of investigations was going on about the possible diversion of around $10 million to $12 million to aid for the Contras in Nicaragua. Both of these defaults, from the standpoint of the normal functioning of the American government, are trivial,[21] but both have attracted attention and are developing into major scandals. In trying to sneak something through, the special interest must always realize that scandal is possible.

More commonly, the program is designed in such a way that there is at least a superficially plausible explanation for it. Designing the program for such superficial plausibility makes it necessary to use inefficient means. Direct cash payments are usually the most efficient way of helping the interest group, but they will not do. The cost of the inefficient method may be high, particularly since, in general, a great deal of complication and indirection is desirable.

21. President Roosevelt lived reasonably openly with his mistress (mildly disguised as a secretary) in the White House, and President Kennedy engaged in a very vigorous sex life in the same august building. Congressman Biaggi, if the decision of his jury is accepted (it is being appealed), diverted more money to Wedtech. Only New York papers seem interested, and even they are only mildly concerned.

Since Anthony Downs' *An Economic Theory of Democracy*,[22] it has been realized that if the voter does not happen to be pursuing politics as a hobby, he will normally be very badly informed. Indeed, if he is rational in his choice of what subject matter to read in the newspaper, he will be "rationally ignorant."[23]

Recently another problem has been recognized. A voter in voting may be motivated not by actual outcome of the matter up for vote but by a desire to express his own emotions, feeling of virtue, and so on.[24] The voter may, in fact, vote directly against his interest because he realizes that his vote has very little, if any, effect on the actual outcome of the election; hence, he can get a feeling of moral satisfaction out of casting a virtuous vote without significant cost to him. Expressive votes may well lead to more waste than corrupt votes.

Granted an ill-informed voter, who, in any event, is apt to be attempting to express his moral principles in the vote, ideology is of great importance also in the voting. Whether this ideology is devotion to the nineteenth-century economic encyclicals of the pope or socialism, it is, in any event, not likely to lead to highly efficient policies. To repeat what we have said before when it comes to rent seeking, we by definition almost are dealing with inefficient policies.

There are two objections to the above line of reasoning. Since the authors are Gary Becker and Samuel Peltzman, they must be given some attention.[25] Becker says: ". . . politically successful groups do attract additional members, e.g. farming became more attractive after being subsidized . . . Subsidized groups try to limit the entry of additional members because that dilutes the gains of established members. One way to limit entry is to lobby for subsi-

22. New York: Harper, 1957.

23. See also *Toward a Mathematics of Politics*, Gordon Tullock (Ann Arbor: University of Michigan Press, 1976), pp. 110–28.

24. This idea was first suggested by Gordon Tullock in "Charity of the Uncharitable," *Western Economic Journal*, Vol. 9 (December 1971), pp. 379–92, but has been greatly elaborated and improved by Geoffrey Brennan and James Buchanan in "Voter Choice: Evaluating Political Alternatives," *American Behavioral Scientist*, Vol. 29 (Nov./Dec. 1984), pp. 185–201. Recent but unpublished empirical work by Gary Anderson and Robert D. Tollison casts a good deal of doubt on the whole concept.

25. See "Public Policies, Pressure Groups, and Dead Weight Costs," Gary S. Becker, *Journal of Public Economics*, Vol. 28 (1985), pp. 329–47. Samuel Peltzman's immensely frequently cited paper is "Toward a More General Theory of Regulation," *Journal of Law and Economics*, Vol. 19 (August 1976), 211–40.

dies that are less vulnerable to entry. For example, acreage restrictions encourage fewer new farmers than output subsidies do. . . ."[26]

But either an acreage restriction or an output subsidy would be dominated both in efficiency and in gain to farmers by an acreage payment on existing farms or a capitation payment for existing farmers. In an oral exchange, Becker agreed. Presumably, his future writing will not uphold the above position.[27] He did not offer any explanation for the inefficiency of the present programs as compared with such direct payments.

I can think of no formal test of my hypothesis. I believe, however, that if the reader just considers the matter a little bit and thinks about the way congressmen act, the way the newspapers report political activities, and so on, he will decide that the conventional wisdom at Chicago (mentioned in a footnote before and endorsed in this article) is more likely to be true than the new Chicago point of view as espoused in Becker's article.[28]

In turning to Peltzman, the situation becomes more complicated because Peltzman has never directly said that the outcomes of government activity are efficient ways of benefiting the special interest groups. He does not, strictly speaking, deny that there might be considerable inefficiency. Nevertheless, the general thrust of his argument implies that is not so.

Peltzman says that the outcome of any given political interchange is the result of a balancing of the forces by the politicians so that both sides gain something. Thus, there is a quota put on Japanese cars, but the quota is not so high as to prohibit imports completely; hence, people who want to buy Japanese cars are not totally exploited. They would, however, be even less injured by an arrangement under which the producers of the cars get the same net benefit by a tax on imported cars dispersed to the producers. Peltzman does not directly deny this.

Note here that the mere beginning of the political fight usually disadvantages one party or the other. Indeed, Peltzman's argument simply ignores the main point of the rent-seeking literature. He does not discuss the matter, but I imagine he would agree that both the automobile producers and the consumers would be better off with a direct tax on automobiles with the funds

26. Becker (1985, p. 342).

27. Probably the basic reason that he uses agriculture for his example is simply that, since the thirties, it has been part of the oral culture at the University of Chicago to say that the agricultural program is inefficient in the sense that direct cash payments would have been better.

28. Becker (1985).

derived paid directly to those people who were in the industry at the time that the Japanese cut into their returns.

The movement of the United Auto Workers (UAW) and the automobile manufacturers to put restrictions on the import of Japanese cars immediately injured the American automobile buyers.[29] The eventual outcome of this squabble is decidedly to the disadvantage of the customers, though not as much as the total victory of the producers would be.

In our opinion, there is always, and in all cases, a third participant in the squabble. American manufacturers and unionists in the automobile industry and the potential purchasers of new cars are only part of the people who take an interest. There are also other American voters who are not directly involved. They are apt to vote, if the matter is brought to their attention, in terms of ideology. It is important that the measure be packaged in such a way that it appears to them to be somehow in accord with their ideology.

A quota is a far better way of doing that than a direct tax and subsidy combination would be. These people who are not directly involved in the squabble are overwhelmingly more numerous than the special interests on either side. It is essential, therefore, that a technique be adopted which keeps them from intervening. The inefficient technology is the answer, and once again, that is what we observe. Thus, we do not directly contradict Peltzman; we simply point out that his model is only part of what is going on in these areas.

There is conflict between different groups, and politicians do balance those interests off against each other. There is, however, an overwhelmingly important additional player in the form of the outsiders to that particular squabble who must be deceived into believing that it is something other than simply a fight for pork.[30]

My position, that the inefficient technique is necessary in order to deceive the voters, is fairly easily but somewhat subjectively testable. I mentioned before, the existence of various efforts to have minor special interest provisions inserted in bills in the hopes they would not attract attention, and the danger of that technique. An empirical study would suffice of the cases in which the secrecy has failed and the matter brought to public attention.

29. It also injured some of the Japanese car manufacturing companies, but it benefited others, so we shall leave that argument aside. In any event, they do not vote in American elections.

30. In some cases, a straightforward fight for pork is regarded by the average citizen as excusable, if not virtuous. The argument that everybody else has a dam in their district and I should have one, too, seems to be regarded as morally unobjectionable. Currently, moral fairness can take the form of everybody getting some of the loot.

As a second empirical test, and this case involves a limited number of cases, the dissolution of the CAB and the current sharp restriction on the Interstate Commerce Commission (ICC) both seem to have come at least in part because of the cartel management characteristics of these two organizations becoming well known. Derthick and Quirk's careful study[31] is in agreement.

I would like to end this chapter by pointing out that although I have been arguing that the required use of inefficient techniques is very expensive to society, it may be cheaper than the direct kind of cash payment that we observe in present-day Mexico. If special interest legislation requires the use of highly inefficient production techniques, then the resources put into the rent seeking for it are much lower than they would otherwise be. It is likely, therefore, that the total amount of this kind of restrictive special interest legislation will be sharply lower than it would be if direct payments were permitted.

Consider, for example, a proposal to make a direct cash payment to some group of people, or a proposal to hire them at a price somewhat above their opportunity costs, for building a dam somewhere. Assume that there is $1 million available. In the first case it would be paid directly to them, and in the second case they would make a net profit of $100,000, but they would spend $900,000 on building a dam which we will assume is totally useless. The net social waste in the two cases is the same.

But although the net social waste in these two cases is the same, the amount of rent seeking that we would expect is quite different. In the society in which the direct payment type of benefit to special interests is permitted, the amount of resources invested in influencing Congress would be much larger. In the above case, $1 million is in contrast with $100,000. Clearly more special interest legislation would get through under those circumstances. Thus, the common citizen, in requiring that those government acts that come to his attention fit sort of vaguely into his rather nebulous ideas of what government should do, is probably "doing good."

There is another advantage to this type of inefficiency from the standpoint of an economist. Almost all economists are, whatever they say, actually reformers who would like to improve the world. The particular tools that they have available in this campaign to help the world is the ability to technically analyze various economic projects. The project that gives a special benefit to some interest group by employing an inefficient technique of production is the kind of thing that the economist is in a good position to attack.

31. Derthick and Quirk (1985).

It is easy to point out that the farm program could give the farmers the same amount of money at less expense to the customers by direct cash payments. It is also politically devastating to the farm program. Indeed, that is probably the reason the farmers have always been so violently adverse to even talking about it in these terms.

The average voter, as we have said before, is apt to be very badly informed but is interested in scandals. The inefficiency characteristic we have been describing makes it possible for an economist to convert a special interest program into a scandal through use of the tools he has learned in his profession. A direct cash payment does not have this disciplinary connection, although economists—like the political scientists or even the philosophers—could complain about it.

The main objective of this chapter has been to put the rent-seeking literature more in accord with what we observe in everyday governmental activity. We end with the suggestion that what appears to be an extremely inefficient characteristic of democracy may actually improve the total efficiency of the system.

EFFICIENT RENT SEEKING, DISECONOMIES OF SCALE, PUBLIC GOODS, AND MORALITY

To most economists, the immediate solution to the problem with which this general section deals would be the possibility of either diseconomies of scale or public goods. I have deferred their discussion up to this point because neither one of them would explain the inefficiency of the means normally used to transfer resources. Also, if used by themselves, rather remarkable parameters have to be assumed. Nevertheless, they can be used to supplement the explanations in the previous two chapters.

Before we deal with these two issues, there is another possible explanation that is not so well known among economists. Some time ago, I wrote an article, "Efficient Rent Seeking,"[1] which examined the situation in which there are either economies of scale or diseconomies of scale right from the beginning. In other words, the cost curve is not U-shaped, it is either continuously declining or rising as the scale is expanded. The article set off considerable discussion because it has rather paradoxical conclusions.

We will confine ourselves here to the diseconomies of scale part of the article. As the size of the individual enterprise goes down, percentage return on investment rises. Returns are always positive, so that entry, with individual enterprises getting smaller and smaller, continues. In the limit of this process there are unexhausted profits. In other words, in the equilibrium state of this model, if it can be said to have an equilibrium, the market does not clear. The total amount invested is considerably less than the total gain.

It would seem that this model would explain the phenomena we are currently interested in if we confine ourselves solely to the apparent underinvestment, i.e., the small size of the industry. In order to get the disproportion

Reprinted, with kind permission of Kluwer Academic Publishers, from *The Economics of Special Privilege and Rent Seeking* (Boston/Dordrecht/London: Kluwer Academic Publishers, 1989), 41–45.

1. *Toward a Theory of the Rent-Seeking Society*, James M. Buchanan, Robert D. Tollison, and Gordon Tullock (eds.)(College Station: Texas A&M University Press, 1980). This article set off a lengthy discussion, mostly in *Public Choice*. The portion of the discussion before 1987 was republished in *The Political Economy of Rent-Seeking*, Charles K. Rowley, Robert D. Tollison, and Gordon Tullock (eds.) (Boston: Kluwer Academic Publishers, 1988).

between expenditures and outcome which we observe in the lobbying market, however, the degree of diseconomy of scale would have to be extreme.

There is a more important problem here. If we face this kind of diseconomy of scale, we would anticipate that the entrants into the business would tend to be small indeed. It would be more sensible to have 250 tiny lobbies pushing for the benefit of the steel industry than 25 small ones, and certainly more than one sizeable one. We do not observe this extreme fragmentation in the existing lobbying industry. If anything, it works the other way, with each particular interest having a single organization in Washington.

This does not prove that we might not have the U-shaped cost curve over scale with a declining portion when the lobby is extremely small and the rising part as the lobby gets bigger. Conceivably all lobbies in Washington are in the diseconomy portion of this U-shaped curve. The efficient size would be at the low point of this curve.

This type of diseconomy of scale, however, does not help us, because assuming that there is an optimal size for lobbies and that it is quite small, the total industry could be immense simply by having a large number of small lobbies. In order for diseconomies of scale to explain the apparent difference between the size of the industry and the size of its effect, there has to be some kind of diseconomy of scale for the industry as a whole; i.e., somehow or other the various lobbies must interfere with each other. Individual lobbies must generate negative externalities for each other.

It is difficult to see how this could be so in the legislative area. Presumably, there is a maximum, apparently a high maximum, on the total number of laws Congress can pass and regulations that our bureaucracy can promulgate. This, however, does not tell us how many lobbies there will be. Suppose, for example, that the total number of laws that can be passed is 100,000 and that each one is worth $1 million to those pushing for it, while the costs of a most efficient-sized lobby is only $100,000. This should lead to a million $100,000 lobbies, each of which has a one-in-ten chance of getting a million dollar prize. The total amount invested in lobbying would be the same as the total return. As I said in my first article,[2] lobbying has some resemblance to buying a lottery ticket.

The degree of diseconomy necessary here is both peculiar and strong. It

2. "The Welfare Costs of Tariffs, Monopoly, and Theft," *Western Economic Journal,* Vol. 5 (June 1957), pp. 224–32.

has to be such that above a certain number of lobbies, the net return on the additional lobby is negative. The return on expansion of all existing lobbies would also have to be negative.

Let us now turn to the public goods phenomenon. Ever since Mancur Olson's *The Logic of Collective Action: Public Goods and the Theory of Groups*,[3] we have realized that pressure groups do generate public goods for their particular industry. This naturally raises an organizational problem. The steel mill that refuses to make its contribution to the steel industry's lobby will benefit from a restriction on Korean steel imports just as much as those who do make such a contribution; hence, one would anticipate underinvestment in such lobbying. What we are trying to explain is not that the investment by the special interest is less than what would be optimal, but that the investment seems to be much less than the benefit conferred.

Let me invent an example. Suppose there were an industry with 100 firms of about the same size, and there is some favor from the government, say, a protective tariff that would benefit that industry as a whole. Assume that the height of the tariff is a positive function of the amount invested, i.e., it would be higher as more money is put in by the lobbyists. Further, assume that the optimal tariff, from the standpoint of the industry as a whole, is one involving the investment of $500 or $5 apiece by our 100 companies.

If one company decided to invest $1 and let the others free ride, there would be some tariff protection. It would itself receive only about 1 percent of that tariff protection so that the total value of the lobbying is about 100 times the size of benefit to the investing firm.

So far so good, but note the rather extreme disproportion of our numbers here. One dollar invested by this one company provides almost 20 percent of the public good purchasable for $500. There must be an extraordinarily rapid deterioration in payoff for each additional dollar invested. Indeed, although I do not want to say these numbers are impossible, they come very close.

This impossibility, of course, is simply due to the size of the numbers. But these numbers do seem to be not too different from what we actually observe in the lobbying industry. The ratio of actual investment in lobbying to the net cost inflicted on the economy is large enough so that the return must be high on the first units invested and low on the units afterwards in order to explain the situation by use of public good arguments.

3. Cambridge: Harvard University Press, 1965.

As a technical aside, there is a possible discontinuity here. It might be that the amount of public goods purchased by the first person, who we assume has exceptional demand for it, is so great that the remaining members of the industry, even if they worked collectively, would prefer to make no investment in moving to the industry optimum. In other words, although for all 100 of them investing $5 apiece would be better than investing nothing, for 99 of them investing $5 apiece when one of them has invested $1 (and assuming that he has added his $4 in at this point) is worse than free riding on the $1 investment by one. This would, of course, be an extreme situation, but the numbers are extreme.

If, however, the arguments in the preceding two chapters are accepted, or either one of them is accepted, then the diseconomies of scale and public goods might be able to supplement them. The general characteristic of the first of these articles is that the total benefit received by the companies is much smaller than its cost to the economy. For the second, the bulk of the incentive to politicians for enacting certain laws is the desire to get reelected. In other words, the voters actually push things through, not the lobbies. If these arguments are accepted, then possible diseconomies of scale and possible public goods arguments could be added on without much difficulty.

This is also true of my final possible explanation: people might think that rent-seeking activity was immoral and not engage in it. Although I do not necessarily see such activity as morally commendable, I see no signs that moral considerations have much effect here. Still, perhaps an ethical aversion to rent seeking on the part of some people reduces its total amount.

Thus, it is not impossible that all the reasons I have canvassed for the rent-seeking industry's being so small are simultaneously true. It is not impossible either that some of them are false, and that there may be some other explanation that I have not thought of.

The problem is a real and important one. Undoubtedly, with modern countries the total cost of the industry's generating special privilege is immense. Further, if we look back at history we realize that before the Glorious Revolution in England (and, more specifically, before the work of Smith and Ricardo), almost all governments in the world had gigantic special privilege industries, which might be a major reason why progress was so slow. The nineteenth century was a halcyon time in which this problem did not exist, and its partial revival in the twentieth century cannot help but have a retarding effect on the growth of our wealth. It is important that we understand it and the political motives leading to its development.

The particular puzzle, that the size of the effort to produce these impediments to growth seems to be much smaller than its effect, has been the motif of the first part of this book. We shall now turn to other areas that do not directly contribute to this problem, although I hope the reader will find them of interest.

ARE RENTS FULLY DISSIPATED?

COMMENT

The measure of the cost of rent-seeking has been difficult, and its theory is complicated. For example, I devoted the first half of my *The Economics of Special Privilege and Rent Seeking* to the mysterious fact that the apparent size of the rent-seeking industry is considerably smaller than the resources obtained.[1] This raises the question of whether there are, in fact, concealed expenses or that entrepreneurs are making mistakes.

The Dougan-Snyder article raises and attempts to answer the problem. They assume a case in which $100 is distributed to the first 1000 people who are at a given point at noon of a specified day. One would expect that this prize would be wholly dissipated by people coming long distances, getting in early in the morning, etc. They call this rent-seeking, and it is a legitimate, although unusual, use of the word.[2]

There is another set of rent-seeking costs. These are costs of impelling the decision- or policy-makers to make the award. It is this second meaning of the term that attracts most attention from students. To repeat, it is not illegitimate of Dougan-Snyder to talk about the first meaning, but they should not ignore the second. In their model the decision-maker simply decides to make a gift to certain people. There is no pressure brought to bear on him; resources are not used to convince him that he should. Altogether, this is quite unlike what we normally see when Congress is handing out money.

I am not alleging that waste in the process of handing out the money is unimportant. However, the pressure brought to bear on policy-makers to make the distribution is what has normally been discussed under the title of rent-seeking.

Take the U.S. agricultural program which provides benefits to the farmers at a cost to society very much larger than those benefits. The benefits them-

Reprinted, with kind permission of Kluwer Academic Publishers, from *Public Choice* 82 (January 1995): 181–84. Copyright 1995 Kluwer Academic Publishers.

1. G. Tullock, *The Economics of Special Privilege and Rent Seeking* (Dordrecht: Kluwer, 1992).

2. W. R. Dougan and J. M. Snyder, "Are Rents Fully Dissipated?" *Public Choice* 77, no. 4 (1993): 793–814. There is also the additional cost involved in raising the money by taxation. They ignore it, and I will also for the remainder of this comment.

selves are modest even to the farmers. The farmers bring a good deal of pressure to bear on the political representatives to keep the program going, and this is what we normally think of as rent-seeking costs, and not the allocative inefficiency waste that the program generates. However, Dougan and Snyder perform a service by bringing these allocative wastes to our attention.

The cost to the United States of the farm program is of the order of $20–30 billion a year (depends upon the weather), and the benefit to the farmers about $2 billion a year. It is even possible that if the program were cancelled, after a painful period of readjustment, the farmers would be as well off as they are now.

Obviously, the farmers would not be willing to put up more than $2 billion a year for this benefit. On occasion economists list the $20 billion as the rents derived, rather than the $2 billion. With these assumptions they find that the rent-seeking costs are very far from being dissipated. In fact, $18 billion of it is dissipated by the kind of activity modelled by Dougan and Snyder, by the equivalent of people going to the corner where the money is to be distributed.

Still, it doesn't seem as if the direct payments by farmers are anywhere near $2 billion. The campaign contributions and other political expenditures seem tiny compared with the amount of money which Congress distributes. Further, congressmen themselves when they retire, although they do not retire to poverty, usually do not retire to great wealth, such as, say, a Mexican congressman normally does.

There are two puzzles here, one of which is why the money is disseminated in such an inefficient way, and the other is why congressmen don't seem to earn the amount that even disseminated in this inefficient way would be justified on a straight cost-benefit analysis.

The answer to these two puzzles is rather simple: the actual decision-maker is the mass of voters. The fact that the voters are systematically badly informed and that they also pay the taxes that are used to support these transfers explains much of the mystery of rent dissipation. Ekelund and Tollison, cited by Dougan and Snyder, are right to point out that when the residual claimant was the king, he had motives for being efficient.[3] In spite of these motives it is not obvious that the royal efficiency was very high.

3. R. B. Ekelund Jr. and R. D. Tollison, *Mercantilism as a Rent-Seeking Society* (College Station: Texas A&M University Press, 1981).

This is the kind of rent-seeking costs that Dougan and Snyder talk about. The other kind that gets the governments to hand out money to favored individuals or groups is somewhat different. If we deal with the latter first it will be easier to understand the former.

Assume then that we are talking about a project to spend $20 billion benefitting the farmers, and that we have two types of rent-seeking, one of which is actually distributing the money. For the time being let us assume that it is inefficient and costs $18 billion. The other type of rent-seeking is getting the Congress to undertake the program which is clearly worth $2 billion to the farmers. Assume that the fundamental decision-maker here is the farmer who makes his decision by campaigning and voting for or against the congressmen, and that the congressmen are simply acting as their representatives. This is a little over-simple, but will do no harm.

Assume there are other voters who have to pay the taxes and will not receive the benefit. If they outnumber the farmers, then getting the bill through will require special arrangements. If the farmers themselves made up 51% of the population so that they could get the thing through on their own,[4] they presumably would either take only $2 billion in direct cash payments or insist on receiving the whole $20 billion instead of wasting $18 billion.

There are a series of problems here. Firstly, the farmers are not a majority. They get the bill through by making deals with other people. In order to get the farm program through, it is essential to have the farm representatives also vote for the Central Arizona Project, for producing a canal parallelling the Mississippi River, making Tulsa a deepwater port, and all the other nonsense that we observe the Federal government understanding.[5]

Since only a majority is necessary, it would be possible for such bargains to spend almost $2 for each dollar that is disseminated to the beneficiaries. The other money would be paid by people who are not members of the bargain. The reader will note that in all of this I am following the log-rolling model of *The Calculus of Consent*.[6]

4. 51% is not really needed. A strong group in a large number of constituencies will do. This makes no difference in the analysis, however, and would lengthen an already long comment.

5. State and local governments do some of this kind of thing also, but their resources are smaller and we tend to ignore them.

6. J. M. Buchanan and G. Tullock, *The Calculus of Consent: Logical Foundations of Constitutional Democracy* (Ann Arbor: University of Michigan Press, 1962).

The ideal system from the standpoint of a simple majority would be to make a permanent coalition which regularly exploited the minority and benefitted the same majority of all votes. In practice, these things are not stable, and that is impossible to do. What happens is a rotating series of majorities among groups that have special things they want, with a result that almost everybody gets something, but the net cost of the marginal projects for all of them is considerably more than the benefit. Perhaps it may be better than not letting any of the projects through.

Unfortunately, the situation is worse than I have just implied. One of the standard, but rather startling, early results of Public Choice, was that the intelligent voter will not bother to become well informed about politics. Empirical evidence confirms theory here. Unfortunately the actual ignorance of the voter has particularly perverse effects because it is not symmetrical. The voter is more likely to know of things that directly affect the small minority of which he is a member than of matters of general public interest.[7]

The farmer knows much more about the farm program than he does about the Central Arizona Project unless he is one of that tiny minority who will benefit, and hence he is apt to mistakenly think that when his representative makes a trade of a vote for the farm program with one for the Central Arizona Project, he is getting a benefit without any cost. The fact that he knows more about the farm program doesn't mean that he knows a great deal. Those people in Arizona who thought they were going to benefit from the Central Arizona Project were ignorant of very well informed criticism by agricultural economists and hydrologic engineers from the university at which I now hold my chair.

They ignored this expert advice. Granted the extremely limited incentives for becoming well informed, we cannot really criticize them for that. They are now paying the costs, but for each individual the cost will be fairly low. It is possible that investing resources in becoming well-informed on the project some 15 years ago would have been unwise. Compound interest for 15 years together with the very slight prospect that any voter could change the outcome, might add up to more than the disadvantage of remaining ill-informed.

7. M. X. Delli Carpini and S. Keeter, "Measuring Political Knowledge: Putting First Things First," *American Journal of Political Science* (November 1993): 1179–1206 (see for data on the actual level of information of voters).

Even this does not fully explain the gigantic difference between the benefit that many of these projects have and their costs. Dougan and Snyder mention that there are "constitutional" prohibitions on making payments to specific individuals in order to avoid the kind of continuous struggle for money which otherwise would exist. None of these limits are constitutional and how firm they are is not clear, but it is clear that large-scale direct cash payments to constituencies are hard to get through Congress. Disguise is necessary. Since the voters are ill-informed these disguises work, but they are expensive and the present method of subsidizing farmers is in essence a gigantic disguise to transfer a rather small subsidy.

To summarize then, the actual distributing of the money discussed by Dougan and Snyder is only a part of the rent-seeking costs. Further, if we look at real government programs, you normally see even that part of the cost is handled wastefully. They are correct that politicians have a motive for spending that money as efficiently as possibly, but also they have a motive for concealing the subsidy from the bulk of the voters. Apparently, the second motive tends to dominate the first.

WHERE IS THE RECTANGLE?

Figure 1, which has been famous since "The Welfare Costs of Tariffs, Monopolies, and Theft," has led to a very large amount of research, and even a larger amount of references to the importance of the rent-seeking cost.[1] Basically, what the article claimed was that the total cost of monopolies, tariffs, and crimes was represented not only by the triangle at the right, usually called the Harberger triangle, but also by the rectangle.

It argued that the development of monopoly, tariff, or other special privilege normally involved the investment of resources. There is no reason why these resources should receive a higher return than resources invested in other activities; hence the rectangle, which represented the return on them, should more or less equal the amount of resources invested. In other words, the social waste from rent seeking was much greater than the previous studies had indicated.

All of this is theoretically correct, but as the person who has written more in this field than anyone else, and who after all wrote the original article, I have been perturbed by the difficulty in finding any actual measurable cost of that rectangle. Consider General Motors. When the Japanese cars began flooding in, they had a problem with the UAW, but it seemed likely that by a large investment of capital they could have produced factories which would have met Japanese competition on even terms. Indeed, after some delay, they obtained concessions from the UAW, and did just that.[2]

Still, the first response was to turn to Washington, and ask for restrictions

Reprinted, with kind permission of Kluwer Academic Publishers, from *Public Choice* 91 (1997): 149–59. Copyright 1997 Kluwer Academic Publishers.

1. G. Tullock, "The Welfare Costs of Tariffs, Monopolies, and Theft," *Western Economic Journal* 5 (June 1967): 224–32.

2. This article will be devoted to government-provided privilege achieved by rent seeking in a democracy. This is not because I believe that privately designed monopolies do not exist, but today, in contrast to the days of J. P. Morgan, they are relatively minor. Further, it is much harder to get any idea of the actual rent-seeking costs because they are normally well concealed. The same is true of rent-seeking costs in non-democratic governments, but see R. B. Ekelund Jr. and R. D. Tollison, *The Institutions and Political Economy of Mercantilism* (College Station: Texas A&M University Press, forthcoming).

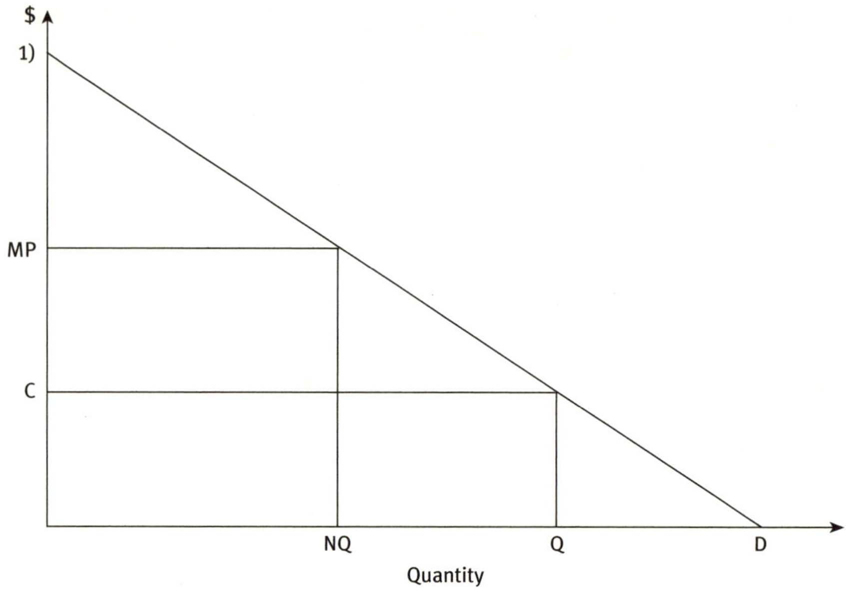

FIGURE 1

on the entry of Japanese cars. They got them.[3] Presumably, they thought that the cost of getting this kind of protection was less than the cost of putting in the new plant. I do not disagree with them, but they eventually did build new factories and re-equip old ones. They clearly felt there were circumstances in which the factories would be cheaper than getting the necessary protection out of Washington.

To repeat, they did get protection, and any thought at all about this protection will indicate that it was worth many billions of dollars to General Motors. There is no evidence that they paid those billions of dollars directly. We now have various statistics on lobbying activities, etc. They are not complete, but they show actual expenditures which are trivial compared with the size of the gain. Presumably, there are expenditures which do not appear in the official statistics, but surely 5 billion dollars invested by General Motors to get protection against Japanese competition (a bargain) could not have been concealed.

3. I am talking about General Motors primarily here. The other automobile manufacturers were also involved. Actually, I am using General Motors as a "representative corporation."

Turn to another case, milk. I used to live not very far from the headquarters building of the milk lobby in Washington. It was a nice, small office building, and it was clear that it could not account for anywhere near the 500 million dollars a year, more or less, that the milk producers were taking out of the pockets of the American consumers. Again, the farmers could have done various things to cut their costs, but they preferred to run the lobby with their resources. Still they did improve efficiency, and it seems likely that the two ways of making profits were not wildly out of equality in marginal cost.

Superficially, it would appear that the people who engage in pressing government for special protection are making absolutely immense returns on rather small investments. This, of course, is conceivable, but then we have to explain why they invest funds in other areas. After all, General Motors could have continued with their previous production methods if they had been able to obtain enough government protection, but they didn't. There must be a sizeable cost of rent seeking.

The same reasoning applies from pure theory. People can be expected to invest capital in various areas until such time as the marginal returns are equal. Since we do observe companies investing money in improving their efficiency and in cutting costs, it must be true that the last dollar invested in such activity brings about as much return in profits for the company as the last dollar spent in lobbying in Washington for some kind of special protection.

Where are these expenses for protection? To repeat what I said above, there does not seem to be any obvious record of them. The lobbying industry in Washington is certainly big, but it is trivial compared with the value of the services which apparently it renders. The rectangles in all of those special privileges areas are immensely greater than the sum total of all the lobbying expenses.

This problem has bothered me from the very beginning. You will even find some references to the problem in my original article, and many more later. I have developed a number of apparent or partial explanations for the inability to firmly pin down the actual cost. The point of this article is not only to summarize my previous work in this area, but to explain what I believe is the major true explanation, in other words where that gigantic rectangle appears in our economy. The reader will not be surprised to find that I think this is a rather indirect expenditure.

There are several areas where this expenditure can be traced. Some of them are mentioned in my previous work, but I summarize all of them here as well as producing the new and gigantic if indirect cost.

In my original article, I pointed out that rent-seeking activities are essentially gambles.[4] It is not true that everyone who invests money in hiring a lobby in Washington gets the special privilege that he wants. It is like buying a ticket in the lottery: the individual expenditure on the ticket, or on the lobby, is much less than the return which occurs to only some of the people who invested.

I am particularly well equipped to say this, as I am on a Board of Directors of a small company in Iowa. It is much too small to maintain permanent lobbying facilities, but has twice had to turn to the government to ask for certain changes in regulations. We spent sizeable resources, won one and lost one. Unfortunately the one we lost was by a large margin the more important.

Although this would explain why individual companies may make large returns on their lobbying investment, it would still be true that the total investment of all companies in lobbies in Washington, state capitals, etc., would be roughly the same, or larger than the total privileges they receive. In lotteries the total spent on tickets is larger than the total of prizes.

Once again, we do not observe the gigantic lobbying industry which would be necessary if we just assume that a dollar spent on lobbying in Washington has about the same chance of getting a return as a dollar spent on the Arizona lottery. The total return is very much larger than the total cost of this collection of lobbies, although here I must concede that there may be concealed lobbying activities which we have not noticed. If any of the readers feel there are, I would appreciate having them pointed out.

The second explanation is that in many cases, as part of the lobbying activities, the company that seeks the special privilege is forced to engage in some kind of inefficient production method in order to conceal the privilege. The obvious case is the farm program. I am informed by my agricultural economics colleagues[5] that the various crop restrictions, acreage limitations, etc., cost the farmers a great deal of money. Some of my agricultural economist friends think that although there would be great confusion when it happened, cancelling the program would not actually reduce total farm income. It would redistribute it.

4. Tullock, "Welfare Costs of Tariffs."

5. We used to share the same building.

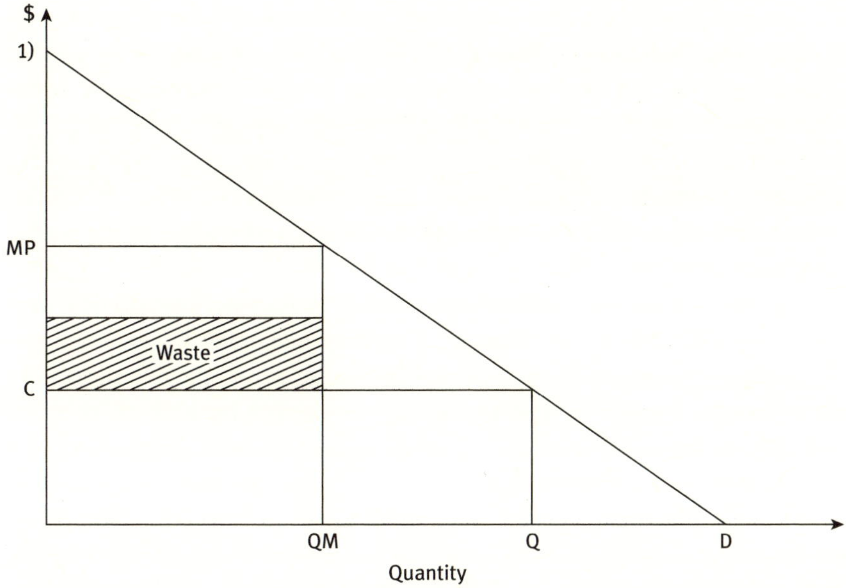

FIGURE 2

We could represent this by a modified figure as shown above in Figure 2. In this case, part of the rectangle [one-half for convenience only] is shown as extra expenses in production which are necessary in order to get it approved.

The problem here is that straight-forward cash transfers to people who are already well off would probably not be acceptable. They would be noticed by the newspapers, and the politicians who voted for them would be in trouble. It is necessary to disguise the transfer one way or another. To take an example from above, if General Motors instead of asking for restrictions on Japanese cars had simply asked for 5 or 10 billion dollars a year in cash, probably the rough value to them of the restriction, they would surely not have received it.

The benefit to General Motors of the protection was large, but it was less than the cost inflicted on the American people by the higher prices of the cars they purchased. The cost of producing the cars in American plants would not be the welfare triangle, but a good part of the rectangle. After all, if the price rise had been a pure transfer, the resources would not have been wasted in producing cars at a higher cost than purchasing them from Japan.[6]

6. See S. Coate and S. Morris, "On the Form of Transfers to Special Interest," *Journal of Political Economy* 6 (December 1995): 1210–35 for evidence on the point.

These two costs have been mentioned in a number of my articles in this area, and the basic point of this article is to add an additional cost which I think is much larger than those two put together. Granted the fact that we cannot strictly speaking measure these costs, or at least no one so far has invented a way of doing so, the factual evidence I must depend on here is an appeal to the judgment of the reader.

I suspect there will be few who will disagree with me, but we must concede that actual measurements would be far better than this kind of judgment call. There are a number of indirect measures in the literature. The lowest is 3% of GNP by Posner, and the highest is 50% of GNP by Leband and Sophocleus.[7] If any of the readers can think of a way of directly measuring the rectangle, I would appreciate their doing so, or at least tell me so that I can make the measurement.

Before turning to my general solution, I should like to discuss two other possibilities. The first is normally attributed to Becker, and I think it involves a misunderstanding of his thought.[8] Becker argued that when you have a number of pressure groups and they contest for policy, the outcome is in essence efficient. This does not mean efficient in the sense that the tariff on Japanese cars is efficient, it means efficient in the sense of the political machine being at its equilibrium.

The tariff protection against Japanese cars was for a long time an important part of American policy, and would be this equilibrium. I take it no one will argue that this was an efficient way of running the economy. It may be an efficient way of running the government, and it may provide efficiency by reducing fights in the political sector, but strictly speaking it is not efficient economically.

The basic problem here, from the standpoint of rent seeking, is that Becker does not actually discuss the cost of reaching his equilibrium. It is rather like saying that the outcome of the Wars of the Roses was efficient[9] and ignoring the resources consumed. Even if we agree that the outcome was efficient, we should also count the waste of resources. The same problem arises with pressure groups pushing Congress.

7. R. A. Posner, "The Social Costs of Monopoly and Regulation," *Journal of Political Economy* 83 (August 1975): 807–27; D. N. Laband and J. P. Sophocleus, "The Social Cost of Rent-Seeking: First Estimates," *Public Choice* 58 (1988): 269–75.

8. G. S. Becker, "A Theory of Competition among Pressure Groups for Political Influence," *Quarterly Journal of Economics* 98 (1983): 371–400.

9. Henry VII was perhaps the cleverest man who ever sat on the throne of England.

Turning once again to the automobile producers' protection against the Japanese enterprises, the American automobile manufacturers and the UAW were a well-organized pressure group in favor of it. The Japanese were against it, but at that time were not well organized in Washington. The average automobile purchaser had a rather confused attitude with patriotism [in my opinion, misplaced patriotism] contesting with the desire for a cheap car, but in any event they were not organized and had little or no influence on the outcome.

It was a rather one-sided war, and whether the ultimate outcome is efficient in some sense is different from the question of how much it cost to get there. Granted that anybody in Washington can lobby, we would anticipate that the expenditures, one way or another, would be about as much as or more than the value of the gift received. To repeat, they would build plants themselves only if there were costs to lobbying which were greater than the cost of the plant.

Once again, it would appear that the total costs of the rent seeking should be roughly the same order of magnitude as the gains. In other words, there should be costs representing the rectangle.

Another possibility, which seems not improbable on first glance, is simply that investments in rent seeking in Washington, or for that matter in Phoenix, are like most industrial activities subject to increasing returns in the early range, and then declining returns, and even sharply declining returns in the later range.

The returns on rent seeking as the resources were increased would then look much like the solid line shown on Figure 3. The argument could be that if you invest too much money in rent seeking it becomes conspicuous and has a negative payoff, or at least a reduced payoff. The solid line shows a reduced payoff, the dotted line indicates that eventually you could get a negative payoff, as the tobacco industry seems to be doing at the moment.

I should digress here to talk about something which is only a minor phenomenon in the United States, but in many other places is sizeable, straight-forward corruption in the form of cash bribes to higher officials. Anyone who is reading the current news from Korea knows they can be very sizeable. Speaking as somebody who has spent much time in the Far East, including Korea, I don't find this at all surprising. I should also mention that I live within 100 miles of the Mexican border.

Even speaking about straight-forward corruption, there are clearly maximum amounts. It is notable that the presidents of Korea who received these very large sums of money do not seem to have been spending the bulk of the

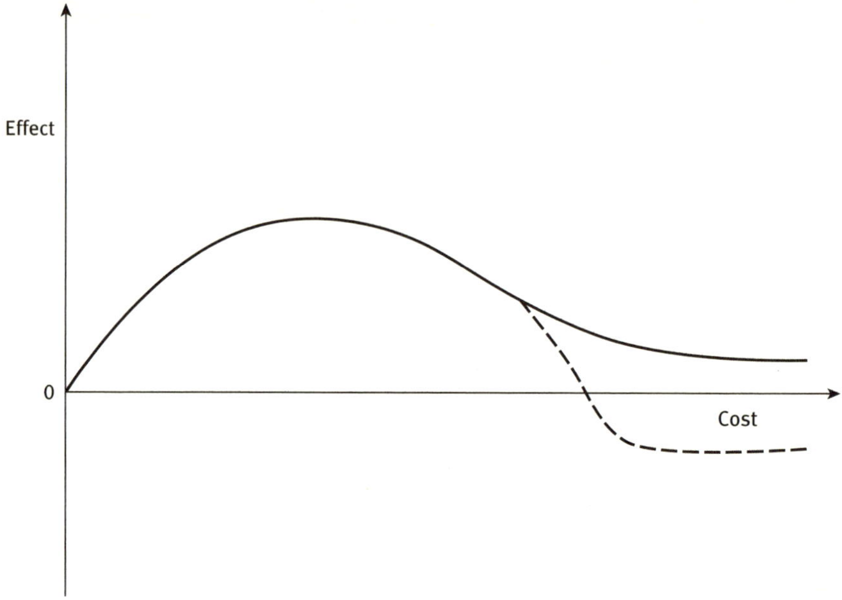

FIGURE 3

money for their own personal consumption, presumably because they did not want to advertise their size.

In any event, in the United States this kind of direct payment is generally speaking a minor matter. I don't doubt that Gabriel has in his books some records of payments received by politicians that we have not heard of, but they cannot be gigantic.

As an obvious example, the Texas Railway Commission governed American oil production to a large extent, and distributed to the oil companies gifts that were worth billions of dollars. The members of the Texas Railway Commission were ordinary politicians; normally when they retired they settled down as moderately upper-middle-class retirees.

Clearly, they had not received anywhere near the value of the gifts they handed out from the companies to whom they handed them. Indeed, looking at their performance you get the general idea that they were trying to simply maximize the profits of the Texas petroleum industry. They could have easily got from the Texas State Legislature the idea that was what they were hired for. That is not corruption in the sense of receiving bribes.

But enough of the digression; the above-outlined theory of diminishing returns beyond a point would imply that individual companies do have a maximum amount they would invest, and the individual lobbies would be fairly small. It would also imply that the number of such lobbies would be very great because the opportunity to get a very large return on a small investment would lead other people in to make similar small investments. This is not what we observe because that again would lead to the total amount of lobbying expenses being equivalent to the total gains.

It might be true that each lobby not only tended to get a sharply diminishing return on its own investment above a certain point, but also tended to reduce the likelihood that other lobbies would be successful. This must to some extent be true. Thus, there might be an optimal or maximum return for total amount of lobbying, as well as a maximum for the individual lobby.

This again raises difficulties, because it would imply that a lobbyist deciding not to start a lobby would be generating a public good for the people who already have lobbies. We do not expect private citizens to voluntarily provide public goods in this manner. It would be like grazing on the common.

We would anticipate if this were so that the total amount spent on lobbying would be about the amount gained in return, although because of the inefficiency of the over-investment in lobbies, the amount generated would be less than it would be with a smaller set of lobbies. This again would be like the over-grazing problem where if the number of cattle on the plot is managed, the actual amount of beef that can be produced is greater than if you have a number of independent entrepreneurs who are not under control. Insofar as I know no one has suggested that there is an entrepreneur who controls the total amount of lobbyists.

Let me now turn to what I think is the major way in which the rectangle appears in our society. Surprising as it may seem, the voters themselves are the rent seekers. Since they are badly and asymmetrically informed, they do a bad job and pay much more than they get back. The congressmen and many of the lobbyists are merely their agents in this process.

My first article on Public Choice was "Problems of Majority Voting," which dealt with logrolling.[10] It was, I believe, the first formal analysis of logrolling, although if one looks back at the political science literature, you will find that political scientists knew that the phenomenon existed, they just didn't talk about it much.

10. G. Tullock, "Problems of Majority Voting," *Journal of Political Economy* (December 1959): 571–79.

Basically what happens is that votes are traded. The above-cited article shows government expenditures were larger than they should be because the individual interest group, in this case people who lived on a given road, had to accumulate only a simple majority, and the total cost of the project to people pushing it was thus a little more than half of its actual cost. This would lead to over-investment.

In this case the entire cost of the "interest group" was the individuals' voting for projects in which they had no interest in order to get their own projects through. Presumably the congressmen would not sell their votes for a project unless what they got in return would fully reimburse their voters for their sacrifice. These votes, this article will argue, are today the principal real cost of pressure groups and represent the rectangle.

Unfortunately, the real world is worse than that, because voters are not only badly informed, they are asymmetrically informed. They are aware of the benefit they receive, and they are aware that is a major benefit in most cases. They don't know about the other projects their congressmen vote for in order to get them that benefit.

We have in Tucson a major example of government waste in the form of the Central Arizona Project. Previously, I always used the Tulsa Ship Canal and the canal paralleling the Mississippi as examples of logrolling waste, but the CAP[11] situation in Tucson is even better.

We, at vast expense to the taxpayers of the United States, have a water supply which is more expensive and of a poorer quality than before the project was built. Needless to say the voters in the City of Tucson who favored and pressed their congressmen to vote for this project did not realize the outcome would be that bad, but they did realize the hypothesized benefit to Tucson would be much less than the cost to the national taxpayer.[12]

There is another problem which I raised in an article entitled "Efficient Rent Seeking." This article produced some mathematics implying that rent seeking could either under-consume the entire value of the gift, or exceed

11. The CAP (Central Arizona Project) brings water across the entire state, dropping some off at various places. The whole thing is both wasteful and environmentally suspect, but the last segment reaching Tucson sets new records for waste.

12. In this case there was a lot of good technical advice. The economists, the agricultural economists, and the hydrology engineers at the University were strongly opposed to the project, and devoted a good deal of time and energy lobbying and arguing against it. Unfortunately, the voters did not seem to believe them.

it.[13] It led to a very long series of comments, replies, etc., which as a matter of fact I am planning to put out as a book. The whole thing is paradoxical, and I don't think we need any more paradoxes in economics even though I invented this one and have been defending it against various people who maintain that they have a solution.

Leaving the confusing efficient rent-seeking literature aside, the CAP went through by logrolling, i.e., trades. The entrepreneurs for this were the congressmen, but it was actually the votes that they were attempting to trade, while the actual cost of the whole thing, as well as the benefits, fell on the voters.

Representative Udall (Arizona) would agree to vote for various projects for raising the price of farm products consumed in Tucson, in return for farm-state representatives' agreeing to put up money for the CAP.

This was not the only trade that he made. One rather amusing example is a trade that he made with environmentalists. He always voted against any development in Alaska, in return for the environmentalists' voting for or putting pressure behind the building of the CAP, although the CAP is certainly an environmentally suspect operation. Both Udall and the environmental organizations could gain from the trade, but the net effect of a large collection of projects which pay off to the people who gain much less than total costs is negative. This is true of the agricultural program and the CAP and perhaps of the Alaskan development block, although I really know nothing about the latter.

Projects of this sort are common in the American government. Even in cases where there is a genuine public good, such as the military, the congressmen work strongly for getting projects in their district, even if their district is not the most efficient place to put them. Normally, the efficiency of the location is almost ignored in deciding where to spend various parts of the military budget. In most cases such logrolling does not lead to as colossally inefficient outcomes as the agricultural program and the CAP, but it is almost certain that in every case where something is put through by logrolling the net cost is greater than the benefit.

The reason that this can be done is that the average citizen is not very well informed. As I mentioned above, most of the experts in Tucson thought the

13. G. Tullock, "Efficient Rent Seeking," in *Toward a Theory of the Rent-Seeking Society*, ed. J. M. Buchanan, R. D. Tollison, and G. Tullock, 571–79 (College Station: Texas A&M University Press, 1980).

CAP was an undesirable project, and would injure Tucson. This information simply did not get to the average voter even in Tucson in spite of extensive efforts on the part of a number of people at the University. If this information did not enter the knowledge of the individual voter in Tucson, think how badly informed the individual voter in St. Louis was.[14]

What we see then as a result of this kind of rent seeking in Washington is a number of congressmen who are able to stay in office because they made these trades, and their constituents know something about the part of those trades that directly benefits them. The costs are widely dispersed and are not noticed on a project-by-project basis by the other voters. Thus things for which the total benefit is much less than the total cost can be put through by logrolling.

Thus General Motors in lobbying for protection against Japanese cars was in essence pointing out to the congressmen that there were a lot of votes to be gained. The UAW, of course, could mobilize their members, but the votes of the vast dealer network were no doubt more important.

This provides, for this particular type of rent seeking, an explanation of where the cost rectangle is. Further, the amount is very large. I do not deny the costs which I discussed previously, but it seems to me that the sum total of those costs is not as large as needed to explain the rectangle. I would argue that because poor information of an asymmetrical nature is involved, the total cost is actually much greater than the rectangle of the rent-seeking literature. The reader may not agree with me, but I feel that if he does not, he should suggest someplace else where the cost would occur.

14. I should say here that the water in Tucson turned out to be even poorer quality than the experts anticipated. It interacts with the pipes in the older part of town with the result that the water coming out is yellow. This led to a public vote to refuse to accept the water. We had already built the water purification plant, and will have to pay a sizeable amount to the government for the water even if we don't use it. We now must dispose of it by some method other than putting it in our pipes. All of this greatly increases the total cost.

WHICH RECTANGLE?

I have noticed in the literature recently, that not only is the monopoly square in the case of rent-seeking, sometimes referred to as the Tullock rectangle, but the question of why we do not seem to have any obvious representation of that large cost in the real world is now sometimes referred to as the Tullock paradox. The purpose of this article and its predecessor, "Where Is the Rectangle?" is to, at least partially, clear up the Tullock paradox.[1] In this article I will also produce another Tullock rectangle, which perhaps we should call T′.

Let me begin by referring back to my article "Where Is the Rectangle?" In this article I referred to my still-earlier article, in which I argued that the rectangle representing the monopoly profit is as much a cost to the society as is the triangle to the right, the Harberger triangle. The argument quite simply was that God does not come down and give people gifts, they have to work for them.[2]

The problem, which is referred to above, the Tullock paradox, is where do we find that cost in the real world. I have been worried about this from the very beginning, and in "Where Is the Rectangle?" I summarized a number of possible solutions from my earlier articles and introduced another. I am not withdrawing any of this here, but I am going to extend the analysis. Figure 1 is a conventional demand and supply diagram with some product, which can be produced at the cost C, and the demand DD.

The government provides somebody a monopoly in producing it, and the price goes from C up to M and the quantity produced falls from Q_c to Q_m and the rectangle marked T is both "profit" and the cost of getting the government to provide it. In "Where Is the Rectangle?" I said the beneficiaries of this particular monopoly obtained it by log-rolling, and hence, they accepted other projects which are to their disadvantage in order to get it. That is the cost of rent-seeking.

Reprinted, with kind permission of Kluwer Academic Publishers, from *Public Choice* 96 (1998): 405–10.

1. G. Tullock, "Where Is the Rectangle?" *Public Choice* (1997): 148–59.

2. G. Tullock, "The Welfare Costs of Tariffs, Monopolies, and Theft," *Western Economic Journal* 5 (1967): 224–32.

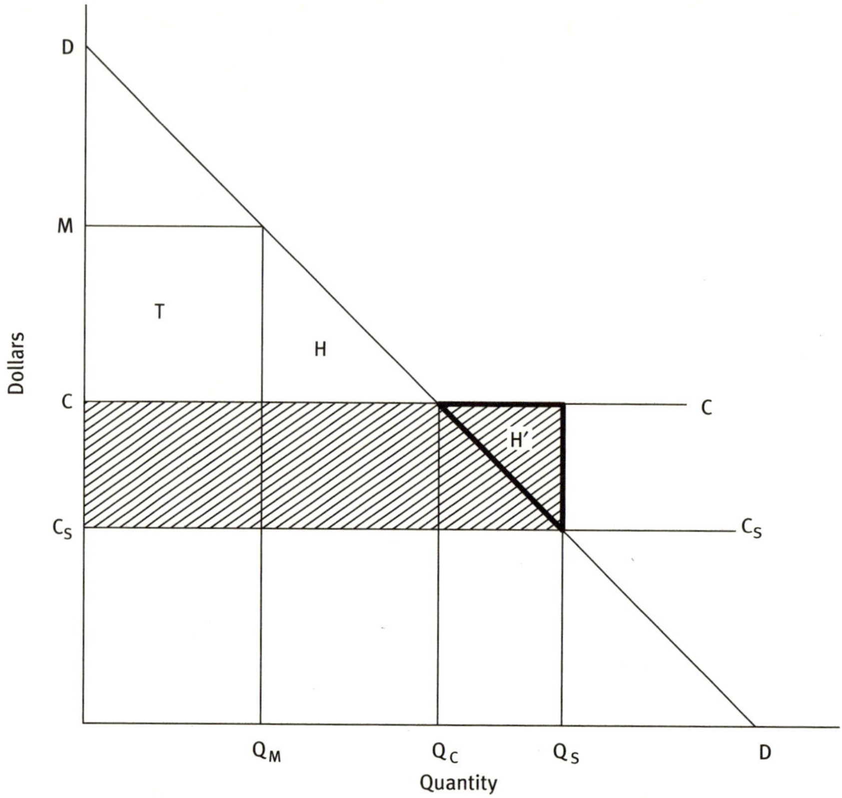

FIGURE 1
Return from monopolies

But governments "helping" voters do not always do so by providing monopolies. Sometimes and in fact very commonly they provide subsidies. I now live in the West, and the West is full of government water projects of one sort or another. Almost all are drastically inefficient in the sense that they produce water at a cost which is very much higher than its value.

Once again, in Figure 1 we show the situation, the cost of the water is, of course, CC as it was before, but this subsidized price is lower and is shown by C_s. Under these circumstances the amount demanded is Q_s, and the government's cost in providing it is shown by the lined rectangle. You will note that this is much larger than the T rectangle, but that, of course, is to a considerable extent simply a drafting decision. The fact that it would be large, I take it, is obvious.

If we are talking about Western water projects there is no problem putting your finger on the cost. You can leave Tucson a very short distance and see the canal which was built to bring water here, and this is water which the city of Tucson appears to think is of less than zero value.[3] Many citizens of Tucson seem to think that we should extend the demand curve down below the horizontal axis in order to show the real situation.

Tucson's water is obviously a special case. More normally the subsidized product would have been accepted. Note that in this case there is a sort of equivalent of the Harberger triangle, heavily outlined and marked H′. This is that part of the government subsidy which goes to providing the subsidized good, where its value is less than the citizens' benefit plus the government subsidy. It is a deadweight cost like the Harberger triangle in a monopoly. The rest of the lined rectangle shows the benefit which people would have achieved as a result of consuming the monopolized good at a subsidized price if they did not have to buy the subsidy through rent-seeking. In any event, we have here a pretty obvious and open waste.

I take it no one will doubt that these water projects are always the result of rent-seeking in the form of log-rolling on the part of the residents in the area affected. Sometimes the source is not narrowly limited geographically. For an example, the people in Europe who subsidized the airbus for such a long period of time. These projects are obtained essentially by log-rolling. Returning to my first article on log-rolling long ago, "Problems of Majority Voting," you would expect that the voters would not take the full cost into account when making decisions on how large the project will be because a majority of voters will pay taxes for only slightly more than half of that total cost.[4] In other words, they act as if they were buying it cheap, and indeed they are for that particular project. Under the circumstances they purchase Q_s quantity.

All of this assumes good information, but the voters are normally very poorly informed on such projects. This can further increase the costs. Thus the two rectangles may greatly underestimate the actual social cost.

From the standpoint of the individual making these decisions though, he is correct to choose Q_s as the quantity he would take. The cost which will be

3. Twice the citizens have voted not to put it in their pipes. Unfortunately they must still pay for it, although not even close to approximating its cost to the federal government.

4. G. Tullock, "Problems of Majority Voting," *Journal of Political Economy* 67 (1959): 571–79.

inflicted on him by log-rolling for other projects would be only slightly reduced by his defecting from the log roll. The bulk of the rent-seeking cost is something he must bear. Cutting back his consumption to, let us say, Q_c would benefit other people and injure him.

The nice feature of the use of water projects for this discussion is that one must only go about the world to see the physical representation of the rent-seeking cost. I mentioned the Tucson water project; one can easily find many others.

In general then government log-rolling activity can raise the price of a product for the benefit of the producers, and this leads to the triangle and rectangle above the cost. In this case the cost of the Tullock rectangle is not immediately visible, but we know it must exist. Indeed if you look at the actual voting patterns in Congress you will normally find that congressmen from areas where benefit occurs are also voting for things which do not benefit their own constituents and thus paying for it. We see that the argument of "Where Is the Rectangle?" is perfectly correct.

The addition produced by this article, however, is that there are many cases in which as a result of a government activity something is sold at less than its cost. In this case we have a physical representation of the cost, and what happens is that the product is purchased in greater quantity than it would be if the cost were directly allocated to the people who benefit.

There is an extreme case of this. Many of our government activities are not directly charged for at all. Many of them are small-scale activities, and I doubt that they enter the decision process of the voters at all. For two examples, there is a park maintained by the federal government on the outskirts of Tucson (a very beautiful park), and there is a road running up the mountains which is maintained by the federal government also. For many years they were provided free.

The federal government is now turning to putting fees on both of these facilities. Clearly this will lead to a lower consumption in which the cost of consuming moves from zero to positive. Probably this fee will be less than the cost of maintaining the facilities.

Returning to Figure 1 we could assume that in some cases the bulk of the lined rectangle represents expenditures to generate a genuine public good, and only a small part represents rent-seeking. Note that it would still be true that it would be over-consumed. For a particular example of over-consumption, when I moved into Tucson I installed a burglar alarm and for some time had a habit of forgetting to turn it off when I came home. As a result of this and

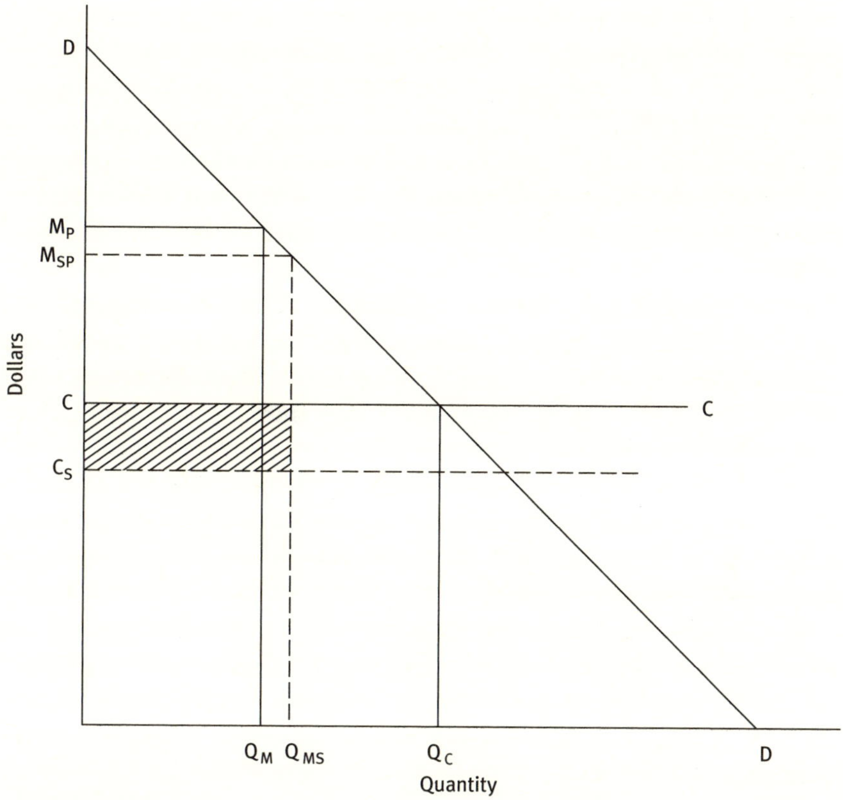

FIGURE 2
Change of cost

without any charge to me, the sheriff's office turned up fairly regularly. They were efficient and polite, but insisted on making certain that I was in fact the person that lived in that house. Clearly, this is a case in which I was overconsuming their activities.[5]

Of course the police department is a producer of valid public goods, and we should talk about it in those terms but the particular problem that shows up on Figure 2 also would apply. The public good would tend to be over-

5. To introduce a note of self-discipline, I began a policy of sending a check to the sheriff's office every time one of these false alarms was set off. After considerable delay I received a very nice note from the sheriff in which he said that he had given the whole matter careful thought and felt he couldn't cash the checks.

consumed. Basically, we distinguish between rent-seeking activities and the imposition of costs on people for public goods, or reducing externalities essentially in terms of whether the outcome is desirable or not. Clearly, the Tucson supplementary water supply drawn from the Colorado River is undesirable, and the sheriff's office is desirable.

Let us turn to another problem which is what happens if both of these types of rent-seeking are produced at the same time. This is not particularly uncommon in the real world. Agriculture is a pretty clear case. Farmers benefitted until recently from a form of cartel run by the government to get prices up and very extensive subsidies mainly in the form of research to lower costs.

In order to discuss this, consider Figure 2. Here we have the usual demand and cost lines, and the usual monopoly rectangle shown as solid lines. If there is a subsidy, the cost to the producer, not the cost to the government, but the cost to the producer, will fall, and this is shown by the dashed line. With this new dashed line the optimal monopoly price is shown by the rectangle formed by the dashed lines. Note that production would be somewhat larger and the price lower with this subsidy.

The simple conclusion is that the social cost of this combination of two different rent-producing activities could be either greater or less than either one of them individually. Presumably, there is some equilibrium, but I have not been able to deduce it. If the reader can do so I hope that he will inform me.

In the meanwhile, the major point of this article is to clear up some difficulties still remaining in rent-seeking theory. Unfortunately, there are a great many more difficulties in rent-seeking theory, but I hope I have at least made a few steps forward in the 10,000 Li march.

PART 5

EXCHANGES AND CONTRACTS

EXCHANGES AND CONTRACTS

Exchanges and Contracts in Economics and Politics

Adam Smith spoke of the human propensity to truck and barter. Today we think that trades come from recognition of mutual advantage followed by action to obtain that mutual advantage. It is of course true that only humans engage in real trade. Further, only humans trade promises or goods for promises. Thus it may be that there is something about human heredity that makes trades likely. It seems reasonable that the hereditary factor is the human higher intelligence that makes it possible to perceive an advantage that for the less intelligent animals remains hidden. In any event human beings do trade object for object, object for promise, and promise for promise.

Since a trade involves consent by both parties, it is generally thought that trades are beneficial. In general this is true, but there are difficulties. In the first place force, deception, ignorance, or simple stupidity may be present. In addition, the trade almost always has at least some effect on third parties. Thus, the very simple line of reasoning found in so many economics books is an oversimplification. Further, trades in the political sphere are normally left out completely in these discussions. Since such trades are as important to the functioning of politics as economic transactions are in the market, this omission is important. In this monograph we shall deal with politics and market transactions, starting with private transactions. Private transactions do not directly involve government, but government is important to them. As we shall discover, private market transactions are also important in government action.

For the next few paragraphs we shall assume that the parties to a contract make no mistakes. I should say that this assumption is implicit but seldom explicit in much economic discussion of commerce. Another problem with transactions much discussed in the economic literature is the possibility, indeed almost the certainty, that the transaction will affect third parties. This is called an "externality," and there is much discussion of it in the literature. Indeed it is a principal justification for government action.

In the first place governments frequently generate externalities them-

Reprinted, with permission, from *The Blackstone Commentaries*, no. 3, ed. Amanda J. Owens (Fairfax, Va.: The Locke Institute, 2000), 1–54.

selves. The Serbian citizens had a particularly good exposure to this matter recently. In most countries, certainly the United States, it is illegal to offer anything of value to someone in return for his vote. It is also illegal for the potential voter to accept the something of value for his vote. I presume that legislation like this exists even in Serbia and certainly in most civilized countries. President Clinton initially said that the United States would send aid to Serbia to repair the externalities inflicted on them by NATO forces if they voted the present government out of power. If they did not, the United States would refuse to aid them and would keep them under blockade. Clearly this is a violation of the standard of not giving things of value to people in an effort to change their votes.

Therefore governments can deliberately create externalities. This should be a part of the elementary economics course everywhere. It is not, however. The Chairman of the President's Council of Economic Advisers, Joseph Stiglitz, showed ignorance of this point that led to my article "Externalities and Government."[1] Apparently this article surprised many economists, although it should not have done so.

But let us return to private contracts and their externalities. If a private citizen enters into a contract with a thug to threaten a voter with injury if he does not vote as the contractor wants, this is not only a crime but also a tortious externality. No court would enforce the agreement between the contractor and his thug. In fact, they would make every effort to put the perpetrators in jail.

There are few examples of an agreement that does not affect at least some third parties. To take an extreme example, suppose I buy a candy bar. My purchase affects the price of the candy bar. The effect is of course trivial—it would require mathematical precision out to the eighth or ninth decimal place to notice it. No one would suggest that we attempt to eliminate this type of trivial pecuniary externality. However, large purchases sometimes lead to significant price effects, and create a significant pecuniary externality.

To take a different case of a nonpecuniary externality, suppose that at 3:00 in the morning I go out on my balcony and play a trumpet. The local police would promptly deal with this action. It is an externality but one which society is more than ready to ban. All my readers will, I presume, agree that the trumpet should be banned. But do we have any general principles? Do we simply make ad hoc decisions on each instance?

1. G. Tullock, "Externalities and Government," *Public Choice* 95 (1998): 411–15.

Another example is the purchase of a house. Suppose the neighbors object to the house purchase based on the use the buyer plans to make of the house. Suppose the buyer always invites people in to engage in gambling. Or suppose he is planning to put an extra story on the house. Either of these activities and many others might annoy his potential neighbors. They might simply dislike him. This all adds up to an externality, but one that may not easily be prohibited. Indeed, if you had to get permission of your neighbors and other people in the same general area in order to move in, land would become relatively nonnegotiable. But having said that we do not want to eliminate *all* externalities, which ones should we eliminate? Any list of externalities to be eliminated and those to be kept would be long and cumbersome. The list itself would be an externality. It would make transfers difficult. The price at which the transfers were made could adversely affect the price of neighboring property.

At the moment in the United States there are large numbers of people who feel that the Japanese are selling their cars too cheaply in U.S. markets. They feel that the government should stop them, and have successfully lobbied for restrictions on the import of Japanese cars. This situation generates three types of externalities. The restrictions are government externalities; the low price is a negative externality to workers in the automobile industry and a positive externality to potential purchasers. Additionally, purchasers of non-Japanese cars also gain from the low price of the Japanese cars since they force, through competition, lower prices for other cars.

A mainstream economist would say that side payments could take care of all of these problems. Automobile workers could pay the Japanese companies to raise their price. Similarly those who want to buy a General Motors car could offer money to the Japanese companies in return for their rejecting the proposal of the automobile workers. A market could develop, and a mathematical economist could set out the necessary optimality conditions. This is a clear indication that mathematical economics can be carried too far.

What we need is an efficient set of rules for such exchanges. However, we must keep in mind that the rules themselves generate an externality, because potential purchasers and sellers must know them and this takes time and energy. The rules will not be optimal in the pure sense. They will be simply the best we can do.

So far I have been talking about externalities arising out of transactions. The failure to transact also can have external effects. In the example given above, suppose that I decided not to buy a candy bar. The effect would be to infinitesimally lower the price. Inaction as well as transactions can affect other people. To give a very minor example: my house in Tucson would have had a very nice view of the sunset except that my neighbor had a house that blocked the view. I bought the house knowing that his house was there. Still it would have been nice if he had torn his house down. Was this an externality? Was I exerting an externality if I complained about the location and height of his house? Almost all of our action or inaction affects other people.

The reader may feel I am raising trivial problems. But let him give me the benefit of the doubt and continue to follow my reasoning. Anything you do may have an effect on someone else. Contrarywise, inaction also makes the world different for other people. In most cases the effect or absence of effect will be trivial, but sometimes it can be sizable. The same line of reasoning applies in reverse. You may be affected by things other people do or via a failure to take action on their part.

What should we do? There is an easy general answer. We should arrange for everyone to maximize their future income stream. Reductions in the net income stream, either by the activity of other people that affect the person of interest, or restrictions on his action in order to avoid affecting other people, should be taken into account. We should try to maximize the net product. Normally this type of scheme would be introduced with a legal and property regime affecting transactions in a maximizing way.

We should favor the set of institutions that give us the prospect of the highest net satisfaction. Thus any restriction on transactions or actions that produce negative externalities would be of benefit. The possibility of positive externalities in both directions should also be considered.

There are some problems with this suggestion. Since this matter deals with the unknown future, no precise calculation is possible. You are presented with a bundle of lottery tickets, each of which presents the future as a gamble with different sets of institutions. You can choose one, but that does not insure success. It is like any constitutional decision in that it is a lottery, and any ticket could be the winning ticket.

The other problem is that we are choosing a government policy, and government tends to be inept when not perverse. A significant problem arises as to whether the rules will be enforced effectively. The legal system is not perfect, or even close to perfect, and in addition, lawyers have much to gain from complexity in the legal rules. Thus even apparently optimal rules may turn out to be a far from optimal solution.

Government-Created Externalities

In this chapter we shall turn to the main subject of this monograph, bargaining and contracts within the government. Private and government contracts are similar in that they create externalities.

Some would argue that there is not an externality, because the government is an attachment of mine, or I am subsidiary to the government, and hence the externality is simply a part of government affecting its subjects and so is not truthfully external. I do not like to quarrel over the meaning of words. If the government drafts me and sends me off to risk my life in a war of which I disapprove, I would say it is an externality, but those who object to that use of words can substitute whatever else they wish whenever they encounter "externality" in my text.

In this chapter I shall discuss only democratic governments. This means that I shall be discussing a minority of all governments. Almost half of the world's population now lives in a democratic society. Since I am going to confine myself to democracies in this analysis it may be sensible to pause for a discussion on the definition of democracy. Normally I define democracy as a system in which the government is chosen by a free election in which considerable numbers of people are permitted to vote. Thus Ancient Athens was a democracy as was the Roman Republic. In both of these countries women could not vote, nor could slaves, nor could a fairly large category of people who were free but not citizens. Further, Switzerland has a democracy in spite of the fact that a large part of their less-well-paid workers are foreigners admitted on temporary permits, prohibited from becoming citizens as are their children, and not permitted to vote. Until recently women could not vote in many cantons.

The restrictions on who can vote have a direct implication for externalities. Some people, not I, believe that if you are permitted to vote on a particular subject then you are not the victim of an externality even if you are in the minority or feel that the issue was improperly phrased. Thus, by this definition, if you are permitted to vote and in fact vote, the election consequences are not externalities. Normally people adopting this approach ignore the question of whether your vote actually made a difference to the outcome.

For this definition of externality to make sense, the actions voted on must be broken down finely. Suppose, for example, that there were direct public votes on one of the gigantic bills, covering many topics, which are typical of Congress. Suppose that you on the whole favor the bill and vote for it although many parts of it you would strongly oppose if they were presented one at a time. This is an externality, externally imposed by the drafting of the bill that made it necessary for you to accept or reject the whole thing. The difference between this situation and electoral voting is that you are motivated to think about the matter carefully and to make an individual and decisive choice. The bargaining process by which the bill was made up was carried on without any input from the voter. Thus an externality is imposed on the electoral voter.

Externalities can be positive or negative. In the governmental field people who cannot vote may benefit from government activities. Children, of course, cannot vote and are subject to a great deal of government activity. Most of this is intended to benefit the child. The child may not like being forced to go to school, but there is no doubt that this is intended to benefit him.

Externalities may be imposed on nonvoters. During World War II men aged from eighteen to twenty-one were drafted but could not vote. Women who could vote from the age of eighteen were not drafted, although I doubt that the difference in voting power was an important factor in the distinction. There are other cases where people who cannot vote are subject to action by democratic governments. In many cases this is for the benefit of the subject; but in other cases, imprisonment for example, it is emphatically not to their advantage.

There are people who would say that in a democracy there are no externalities, because in essence we do it to ourselves. Economists will recall that it used to be said that government debt was not a burden because we owe it to ourselves. This slogan, important in the last days of Keynesianism, has died out. It has been replaced by the opposite error. Now we are taxed under the Social Security Act for an amount that allegedly is to be saved for future use when the demographic structure of society changes. In fact it is not saved but spent. In the trust fund are a number of IOUs that will have to be paid for by the taxpayer just as if the additional money had not been taxed. The alleged "savings" are actually government expenditures.

If it is true that the majority in a democracy takes action that they think will benefit them, then there is no reason to believe that the minority will gain particularly from each action. The obvious modern cases are the graduated income tax and the corporation tax that fall very heavily on about five percent of the population. To some extent this is compensated for by the

Social Security tax that falls most heavily on the lower brackets in the income stream.

But these are externalities imposed by the voting group on part of itself. How about people who cannot vote? Before women got the vote in the United States they were subject to a number of legal disabilities. The granting of votes to blacks in the southern states in the early 1960's led to a great improvement in their status.

Most classical democracies permitted only some of the citizens to vote. There was no representative democracy with respect to legislation. The voter actually had to go to the forum or the Pynx in order to vote. In the case of Rome, with its extensive empire, this was a very severe restriction. Athens made it less of a problem by transferring some minor legislative tasks to a randomly selected group of citizens.

In the Middle Ages voting bodies and free cities developed into parliaments of one sort or another. In all cases there were many residents of the area who could not vote. There is no doubt that these elected bodies benefited themselves at the expense of other members of society. However, the electoral bodies had to limit their profiteering because the support of some of the nonvoters was required for military reasons if the state was to survive.

Among the people who cannot vote are foreigners. In some cases they are subject to severe negative externalities imposed by governments other than their own. The bombing of Serbia and Iraq are examples, but we need not go to actual acts of war. The tariff policy of most countries is intended to benefit their own citizens at the expense of foreigners. People who do not know economics usually design the tariffs, and although the tariffs do not achieve their domestic objectives, they do succeed in injuring foreigners. This is a clear-cut externality.

How about the benefits? The U.S. government does improve the well-being of foreigners, for example with aid programs. This is a positive externality. It should be admitted, however, that frequently aid programs are distorted to benefit domestic citizens who can vote. The aid characteristically provides a market at above-market prices for various domestic producers. It is not clear whether the rather high salaries and superior living conditions of our citizens who administer this aid should be regarded as an externality.

The striking feature of our aid programs abroad is how small they are. If the citizens of India were permitted to vote in American elections they would no doubt transfer enough of the American national product to themselves to impoverish us and to raise their living standards to about one-third of our poverty level. This move would not gain the approval of the American public.

This aversion is particularly clear in discussions of the United Nations. There is fierce opposition to making the United Nations a genuine government with redistributive powers. I find that the objections to converting the United Nations into a real government are normally strong but incoherent. In my opinion the unexpressed objection is the fear that egalitarian policies would be followed by a powerful United Nations, and this would lower the income of almost every American.

The above discussion of externalities is odd in that it is both orthodox and revolutionary. These actions affect people who are not decision-makers. Thus these actions are externalities. While Chairman of the President's Council of Economic Advisers, Joseph Stiglitz gave a speech in which he said that government was necessary because of the widespread externalities in the market. He was correct but did not consider *governmental* externalities. I wrote an article filling this gap by discussing governmental externalities.[2] A referee said that I had got Stiglitz "dead to rights" and that most economists did not know that government cures some externalities and creates others.

Domestic Governmental Externalities

Government is frequently urged as a solution to the externality problem. As we have discussed, the existence of rules to limit externalities are generally in themselves externalities, since they require parties to transactions to know what they are and this process in itself is costly.

We now turn to direct imposition of externalities by governments. We have already mentioned some cases, such as bombing, which inflict externalities on people outside the government control. We will now direct our attention to the internal imposition of externalities by the government. For the first part of our demonstration we will assume that we are dealing with a simple democratic government in which all issues are voted on directly by the population, such as a village.

Suppose that someone in the village decides to establish a small automobile repair shop. This leads to the usual collection of externalities, both posi-

2. Ibid.

tive and negative. In this case there is a special positive externality in that the shop will provide convenient repairs for some of the citizens. I suppose that cars coming to be repaired might generate some negative externalities too.

Alternatively, suppose that the village by popular vote decides to build a small repair shop for its own vehicles. Let us assume that this generates the same conventional externalities as the private shop. There are, however, some further externalities due to the combination of the vote and the method of financing. For simplicity assume that fifty-one percent of the voters favored the shop and forty-nine percent were opposed. All of the voters will pay taxes to support it. Thus, those who voted against the facility not only find its presence annoying, but also suffer an externality in that they are taxed to pay for it.

The voters who favored the repair shop, however, find that they pay only fifty-one percent of the total cost. They receive a positive externality from the project. The size of the externality would be hard to evaluate. Perhaps some people who voted against the shop thought it was basically desirable but not at the price. Their negative externality would be only the difference between their tax price and what they would have paid for it. On the other hand those who favored it might have been only mildly interested and hence are benefited only a small amount. Perhaps if the cost had been allocated only to the people who favored the project the increase in cost would mean that they would no longer have favored it.

The actual value of this political externality is always hard to figure out. Only if there is a transaction can we say that the transactors gain. Since a basic reason for voting and compelling the minority to go along is minimizing bargaining costs, the difficulties raised by the alternative mechanism are insuperable. Earlier we discussed the rules with respect to externalities in ordinary market transactions. The optimal rules were those that balanced the relative disadvantages of direct externalities with the disadvantages imposed by the rules.

The situation changes when many projects are advanced instead of a few. In the real world of politics, a government deals with many things. A permanent coalition could exploit the minority and make gains for itself. Such permanent coalitions are unlikely. The victims can always attempt to buy the votes of marginal members of a voting coalition. Thus we would expect a rotating majority with all projects being provided, using more resources than are optimal.

What is the solution? Requiring unanimity would solve the externality problem but would provide an impossible bargaining problem. Public choice scholars have proposed simply that the required majority be raised so as to reduce the exploitation of the minority, while not making the bargaining problem impossible. But how much should we raise it? There are no empirical data upon which we can found a formal solution.

There are, however, institutions that try to solve this problem. In the United States, for example, there are many condominiums or collective housing estates that are produced by profit-seeking real estate firms. These firms are motivated to choose a voting rule that they believe will attract the individual purchasers to make decisions on communal issues.

As a general rule the condominium constitutions provide for an elected body much like a city council. Important decisions, however, are usually left to a direct vote of the owners. For unimportant matters a simple majority is the voting rule. For matters involving significant expenditure, however, most of these privately organized governments use an eighty percent majority rule. Decisions can be deferred if there is not an eighty percent majority until there is more agreement. From this example it seems that some majority higher than fifty percent and less than one hundred percent would work better than simple majority.

But returning to simple majority voting and continuing with our present system in which the voters vote directly without the intervention of politicians, we are led to watch for complex problems where there are many possible projects under consideration, each of which would be favored by some voters and not by others. It is possible for one coalition of voters to make a deal in which several projects win vote majorities, even though none would secure a majority vote by itself.

In reality, projects tend to be different from each other and to be favored by different groups of voters. Thus we have a set of projects that are favored by different groups of voters, many of which cost more than the tax revenues from voters who favor them. In other words, some voters gain and others lose. It is again an example of political externalities.

Let us consider the various groups of voters who propose various mixes of projects. In general each mix proposed would benefit a majority of voters but might very well injure a minority who have to pay taxes for this group of projects. This raises the potential prospect of a cyclical majority, first discovered by French scholars in the eighteenth century and investigated mathematically by many scholars, but apparently not existing as a practical problem in the real world. My explanation of why it does not exist in the real world is given in "Why So Much Stability."[3] Let us for the time being simply consider an example of potential cycles.

Suppose a group of voters composing a majority put together a bundle of projects that will benefit each of them if taken as a whole, even though many of the projects considered individually would injure part of the group. The bundle is a bargain that is mutually acceptable but injurious to the voters who were not part of this particular bargain. These voters then create another bundle of projects in which they gain and in which at least a few members of the majority coalition will gain more than in the rest of the majority coalition. In essence they are buying votes, and, if they have calculated correctly, then they will obtain a majority for themselves and eliminate the previous majority.

Suppose, however, that members of the previous majority who have not been purchased in this deal produce a new coalition in which a significant group of voters switch allegiance to them. Obviously this process can continue indefinitely. Although I have not taken the trouble to do so here, it is clear that a number of such special combinations could be arranged so that the original majority coalition eventually became a majority again. This is called a cyclical majority and with simple voting structure is easy to demonstrate, as in "Why So Much Stability."

Logrolling

In this chapter, we will begin a discussion of logrolling. My article "Problems of Majority Voting"[4] was the first formal economic analysis of logrolling. We shall start our current study of logrolling with a repetition of that very simple model. Later we shall turn to more complicated models that reflect the research since the 1960's.

The common model of lawmaking assumes that the legislators, whether elected officials or hereditary monarchs, consider a general law in terms of its general desirability. For example, most countries need and maintain a military machine. In the United States, if we consider the actual progress of the appropriations bills for the Department of Defense, we discover little objection to the department itself but immense interest in the details of the bills.

3. G. Tullock, "Why So Much Stability," *Public Choice* 37 (1981): 189–202.

4. G. Tullock, "Problems of Majority Voting," *Journal of Political Economy* 67 (1959): 571–79.

Which, if any, bases shall be closed? Should new aircraft be purchased, and if so, which ones? Congressmen are very interested in what happens in their own constituencies. The same process goes on in almost all appropriations bills, and even mere rules of court procedure seem to be the outcome, in their details, of bargaining.

The bargaining process is what we call logrolling. It is important in all governments. Until recently it was discussed only in general terms. My contribution to this process was to produce a formal model. The model in its original version was very simple, but in my opinion a big help in understanding the process. I will reproduce it here and then go on to the more complicated analyses that proceeded from the simple model.

Assume that there are one hundred farmers living on a series of feeder roads leading into a major road. The state maintains the main road but a local government of the hundred farmers provides for maintenance of the feeder roads. For simplicity's sake, let us assume that there are twenty roads with five farmers living on each. When one road is worn enough to require maintenance all of the hundred farmers vote for or against an appropriation to repair it, and the majority will is carried out. Each farmer is taxed for his share (one one-hundredth) of the cost.

One pattern of behavior for the farmers would be for each farmer to decide individually on the standard of repair for the roads. He would then look at each road and vote for repairs depending on his own personal standard of acceptable road conditions. Different farmers would have different standards. The outcome would be that all roads would be repaired at the level thought optimal by the median farmer. This, I think, is what the conventional view of democracy implies.

Unfortunately the farmers can devise a different decision-making system. Farmers from one road can make a deal with the farmers of ten other roads. They can offer to vote for additional repairs on the other farmers' roads in return for votes to repair their own roads to a higher standard. The cost of repairs to the farmers on the eleven roads that are part of the bargain is only eleven-twentieths of the cost actually inflicted on the collective. Thus the farmers will choose a higher standard but pay no more.

The bargain could take two forms. Firstly, the inhabitants on the eleven roads could form a permanent organization to vote for repairs on their roads and against repairs on the other roads. I will put this possibility off for a few paragraphs. The alternative is that the individual farmers on each road agree to vote for repairs on the roads of the farmers on ten other roads, but do not form a permanent collective.

Negotiations might fall into several different patterns. Everyone would be trying to get the best bargain, and so it is likely that the farmers on two roads would make more or less equal bargains with the farmers on nine additional roads. Each of the additional roads would make their own bargain. Any road that was left out could offer exceptionally good terms to get in. This system would result in the same level of repair for all roads because eventually all of the roads would be part of a bargain. Thus, everyone would be paying for the maintenance of all roads, including their own, at a higher level than they would have chosen if this bargaining or logrolling had not taken place.

Why not form a permanent coalition of the farmers on eleven roads? The coalition would be unstable. The nine roads left out of the coalition could offer very good terms to two of the members of the coalition if they defected. Therefore, any effort to form a strong coalition to provide permanent good roads for its members would fail. I suppose I do not have to explain why a simple agreement on the part of all farmers not to form such bargains would fail.

In practice this kind of coalition does not hold. In the United States, a powerful governor or president with a majority in the legislature is occasionally able to keep the minority weak. Normally however this is true only with major legislative matters and not with respect to the various items pertaining to each constituency or pressure group that make up the bulk of the logrolling.

The only case I know of in which a coalition remained solid was in the old South. After the Civil War, when whites once again were able to vote, they formed a solid Democratic coalition. Republicans who were suspected of too much sympathy for blacks were not admitted. This led to the creation of the Solid South because voters elected only representatives to the legislature who brought back pork for the constituency. The Solid South is still in effect in the southern states today, although it is gradually eroding, starting with the president and gradually working its way down through senators, governors, and representatives to Washington.

What role do externalities play? If we take the original system in which each person votes for all roads in accordance with his own preference for the degree of maintenance required and does not make special decisions for his own road, assuming single-peaked preferences, the roads would be maintained at the level of the preferences of the median voter. Note that under these circumstances only the median voter would actually get his first preference. All of the others would be compelled to follow his preference, and in about half of the cases this would be less than their wants and in about half, more. Strictly speaking this is an externality, albeit a small one, inflicted by the choice process.

Interestingly enough this same externality is inflicted in the market. Producers select designs that they think will be acceptable to a large number of customers. Only the customer whose desires are right in the center of the preference spectrum receives his first choice. Once again it seems likely that a minor externality is inflicted. We can imagine the most exact duplicate in politics if voters selected a general standard and then appointed an engineer to apply it. The outcome would be the median preference in both maintenance and taxes.

Now let us turn to an alternative form of logrolling in which there are many individual bargains in each of which only a majority are participants, but all of the voters are members of at least one bargain. This leads to the voters choosing a degree of road repair in which only a little more than half of the tax cost is taken into account because the rest falls on people who are not part of that specific bargain. This is in a way a self-inflicted externality. Only by changing the Constitution so that voters chose a general standard and then somebody applied that standard could the externality be avoided.

The real world does not lend itself to the same solution to these problems. A subsidy for farmers, improved water supply in some western state, and a tariff on Japanese cars may all be the constituents of the same bargain. The president may act as a representative of the whole, and no doubt this does improve things. However, normally he represents only a little more than half of the voters.

Note the externality situation here. Everyone is a member of coalitions of various people receiving various benefits. For each person the benefits from this web of coalitions are greater than the cost. He suffers external costs for the projects for which he votes although he does not want them, because the bargain as a whole benefits him. One of the reasons it benefits him is that much of the cost of the bargain falls on people who were not members of his coalition. Thus in getting the best deal he can he inflicts externalities on others. He is not a member of all of the bargains made, however, and for those cases where he is not a member he suffers an externality. Being a member of the constitutional group may be in net to his advantage; indeed, but that means that he suffers negative and not directly compensated external costs.

Constitutional methods of fixing this were the subject of Buchanan and Tullock's book *The Calculus of Consent.*[5] In essence, we recommended going to a reinforced majority that would reduce but not eliminate the problem.

Politicians, Ignorance, and Rent Seeking

According to the type of political science taught in most high schools, the professional representatives of the voters, the elected politicians, are expected to carry on the actual business of the government, subject to periodic elections that keep them interested in efficiently performing government tasks in accordance with the desires of voters. As you will see below I have no major quarrel with this model. The politicians devote much attention to the voters' needs because they want to be re-elected.

Here, as in many other parts of our society, motives are not really unitary efforts to gain or retain position and wealth. Politicians are like the rest of us, and most of their efforts are devoted to personal gains. But like the rest of us to some extent they sacrifice their well-being in a material sense for spiritual well-being, acting with charitable or moral motives rather than self-interest. Nevertheless, most of the time they, like us, are engaged in maximizing their own interest.

In all societies and in all times politicians, who in royal societies are called courtiers, have had poor reputations for honesty and good morals. Whether this reflects their actual moral and charitable defects or simply that their actions are much better known and hence have a greater effect on their reputation than an ordinary individual is not clear. It is also, however, quite possible that they are really less moral and charitable than ordinary citizens. This could reflect partly the type of people who go into political activity and partly the effect of having power with incomplete checks.

In any event we shall argue that leaving the government to its high-ranking and unchecked employees is unwise. In democracies, hopefully the voters provide checks on elected officials. In monarchies and dictatorships supervision comes from the top. Usually people criticizing monarchical rule

5. J. M. Buchanan and G. Tullock, *The Calculus of Consent: Logical Foundations of Constitutional Democracy* (Ann Arbor: University of Michigan Press, 1962).

confine themselves to criticizing the difference between the view of the monarch as to desirable policy and that of the people. Such differences may of course exist but they are not the only problem for monarchies.

A monarchy centers control onto one man with limited time to spend governing his country. It is true that some monarchs sometimes are very hard workers. Stalin, for example, personally read the reports from his spies in the American atom bomb laboratories during World War II. However, he must have had many areas that he was unable to supervise simply because of lack of time. There must have been many other areas where he gave poorly informed orders that did not conform with his long run interest.

We are, however, primarily interested in democracies, and in these situations lack of information and lack of interest on the part of voters are very important. Anthony Downs pointed out in his first book that the likelihood of any individual voter casting a decisive vote in any normal election is very small.[6] In general you are more likely to be killed in an automobile accident on the way to the polls than to cast a vote that changes the outcome. Under the circumstances if you enjoy voting or feel that you have a duty to do so, or have not thought about the implications of voting since your high school political science course, you are likely to vote. U.S. voters are more likely to guilt-tinged abstention than voting.

In your high school political science course, not only were you told to vote, but you were also told that your vote should be informed. As we mentioned above it is easy to deceive yourself about whether or not your vote is informed. In the early days of polling, pollsters frequently asked people specific questions in order to find out whether they were informed. They quickly found out that the people frequently gave wrong answers.

A strong example of voter ignorance comes from the Reagan campaign for president. Republican television advertisements ran again and again a picture of Reagan taking the oath as governor of California. The reason for this was that pollsters discovered that most voters thought that Reagan was simply an actor. At the same time the Republicans found out that many voters were irritated by actions taken by the government in the previous eight years. A great many voters thought that the past two presidents and the legislature were Republican. In focus groups there was vigorous opposition to the statement that the legislature was Democratic. Members of the focus group would claim that this was just a Republican lie.

When we turn to details, voters are almost totally ignorant except for the

6. A. Downs, *An Economic Theory of Democracy* (New York: Harper and Row, 1957).

few issues that directly affect them. I used to live in Tucson. Tucson was at the end of what was one of the most wasteful government projects in the West. This project took water from the Colorado River and shifted it across the state, ending at Tucson. Part of the water was used for irrigation for farmers' crops that were then purchased by the government to keep prices up. Much water was used by the city of Phoenix, which had an adequate nearby source, but preferred to have the federal government provide water from far away rather than to spend its own money in getting water from nearby. The water that reached Tucson was so polluted that the city refused to allow it in the water mains. Tucson dumped the water on the ground in the hope that percolating the water through two hundred feet of sand would purify it enough to make it drinkable when it reached the aquifer. The U.S. taxpayers paid for this project, and yet only a few benefited. I have used this as an example of wasteful government many times, but have never met anyone outside Arizona who has even heard of the water pipeline.

Let me modify my previous simple model of farmers and roads from Chapter 4 to illustrate this kind of asymmetric information. Suppose the farmers knew the condition of their road and the cost of repairs. They also knew their total tax bill, but they do not know that a large part of that tax bill comes from bargains made by their representative with other road representatives for votes. In other words, they see the world as one in which they get road repair on their own road very economically but have to pay considerable taxes for projects of which they are ignorant.

This may seem unrealistic, but fairly minor investigations of voters show that this kind of ignorance is common. Voters have a general idea that many projects other than those from which they reap benefits are wasteful, but rarely have any further information about these other projects. One result of this asymmetric information is that polls show that most voters like their congressmen and dislike Congress. This is not irrational. Congress passes many bills that injure them by inflicting taxes for projects in other parts of the country. Their own congressman does his best for them, and they know of certain specific projects which benefit them and for which the tax cost on them is much less than the benefit.

Legislation is often lengthy and complex. In one case, a secretary's phone number was enacted into law because no one had actually read the full text.[7] Indeed, it seems unlikely that the full texts of these gigantic portmanteau bills

7. David A. Stockman, *The Triumph of Politics: How the Reagan Revolution Failed* (New York: Harper and Row, 1986), 227.

are actually read by anyone. The congressman's own office personnel no doubt read those parts of the bill that affect their constituency but not the rest. Any part that gets into newspapers may be read more widely, but even then it is more likely that only the newspaper accounts are read.

All of this is, I think, a correct but discouraging view of democracy. The basic question is not whether democracy gives perfect government but whether it is better than the alternatives. There has been little in the way of good comparative studies.

In any event democracy is not a new form of government, and there is little evidence that the Greek and Roman democracies were markedly more prosperous than the surrounding non-democratic states. The development of large numbers of independent city-states in the late Middle Ages also did not bring prosperity.

There is a sort of compromise between democracy and monarchy. There were a number of cases, the Roman Republic, Athens, Venice, Berne, and England under the Whig predominance, in which a considerable number but by no means all of the inhabitants could vote. Superficially the states following this form of government seem to have done well. I suspect that the same kind of bargaining that we observe in the real democracy and in our models prevails there also. There have been almost no serious efforts to compare different forms of government in a scientific way. Indeed, if we confine ourselves to democracies, there have been little or no scientific comparisons of the different forms of government in democracies. I think such research is very important and would like to see it performed.

Politics

So far our discussion of how democracy actually works has not been very encouraging. Clearly there are severe defects. But most institutions have defects, and the fact that democracy has these defects does not prove it is inferior to other methods of running a government. To some extent any government has defects as compared with the market or other methods of achieving our goals. But then the market and the other methods also have defects. It would be nice if we had a perfect system, but given the actuality of the world, we must be content with having as few defects as we can.

To repeat here a favorite saying of mine, an engineer knows from Cournot's equations that no heat engine is perfect. Nevertheless he is able to choose between diesel and steam in designing a ship. He selects the one that for his particular use has the fewest defects. We should follow his model in choosing social structures. We should not be disturbed by the fact that we will not obtain a perfect solution. It is not given to us here below to reach perfection.

We can, in general, divide government activities into those which benefit or injure almost everybody, like the military when fighting a generally approved war or preparing for one, and those which benefit only specific groups of citizens, like the traditional pork-barrel projects. With respect to the first, democracy does provide such services—on the other hand so does a hereditary monarchy.

We have already discussed the limitations on the information of voters. Summarily, voters are not motivated to become well informed because their individual vote does not make a difference. They may, as a sort of hobby, follow the news. All my life I have been interested in foreign affairs and keep up with it insofar as reading to a more than casual level. This does not mean that I am really very well informed, only that I know more about foreign affairs than most of my faculty colleagues. In domestic affairs I am less interested and hence know less. Still, compared with the average voter my information is much larger.

Yet, if I voted, the superior information would have almost no effect. My vote would be dominated by the votes of people who knew much less. Thus, the outcome is apt to be erratic. To a considerable extent we depend not on voters but on professional people in government. Some of these are elected and others are career civil servants. They are not ignorant or unmotivated but they do have personal motives. In general civil servants tend to develop personal views as to what should be done in their particular field. These motives are not necessarily in accord with the public good.

In absolutist governments there is a similar collection of people at the lower levels with the same motives. They too have objectives for their particular bureau that are not entirely in accord with those of their superiors. The basic difference between democracy and absolutist rule is the governing person or persons and objectives. Further, the information contained in the mind of the absolute ruler is limited.

All of this, of course, is an argument for limited government. Only if we confine our actions to an area that we can understand, will we be able to choose good policies. So far we have been talking about matters of general interest, like a military organization, the police, and the highway system.

When we turn to more detailed policies things change. It should be emphasized that general policies contain within them innumerable special decisions that are of interest to various small minorities. This is as true in absolutist governments as in democracies, but I am going to confine my discussion to democracies. Thus the type of fighter plane which the Air Force will buy is interesting not only from the general defense standpoint, but also from the standpoint of the manufacturer, the people who work for him, merchants in the area where his factories are located, and, in particular, the congressman who is elected from that area.

The Navy understands the importance of the latter consideration. Every year it publishes a listing of naval expenditures by each state. This emphasizes the importance to congressmen of a good Navy and expenditures in their districts. Fighting in Congress is more likely to focus on the pork to be handed out to the various electoral districts than on matters of national armed strength. This is not because the congressmen are more interested in pork, but because pork allocation has a much greater impact on their personal reelection prospects.

Thus we have a situation in which almost everybody is interested in the provision of general public goods, even public goods that affect only a small part of the country. For example, the direct beneficiaries of the traditional water works of western United States would not finance the project because there are not enough of them. This illustrates the public good problem in which it is wise to hold out and let other people pay for the project. All of the people in a localized area are better off if they can get the national government taxes to pay for assistance instead of doing it themselves with local taxes.

It is likely that the voters in the benefited area will have to pay for support by voters in other areas in order to get national action. Thus logrolling will be put into action. If the transactions were perfect between different areas then this could be efficient. There are, however, two significant sources of inefficiency. First, a flood, for example, affects different people differently. Second, most tax systems are incapable of adjusting costs to that level of precision. Indeed a single tax for the entire area is likely to be the only feasible method of financing flood control measures.

But this assumes perfect information and perfect bargaining. The individual voter working to obtain this kind of bargain is investing his own resources to access a public good. Although the voter understands his own flooding problem, he probably does not know much about the other projects for which he is trading votes. Thus we have another source of inefficiency.

Let us summarize the various problems we meet when attempting to achieve our objectives. First, we have two major instrumentalities to use: the market and the government. The market and the government have two major difficulties. If I buy something in the market, it will exert externalities on other people. These externalities can be negative or positive. Other people will only object to the negative externalities.

The same problem arises with the government. Assuming a democratic government, the majority may exert externalities on the minority exactly the same as the externalities produced in the market. Whatever is generated may affect people other than those who favored the proposal. Further, because of the public good aspects, payment is compulsory whether you want the public good or not.

In principle, we choose public provision of goods when we feel that the negative externalities generated by public provision are less important than those generated by private provision. It is also easy to think of many examples where the government provides something that would be better provided privately. The Post Office is an excellent example, and indeed seems to be being gradually competed out of existence by private means of transmitting information.

Until recently there were strong intellectual currents favoring putting the whole economy under direct government control. This particular drive seems to have passed away but did much damage when it was in ascendance. It is still true that the division between government and private provision in all modern societies is mainly something that, like Topsy, just grew.

Creation of externalities is not the only area of similarity between government and market. The other resemblance is that both the government and the market operate by trading and bargaining. This is true with all forms of government but we will talk primarily about governments of a democratic character. We now turn, in the next chapter, to a discussion of bargaining and negotiation in the government. As we shall see it is not all that much different from bargaining and negotiation in the market.

To Truck and Barter

TRUCK

Political negotiation is very similar to negotiation in the private market. In both cases there are customers, suppliers, and people who will be affected by the decision but cannot directly control it. The specific project that results from the negotiation, whether it is a new model car or a military appropriation, is a result of compromises within the bargaining coalition pushing for the project.

Consider the decision-making process of the engineering section of Ford Motor Company when they want to develop a new model. The objective is to produce a model that will sell. Part of the sales-worthiness is the price. Decisions on the detail of the design turn on whether the new gadget will be attractive and how much it will cost. Further, different engineers and indeed whole engineering departments will have different ideas about this. The eventual outcome will be a compromise between various "pressure groups" mediated by the higher management. The customers, however, will make the eventual decision. They will decide whether to buy or not. In the long run, consumer decisions determine which companies will supply the market.

I should like to re-emphasize that there is no claim that the market or customers are perfectly informed. Of course they are not. It is clear, however, that the information held by the average purchaser of a car on the details of its design is greater than the information the average voter has about the details of government behavior and of the behavior of its opposition.

There is a striking difference between people opposed to a public or private project. For example, suppose that someone proposes to erect an ugly building near my house. I object and my objections are overridden. If the building is private, I may have the value of my house reduced. If the government constructs the building, not only is the value of my house reduced, but also I have to pay for part of the building. Taxes fall on those who vote against a project as well as on those who vote for it.

If it were not for the externality problem, we could simply shift everything to the private market. Unfortunately, in areas like the police, military, and some environmental matters, the market simply does not work. I take it that all of my readers will immediately recognize the absurdity of any proposal to reduce air pollution significantly by the private market method. For example, I would be foolish to put a catalytic converter on my car and buy more expensive gasoline, because the effect on me of the reduction of pollution would be too trivial to notice. The cost would not be.

The government solution also has limitations. The new cars ordered to reduce pollution also increase fatalities in accidents because they are smaller, lighter, and hence less resistant to damage to the passengers in an accident. We are unlikely to get a perfect solution to these problems either from the market or from the government. When externalities are large it is likely, but far from certain, that the government will do better than the market.

With respect to any given project there will be those in favor and those opposed. Everyone would like a project to be cheaper. The bargaining is likely to be complicated. Further, the people actually doing the bargaining, our elected officials or in some cases civil servants, are responsible directly or indirectly to voters.

Each individual voter is informed, mostly poorly informed, about only a small part of the alternatives. Politicians are aware of this and bundle projects which will, on the whole, attract a sufficient number of votes. But note that some voters may be attracted by part of the bundle and others by other parts. Further there will be some voters who find that, on the whole, this particular politician's bundle is less attractive than someone else's. The politician aims not at pleasing them all, but only a majority.

BARTER

There is another more serious problem, which is the absence of any political money. For example, the politician trading a particular environmental rule for the elimination of the death penalty does not have any common denominator. It would be helpful if there were some kind of money. The situation resembles the market before the invention of money.

Long ago there was a colony of Assyrian merchants in central Turkey. Money had not yet been invented, and they traded as agents for their principals in Assyria one bundle of goods against another using a barter system. They kept records of their trades on baked clay tablets. Many of these tablets have survived. Unfortunately only a few have been translated. The same type of problem faced by the Assyrian merchants now is confronted by a politician who is trying to make a set of bargains pleasing to his principals, the voters, without the use of any common denominator like money.

Economists have pointed out many times the difficulties of barter trading. There are problems of indivisibility. There are also problems of imperfect knowledge. The merchant has one bundle of goods and his Turkish customers have another. How can they determine equality of bundles?

Let me invent a modern equivalent. Suppose there are furnished houses, and the market involved trades rather than the purchase and sale of the houses. In each case the owner of a house hires an agent to handle the trade. Assume further that there are several house owners with furnished houses in the market and with other agents. The trade is to be made directly, without money. The bargaining would take the form of, let us say, one agent insisting on the addition of a sofa in the living room and another complaining about the dining room suite. The bargaining would take a long time and be much less efficient than if we used money. Assyrian merchants solved these problems, probably with less-than-perfect efficiency. Our political representatives face the same problems and solve them, once again, probably with less-than-perfect efficiency.

These problems are of course aggravated by the fact that only a majority of the voters must be pleased, and even they are rather badly informed and have poor memories. Also there are general problems of externalities using majority voting, aggravated by the fact that the bargaining itself is for barter rather than for monetary transactions. Altogether we should not expect a high degree of efficiency and of course we do not receive such efficiency.

REMEDIES

But what can we do about this? There are a number of people who do not think that their representatives should engage in this kind of bargaining. They think that they should simply try to implement the public good. Of course some of the outcomes of logrolling are in accord with the public good, and most of them are only a minor reduction in the public good. Mostly they are minor expenditures for something that benefits one small group of voters. In many cases a cost-benefit analysis might well show that the benefit to the minority is greater than the tax cost falling on the majority.

Voting bodies not infrequently pass rules prohibiting vote trades. The cynic, like myself, would expect these rules to be passed with the aid of vote trading. In any event even the most cursory acquaintance with actual legislatures indicates that this is the way they mainly work. Occasionally some proposal will obtain majority approval without logrolling, for example the United States' declaration of war against Japan in World War II. On the other hand, congressional approval of the Gulf War required a great deal of maneuvering and logrolling on the part of President Bush.

Rents

So far we have talked mainly about the externalities inflicted by government projects upon others and the injury to the minority that is out-voted. Unfortunately this is not the whole story. The winning majority will normally make some gains, but they may be small. Further, members of a winning majority in one case may be members of the losing minority in another.

One of the newer developments in economic theory has been rent seeking. As the first discoverer of this particular phenomenon, although not the

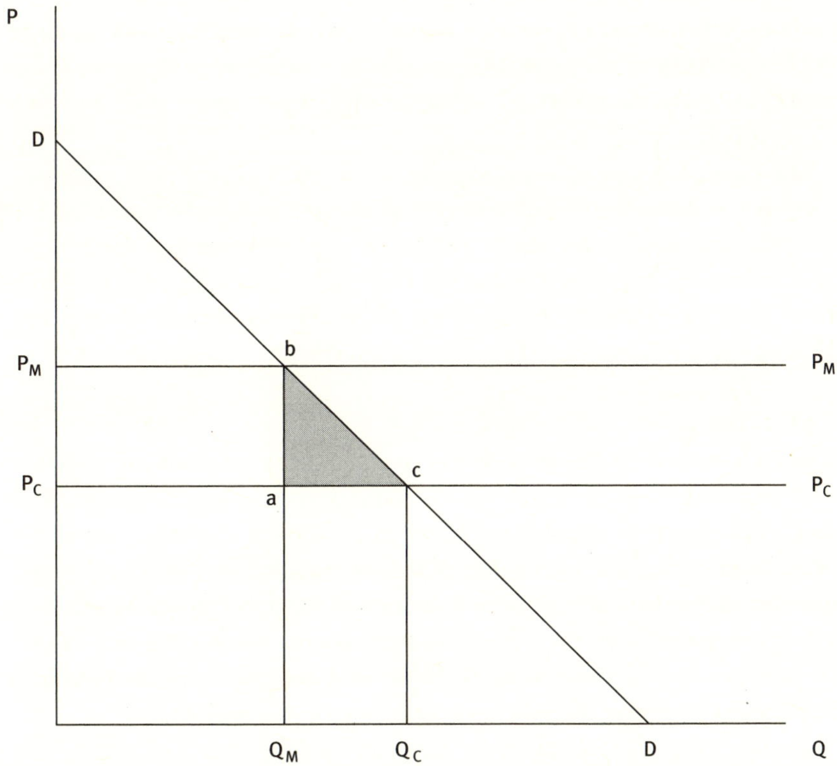

FIGURE 1

person who gave it the name rent seeking, it is surprising that I have not dealt with this subject earlier in this monograph.[8] Let me now take up the example of a narrow coalition of minor groups, the kind that back most pork-type legislation, to illustrate a discussion of rent seeking and its role in politics.

Let us turn to the technical side. Until recently, most elementary economics texts had a figure like Figure 1.

This figure would be accompanied by an explanation of monopoly profits in which it would be pointed out that at the nonmonopoly price people could buy a good at the P_C line and would buy quantity Q_C. This gave them a consumer surplus equivalent to the triangle above the cost line and below the demand line.

8. G. Tullock, "The Welfare Costs of Tariffs, Monopolies, and Theft," *Western Economic Journal* 5 (1967): 224–32; A. O. Krueger, "The Political Economy of the Rent-Seeking Society," *American Economic Review* 64 (June 1974): 291–303.

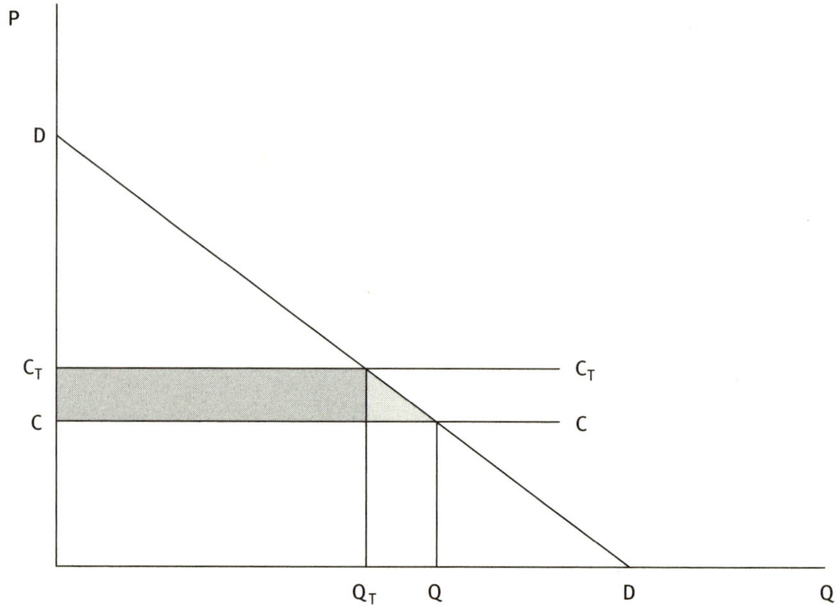

FIGURE 2A

If a monopoly were formed, it would charge the price shown by the line P_M. The product shown by the shaded triangle abc would be the consumer surplus that was lost to the world, since the consumers would not buy commodities beyond line Q_M. The standard text then said that the rectangle P_mP_{cab} was not a social cost, since the monopolist himself was a member of society. It was simply a transfer without cost to society as a whole.

I found that my students normally disliked this line of reasoning. After teaching it for a number of years I realized it was wrong. It assumed that the monopoly was costless to the monopolist. This does not seem likely. The resources involved in creating a monopoly are competitive. There are no barriers to enter the competition to create a monopoly. Anyone can conspire with his competitors or buy them out. Therefore, the average return on monopoly investments, i.e., resources put into creating a monopoly, would be no higher than the return elsewhere. Thus the rectangle now sometimes referred to as the Tullock rectangle was a cost not a transfer. Society as a whole was much worse off as a result of such monopolies.

All of this was revolutionary when first proposed. Indeed my first article was turned down by three leading journals and ended up in a minor one. My

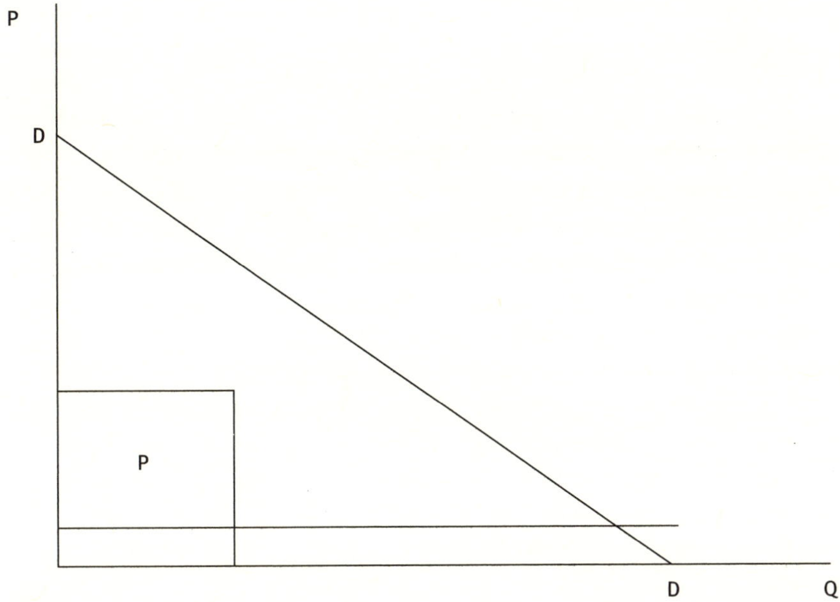

FIGURE 2B

second article, which dealt with direct transfers, was placed in a fairly good journal, but it was published in Europe. Anne Krueger broke the blockade with an article in the *American Economic Review* that referred to a special kind of society found in Asia.[9]

We now turn to Figure 2a that is intended to show the result of special-interest legislation in the same general way. We have some product being produced with the demand and cost lines shown. We assume that the citizens of Tulsa think they will benefit from dredging a deep-water channel to Tulsa. The cost is to be met by general taxation, thus the retail price of the taxed commodities rises slightly from CC to C_TC_T as shown by the darkly shaded area. Total quality purchased falls to Q_T and there is a tiny conventional welfare triangle shown by the lightly shaded area.

The citizens of Tulsa also must pay the tax, and so some of them may be among those excluded from purchasing by the new high price. On the other hand, they benefit from the ship canal to the amount shown by the rectangle on Figure 2b. Note that the demand in Figure 2b is the demand for the ship

9. Krueger, op. cit.

canal. It is downward slanting. It seems likely that at least some of the citizens of Tulsa find the very small tax that they must pay for this project greater than any benefit that they receive. Thus the citizens of the rest of the United States are made worse off by the tax, and most of the citizens of Tulsa are in the net made better off by the P rectangle minus that part of the rectangle that is represented by the taxes they pay.

It is not obvious whether the cost of this project to citizens of the United States as a whole is greater or less than the gain to citizens of Tulsa. If the gain to the citizens of Tulsa is greater than the national tax cost, then the project is a beneficial but highly limited public good. If a benefit to the citizens of Tulsa is less than the tax cost, then it is a wasteful limited public good.

This line of reasoning, like that used for all monopolies before the discovery of rent seeking, assumes that the government project did not cost the citizens of Tulsa anything except their share of the taxes. But once again this seems unlikely. Projects like this are produced in a highly competitive market. Their congressman must have promised his vote for various unrelated projects. His votes are like the resources invested in creating a private monopoly. These should be included in assessing the cost. Unfortunately there is no way to directly measure the cost of monopolies.

Once again, it does not seem likely that resources invested for the purpose of obtaining a government project pay higher returns than resources invested elsewhere. Thus the cost of the project to the citizens of Tulsa should be roughly equal to the benefit. Their congressman has obtained a profit on his negotiations, but the profit is not gigantic and is very unlikely to be greater than the cost of the canal. Indeed it is very unlikely to even approximate the cost of the canal.

The citizens of Tulsa would gain if the benefit of the canal were greater than the taxes collected in Tulsa. Thus the benefit could be less than one percent of the total cost for the citizens of Tulsa to favor it. Voting for a congressman who would refuse such a gift is unlikely.

Consider a constituency refusing to enter into a logrolling bargain with other constituencies. Their only advantage will be slightly lower taxes. They get no positive gain of any sort. If Tulsa does not participate it will make a net loss in the form of slightly higher taxes and no benefit of any kind.

It is extremely unlikely that the voters in Tulsa know for what projects their votes are being traded. The problem is one of a negative sum game. If a coalition is not formed then you are better off, but if it is formed you are worse off than if you are not a member. It is unlikely that your vote or the vote of your congressman will actually prevent the formation of a coalition.

All a negative vote can do is to remove you from the coalition, with subsequent losses.

Professional lobbyists, either government employees or private, frequently carry on negotiations in Congress. Lobbyists frequently analyze legislation, for example appropriations, by their effect on congressional constituencies. They clearly think congressmen are more interested in the effect on their constituency of a given expenditure than of more general policy issues. Of course it is not true that congressmen, and for that matter the voters, are completely uninterested in the public good. Within the public good they want to do as well as they can. Many of the pork projects are limited public goods in their particular area.

Envoi

This monograph may be generally discouraging. I am reminded of the summation of a distinguished economist talking about international currency problems: "the world is an unsatisfactory place." The economic situation seems to be in a similar position to that of medicine between about 1900 and 1940. We know what is wrong, but we do not know how to cure it. We obviously need more research, and there is great room for important discoveries. I urge you all to see whether you cannot invent the economic equivalent of penicillin.

If we cannot, and indeed may not want to abolish logrolling, can we make it more efficient? Since I have devoted the bulk of my intellectual life to the study of government and how to make it work better, I am reasonably well qualified to answer this question, although it is somewhat difficult.

One of the problems is that generally in political markets there is a tendency to use barter rather than some sort of currency. The demand-revealing process invented by Clarke attempts to provide an alternative currency for determining the extent of political action.[10] Voters can express not only which side they are on, but also how strongly they feel by putting a value on their vote. This value in most literature is expressed in dollars but need not necessarily be so. Extensive experimental efforts have used hours of labor, and there have been suggestions using percentages of annual income.

For simplicity, I will present the idea using dollars rather than one of many

10. E. H. Clarke, "Some Aspects of the Demand-Revealing Process," *Public Choice* 29 (Spring 1977): 37–39.

other things that have been suggested as the currency in the process. Note, however, that this system presents a way of moving from a barter economy to an economy with a common denominator no matter which of these diverse currencies is used.

The idea is simple, but the details are hard to understand. The individual voter not only indicates which candidate or proposal he favors but also tells how much it is worth to him to get his favorite choice. The cleverness of Clarke's idea is to provide a system under which an intelligent, or even a dishonest, voter would actually tell you the truth.[11]

Clarke's idea has been discussed among specialists, but most people are skeptical about ever getting it adopted. There are two problems. The first is "Can the voter understand it?" Secondly, "Could he give an estimate of the value of a particular project or election of a given candidate to him?" We normally do not think about politics in this manner. Experiments showed that naive subjects simply did not understand the system.

Another way of improving the voting process and hence getting better quality policies was first introduced seriously by Buchanan and myself almost forty years ago.[12] As of now, most economists but very few political scientists accept that our assertions are correct. *The Calculus of Consent* suggests that simple majority voting is simply a hangover from tribal customs and that a reinforced majority would work better. Clearly this would mean that fewer people would be subject to taxes that they did not approve for projects that they thought were not worth it. The political scientists point out that many people would fail to get their desire even though a majority favored it if that majority was not large enough. In practice, logrolling means that the voting majority can be increased by offering more benefits to objecting voters. Thus this objection is of limited, not overwhelming, validity.

Reinforced majorities have been analyzed in depth in the public choice literature, and I will leave the reader, if he has doubts, to that literature.[13] There is, however, an interesting variant. Countries that once formed part of the British Empire normally elect legislatures by what is known as the "first past the post" method. The candidate with most votes wins regardless of how

11. The methodology is too complicated to be explained in this monograph, but the reader may refer to T. N. Tideman and G. Tullock, "A New and Superior Process for Making Social Choices," *Journal of Political Economy* 84 (1975): 1145–59, or G. Tullock, "Practical Problems and Practical Solutions," *Public Choice* 29, no 2 (suppl. Spring 1977): 27–35.

12. Buchanan and Tullock, *The Calculus of Consent.*

13. Ibid.

slim the majority vote. Lincoln, for example, faced three opponents and won with thirty-five percent of the popular vote. A legislature made up by this kind of voting may have a majority with less than fifty percent of the popular vote. The British House of Commons, for example, for many years has had a single-party majority although the winning party normally has only forty-five percent or less of the popular vote.

Most democracies that have not descended from the British Empire, however, use what is known as proportional representation. To explain proportional representation it is easier to use the Israeli method that represents a very simple example. All parties present lists of candidates. The voter then checks the list he likes most. The seats in the legislature are divided among the parties in strict accord with the number of popular votes. Thus a very small minority will have representatives although they will be a small minority of the legislature.

If, however, we have one house of the legislature elected by proportional representation and the other by the English method, then a majority in each house would represent different voters. Thus for a bill to get through both houses it would need to represent a majority of voters in each of these classifications. The net effect would be that for any bill to pass, representatives of more than a majority of the population would need to be in favor. It would have much the same effect in reducing the size of the exploited minority as requiring a higher majority in a single house.

It should, however, be kept in mind that our system does something rather like this. To some extent a majority in the Senate represents different voters to the majority in the House. Further, the president is elected in yet a third way which means that the voters who elect the majority of both houses and the president are more numerous than those who elect one house. My off-hand guess is that the system is roughly equivalent to requiring about a sixty percent majority in a single house.

When drafting the U.S. Constitution, modern public choice was unknown, but the participants clearly realized that bills that could get through one house might well fail in the other and hence they insisted on two non-identical majorities. The public choice recommendation of reinforced majorities is not so radical as it appears. Madison, Hamilton, and Jay might well have approved of it even without reading *The Calculus of Consent.*

PART 6

FUTURE DIRECTIONS FOR RENT-SEEKING RESEARCH

FUTURE DIRECTIONS FOR RENT-SEEKING RESEARCH

In the existing literature there is not a single direct measure of rent-seeking cost. It is true that there are a great many indirect measures, but these involve both theoretical and practical problems. Direct measures would clearly be much more useful. The problem here is very much like the problem of measuring the black economy. Indeed, it can be argued that the rent-seeking industry is a very important part of the black economy. A large part of the total cost of rent-seeking activity is concealed by the people who bear it, partly because in many cases it is actually illegal (bribes, for example), and partly because publicity would be counterproductive. Nevertheless, it would be highly desirable that this screen be penetrated, and that we obtain direct measures. Theoretical reasons, which will be discussed below, indicate that these measures would almost certainly be partial, but still better than nothing.

Having said that direct measures are desirable, I should, I suppose, at least point in a direction for accumulating such measures. Unfortunately, this is an area where my own abilities are not very great. I can only suggest two areas where there are some data which could be used to at least make some kind of direct estimate of the cost of certain types of rent-seeking.

The first of these is the cost of legal proceedings. Legal proceedings sometimes are rent-seeking, e.g., a particular company attempting to enforce some kind of a restriction on its competition. More often they are simply fights about a given sum of money. Nevertheless, they are clear-cut cases of what we might call civil conflict; places where there is a strong incentive for both parties to invest resources in attempting acts of persuasion. In other words, they do to some extent resemble lobbying activities.[1]

Reprinted, with kind permission of Kluwer Academic Publishers, from *The Political Economy of Rent-Seeking*, ed. Charles K. Rowley, Robert D. Tollison, and Gordon Tullock (Boston/Dordrecht/Lancaster: Kluwer Academic Publishers, 1988), 465–80.

1. There is now quite a large body of data on the cost of legal proceedings collected by the Rand Corporation. Since the project is continuing to produce data, I see nothing much to be gained by giving specific citations. The interested student can write to the Rand Foundation and get a list of their publications.

Rent-seeking would no doubt be quite inexpensive if there were no conflicts of interest. The rent seeker is characteristically trying to get something which will injure other people. Those other people may fight back, either by hiring a contrary lobbyist or by their vote at the next election. Thus, the resemblance between rent-seeking and a lawsuit is somewhat closer than one might think at first glance. If the analogy is accepted it should perhaps be pointed out that under the present circumstances in this country, the total sum invested by the two parties in attempting to win lawsuits is characteristically about the same as the total value of the amount at issue. Thus what is now called the "Tullock Rectangle" is indeed totally consumed.

As another area where direct measurement is possible, in South America there are a number of places where the black economy is at worst light grey; i.e., it is very visible indeed. Forty percent of the land area of Lima is occupied by illegal entrants. Further, these people engage in a large number of activities which have not been properly licensed. Research has begun in Lima, and to a lesser extent in Caracas, on the actual behavior of this part of the economy. Measures of the size of the bribes that they have to pay would be fairly easy to obtain and fairly reliable.

Further, most of the entrepreneurs engaged in this kind of business would be quite willing to explain any inefficiency in the production process imposed upon them by the quasi-legal character of their business. We thus have possible direct measures of at least a very large part of the rent-seeking cost. I do not wish to argue that it would be easy. It would be necessary for somebody to spend quite a lot of time poking around in the less pleasant parts of Lima and Caracas. It could, however, be a very significant contribution to our knowledge of rent-seeking.

But these are direct efforts to obtain information which only bears indirectly on rent-seeking in the United States and indeed in Western Europe. Most actual efforts to measure the size of the rent-seeking cost have simply accepted the statement made in "The Welfare Costs of Tariffs, Monopolies, and Theft," that the monopoly profit now sometimes referred to as the "Tullock Rectangle" would be completely exhausted by resources invested in attempting to get it.[2] I can hardly criticize people for following my advice, but I now think that this is at best an approximation. My first reason will be ob-

2. Gordon Tullock, "The Welfare Costs of Tariffs, Monopolies, and Theft," *Western Economic Journal* 5 (1967): 224–32.

vious to anyone who has read the exchanges which make up chapters 7–12 of this volume.

My "Efficient Rent Seeking"[3] raised a mathematical issue having to do with the lack of an intelligible equilibrium in many rent-seeking cases. The lack of equilibrium could lead to either overinvestment or underinvestment of resources in rent-seeking, proper investment being taken as fully discounting the profit of the rent-seeking. Thus the Tullock Rectangle remains as only an approximate measure of the cost of rent-seeking.

We need a more rigorous specification. So far, this problem has turned out to be mathematically intractable. It should be pointed out, however, that it is just possible that empirical work could get rid of our mathematical difficulties. I do not say this because I think we should stop working on mathematics. Indeed, I think we should try and solve the problem mathematically as well as practically.

The basic reason for the problems raised in "Efficient Rent Seeking" and further canvassed in this volume is the fact that rent-seeking apparently does not have a U-shaped cost curve. The general view of most economists is that almost any production activity has a U-shaped cost; i.e., the cost per unit falls as production is increased and then begins rising again after a period. Public utility economics is almost the only place we ever worry about continuously declining marginal cost. Even there no one believes that it continues declining forever, only in the relevant range.

Just as there is no solution with any degree of elegance for the natural monopoly, there is no solution for rent-seeking in the area of declining marginal cost. There is on the contrary the possibility of rising marginal costs. This also leads to absurd results, except in special cases.

If empirical work on rent-seeking led to the conclusion that we have a U-shaped cost curve, then the problem would vanish. Theoretically, there doesn't seem to be any reason why the cost curves should be U-shaped, but it is not obvious that theorists would have deduced that the market cost curves were normally U-shaped if we did not have a lot of empirical data. Thus, my conclusion is that we should both continue the mathematical work and simultaneously try and get measures of the productivity of investment in

3. Gordon Tullock, "Efficient Rent Seeking," in *Toward a Theory of the Rent-Seeking Society*, ed. James M. Buchanan, Robert D. Tollison, and Gordon Tullock (College Station: Texas A&M University Press, 1980).

rent-seeking. If it turns out that the cost curve is U-shaped, the mathematical puzzle will cease to be anything more than an intellectual exercise. Until such data have been produced (and it is by no means obvious they ever will be) we must continue with the mathematical research.

In chapter 4 of this volume I raise another empirical problem. I argue that the total cost of rent-seeking in most cases is considerably larger even than the sum of the Harberger Triangle and the Tullock Rectangle. Specifically, the benefit to society from the alternative investment of the resources which are otherwise wasted in rent-seeking should also be taken into account.

If we knew the size of the resources invested in rent-seeking, this would be comparatively easy, because we already have some measures by Mansfield on the degree to which cost-saving inventions are transmitted to the general populace rather than being retained by the inventing organization. Duplicating this research in other areas should be fairly easy. In fact, simply taking Mansfield's results, which imply that the innovator actually retains only about one-third of the social value of his innovation, would be a good first approximation. But for this purpose we again need a measure of the actual size of the rent-seeking activity.

All of this depends on some method of measuring direct costs of rent-seeking. This could be divided into two general categories: firstly, the direct expenditures on lobbying, etc., engaged in by individuals, corporations, and, for that matter, trade associations; secondly, dispersed resource investments, involved in such things as putting your factory in the constituency of a relevant congressman, or endowing a distinguished visiting chair at Baruch School,[4] etc.

I am by no means discouraged about obtaining accurate data on the first category. After all, corporations and trade associations all publish their accounts. It should be possible with some ingenuity to get inside the published accounts, to the actual detail of the accounts, in at least a sample of corporations. To say this can be done, however, is not to say that it would be easy or that the standard economic technique of looking at published statistics and putting them in a computer would be of much help. Hiring private detectives to penetrate the accounting system of General Electric would be a more highly paying approach to this particular kind of research. Still, to say that it is difficult is not to say it is impossible.

4. I will be occupying such a distinguished chair in the Spring of 1987.

The second category, the indirect expenditures, is much more difficult. It is particularly difficult because a lot of these indirect expenditures take the form of people voting for politicians whom on general grounds they detest because those politicians are in favor of some expenditure by the government which will benefit the voter. To take an extreme example, in 1964, a wealthy man who was in his spare time the head of the finance committee of a small private college was an extreme conservative. His general political position was well to the right of Goldwater, but he strongly opposed Goldwater because the latter opposed large-scale payments supporting higher education.

The total cost of this kind of activity and this kind of voting spread over society may be very great. Then again, it may not. We do not know how much of it is done, and it is very hard to decide what the social cost is, or indeed whether there is a social cost.

Here we have a problem rather analogical to that of advertising. It is clear that to some extent advertising increases the information of the purchaser, and hence makes the market work better. It is also clear that to some extent advertising simply is a competitive arrangement in which one firm's advertising cancels another's. We like the first kind of advertising and dislike the other, but there doesn't seem to be any way of disentangling them in practice.

The Calculus of Consent had as one of its main themes the desirability of a sort of market in which people traded votes on "projects" which were of benefit to themselves.[5] We emphasized that the desirable data here was that a market should exist and that it should not be too perfect. In other words we wanted a market of the right degree of inefficiency. This kind of cost of vote specialization raises somewhat the same issues. We do indeed want people to both vote for and especially press for things which are to their advantage, but only to a certain degree, and it is very hard to say exactly how much.

Since this chapter is devoted to suggesting future research, I do not have to solve the problem here. I simply suggest that other people work on it. Speaking truthfully, I have thought about it a good deal myself but do not have any solution. I will continue thinking about it. I hope someday to solve it, but I certainly would not be unhappy if one of the readers beat me to it.

There is still another problem which requires much research. As Charles Rowley points out, the rent-seeking perspective raises difficulties for the

5. James M. Buchanan and Gordon Tullock, *The Calculus of Consent: Logical Foundations of Constitutional Democracy* (Ann Arbor: University of Michigan Press, 1962).

whole analysis of *The Calculus of Consent*. Further research is most certainly called for to integrate rent-seeking and the theory of constitutions.

There is another problem which has been bothering me ever since I wrote "The Purchase of Politicians," a long time ago. This is that the total amount spent in lobbying, etc., in Washington, does not seem to be even close to the economic value of the favors dispensed by the government. Note that I say in Washington. I suspect that in Mexico City the two are in quite close agreement. One of the co-editors of this volume, Robert Tollison, has done work on the mercantilist societies of the sixteenth and seventeenth centuries. He found royal governments, in essence, put this kind of favor up to auction. This presumably obtained the full economic value. Since they used the funds for various governmental purposes, this was a kind of taxation. We may regard building Versailles as a waste, but is it not the same kind of waste we normally associate with rent-seeking?

In any event, the amounts derived were much larger as a share of GNP or even of government activity than the apparent expenditure on rent-seeking in most modern democracies. There is a sort of canonical explanation for this, which is that much rent-seeking is a public good for the members of the special interest. One would anticipate that the individual people who are potential members of pressure groups would choose not to invest funds in attempting to get a favor for that entire pressure group. Hence the investment of funds would be less than "optimal."

The basic problem with this "solution" is that it assumes that only the present collection of special government favors is feasible. Its proponents normally offer no intrinsic reason why people should not seek out very special narrow government favors and then invest the full amount in them. If there were no restrictions on the kind of things that can be bought by rent-seeking, then these public-good-type monopolistic restrictions, tax exemptions, etc., would not exist at all, because they would lose out on the competition from the better-financed special gifts.

In other words, we might expect that the bulk of rent-seeking would be devoted to fairly narrow, specific gains to small groups, and that they would in general pay the full value. There would be little or nothing in the way of special gifts to large groups of people because of the public good problems of organizing such an interest group.

The first thing to be said is that it is conceivable that this is a correct albeit partial description of the way our government operates. It is possible, although I do not believe it is true, that all special privileges and advantages distributed by the government to large numbers of people are distributed to them entirely in return for their vote. Thus for example, farmers vote in terms of the farm program, and older people in terms of Social Security. It must be assumed that the people who are taxed for these expenditures are badly informed, or that they are themselves voting in terms of some other special interest.

What would then be added on by direct lobbying is the gigantic collection of minor clauses which make up the bulk of almost every one of the immensely long bills passed by Congress. Most of these special clauses would have been purchased at their fair prices by groups of people small enough so that the public good argument does not apply.

But having said that this is feasible as a description of our present system, I shall go on and say that I do not believe it is accurate. Nevertheless, this would be an area where I think that valuable research would be possible. It would be difficult and tedious, but not impossible.

This still leaves us with the puzzle of why the total expenditure on seeking special favors in Washington, immense though it is, is still rather small compared with the value of the favors. I have a theory which points in the direction of future research to either confirm or disprove it. But before turning to this theory it is necessary for me briefly to deal with a recent twist in what we may call the "Chicago" doctrine.

When I was in the University of Chicago, it was fashionable to point out that the farm program was hideously inefficient. It would have been far cheaper to simply pay farmers the real value of their special privileges rather than establishing the complicated set of quotas and subsidies which in fact were being used.

Recently Chicagoans, Becker in particular, have attacked this farm orthodoxy. They point out that it would be quite difficult to produce a set of cash payments to farmers that would exactly duplicate the benefits that different farmers are now receiving. Indeed, the gradual development of agriculture under these government programs, with some farmers actually being driven out of existence by the program and many farm laborers suffering, the great expansion of the fertilizer industry, etc., would have been quite difficult to reproduce if the technique had been direct cash payments.

Clearly, these claims about the difficulty of reproducing the present pattern by cash payments are correct. It would be difficult or almost impossible. The problem with this line of reasoning as an explanation of why we do not use "efficient" means is that it assumes that the pattern of payments that was in fact made was the politically optimal pattern. The only evidence for this assumption is that it was the pattern which was adopted.

There is of course another explanation, one which was in fact believed by the people who presented the original or the older Chicago view. This is simply that for political reasons, direct cash payments were not possible, and hence the politicians were forced to turn to an inefficient method of rewarding some of the farmers. The present pattern could be explained by either of these two explanations, but it seems on the whole absurd that the people starting this program (actually under President Hoover) properly foresaw all of the developments which would occur. There is certainly no reason to believe that they consciously intended to help one group of farmers, injure another, injure farm laborers, etc. It is certainly more plausible that they were simply trying to get the votes of a large number of farmers and were compelled by the circumstances they faced to choose a relatively inefficient method.

Thus we have two possible explanations for the present farm mess. One of these is that it is an ideally efficient method chosen by the politicians to reward exactly the people who in fact were rewarded and penalize exactly the people who were penalized. The other is that the politicians were in general trying to increase the incomes of farmers, but were faced with political difficulties in making direct cash payment and so turned to inefficient methods. Both of these would explain the present distribution of income among farmers. They would also explain the evolution from the beginning of the program with President Hoover to the present day. But the modern Chicago theory requires really quite extraordinary foresight on the part of the politicians. Perfect information has never been carried this far before.

Moreover, the Becker-Chicago theory would require some explanation of why the politicians who put this particular program through didn't get a very large part of the return on it themselves. That is the problem which I was addressing when I found it necessary to digress and deal with this new Chicago position. I believe that the basic problems here are a combination of knowledge or ignorance on the part of most voters, most politicians (and indeed many other people), and a set of political beliefs which are very widely held.

Two European scholars say: "The first and decisive stage of decision making is determined by constraints and knowledge about the alternatives available to an individual."[6] We will begin with information, and then turn to my

6. Bruno S. Frey and Klaus Foppa, "Human Behavior: Possibilities Explain Action," *Journal of Economic Psychology* 7 (1986): 137–60, p. 137.

view about the views which most people have about politics, and then once again turn to the effect which all of this has on rent-seeking. Finally we will consider the effect that rent-seeking has on information.

That people are not very well informed about political matters is something that most of us know, although political scientists argue that they should be informed. I do not quarrel with the political scientists' view that people should be informed. I merely point out that they usually are not.

Almost any empirical examination of what the common man actually knows immediately indicates that it is not very much. He does not even think very much about his opinions. To take but one example, the November–December issue of *Public Opinion* contains a lot of data on ethics.[7] From it we discover that 71 percent of all people asked thought that congressmen "will tell lies if they felt the truth will hurt them politically," and 44 percent thought they "have a high personal moral code."[8] It is obvious from these numbers that either at least 15 percent of the respondents to these polls must have thought that "telling lies if the truth will hurt" is consistent with "a high personal moral code," or, more likely, that a considerably larger number of the respondents literally did not think very much about what they were saying. This is but one example. We could easily get many more.

This of course is a statement about reality. Since Anthony Downs wrote *An Economic Theory of Democracy*, most public choice scholars have realized that the individuals are behaving quite rationally in being ignorant. There is little or nothing to be gained from an individual looking into the details of government policy, unless he actually enjoys it. Since most of the readers of this article probably do follow politics to at least some extent, they are abnormal in this regard, but even they would turn out not to be very well informed if we asked them any significantly detailed questions.

There are nevertheless, in addition to this general lack of information, some fairly strong opinions held by most people. Firstly, they have a "general image" of what government should do. This general image includes most of the major duties of the government. For example, most people think that the government should repress crime. For a less pleasant example, most Aztecs thought their government should engage in large-scale human sacrifice. For most modern societies, direct payments to well-off people are not part of that public image.

7. *Public Opinion* (November–December 1986). The quotation is taken from p. 26.

8. Fifty-six percent of them also thought that the congressmen "make a lot of money by using public office improperly."

In addition to this general image, most citizens would also like to get various special privileges from the government. But they realize that the government can be expected to do things in their personal interest only if it at least superficially fits the public image. This rather vague public image is, of course, not a well-calculated view of the world.

What I am trying to say here is that the government's activities must almost always have at least a veneer fitting the public image or be so inconspicuous that most people don't notice them. Granted the poor information of the average voter, the latter possibility is quite significant. The collection of special provisions in the Internal Revenue Code, for example, miss the notice of most people. Indeed, the author of this chapter must concede that he knows almost none of them.

What we observe then is a government which is engaging in a number of rather traditional activities which are part of the public image. It is also engaging in a lot of activities which are in the special interest of reasonably organized groups, but which are camouflaged to fit the public image. The farm program discussed above was in its early years pushed very heavily on the grounds that having a strong group of "yeoman farmers" was important for the success of the United States as a nation. Indeed, the same argument has been used in Switzerland, where the farmers are generally even more prosperous than those in Iowa.[9]

Assume that the above remarks are correct, as I believe they are. Imagine that a politician in the 1930s had proposed simply paying the farmers cash with the intent that a good many of them would stop farming and retire to Florida. It would have been cheaper than what we did, but it would have been very hard to camouflage it to fit the public image.

The farm program is a conspicuous program which had to be camouflaged and hence could not be done efficiently. A great deal of other special interest legislation depends on being inconspicuous. Most Americans were not aware of the fact that aid-program wheat had to be carried on American ships. If they had become aware of it, and some did, the shipowners could claim it fit the public image as providing reserve shipping for military use.

The latter kind of program is probably the commonest single output of

9. The Iowa farmers have recently undergone quite a financial crisis because a number of them had borrowed too much money against their land. The bulk of them, however, did not have large mortgages, and the crisis meant that their personal wealth fell from, let us say, three-quarters of a million to half a million.

rent-seeking in Washington, i.e., something which escapes the notice of the bulk of the population, which is not strongly opposed by any special group, and for which there is at least a superficially plausible explanation which fits the public image. There are two other kinds of programs which can get through. Firstly, there are fairly direct applications of the public image, which will have large-scale voter support. Details of the military budget do not fit that description, but the general structure of it does. The second type are things like old-age pensions or large-scale medical aid to large parts of the citizenry which can be sold as respectable duties for the government, primarily because a very large part of the population will (sometimes mistakenly) think that they benefit by them.

In these cases (which we may refer to as public image or possibly widespread benefit types of action), the amount of lobbying and rent-seeking done in Washington can be quite significantly less than the actual cost of the project. Carolyn Weaver, in her study of the origin of the social security act, discusses at great length the activity of a group of people whom she refers to as "potential administrators." It is likely that they were in fact rent-seeking, but the profits that they were anticipating were quite modest. Hence the resources they were willing to invest were also quite modest. The bill went through because with quite modest resources it was possible to convince the average voter and the average congressman that it was desirable.

If we turn to more definite private interest legislation, private interest has to be at least disguised. In some cases of course this disguise takes the form of simply hiding a minor provision in a long bill. In other cases, e.g., the farm program, efforts are made to confuse the average voter, while the principal political payment for the program is made by farmers actually voting for people who will support it.

So far I have not directly referred to logrolling. As the originator of the present analysis of logrolling, I assure you that this is not because I am unaware of its existence. Indeed, it is vital to all of these programs. Here, however, we are talking about another aspect of the matter. All of these special interest bills are put through by logrolling, but I am now saying that there are certain restrictions on what can be done, because the public image, whether we think it is rational or not, restricts the alternatives which are available.

In a way, the public image has the function of keeping some expensive items off the budget. It should of course be kept in mind that it also leads to great inefficiency in some areas. The American foreign policy from its earliest days to the present has been severely damaged by the fact that the voters think that one of the government's duties is to spread the American ethical system to other countries. They don't think that much effort should be expended in this direction, but they are sufficiently interested in it, so that efforts to carry out this objective seriously handicap more genuinely important aspects of foreign policy.[10]

Since the public image changes from time to time, there is some possibility for special interest groups to influence its general structure. In general, however, that is too expensive. The public image does, however, often make returns from rent-seeking much lower than you would otherwise expect. If we think of the federal government budget as "all up for grabs," it is hard to explain the relatively small size of the rent-seeking community in Washington. If we assume, however, and I think this is correct, that anyone attempting to get hold of parts of the federal budget must, because of public image considerations, choose a very inefficient way of getting that money, then we have at least a partial explanation for the small size of the establishment.

Suppose for example that we have a nearly bankrupt company which makes aircraft engines. It can, through influence on Senator Kennedy who represents the area in which they are operating, get the federal government to buy a number of its not-such-wonderful engines. This will permit it to continue employing its workers at an income which to the workers is $100 million more than they would make if they were fired and had to seek other employment. The company will pay its stockholders and higher management another $50 million. The excess cost to the American government of buying these inferior engines is, shall we say, $500 million.

The economist traditionally would look at this and say: "Aha, the government should simply give the company $151 million and buy its engines elsewhere." The Beckerite Chicagoan would say that it was impossible to distribute the money to give exactly the same pattern of benefits as the purchase of the engines.

As the reader will guess, I do not accept either of these explanations. I

10. I am not saying it would not be nice to have foreign countries carry out our ethical system. The fact is, however, that we do not have enough power to achieve this goal. Hence efforts to do so normally have no effect on ethics and a considerable effect on our relations with the government which we are attempting to influence. When I was in Korea as an American diplomat, it was perfectly obvious that President Rhee thought of the United States as his principal foreign ally and his principal domestic enemy. This led to a series of difficulties on policy, which could have very easily been avoided if he had not suspected us (correctly) of attempting to overthrow him.

would say that a straightforward payment of $151 million to the company would fail to fit the public image and hence is politically impossible. Purchasing these defective engines fits the image, particularly since the government can claim that the engines are really pretty good. The voters will have neither the motive nor the technical knowledge to test the claim.

The company would be willing to invest a maximum of $50 million. The workers would be willing to invest more, but they will use their votes rather than cash. For a billion-and-a-half-dollar contract, it looks like an awfully small payment. But the bulk of the "rent" is eaten up in inefficiency which is required to fit the public image.

Note here that I am not saying that the dominance of the public image leads to an inferior result. If it were possible to get cash directly in the economist's efficient way, manipulating the government would become the primary activity of the American people. We would be much poorer. I am also not saying the public image leads to optimal efficiency. It leads to a mixed system which can be supported only on the grounds that there are other systems that are worse. We have only to look across our southern border to see a system which I am sure all of us would agree is very much worse.[11]

But all of this functions only because the average voter is badly informed. We have mentioned that he is rational in being badly informed, but it should also be pointed out that the rent-seeking activity probably means that he is even worse informed than he otherwise would be.

Take a very traditional example, the protective tariff. Anyone who has taught elementary economics knows that it is hard, indeed very nearly impossible, to convince the students that protective tariffs are a bad idea. Students who get an A in your course and regurgitate the standard arguments against protective tariffs on your exams may not believe a word of it.

The explanation is fairly simple, i.e., that the arguments for a protective tariff are simple and superficially obvious, while the arguments against it are unfortunately complicated and indirect. Granted that the voter has no motive for becoming well informed, he or she will buy the simpler of the two explanations.

Under these circumstances, a rent seeker seeking protective tariffs does not actually have to engage in too much lobbying. The system is already bent in his direction. Suppose that some particular industry does not now have a protective tariff and would like it. They do not have to use their votes, their

11. Two such systems; Cuba is somewhat different, but even more unpleasant.

campaign contributions, and other kinds of influence to move the government from opposition of the protective tariffs to actively favoring them. What they have to do is move the political system from a sort of vague feeling that the American worker must be protected against unemployment[12] to actual application in this case. Suppose that a tariff will be worth $100 million; the cost might be as low as $10–15 million[13] because the government is rather inclined that way anyhow. It is just being pushed from a 90 percent chance of passing the tariff to 100 percent. This is worth only $10,000,000, although the apparent gain is $100,000,000.

Thus the direct cost might appear to be quite low. Unfortunately there may well be an indirect cost not borne by the special interest group, but by the population in general. This is what we might call the expansion of ignorance. The economics of information usually takes the form of discussing a situation in which different people produce different bits of information with the result that the recipient over time becomes better informed. This is unfortunately not particularly typical of the real world. In addition to information there are lies[14] and deliberate fraud.[15]

It should be emphasized that not all of this is done by deliberate villains. The student who did not understand the arguments against protective tariffs, and who is later hired as a lobbyist by the cotton textile industry, probably operates with a good conscience when he retails false economic arguments. It is true that if he is presented with correct arguments, and they at least temporarily convince him, he is likely to deliberately turn away from thinking further about the matter. If really pressed, he will in all probability deliberately lie or mislead, or engage in other "opportunistic behavior." Primarily, however, he simply remains ignorant in the area and spreads his ignorance.

The result may not only be that a particular tariff is adopted. Indeed, the lobbyist may fail to get his tariff. But in his lobbying activity he in a real sense lowers the information held by the politicians and the public by introducing falsehood. This would be true even if what he said was literally true, but led to people forgetting truthful arguments on the other side. Adam Smith's re-

12. Frequently the voter is sufficiently badly informed so that he believes both that the American voter must be protected against the Japanese competition which would unemploy him, and that free trade is a good thing.

13. Including the vote somehow as part of this value.

14. Oliver Williamson usually refers to this kind of thing as "impacted information."

15. Once again, Williamson usually refers to this as "opportunistic behavior."

marks about protecting strategically important industries, for example, are probably better known in Washington than any other part of his discussion of tariffs.

Suppose then that we have ten tariffs, each of which in net would increase the value of an industry by $100 million. Some of them are regarded as reasonably likely bets for the next two years, and the stock market has discounted them by valuing the stock in these industries at about $90 million more than it would be worth if there were no prospect of a tariff. Each of these industries sends lobbyists to Washington to promote those tariffs, spending about $1 million on the task. One of them wins this time; the others very likely will later. The direct rent-seeking cost here is $10 million, and the apparent gain to the industry affected is a net of $99 million. Actually, however, its stock only goes up $10 million, because the possibility of this gain had already been discounted. There is of course somewhere in the economy, probably in the United States, possibly entirely abroad, a place where stock goes down in value because this change in tariff policy had been thought likely but not certain, and hence there was the company whose stock was selling at less than its value would be if the tariff were known to be impossible. The cost then seems to be very much less than the apparent benefit to the rent seeker, but they were moving not from a zero possibility of tariff to certainty of tariff, but from a 90 percent probability to certainty.

Unfortunately, there is here another very major and very hard-to-measure cost. The reason that the tariff was a reasonable possibility is of course widespread public ignorance and misinformation. Further, it is not just a congressman. Politicians and bureaucrats very likely share this misinformation. The activity of the lobbyist has surely strengthened and reinforced this unfortunate public image. The general feeling that it is one of the duties of the American government to protect its industries against vicious competition from the "gang of four" has been reinforced.

It will be harder for future economists to push for lower tariffs after this lobbying campaign than it was before. There is no way of measuring this change in money terms, but it does seem to me it might be possible to measure it in terms of the change in attitude of citizens, politicians, and bureaucrats. In any event, I would be very much interested in seeing people attempting to measure this phenomenon or, for that matter, merely obtaining some empirical evidence proving or disproving the theoretical argument.

We note here that although lobbying activities will have this kind of unfavorable externality, there is no law of nature that says that they will win.

Opinion is affected by things other than the professional lobbyist. Further, there actually are some professional lobbyists who are pushing for lower tariffs. Such organizations as Brookings, Cato, Heritage, etc., may not like to think of themselves as professional lobbyists, but as a matter of fact, they are. All of them of course do favor lower protective tariffs.

Another important group in this regard is the professors of economics in the United States. It is true that many professors of economics have left the real world for the abstractions of mathematics, but most of them do at least occasionally tell their students that protective tariffs will not achieve the goals for which they are normally urged.

There have been successes in reducing rent-seeking. The CAB is no longer with us, the ICC is much less dangerous than it was, and the banking industry is very largely deregulated. From about 1930 to about 1975, American tariffs and indeed tariffs all over the world were steadily lowered. Towards the end of that period, there was of course a rise of nontariff barriers, but I believe that up to about 1975, the net effect was a freeing up of American trade. Unfortunately, since that time, that trend has reversed. All of this is evidence that ignorance will not necessarily prevail in public affairs. It is usually true however that rent-seeking activity which is directed at obtaining government favors will have as a by-product an increase of public ignorance in the area concerned.

If we look at history, the world in, say, 1600 was a place in which rent-seeking was overwhelmingly the most common way of becoming wealthy. The "mercantilist" society was a society organized by rent-seeking. For a variety of reasons, this fell away, in England and to a lesser extent in Europe. It was still quite strong even in England in 1800. From 1800 to about 1870, England steadily dismantled the remaining mercantilist rent-seeking structure of its government.

As a result, we had the industrial revolution, and through the copying of the English system by other countries, the spread of prosperity throughout most of Europe and, to a lesser extent, the world. There seems to be no explanation for this radical change in society, except intellectual conversion of a very large number of people, including of course Mr. Gladstone and Napoleon III, to the economics of Adam Smith and Ricardo. Unfortunately, beginning with the inventions of Bismarck, this trend was reversed at the end of the 19th century.

I have ended this chapter on future directions of research in rent-seeking by this discussion of changes in information, not only because I think they are important areas of research, but also because I think it is a practical matter. We know from the study of history that an elaborate rent-seeking state was dismantled once in the early 19th century. If it happened once, it can happen again. Economists today know much more than Ricardo and his friends did. It is to be hoped that their political and propaganda activities will also be more effective than those of their predecessors.

INDEX

References to bibliographic information appear in italics.

AAA (Agricultural Adjustment Act), 212
AAA (American Automobile Association), 50
ABA (American Bar Association), 51
academic journals: motives of editors of, 20–21; referees, 21. *See also* economics journals
advertising: calculating effective, 299; and rent seeking, 171–72; restrictions on, 4–6
Agricultural Adjustment Act (AAA), 212
agricultural subsidies: allocative costs of, 236–37; Chicago doctrine on, 301–6; vs. direct cash payments, 222; as examples of "iron triangle," 58; and land use restrictions, 219; as rent seeking, 29; and tobacco taxes, 198. *See also* farm lobbies
aircraft industry lobbying, 306
Alaska oil revenues, 136–38, 139, 140, 141–42, 145
alcoholic beverage taxes, 196
American Automobile Association (AAA), 50
American Bar Association (ABA), 51
American Economic Review, 19, 24, 25
Anderson, Gary, *218nn. 11, 12, 221n. 15, 226n. 24*
Anglo-Saxon system of law, 186, 188–89; erroneous interpretations under, 192–93
Arab countries: oil revenues, 137, 138, 139, 140, 141, 142
Argentina, government in, 128, 129
Armed Services Committee, 158
Arrow's paradox of voting as applied to dictatorships, 131–32
Asian countries: buying of government jobs in, 111
attorneys. *See* lawyers
Autocracy (Tullock), 132n. 11
automobile manufacturers, 247; competition among, 241–42; import restrictions on foreign, 228, 263; new automobile development, 282

banking industry deregulation, 310
bankruptcy as cost for efficient economy, 107
bargaining costs and government-created externalities, 269–70
bargaining in government. *See* logrolling; political negotiation
barter in politics, 283
Barzel, Yoram., *43n. 46*
Becker, Gary, *66n. 85*; on agricultural subsidies, 301; on collective action, 51–52; on interest group competition, 36, 46–47; on rent seeking, 246; on rent-seeking costs, 52–53; on subsidies, 226–27; "A Theory of Competition among Pressure Groups for Political Influence," *145n. 12*
begging in China, 22, 25
Bélanger, G., *59n. 71*
Bentham, Jeremy, 208–9, 212
Berman, H., *81n. 106*
better-informed voters, 210. *See also* ill-informed voters; well-informed voters
Bhagwati, Jagdish, 27; compared with Anne Krueger, 30–31
Biaggi, Mario, scandal, 214, 219, 225n. 21
bicameral legislatures with different constituencies, 291
bills. *See* legislation

Bismarck, Otto von, 310
blackmail, legal: by politicians, 72–73
black (underground) economy, 295, 296
Borts, George H., 24, *24n. 25*
Boston Tea Party, 162n. 3
Brady, G., *19n. 13*
Brazil, government in, 128
Brecher, R. A., *27n. 28*
Brennan, H. Geoffrey, *54n. 67*, *226n. 24*
bribery: of government officials, 112–13, 115, 247–48; of politicians, 214, 295; of voters, 262
Britain, industrial revolution in, 160–70
British Parliament: history, 164–65; seventeenth century, 161; voting in House of Commons, 290–91
broadcasting. *See* cable television industry
Brock, W. A., *65n. 83*, *74n. 95*
Brough, W., *128n. 6*
Browning, Edgar K., 23, *24n. 23*
Buchanan, James M., *53n. 64*; *The Calculus of Consent*, *33n. 37*, *46n. 48*, *78n. 102*, *176n. 2*, *238n. 6*, 299, 300; *Deficits*, *77n. 101*; *The Power to Tax*, *54n. 67*; *Public Principles of Public Debt*, *79n. 103*; solution to rent seeking, 181; *Toward a Theory of the Rent-Seeking Society*, 28, *95n. 2*, *189n. 13*; "Voter Choice," *226n. 24*
budgets: balanced federal government, 79; discretionary, 59
bureaucracies: Chinese, 104–8; pay scales in, 118
bureaucrats: definition, 55; under dictatorships, 127–29; misinformed, 309; role in rent seeking, 54–60. *See also* government officials
businessmen: rent avoidance by, 114–17, 118–20; rent seeking by, 120; who become government officials, 133
Byers, Edward, *141n. 9*
C.A.B. (Civil Aeronautics Board), 224, 229, 310
cable television industry, 157–58
Calculus of Consent, The (Buchanan and Tullock), 275, 299, 300
California, government in, 78
campaign contributions, 41–42; small size of, relative to returns, 214–15
Cao Garcia, R. J., *134n. 14*
CAP (Central Arizona Project), 250, 254–55, 277
capital investment: impact of "perpetual gale" on, 153; riskiness of, 150–51
"capitalist" dictatorships, 123–24; rent seeking in, 122–23
Caracas, Venezuela: black (underground) economy, 296
cartels: combining with subsidies, 258; as form of rent seeking, 6; government regulation as, 220; OPEC, 138, 141, 142; resulting from government taxation, 5; taxi medallion, 67; transfers of oil revenues from, 138–42
casually informed voters: definition, 44; lying to, 44–45, 46
cattle-grazing example, 249
Central Arizona Project (CAP), 250, 254–55, 277
certification examinations: in China, 104–7; higher education as, 143
charitable giving: effect on recipient organizations, 22–23; utility of, 208–9
charitable motives, paternalistic, 210
charities: lobbying by, 179; subsidies for, 174
checks and balances in U.S. government, 60; intention behind, 81
Chicago School of Economics: transfer models, 66; view of agricultural subsidies, 301–6; view of subsidies, 227
China: beggars' tactics, 22, 25; bureaucracy, 104–8; U.S. foreign policy toward, 207

choice and externalities, 273–74
Chrysler Corporation, 214
cigarette taxes, 196–200
Civil Aeronautics Board (C.A.B.), 224, 229, 310
Clarke, Edward H., 289
Clifford, Clark, 116
Clinton, William (Bill), 262
coalitions: externalities from, 274–75; Keynes' point about, 77–78; permanent, 273–74; relation with rent seeking, 239; that can remove dictators, 131
Coase, Ronald H., 150
Coate, S., *245n. 6*
coercion by governments, 75–76
collective action: asymmetric impact on free riding, 48–49; selective incentive toward, 49
committees: Armed Services Committee, 158; Congressional, 59
communist countries, poverty in, 124–25
compensation for losses from competition, 150
"Competing for Aid" (Tullock), 25
competition: compensation for losses from, 150; costs vs. gains from, 6–8; duplication of efforts in, 3–10; "handicapped," 220; impact on management of firms, 15; not always a good thing, 117; by political parties, 80; among special interest groups, 246; between U.S. and foreign manufacturers, 241–42
computer, hypothetically perfect utility-maximizing, 207–10
condominium constitutions, 270
congressional committees, 59. *See also* Armed Services Committee
congressmen: costs of intervention by, 41; failure to read bills, 37; influence of political donations on, 41–42; motives for brokering rent seeking, 36; requiring to read bills passed, 80; voters' attitudes toward, 38. *See also* congressional committees; politicians
Constitution of United States: dual majority voting provision, 291; relation with three branches of government, 81; vulnerability to special interests, 52. *See also* checks and balances in U.S. government
consumers, well-being of, 153–54
contracts: assumptions made about, 261; drawing up of, 191–93; enforceable, 188–89; externalities from, 262–63
Corcoran, Thomas (Tommy the Cork), 111–12, 116
Corcoran, W. J., *64n. 82*, 88–92
corporations: backgrounds of CEOs, 118; decision making by, 282; relation with associated lobbying organizations, 50; rent seeking by, 120
costs: bargaining, 269–70; of congressional intervention, 41; contracts, 262–63; court, 186–87; deadweight, 255; government created monopoly, 126–30; from ill-informed voters, 203; for individual of voting, 43; of inventions, 158–59; lobbying for protective tariffs, 309; logrolling, 288; monopoly, 19, 286; of specific policy output, 36; U-shaped curve, 231, 297; vote specialization, 299. *See also* lobbying costs; rent-seeking costs; social costs
"Court Errors" (Tullock), 186
Court of the Star Chamber, 164, 166, 170
courts: as bureaucracies, 118; costs, 186–87; duties, 38; in historical England, 164; without lawyers, 193; role in promoting rent seeking, 61. *See also* judges; juries; legal proceedings; U.S. Supreme Court
Crain, W. Mark, *33n. 38*, *62n. 76*
Crew, M. A.: "Dispelling the Disinterest in Deregulation," *64n. 80*, *71n. 90*; "On Allocative Efficiency,

Crew, M. A. (*continued*)
X-Efficiency and the Measurement of Welfare Loss," *16n. 9*; "Rent-Seeking Is Here to Stay," *69n. 87*; "Toward a Public Choice Theory of Monopoly Regulation," *52n. 59*; "X-Theory versus Management Discretion Theory," *15n. 7*
Cromwell, Oliver, 165
Cuba, 307n. 11
cyclical majority: as applied to dictatorships, 270–71

Dales, J. H., *180n. 5*
deadweight costs, 255
decision making: corporate, 282; individual, 208–9; political, 302–6; relation with externalities, 268
defense industries and lobbying, 158
Delli Carpini, M. X., *239n. 7*
demand-revealing process, 289–90
democracies: compared with monarchical governments, 278; crucial weakness, 44; definition, 265; differences from dictatorships, 132–34; efficiency of, 230; externalities in, 266; limitations, 278–81; strength of bureaucrats in, 54–55. *See also* nondemocratic systems; voting
deregulation of industries: banking industry, 310; and transitional gains trap, 67–69
Derthick, Martha, *216n. 8*, *229n. 31*
dictatorships: "capitalist," 122–24; compared with monarchical governments, 122; difference from democracies, 279; motives of dictators, 127–29, 130. *See also* monarchies
diplomatic service, 120
directly unproductive profit seeking (DUP), 30–31
direct popular voting. *See* referendum on government policies
diseconomies of scale, 231–32
Dominican Republic, 127–28
Donahue, John D., *214n. 3*
Dougan, W. R., 236–37
Downs, Anthony: *An Economic Theory of Democracy*, *39n. 43*, *42n. 45*, 226; on importance of individual vote, 276; *Inside Bureaucracy*, *54n. 68*
DUP (directly unproductive profit seeking), 30–31
DuPont Corporation, 118
Durden, G. C., *19n. 12*

economic growth, 153–54
economics: neoclassical, view of social cost of monopoly, 14; public utility, 297
economics journals: rejection of Tullock rectangle, 19–20; rejection of Tullock rent-seeking article, 25
Economics of Special Privilege and Rent Seeking, The (Tullock), 75, 236
Economic Theory of Democracy, An (Downs), 226
economists, importance of, 310–11
editors of academic journals, motives, 20–21
efficiency: bankruptcy as cost of, 107; of democracies vs. dictatorships, 135; of government transfers, 147; "process efficiency," 116n. 9; of rent seeking, 63–66; of special interest groups, 47
"Efficient Rent Seeking" (Tullock), 221, 231, 250–51, 297; mathematical problem solutions, 95–100; revisited, 85–87
egalitarianism (Mises), 114
80 percent majority rule, 270
Ekelund, Robert B., Jr.: *Economic Regulation in Mercantile England*, *162n. 4*, *164nn. 6*, *7*, *165n. 8*; *The Institutions and Political Economy of Mercantilism*, *241n. 2*; *Mercantilism as a Rent-Seeking Society*, *122n. 1*, *126n. 5*, *237n. 3*
Elgin, R. S., *59n. 70*
Ellis, L. V., *19n. 12*
employment, waste of resources in obtaining, 110–12

England, industrial revolution in, 160–70
Epstein, R. C., *12n. 2*
ethical imperialism, 206, 207
European Common Market, 121
European vs. Anglo-Saxon system of law, 186, 188–89
excise taxes and rent seeking, 196–97
externalities: from coalitions, 274–75; from contracts, 262–63; from externalities, 268; from failure to transact, 263–64; foreign aid as, 267; impact on vs. cost to individuals, 204; imposed on nonvoters, 266–67; among individual lobbies from each other, 232; merely pecuniary, 155–56; principle for dealing with, 264; self-inflicted, 274; synergism with poor information, 211–12; from tariffs, 267; from transactions, 262–63; from voting, 265–66, 273–74. *See also* government-created externalities
"Externalities and Government" (Tullock), 262

farm lobbies, 49. *See also* agricultural subsidies
FCC (Federal Communications Commission), 34–35
firms, cause of X-inefficiency in, 15. *See also* corporations
Fisher, F. M., *74n. 94*
Fitzpatrick, Thomas B., *141n. 9*
Foppa, Klaus, *302n. 6*
Ford Motor Company, 282
foreign-aid programs, 267–68
Fortas, Abe, 116
France: government of, 123–24; tax farmers, 127
Franz, R., *30n. 33*
free riding: asymmetric impact on collective action, 48; Mancur Olson proposition, 49; by special interest group members, 47, 48–52
free trade: effect on rent seeking, 168–69
Frey, Bruno S., *302n. 6*
Friedman, David, 66
Fukuyama, F., *76n. 97*
funding: impact of tobacco taxes on, 200; of U.S. military, 58

Gallman, Robert E., 20
gas shortages in U.S., 141n. 9
General Motors, 241, 242, 245, 252
Ghana: government officials, 111, 112
Godwin, R. Kenneth, *215n. 4*
government actions: involving items sold at less than cost, 256; motivation of, 9
government agencies: budgets, 56–58; discretionary budgets, 59; with no real output, 60; for planning the government, 9; rent-seeking potential of, 55–60
government-created externalities, 261–62; external, 265–68; internal, 268–71
government-created monopolies: costs of, 126–30; in democracy vs. dictatorships, 134–35; in dictatorships, 122, 123–24; in historical England, 164–65; and protective tariffs, 125; riskiness of investment in, 153; vs. taxation, for collecting revenue, 126–27
government expenditures. *See* funding
government income transfers. *See* transfers
government officials: bribery of, 112–13, 115, 247–48; in democracy vs. dictatorships, 134; denial about own privileges, 125–26; lifestyles, compared with expenditures by, 248; purchasing of own positions, 108–12; who were businessmen, 133. *See also* bureaucrats; politicians
government policy: cost of specific policy output, 36; costs from fragmentation of, 37. *See also* referendum on government policies
governments: coercion by, 75–76; deficit finance by, 79; direct limits

governments (*continued*)
on size and growth of, 79–80; inefficiency in, due to rent seeking, 113–14, 115; justification for, 76; purpose of, 212; role, 54; transfers among different levels of, 25; vague public image of, 304–6, 307. *See also* bureaucracies; democracies; funding; legislatures; nondemocratic systems; political negotiation
government vs. market problem, 282–83
gray economy. *See* black (underground) economy
Gurley, John, 19, *19n. 14*

Harberger, A. C., *11n. 1*, *20n. 15*; interpretation of Tullock rectangle, 18–19
Harberger triangle, 12; equivalent, 255; Leibenstein's challenge to, 14–17
Harvard Law School graduates: careers, 111–12
hawk/dove equilibrium, 88n. 2; applied to rent seeking, 99–100
Hieder, F., *129n. 7*
Higgins, R. S., *64n. 82*; on efficient rent seeking, 88, 91–92
higher education, transitional gains from, 142–44
Hillman, A. L., *64n. 82*, *65n. 84*
Hillman's equilibrium, 93–94
Hochman, Harold M., *22n. 21*
Hollywood movie producers, 99–100
Huddle, Donald L., *111n. 8*
Hume, David: views on dictatorship, 131

ICC (Interstate Commerce Commission), 229, 310; and rent seeking, 167, 169
ideology: importance in voting, 226
ill-informed voters, 276–77; benefits to society from, 210; biased ignorance of, 39–40; consequences from, 42; contradictory ideas held by, 303; costs from, 203; disadvantages due to, 210–11; impact of rent seeking on, 307–10; as inefficient rent seekers, 249; public opinion pollsters' experiences with, 38–39; role in rent seeking, 237, 239–40. *See also* better-informed voters; well-informed voters
illth, 218n. 13
import restrictions on Japanese cars, 263
income tax in United States, alternative to, 173
income transfers. *See* transfers
individuals: impact vs. cost of externalities on, 204; knowledge of others' utility, 210
Industrial Revolution, 160–70
inefficiency: in government, due to rent seeking, 113–14, 115; of policies created by rent seeking, 226–30; rationale for inefficient transfers, 144–48; rent-seeking costs from, 222; of rent transfers, 215–18; in scientific research, due to patents, 3–4; of socialism, 124. *See also* X-inefficiency
information: causes of poor, 210; impacted, 308n. 14; proprietary, 298; relation to externalities, 211–12; results of asymmetric, 277. *See also* rational-ignorance model of voting
insurance as proxy for rent seeking, 74
Internal Revenue Act, 37
Interstate Commerce Commission (ICC), 229, 310; and rent seeking, 167, 169
inventions: competition for, 7–8; costs, 158–59; government support for, 159; lobbying for and against, 154–55; measuring social value of, 298; under monopoly, 156–67. *See also* patent system; scientific discoveries
inventors: compared with lobbyists, 152

investment. *See* capital investment
"iron triangle" in Washington politics, 58
Islamic legal system, 194
Israel, government in, 130, 132, 291

Japanese cars, 228, 241–42, 263
Johnson, Harry G., *13n. 3*
Jones-Lee, M., *15n. 7*
judges: as bureaucrats, 118; powers, relative to jury's powers, 169–70
juries: powers, relative to judges' powers, 169–70; and rent seeking, 166–68, 169–70

Karels, G. V., *64n. 82*; on efficient rent seeking, 88–90
Katz, E., *64n. 82*, *65n. 84*
Keeter, S., *239n. 7*
Kennedy, Ted, 306
Kenya, government in, 127–28
Keynes, John Maynard: point about coalitions, 77–78
Korea, 114–15, 123–24, 306n. 10
Krueger, Anne O.: article on rent seeking, 25–26; compared with Jagdish Bhagwati, 30–31; "The Political Economy of the Rent-Seeking Society," *74n. 93*, *110n. 7*, *285n. 8*, *287n. 9*

Laband, David N., *74–75n. 95*, *246n. 7*
Landes, W. M., *61n. 74*, *62n. 76*
lawsuits. *See* legal proceedings
lawyers: as proxy for rent-seeking waste, 74; role in drawing up contracts, 191–93; social costs of, 194–95
Lebergott, Stanley, *179n. 4*
Lee, Dwight R., *147n. 14*
legal proceedings: resemblance to lobbying, 295–96; similarity to rent seeking, 184, 186–90
legal system: European vs. Anglo-Saxon, 186, 188–89; Islamic, 194; relation with politics, 81–82; Tullock's views about jury system, 170; Western, 81–82, 186. *See also* Anglo-Saxon system of law; courts
legislation: about billboards, 4; complexity of, 277–78; congressmen's failure to read, 37; effective special interest, 304–5; impact of lobbying on content of, 301; "milker bills," 73; pork-type, 285–89; requiring congressmen to read, 80
legislatures: bicameral, with different constituencies, 291; efficient rent seeking from, 63–66; influence of bureaucrats on, 55; process of, 37. *See also* British Parliament; U.S. Congress
Leibenstein, Harvey, 14–17, 21; "Allocative Efficiency vs. X-Efficiency," *13n. 4*
lesser developed countries: impact of rent seeking on, 120–21; rent seeking applied to, 27; socialism in, 29
Libecap, Gary D., *215n. 6*, *216n. 7*
Lima, Peru: black (underground) economy, 296
lobbying: aircraft industry, 306; for charities, 179; compared with related government outlays, 75; diseconomies of scale, 231–32; impact on industries/products lobbied for, 158; impact on technology, 220–21, 222–25, 228–30; for and against inventions, 154–55; limitations to, 90; maximum investment in, 249; optimal size and number of lobbies, 232–33; as productive activity, 184–85; for protective tariffs, 307–10; against regulation, 154–55, 157–59; relation with associated businesses, 50, 51; relation with transfers, 23; resemblance of lawsuits to, 295–96; size of payments for, 214; and tax reform, 174–76. *See also* farm lobbies; lobbyists; rent seeking; special interest groups
lobbying costs, 23; vs. gains, 300

lobbyists: compared with inventors, 152; lying by, 308; pressures on, 96–100. *See also* lobbying
local politics: logrolling, 33
Logic of Collective Action, The (Olson), 233
logrolling, 271–75; costs, 288; currency for, 283–84, 289–90; by majorities, 273; the need for, 284; original Tullock analysis of, 249; reducing, 79; relation with rent seeking, 33, 238, 239; restrictions on, 305. *See also* vote trading
loopholes. *See* tax loopholes
lottery metaphor for rent seeking, 85–94; ticket price equilibrium, 95–96
Louis Harris & Associates, 38
Luddism, 218
luxury taxes, 196–97
lying: to casually informed voters, 44–45, 46; by lobbyists, 308; by special interest groups, 212–13; to well-informed voters, 44–45

Magee, S. P., *65n. 83*, *74n. 95*
majority voting: effect of, 77–78; with two nonidentical majorities, 291. *See also* demand-revealing process; reinforced majorities
markets: areas where they don't work, 282; externalities from choices in, 274; where equilibrium does not clear, 231
market vs. government problem, 282–83
mass media: cable television industry, 157–58; coverage of socialist countries, 124–25; impact of ad revenues on, 5; rent-seeking role of, 44–46
mathematical problems of rent seeking, 85–87, 95–100
McChesney, Fred S., model of rent extraction, 71–73
McCormick, R. E., *33n. 38*
median consumer, 273
Medicare, 33
mercantilism, 122–23, 310
Mexico, 307n. 11
Mexico City: lobbying costs vs. gains, 300
middle class, transfers among, 24, 145–46
Migué, Jean-Luc, *59n. 71*
military: funding, 58; governments, 128, 129; purchasing of officers' commissions, 108; as special interest group, 178–79; taxing rich people to support, 181–82
Mill, John Stuart, 218n. 13
Miller, D. T., *129n. 7*
Miller, James C., III, *215n. 5*
Millsaps, S. W., *19n. 12*
Mises, Ludwig von, 114, 153
Mitchell, William C. (Bill), *52n. 60*, *54n. 66*
Mitterand, François, 123
monarchies: compared with democracies, 278; compared with dictatorships, 122; historical English, 163–64; problems of, 276. *See also* dictatorships
money, absence of political, 283
monopolies: costs of, 286; Harberger triangle omission of costs of, 19; inventions under, 156–57; justifications used by, 224; main effects, 11; patents as, 3; relation with rent seeking, 6; riskiness of investment in, 153; on scientific discoveries, 8; taxi company, 67. *See also* welfare losses to monopoly in U.S.
monopoly costs and traditional theory of rents, 151–52
monopoly prices: percentage above competitive prices, 14
Moran, M. J., *59n. 70*
Morris, S., *245n. 6*
motives: of academic journal editors, 20–21; of dictators, 127–29, 130; of politicians, 36, 240, 275; of voters, 226
Mueller, Dennis C., *216n. 8*
Mundell, Robert A., *17n. 11*

Munger, M. C., *52n. 60*, *54n. 66*
Murphy, K. M., *74–75n. 95*
Mwangi, K., *128n. 6*

Namier, Phillip, *161n. 1*
neoclassical economics: view of social cost of monopoly, 14
newspapers, lying by, 46
Niskanen, William A., *54n. 68*; process efficiency, 116n. 9; view of bureaucracy, 55–58
nondemocratic systems: and rent seeking, 122–35. *See also* dictatorships; monarchies
North, Douglass C., *54n. 67*, *191n. 15*

oil shortages in U.S., 141n. 9
Olmstead, A. L., *141n. 8*
Olson, Mancur: criticisms of his theory about interest groups, 54; free rider proposition, 48–49, 50, 51–52; insights related to rent seeking, 52; *The Logic of Collective Action*, 233
OPEC, 138, 141, 142
Organization of Inquiry, *The* (Tullock), 20
Ostrom, Vincent, *76n. 96*
overgrazing problem, 249

PACs (Political Action Committees), 41–42
paradox of the liar: and rent seeking, 89
paradox of voting as applied to dictatorships, 131–32. *See* cyclical majority
patent system: in England, 165; relation with rent seeking, 3–10. *See also* inventions
Peacock, A. T., *60n. 73*
Peltzman, Sam: "How Efficient Is the Voting Market?" *42n. 45*; on subsidies, 226, 227–28; "Toward a More General Theory of Regulation," *63n. 78*, *69n. 89*, 226n. 25; on transfers, 34, 35
Perez-Castrillo, J. David, 95–100
police services as proxy for rent seeking, 74
Political Action Committees (PACs), 41–42
political advocacy through media, 45
political candidates: campaign tactics, 40; in U.S. presidential races, 276. *See also* campaign contributions
Political Economy of Rent-Seeking, *The* (Rowley, Tollison, and Tullock), 28
political information: probability of accurate, 43; reasons for acquiring, 39
political negotiation, 281–83
political parties: compared with sports teams, 39; conflicts with U.S. president, 62
political persuasion by media, 44–46
political reform to protect property rights, 77–82
politicians: bribery of, 214; constituency work, 40–41; interaction with bureaucrats and special interest groups, 58; legal blackmail by, 72–73; lifestyle, compared with influence peddling by, 215; limits to power of, 132–34; misinformed, 309; motives, 36, 240; nonunitary motives of, 275; rent protection and, 71–73; reputations, 275; role in rent seeking, 32–38; use of media, 45; votes for detested, 299
politics: bartering in, 283–84; relation with law, 81–82
poor people in democracies: transfers by rich people to, 24; transfers to rich people from, 225
pork-barreling, 285–89; getting rid of, 177; vs. tax loopholes, 175, 178
Posner, Richard A.: exact dissipation hypothesis, 63; "Independent Judiciary in an Interest-Group Perspective," *61n. 74*, *62n. 76*; on regulatory agencies, 34; "The Social Costs of Monopoly and Regulation," *64n. 81*, *74n. 94*, *246n. 7*
poverty in communist countries, 124–25

power: within dictatorships, 131–32; judges vs. juries, 169–70
presidential elections in U.S., 276
presidential role in rent seeking, 61–62
pressure groups. *See* special interest groups
private local governments: condominium constitutions, 270
"Problems of Majority Voting" (Tullock), 249, 271
"process efficiency," 116n. 9
property rights: political reform to protect, 75–82; and rent seeking, 159
proportional representation, 291
proprietary information, 298
protective tariffs. *See* tariffs
public choice theory: linkage with rent seeking, 31
public goods: difference from market goods, 282; overconsumption, 256–57; paying for, 280; pork-barrel projects, 289; as product of rent seeking, 147; vs. rent seeking, 258; from special interest groups, 233–34; wasteful, limited, vs. beneficial, 288
public health examples: smoking, 198–200
public interest, damage done in name of, 206
public opinion, rule by, 131
public opinion pollsters: approach to voters, 38–39
public utility economics, 297
"Purchase of Politicians, The" (Tullock), 300

qualified majority voting. *See* reinforced majorities
Quirk, Paul J., *216n. 8*, *229n. 31*

Rand Corporation, 295n. 1
rational-ignorance model of voting, 42–43
Reagan, Ronald, Sr.: campaign for president, 276; tax reforms, 178
real estate agents, 103–4
referees of academic journals, 21
referendum on government policies: pros and cons, 41; and rent seeking, 78–79
regulation: of automobile imports, 263; as cost of rent seeking, 114; vs. direct cash payments, 301; improving, 80; of land use for agriculture, 219–20; lobbying against, 154–55, 157–59; rent extraction measures, 71–73; rent seeking, 117–18
regulatory commissions, 34–36
Reich, Robert B., *214n. 3*
reinforced majorities: eighty percent majority rule, 270; share of costs borne by members, 78; variants, 290–91
rent avoidance, 112; by businesses, 118–20; examples, 114–15, 115–16
rent extraction: McChesney model, 71–73
rent protection: definition, 69; social cost, 70–71
rents: definition, 104; good, vs. bad, 148, 154–58; traditional theory of, 148–54; types of investments that produce, 109
rent seeking, 284–89; and advertising, 171–72; applied to lesser developed countries, 27; coalitions in, 239; from competition for jobs, 110–12; data about returns on investment in, 297–99; definitions, 9–10, 28–29, 104, 171, 236; in democracy vs. dictatorship, 132–34; and drawing up of contracts, 191–93; early beginnings, 11–14; effects of idea of, 27–28; ethical aversion to, 234; general agreements to eliminate all, 177–79; through government regulation, 117–18; Hillman strategy, 93–94; in historical England, 160–61, 162–63, 164; in historical United States, 168–69; ideological cover for, 122–

24; impact of free trade on, 168; impact of juries on, 166–68, 169–70; impact of transfers on, 31; impact on voters, 307; inefficiency of rent transfers, 215–18; inefficient policies from, 226–30; limits of Tullock's inquiry, 29–30; mathematical problems of, 85–87, 95–100; measuring, 241; most desirable outcome, 66; necessary subterfuge in, 224–25; as negative sum game, 106–8; origin of term and concept, 25–27; of Parliament after Charles I, 165–66; political market in, 30–32; problem with Tullock model of, 88–94; and property rights, 159; protective tariffs and, 183; proxies for, 74; real loss from, 218–19; reduction of, successes in, 310; reduction of, via tax reform, 181–82; relation with government transfers, 147; relation with logrolling, 238, 239; relation with patents, 3–10; relation with rent avoidance, 117; resource investment in, 214–15, 219, 231–35, 243–45, 300–306; returns on resource investments in, 247, 248; role of bureaucrats in, 54–60; role of ill-informed voters in, 237, 239–40; role of media in, 44–46; role of politicians in, 32–38; role of special interest groups in, 46–53; role of U.S. president and courts in, 60–62; role of voters in, 38–44; similarity of lawsuits to, 184, 186–90; and stock market, 309; that is badly informed, 206; and theory of constitutions, 300; three types of investment in, 96; and transitional gains trap, 68; zero dissipation result, 63–66. *See also* rent avoidance

rent-seeking costs: Becker's view of, 52–53; from bribery of government officials, 112–13, 115; calculating, 299; vs. costs for public goods, 258; data for estimating, 295–96; defining, 204–5, 212–13; vs. efficiency, 246; empirical estimates, 73–75; from inefficient use of technology, 222; from logrolling, 249–50, 251–52; relation with risk premium on capital, 155; size, 243, 296–97; total size, 298; true total of, 220–21; types of, 236–40, 298; in United States, 114–15, 117–21

Rhee, Syngman, 114–15, 123–24, 306n. 10

Rhode, P., *141n. 8*

Ricardo, David, 148–54; influence, 310

rich people: taxing, 181–82; transfers from, to the poor, 24; transfers to, 224, 225

risk premium in capital investment, 150–51, 153

road repair examples, 272–74, 277

Rogers, J. R., *22n. 21*

Rogerson, W. P., *64n. 82*, *65n. 84*

Ross, M., *129n. 7*

Ross, V. B., *74n. 94*

Rowley, Charles K., 299–300; *Antitrust and Economic Efficiency*, *17n. 10*; *Deficits*, *77n. 101*; *Democracy and Public Choice*, *77n. 99*; "Dispelling the Disinterest in Deregulation," *64n. 80*, *71n. 90*; "Gordon Tullock: Entrepreneur of Public Choice," *20n. 17*, *21n. 19*; "Interest Groups as Deficits," *32n. 36*, *53n. 63*; "On Allocative Efficiency, X-Efficiency and the Measurement of Welfare Loss," *16n. 9*; *The Political Economy of Rent-Seeking*, 28, *29n. 32*, *64n. 81*, *214n. 1*, *224n. 20*; "Rent-Seeking and Trade Protection," *69n. 88*; "Rent-Seeking in Constitutional Perspective," *77n. 98*; "Rent-Seeking versus Directly Unproductive Profit-Seeking Activities," *31n. 35*; *The Right to Justice*, *51n. 58*, *62n. 77*; "The Supreme Court and Takings Judgements," *61n. 75*; "Toward a Public Choice Theory of Monopoly Regulation," *52n. 59*; "Toward a Theory of Bureaucratic Behaviour," *59n. 70*;

Rowley, Charles K. (*continued*)
"X-Theory versus Management Discretion Theory," *15n. 7*

salesmen, rent avoidance by, 119
Saudi Arabia: oil revenues, 138, 139, 140
Schattschneider, E. E., *184n. 1*
Schleifer, A., *74–75n. 95*
Schumpeter, Joseph: on American foreign policy, 205–6; "perpetual gale," 153
Schwartzman, D., *13n. 3*
scientific discoveries: monopolies on, 8. *See also* inventions; patent system
scientific research: inefficiency, due to patents, 3–4; progress too fast or too slow, 3, 4
secrecy about scientific discoveries, 3
self-serving attribution, 129n. 7
Shapiro, Irving S., 118
Shughart, William F., II: on efficient rent seeking, 88, 90–92; "Free Entry and Efficient Rent-Seeking," *64n. 82*; "Interest Groups as Deficits," *32n. 36*, *53n. 63*
Silberberg, Eugene, *43n. 46*
Smith, Adam: contribution to history, 162–63; influence, 310; view on mercantilism, 123–24; views on protective tariffs, 308–9; *The Wealth of Nations*, *123n. 2*, 160
smoking, efforts to control, 198–200
Snyder, J. M., 236–37
social costs: from fragmented political policy, 37; lawyers, 194–95; rent protection, 70–71
socialism: inefficiency, 124; as rent seeking, 29; rent seeking under, 122–23
Social Security Act, 266–67, 305
Sophocleus, J. P., *74n. 95*, *246n. 7*
South America: black (underground) economy, 296
Southern Economic Journal, 20
southern states, voting block in U.S., 273–74
special interest groups: costs of competition for transfers by, 52–53; cost vs. efficiency, 246; desirable, 206; free riding among, 233–34; inelasticity of government privileges to, 68–69; interaction with politicians and bureaucrats, 58; lying by, 212–13; public goods from, 233–34; role in rent seeking, 46–53; scandals involving, 225, 230; size of individual, 300–301; small, 51; and tax reform, 176–77; use of selective incentives to lure members, 49–51. *See also* lobbying; pork-barreling
Srinivasan, T. N., *27n. 28*
Stein, Herbert, 203
Stigler, George J.: "Free Riders and Collective Action," *48n. 51*; on regulatory agencies, 34, 35; on special interest groups, 49–50; "The Theory of Economic Regulation," *69n. 89*; "Xistence of X-efficiency," *17n. 11*
Stiglitz, Joseph E., 262, 268
Stockman, David A., *277n. 7*
stock market and rent seeking, 309
subsidies, 25; for charity, 174; combining with cartels, 258; vs. direct cash payments, 222–24, 229–30, 238–40, 301; impact on Tullock rectangle, 254–58; inelasticity, 68–69; more efficient, 226–27; negative effects, 219–20; and transitional gains trap, 67–69. *See also* agricultural subsidies; cartels
Switzerland, government in, 78

tariffs: desirability of, 211, 212, 213; in dictatorships, 123, 124; as externalities, 267; lobbying for, 307–10; and rent seeking, 183; and unemployment, 124
taxes: on advertising, 4–5; alternative to income taxes, 173; cutting vs. increasing, 175, 178; excise, 196–97; as externalities, 269; optimal types of, 179–82; in rent-seeking socie-

ties, 114; vs. revenue from government-created monopoly, 126–27; Social Security, 266–67; tax farmers in France, 127; user taxes, 180. *See also* tax loopholes
taxi company monopolies, 67
tax loopholes, 172–76; closing, 177; desirable, 174; vs. pork barreling, 175, 178; for special interest groups, 177
tax reform: definition, 172; and lobbying, 174–76; to reduce rent seeking, 181–82; and special interest groups, 176–77
technical progress. *See* inventions
technology, impact of lobbying on, 220–21, 222–25, 228–30
television. *See* cable television industry
Texas Railroad Commission, 215, 216, 248
theory of constitutions, 300
think tanks, 310
Tideman, T. Nicolaus, *290n. 11*
tobacco taxes, 196–200
Tollison, Robert D., *226n. 24*, 300; *Deficits*, *77n. 101*; "Economic Regulation in Mercantile England," *162n. 4*, *164nn. 6*, *7*, *165n. 8*; on efficient rent seeking, 88, 90–92; "The Executive Branch in an Interest-Group Perspective," *62n. 76*; "Free Entry and Efficient Rent-Seeking," *64n. 82*; "Gordon Tullock: Creative Maverick of Public Choice," *19n. 13*; *The Institutions and Political Economy of Mercantilism*, *241n. 2*; "Interest Groups as Deficits," *32n. 36*, *53n. 63*; "Luddism as Cartel Support," *218nn. 11*, *12*, *221n. 15*; *Mercantilism as a Rent-Seeking Society*, *122n. 1*, *126n. 5*, *237n. 3*; *The Political Economy of Rent-Seeking*, 28, *64n. 81*, *214n. 1*, *224n. 20*; *Politicians, Legislation, and the Economy*, *33n. 38*; "Rent-Seeking and Trade Protection," *69n. 88*; *Toward a Theory of the Rent-Seeking Society*, 28, *95n. 2*, *189n. 13*
Toward a Theory of the Rent-Seeking Society (Buchanan, Tollison, and Tullock), 28
trading, 261
trading of votes. *See* logrolling; vote trading
transfers: in cash, to well-off people, 245–46; to correct monopoly resource misallocation, 12; costs, 22–25, 53; effect on government subsidies, 25; impact on rent seeking, 31; within the middle class, 145–46; of oil revenues from cartels, 136–42, 145; rationale for inefficient, 144–48; relation with lobbying, 23; self-cancelling, within middle class, 24; from wealthy to poor, 24; to the well-to-do, 224, 225. *See also* subsidies; taxes
transitional gains: from higher education, 142–44; from oil, 136–42
transitional gains trap, 66–69
Trucial States (United Arab Emirates), 140
trucking. *See* political negotiation
Trujillo, Rafael, 127–28
Tucson, Arizona: Air Pollution Reduction Program, 222–23; Central Arizona Project (CAP), 250, 254–55, 277
Tullock, Gordon: difficulty in publishing articles, 19–20, 24; time spent in Far East, 27
Tullock, Gordon, writings: "Another Part of the Swamp," *64n. 82*; *Autocracy*, *29nn. 30*, *31*, 132n. 11, *132n. 11*; "Back to the Bog," *64n. 82*, *65n. 84*; *The Calculus of Consent*, *33n. 37*, *46n. 48*, *78n. 102*, *176n. 2*, *238n. 6*, 275, *290nn. 12*, *13*, 299, 300; "Charity of the Uncharitable," *226n. 24*; comment on Corcoran, "Long-Run Equilibrium," *88n. 1*; "Competing for Aid," 25, *66n. 86*;

Tullock, Gordon, writings (*continued*)
"Constitutional Mythology," *81n. 104*; "The Cost of Transfers," *22nn. 21, 22*; "Court Errors," 186; *The Economics of Income Redistribution*, *59n. 72*, *179n. 3*; *The Economics of Special Privilege and Rent Seeking*, *35n. 40*, *42n. 44*, *65n. 83*, 75, 236; "Efficient Rent Seeking," *64nn. 81, 82*, *65n. 84*, *88n. 1*, *90n. 5*, 221, 231, 250–51, *251n. 13*, 297; "Efficient Rent-Seeking Revisited," *65n. 83*; "Externalities and Government," 262, *268n. 2*; "Future Directions for Rent-Seeking Research," *64n. 82*; "Games and Preference," *97n. 7*; "A Generalization of the General Impossibility Theorem," *131n. 9*; "Hawks, Doves and Free Riders," *99n. 9*; "Information without Profit," *208n. 8*; "Intellectual Property," *4n. 2*; *The Logic of the Law*, *170n. 11*, *186n. 3*, *193n. 17*; "A New and Superior Process for Making Social Choices," *290n. 11*; *The Organization of Inquiry*, *4n. 2*, *14n. 6*, 20, *21nn. 18, 20*; *Papers on Non-Market Decision Making*, *20n. 17*; *The Political Economy of Rent-Seeking*, 28, *29n. 32*, *64n. 81*, *214n. 1*, *224n. 20*; *The Politics of Bureaucracy*, *54n. 68*; "Practical Problems and Practical Solutions," *290n. 11*; "Problems of Majority Voting," *77n. 100*, *176n. 2*, *206n. 3*, 249, *249n. 10*, *255n. 4*, 271; "The Purchase of Politicians," 300; "Rents and Rent-Seeking," *64n. 82*, *220n. 14*; *Toward a Mathematics of Politics*, *14n. 5*, *39n. 43*, *44n. 47*, *226n. 23*; *Toward a Theory of the Rent-Seeking Society*, 28, *86n. 1*, *95n. 2*, *189n. 13*; *Trials on Trial*, *170n. 11*, *186n. 3*; "The Welfare Costs of Tariffs, Monopolies, and Theft," *11n. 1*, 17–22, *22n. 21*, 85, 221, *232n. 2*, 241, *244n. 4*, *253n. 2*, *285n. 8*, 296; "Where Is the Rectangle?" 252; "Why So Much Stability," 271
Tullock Economic Development Plan, 222–23
Tullock paradox, 252
Tullock rectangle: approximate nature of, 297; costs that exceed, 252, 298; effect of subsidies on, 254–58; empirical studies using, 74; Harberger interpretation of, 18–19; initial reactions to, 286–87; major way it appears in economy, 249
Tulsa Ship Canal, 250

UAW (United Auto Workers), 228, 241
Udall, Morris, 251
underground economy. *See* black (underground) economy
United Arab Emirates (Trucial States), 140
United Auto Workers (UAW), 228, 241
United Nations, 268
United States: historical rent seeking in, 168–69; rent-seeking costs, 114–15, 117–21; welfare losses from monopoly, 11–13
United States government: checks and balances in, 60, 81; foreign aid programs, 267–68; foreign policy, 205–7, 306; founding fathers, 81–82; southern states' voting block, 273–74. *See also* Constitution of United States
University of South Carolina, 142–43
U.S. Congress: impact on industries/products lobbied for, 158; televising proceedings of, 80; voters attitudes toward, 38
U.S. Supreme Court: as arbitrator of U.S. Constitution, 81; role in rent seeking, 61–62
user taxes, 180

Verdier, Thierry, 95–100
Versailles, 300

veto power of U.S. president, 62
Vietnam, equality of poverty in, 124–25
Virginia State Lottery Commission, 96
Vishny, R. W., *74–75n. 95*
Voltaire, 160
voters: better-informed, 210; bribery of, 262; casually informed, 44–45, 46; costs of specialization of voting by, 299; externalities from votes of, 265–66, 269; government bureaucrats as, 54–55; impact of media on, 44–45; likelihood vote will make a difference, 43; motives, 226; role in rent seeking, 38–44; specialization of voting by, 203; strong opinions held by, 303–4. *See also* ill-informed voters; voting; well-informed voters
vote trading: relation with rent seeking, 33–34; rules prohibiting, 284. *See also* logrolling
voting: costs to individual of, 43; importance of ideology in, 226; model, 42, 43; payoff from, 43; unanimity, 78. *See also* decision making; logrolling; majority voting; reinforced majorities
voting process: demand-revealing, 289–90. *See also* proportional representation; referendum on government policies

Wagner, Richard E., *24n. 24*, *53–54n. 65*, *79n. 103*, *82n. 107*
Wagner-type lobbying, 24
Warren, C., *81n. 105*
water projects, government, 250, 254–56, 277
Watson, Donald S., 20
wealth, word for the opposite of, 218n. 13
Wealth of Nations, The (Smith): historical context, 160
Weaver, Carolyn, 305
Weingast, B. R., *59n. 70*
"Welfare Costs of Tariffs, Monopolies, and Theft, The" (Tullock), 85, 221, 241, 296; Tullock commentary about, 17–22
welfare losses to monopoly in U.S.: challenge to theory of, 14–17; estimated magnitudes, 11–13; Tullock's work on, 17–22
well-informed voters: ineffectiveness of, 279; lying to, 44–45. *See also* ill-informed voters
Wemelsfelder, J., *13n. 3*
Western Economic Journal, 20
Western legal tradition, 81–82, 186. *See also* Islamic legal system
"Where Is the Rectangle?" (Tullock), 252
"Why So Much Stability" (Tullock), 271
Williamson, Oliver, *308nn. 14*, *15*

X-inefficiency, 14; in firms, 15–16; in U.S. federal bureaucracy, 58

Young, L., *65n. 83*, *74n. 95*

The typeface used for the text of this book is Galliard, an old-style face designed by Matthew Carter in 1978, in the spirit of a sixteenth-century French typeface of Robert Granjon. The display type is Meta Book, a variant of Meta, designed by Erik Spiekermann in the 1990s.

This book is printed on paper that is acid-free and meets the requirements of the American National Standard for Permanence of Paper for Printed Library Materials, z39.48-1992. ♾

Book design by Richard Hendel, Chapel Hill, North Carolina
Typography by G&S Typesetters, Inc., Austin, Texas
Printed and bound by Thomson-Shore, Dexter, Michigan